OSWEGO:

Fountainhead
of
Teacher Education

EDWARD AUSTIN SHELDON
Oswego's founder

FOSTER SARGENT BROWN
President in 1961

OSWEGO:

Fountainhead
of
Teacher Education

A Century in the Sheldon Tradition

BY

DOROTHY ROGERS

APPLETON-CENTURY-CROFTS, INC.
NEW YORK

Acknowledgment is made of the material on page 51 taken from THE
STORY OF AN ITINERANT TEACHER by Edward Howard Griggs,
copyright © 1934, used by special permission of the publishers, The
Bobbs-Merrill Company, Inc.

Foreword

OSWEGO: FOUNTAINHEAD OF TEACHER EDUCATION is the centennial history of an institution which has played a key role in preparing this country's teachers. It initiated the first of the three great movements in American education, Pestalozzianism, Herbartianism, and progressivism, and for two decades was the leading normal school in the country. In fact, its alumni played so vital a part in founding and staffing normal schools that Oswego was dubbed "Mother of Normal Schools."

The story is treated by administrations—from Edward Austin Sheldon to Foster Sargent Brown—because of the paramount role played by institutional chiefs-of-staff. Each administration, in turn, is discussed in terms of four topics: general developments, curriculum, students, and staff.

Present-day students and staff are presented in a different manner from those of earlier administrations. The material about today's student was distilled from group interviews with students, several hundred student themes, and from the student annuals and newspaper. It was checked for authenticity by upper-classmen in three general psychology classes.

The staff and key administrators are discussed individually; but the teaching staff has grown so large that it seemed wise to list them, with significant data, in the appendix. Unfortunately, due to modesty, the quantity of this information is often not a valid key to faculty members' achievements.

Naturally any historian faces special problems. In this case, information was sometimes undocumented, often conflicting and frequently missing altogether. Many of the school's records were destroyed by a combination of fires and overzealous housekeeping—and much material which at the time seemed irrelevant was lost. It was difficult anyhow to capture the flavor of times the writer never knew, and to put into words the intangibles which make a school but resist description. Where data conflicted, the consensus was adopted—not always identical with the writer's private opinion.

v

The history could hardly have emerged at all had it not been for the help of persons too numerous to mention. Among the donors to the historical cause are many alumni, identified in the text by date of graduation, or by two dates when two diplomas were earned. Other persons quoted, unless otherwise identified, are present or former faculty members.

Among those to whom special credit is due are Mrs. Hilda Bohall, Mrs. Eileen Poucher, Isabel Hart, Frank Wagg, Charles M. Snyder, Helen Hagger, the library staff, and the Oswego Historical Society. In addition, Louise Ostberg copied numerous pictures; Harry Charlton supplied others; Ray Cornwell drew up printing specifications; Foster Brown, Charles Turner, Don Snygg, Arthur Hauler, and Paul DeVore checked the manuscript for authenticity; Mrs. Joseph Barnes supplied valuable historical data; and Charles Coward and William Huss supervised the drawing of the maps of the campus. The maps were drawn by John Somerville, Arthur Greer, Robert Heller, William Hanks and William Huss.

Dr. Foster Brown initiated the idea and offered full administrative backing. And it was the approval by College Council and Faculty-Student Association that made the project possible—a gesture of trust which the writer has tried to fulfill, however successfully the reader must judge.

—D. R.

Contents

PART VI: First Years of Foster Brown's Administration, 1952–61

PART I

The Sheldon Period

1861-97

CHAPTER 1

Thirty-six Eventful Years in the Life of a Famous School

I N historic Oswego, New York, located on Lake Ontario's waters, lies a bustling college campus that any native can tell you harbors a rich tradition. Keeping watch over the scene is the statue of the founder, Edward Austin Sheldon, using a sphere to teach a small boy. In front of the statue pauses a fledgling freshman, who gazes at it curiously, wondering what it means. The legend provides only a beginning—for a story that goes back a hundred years, to an epochal event for education, the founding of Oswego, mother of normal schools.

But no event has meaning except in the context in which it occurs, in this case the educational scene of the day.

A century ago, despite faint signs of better classrooms to come, education was still primitive, and teachers possessed an unenviable tradition. For their European predecessors, prior to the 1500's, had been local tradesmen—tailors, weavers, shopkeepers—anyone who could ply his trade while hearing recitations.[1] The seventeenth century was the first to see systematic education—by two church-related orders, the Christian Brothers and the Jesuit Order.

In our country, colonial teachers were recruited from indentured servants, common laborers, and literate dames—who combined household chores with lesson hearing. "Everyone," Sam Hall wrote in his *Lectures on School Keeping*, first American work on the science of teaching, "conscious of imbecility in other businesses, esteems himself fully competent to train [others]." Teaching obviously held no trade secrets because teaching was anyone's trade.

Teachers knew little of their subjects and less of the children they taught. Answers were printed after problems in arithmetic books—for the teachers' benefit, not for the pupils'. They looked on their pupils as unregenerated. Human nature was bad. "The will of the child must be broken," was the disciplinary doctrine of the day.

3

Buildings were as rough-hewn as the teachers. Sheldon himself as a boy had attended a "rough stone house with a forest in the rear and a swamp in front. There he had sat for hours with dangling feet on a backless slab, his text a tattered primer."

Such teacher training as existed hardly deserved the name. This type of education, as we know it, originated in the teacher seminaries of Prussia, dating from the seventeenth century.[2] One of these Frederick the Great made into a royal primary school for educating teachers and teachers' clerks. To what extent these schools were responsible for the beginnings of teacher education in America is a matter of conjecture. In 1789 an essay in the *Massachusetts Magazine* urged such education to "fit young gentlemen for schoolkeeping" so that schools should be kept by "a worthy set of teachers instead of by ignoramuses." Then, in 1816 Denison Olmstead gave an oration outlining a plan for an "academy of schoolmasters."

In America prior to the Civil War three systems of teacher education were tried. For a time the monitorial system and academy training classes flourished but neither proved successful. The most promising development was the normal school. The first was opened to three scholars in Lexington in 1819. At least ten other normals appeared in the years prior to Oswego's founding and an equal number had the name, if not all the functions, of a normal school.

The professional work in all the pre-Civil War normals was rudimentary indeed. While patterning after the organization of Prussian models, they manifested no awareness of Prussian methods. Their academic offering was identical with that of the academies, the only distinctive part being the lectures on teaching largely drawn from the instructor's experience. Texts were rare and poor. The two best books, Potter and Emerson's *The School and the School Master* and Page's *Theory and Practice*, encompassed all then known of professional areas within a few hundred pages. Model schools were an essential feature of all the normals, but they had absurdly small classes and only a few grades.

The normals took on new life, however. The public school movement had created a growing demand for teachers. And Oswego's object teaching supplied a method for mass-producing them. As a result, normals sprang up across the country, varying greatly in quality and curriculum. It is undoubtedly significant that Oswego's first fifty years happened also to be the Golden Age of the American normals. Oswego's success stemmed from a fusion of genius, enthusiasm, and the needs of the times.

As for teacher education in New York State, several dates possessed significance for the future of the Oswego Normal School. The first was the establishment in 1787 of a state university on the English model with the Regents of the University of the State of New York charged with general supervision of college, academies and schools in the state.[3] Next was the organization in 1812 of a common school system for the state under the superintendent of the common schools. The administration of New York education thereby became two-headed—responsible sometimes to regents, sometimes to superintendents of public instruction, sometimes to both.[4] Third, came a law in 1827 to promote the education of teachers—first provision for the professional training of teachers in the United States.

Upon passage of this law a vital question arose: Should the state establish separate schools whose special function should be the training of teachers or should teaching departments be added to existing agencies, notably the academies? The academies, fearing loss of their prosperity and support if normals should be established, prodded legislators to favor their cause. Since the academies possessed powerful popular support, the legislators bowed to their will. Thus, from 1827 to 1844, training classes in academies became the chief means of providing New York State with teachers.

Meanwhile, sentiment for establishing normal schools was gaining momentum. The question was debated heatedly at the first New York State Teachers Convention at Utica in 1830. Horace Mann, then secretary of the Massachusetts State School Board and guest of the convention, urged giving them a trial. State Superintendent of Instruction Young lent his support. Finally, in 1844 the legislature authorized, for an experimental period of five years, a normal to be located at Albany, where it might be inspected by legislators from all over the state.[5]

It is against this background that the Oswego State Normal was founded, in 1861—or so the records say. Actually, any of several dates might have been chosen: 1859, when Sheldon opened his first classes for teachers; in 1861, when the Oswego Primary Training School was established; or 1865 when the state assumed charge of the class, thereby converting it to a normal school. However, since the twenty-five-year celebration was held in 1886, we naturally conclude that the early faculty settled on 1861 as the most logical date of founding.

In 1859 the superintendent of schools in Oswego was Edward Austin Sheldon—and a more energetic head a school system never had. By now he had been superintendent for five years, and all was running like clockwork. But Sheldon sensed something amiss in his smooth-running machine. Performance was mechanical because motivation was missing; nor did pupils understand the why's of what they learned. "The child says his tables with no notion what they mean," complained Sheldon. "We use terms like 'parallel' and 'perpendicular' which have no meaning for him."

At this juncture came Sheldon's fateful trip to Toronto, where he found in the National Museum a display of materials used in the Home and Colonial School in London, a training school for teachers, representing a formalized adaptation of Pestalozzian objective teaching. The collection contained a complete set of models, charts, objects, and methods materials—including bells, pictures of animals, building blocks, cocoons of silk worms, cotton balls, samples of grain and specimens of pottery and glassware—and publications of the English Home and Colonial Infant and Juvenile Society. Sheldon saw the possibilities and became a Pestalozzian on the spot.[6] He purchased the entire exhibit for three hundred dollars, approximately one-third a year's salary, out of his own pocket—a gesture so typical as to explain his chronic penury. Without realizing it, Sheldon also brought from Toronto the seeds of the first of the three great movements in American education—Pestalozzianism, Herbartianism, and progressivism.

Unlike the Canadians, Sheldon did not consign his trophies to a showcase. He immediately set them to work to earn their cost and keep. That same fall he introduced his own version of objective teaching, which he called "object teaching." And on Saturday mornings from nine to twelve, all the city teachers were required to attend meetings, devoted to studying the new methods and planning work for the following week.

Two factors led Sheldon to contemplate a regular training class taught by someone thoroughly grounded in Pestalozzian methods. For one thing, he felt inadequate to teach a system with which he lacked first-hand acquaintance. For another, he hoped to insure a steady supply of teachers trained in Pestalozzian techniques. Since 1859 he had required that teachers spend a year in observation and practice before appointment in the system. However, he hardly had classes trained before rival schoolmen raided their ranks, luring them with offers that Oswego could not match. And perhaps those Saturday meetings helped swell the migration.

At any rate, Sheldon wrote to the London Home and Colonial School in quest of a suitable teacher. The reply came that a Pestalozzian expert, Margaret E. M. Jones, would come for all living expenses and a thousand dollars a year. The local board was staggered by such a figure, and finally agreed that the lady be imported, provided that she not cost the city a cent. To make up the sum, several of the teachers—at Sheldon's urging—reputedly contributed half their salaries, which were then about three hundred dollars. This account, first related by Sheldon's daughter, has been often reiterated with various morals attached. However, Dr. Poucher, a member of the class in question, categorically denied the story and attributed the gift instead to a small group of private citizens.[7]

In May, 1861, the English lady arrived, and Mr. Sheldon and Mr. Matoon went to the station to meet her. On boarding the train, however, they saw only an unpromising-looking woman with a weather-stained face, in a stooping position, half buried in boxes and bundles. "We could not entertain the thought that this was our importation and passed her by," confessed Sheldon. To their chagrin, however, she turned out to be Miss Jones. Nevertheless, when her skin was no longer peeled from her face, her appearance improved and she proved no ordinary woman.[8]

The Oswego Primary Teachers Training School opened, with Miss Jones in charge. Originally attending the primary division of the school was a class of nine city teachers. The class met on Saturdays and for two hours each weekday, when the school was closed early for the purpose. Among the scholars was Sheldon himself, who wished to insure his right to teach in the state. Sheldon thereby became an alumnus of the school that he founded.

So impressed was Sheldon with the success of the class that he invited educators from all over the country to come and see for themselves. On February 11 to 13, 1862, visiting dignitaries met in Oswego's Doolittle Hall, where they were given samples of object teaching. According to the local paper: "[The five-to-seven-year-olds] answered questions with rapidity, describing forms and sizes with astonishing exactness." As for the older children, "they drew geometric figures with neatness and readiness surprising in children so young."[9] A committee appointed by the visiting educators to prepare a report on the system was impressed by the staff's polished techniques. They predicted "a great and important revolution" in teaching and agreed that the country was on the threshold of a mighty educational reform. They warned, however, against untrained teachers' use of the new methods.

The committee's report reverberated through educational circles across the country. Oswego immediately became so well known that the second year's class drew students from Connecticut, Vermont, Massachusetts, and Michigan. Seventeen of that year's twenty-three graduates were snapped up by schools in other states.

When Miss Jones returned to London at the end of the year, Sheldon took full charge of the school himself. He had suggested Mr. Weller as head, but Miss Jones insisted on Sheldon, and her choice had prevailed. Simultaneously, one of Miss Jones's pupils, Amanda Funnelle, assumed charge of the practice school, and Hermann Krüsi provided much-needed background in Pestalozzian theory.

For two years the school was supported by the city. After that Sheldon applied to the state for help. In the debate that followed (1863), one senator aired his ignorance by asking whether the training school was for training horses. Anyhow, that same year the legislature voted an annual grant of three thousand dollars and two years later, by legislative act of 1865, the state assumed the training class, placed it under control of the state school superintendent, and made it free.[10] Simultaneously, the class became known as the Oswego State Normal and Training School and the legislature voted six thousand dollars a year for its support, subject to certain conditions. The city must provide buildings and grounds and admit free of charge one pupil from each assembly district.

Meanwhile, in 1862, the school had been transferred to a much larger building, the Fourth Ward School on East Fourth Street, which has since been torn down. The school moved yet again in 1866, this time to the United States Hotel Building, which housed the Normal School, the practice school, and two model schools, devoted to observation and taught by paid teachers.

The transition from a city training class for primary teachers to a school for training teachers for all grades required an expanded curriculum. The one-year course was extended to courses of two, three and four years. Meanwhile, the private schools, fearing competition, bitterly opposed the expansion. Without it, however, the normals' graduates would have been so inadequate as to discredit such institutions altogether.

Other developments followed fast. On April 7, 1866, the state provided for six normal schools—including Oswego, which were to be governed by local boards appointed by the State Superintendent of Instruction. The location of all these schools, except at Albany and Oswego, was influenced by the amount of lands and monies donated.

In March 1867, the Oswego Normal's buildings and grounds were accepted by the state. At the same time, the State Superintendent appointed a local board of thirteen, thus ending the Normal's connection with the city schools—except for the practice school, whose teachers continued for many years to be chosen by the city board. As a result, in 1869, Sheldon resigned as superintendent of city schools and as secretary of the Board of Education, in order to devote full time to work with the Normal School.[11]

From the first, Sheldon welcomed others' reactions to his program— and it is well that he did. For Oswego's object teaching was to sustain a shifting fortune. The report in 1862 was favorable, but shortly thereafter came the first volley of vituperation, from Dr. H. B. Wilbur, superintendent of the New York State Idiot Asylum, a man eminently successful in his work. At the New York State Teachers Convention of 1862 and the National Convention of 1864 he branded Oswego's system as "vicious." In consequence, the National Teachers Association appointed a committee, chaired by Professor Greene of Brown University, to test and report on its methods. Greene's report in 1865—an excerpt of which follows—was favorable and, by order of the Association, several hundred copies were distributed through the country.

Let us enter any primary school at the beginning of the year, with the C class, at the age of 5, fresh from home life, for the first time to enter upon school duties. They come with their slates and pencils, and this is all. Their first exercise is not to face the alphabet arranged in vertical or horizontal columns, and echo the names of the letters after the teacher in response to the question, "What is that?"—a question that the teacher knows they cannot answer, and therefore ought not to ask; but some familiar object, one of the boys of the class, it may be, is placed before them and called upon to raise his hand; the class do the same. This is beginning with the known. Then he is called upon to raise his right hand. This may be an advance into the obscurely known. The class do the same if they can make the proper distinction; if not, the first lesson marks clearly the distinction between the right hand and the left. Something real and tangible is done. The children can now distinguish between the right ear and the left ear, the right eye and the left eye. Here is acquired knowledge applied.[12]

Reinforcing Greene's report at the convention were demonstrations of object teaching by Oswego's master of master teachers, Matilda Cooper. She taught a group of children assembled from the local area (Harrisburg) how an apple might be resolved into its shape, color, and constitutent parts.

Miss Cooper's performance was invariably so lively as to be completely believable. Thus Oswego emerged vindicated and even more famous. "Oswego has gained the 'general voice of the convention,'" wrote a special reporter from the New York *Herald Tribune*. Consequently, in the time-honored manner of humans the world over, educators scrambled onto the Sheldon bandwagon. Everybody who deemed himself anybody at all in education beat a path to Oswego's door. Sheldon's school became the pedagogue's shrine, with pilgrims hailing from coast to coast. Even D. M. MacVicar, one of Sheldon's sharpest critics, succumbed. "I suppose you realize," he said to Sheldon, "that I have changed my coat." And when he opened the new school at Potsdam three Oswego graduates went with him.

In 1872, however, rumblings of local opposition rose to a din. In fact, Sheldon had always had his critics. A letter to the editor signed "Taxpaying Citizen" even carped at Sheldon's holding school on Washington's birthday, thus preventing children from seeing the parade of the Forty-eighth Regiment.[13] Even more snide was the suggestion that Sheldon's faculty capitalized on their position to peddle their own books for profits. Sheldon, they said, lined his pockets with profits from his readers.

What Sheldon called "The Big Fight" began in 1872 when the board offered the following resolution: "*Resolved,* That we discontinue objective teaching in our junior school and substitute instead Cornell's

Primary Geography and Appleton's *Elementary Arithmetic*." [14] This was the blast that set off a series of repercussions lasting for a year. Self-appointed experts on education made all sorts of accusations: that pupils did not pass easily from one grade to another; that teachers and parents wanted books instead of oral lessons; that the children had to buy too many textbooks; that they could not pass the regents' examinations; that they were held in school longer than formerly, etc. One member accused another of switching sides due to fear of Sheldon. Two of them, Wallace and Kellogg, almost came to blows. [15]

Several local educators joined in too. Professors Hamilton and Waldo complained that object teaching discourages study from books and devotes too much time to recitation. [16]

Another party to the egg-throwing was the *Oswego Commercial Advertiser*. On March 31, 1872, a defender of object teaching challenged the editor to set forth clearly his own definition of object teaching. The editor answered this "sneering question" by suggesting that critics of "object teaching" merely presumed to introduce "a little old-fashioned study such as has been relied upon from the commencement of civilization to make scholars."

The papers were also besieged with letters from irate citizens—self-constituted authorities on the subject of education—who signed themselves by such anonymous names as "Taxpayer," "Inquirer," "Clericus," "Fifth Ward," "Observer," "Pedagogue," and "Examiner." [17] Here are a few excerpts:

> The taxpayers of Oswego will see to it that their schools shall be run in the interests of sound, practical education, and not to build fortunes of book-publishing rings and Pestalozzian monomaniacs.

> The Pestalozzian propagandists are just now filling the Press with dreary articles on the great underlying principles of the objective methods of teaching—a system by which the people have been humbugged out of large sums of money and an incalculable amount of time.

> We have yet to find a person not directly interested in the profits of "the system" who does not agree with us that reading, writing, and English grammar, arithmetic and geography, and those branches only, should be taught in the public schools at public expense.

> We should send gymnastics and object teaching outdoors again.

> Object teaching is a cruel humbug.

> Teachers can keep carriages. . . . The common council have to travel afoot. [18]

The fracas came to a head over the issue of adopting a geography book. Sheldon's supporters favored Guyot's *Geography*, prepared with the aid of Mary Howe Smith of the Oswego faculty and utilizing the objective method. His opponents favored Cornell's *Geography*, which took the traditional approach.

Object lessons were discontinued and map drawing ceased. "Cornell's *Geography* and Appleton's *Arithmetic* were adopted," wrote Sheldon, "to the satisfaction of the parents, if not the children." And no teachers were to be employed who were not natives of Oswego. "They pronounced me dead and buried," added Sheldon, "and object teaching with me. But, despite the funeral obsequies in the city papers, [object teaching] has gone to fill the land."

Krüsi was incensed, too, complaining that the board refused to endorse his recently published *Drawing Course*, already widely used. "The enlightened Board of Education of Oswego," he wrote acidly, "never deigned to patronize it. These men were guided entirely by the persuasive power of book agents. In fact, one of the most ignorant and ill-disposed board members followed me to my drawing class, placed himself in the back part of the room, where he could not see the work of scholars, and reported to the board that the new method of drawing did not amount to anything."

The upshot, at least locally, was victory for Sheldon's detractors. Bowing before the verbal blast, the board abolished object teaching from Oswego's schools, while it continued to sweep the country. Before long, however, the board reversed itself; object teaching regained, and maintained, its position—until Herbartianism became the new order of the educational day.

This was the last serious local fight against the new movement; but now trouble came from outside. In the 1870's both Governor and Superintendent of Instruction began to question the worth of the normals, and the normals had to fight for their lives. In 1877 a committee appointed by the legislature went to the normals to see for themselves. They called on each faculty member to defend the usefulness of his department. Sheldon, of course, was always in the thick of the fray, leveling at the papers a barrage of letters, defending the normals and interpreting object teaching. The committee reported favorably, and by 1884 public confidence was restored.[19]

An important milestone in the Sheldon Administration came seven years later, the twenty-five-year celebration of 1886. Miss M. E. M. Jones, by now Mrs. Jones, was induced to come back to the United States for the occasion and Sheldon went to New York City to meet her. However, in mid-ocean her mind had become "unhinged" and on landing she failed to remember either Sheldon or why she had come to America. Her condition required that she accompany him to Oswego, but her pitiful "mental hallucination" made it impossible for her to read the essay she had prepared for the occasion. It was read instead by Matilda Cooper, a member of Miss Jones's original training class.

Apart from this unfortunate fiasco, the celebration was a success. A hundred copies of the *Twenty-five-Year History* commemorating the occasion were presented to prominent educators and normal schools. The remainder was sold at a dollar a copy.

This celebration might be thought of as marking the peak in the succession of Sheldon's triumphs. For about this time the ramparts of object teaching were assailed by legions of loyal Herbartians, destined soon to turn the educational tide.

From 1835, when the Reverend Charles Brooks studied and recommended the Prussian system, Prussian influence on normal schools in the United States was very great. The stream of Americans attending German schools from 1880 to 1890 steadily enhanced that influence. By this time, the theories of Herbart (1776–1841), which had been slow to take hold, had caught on and were sweeping Germany. Several young American men returned and in 1892 formed the Herbart Club, thus initiating the movement which swiftly displaced object teaching. Some of Sheldon's followers shucked their former loyalties and scuttled to the Herbartian corner.

What was this new juggernaut which swept its way into the classrooms? According to Herbart, the chief aim of education is moral character. But instruction cannot be subdivided into intellectual and moral education because the soul itself is not divisible into faculties. New experiences are perceived and assimilated to old ideas, the so-called apperceptive mass. Since knowledge is not innate, however, the teacher must instill proper interests. These aims can be realized through organizing instruction according to these steps: (1) *clearness,* presentation of facts to be learned; (2) *association,* or relation of new material to previous knowledge; (3) *system,* logical organization of associated knowledge; (4) *method,* practical application of system by the student; and (5) *correlation,* or unifying separate items of subject matter into integral parts.

Although Quincy, Massachusetts, and Normal, Illinois, deserve chief credit for spreading the American Herbartian movement, Oswego was in the forefront of schools testing the new theories.[20] Margaret K. Smith, '83, who studied in Germany from 1885–87, returned to her alma mater as "Teacher of Exact Philosophy as founded by Herbart." The work she initiated was carried on by Grant Karr and Mary E. Laing, who also studied at the fountainhead of Herbartianism in Jena, Germany.

Oswego, therefore, became one of the first schools to emancipate itself from the movement it had started. As far as Sheldon was concerned, the only heresy to any chosen doctrine was to follow it simply because it was chosen. Anyway, the problem of reorientation was less severe than it seemed. It was easy to switch from the formal procedures of Pestalozzianism to the equally formal Herbartian steps in teaching a lesson. The new movement also received impetus from Oswego alumna and faculty member Margaret K. Smith who, at the request of the U.S. Commissioner of Education, first translated Herbart's work for distribution in this country. In short, the Herbartians might have had a lesser—or later—heyday had the Oswegonians not helped pave the way.

By present standards, the effect of Herbartianism was both good and bad. On the credit side of the ledger stand: a more scientific approach; emphasis on interest and organization of subject matter around meanings; and rejection of faculty psychology in favor of unity of mental activity.[21] On the negative side must stand: slavish submission to the formal steps; rigid organization of subject matter; and a subject-centered curriculum.

The problems of the normal schools included funds, physical plant, and curriculum. Financial problems, especially, are traditionally the administrator's. From the early days, tuition had been low—only thirteen dollars at Dartmouth in 1779, for instance. In fact, even that amount was sometimes paid in kind—grain, cotton, sheep, pewter and the like.[22] The normal school student paid no tuition at all—but had to rely on a budget-conscious legislature and local aid. A long article in the *Oswego Daily Palladium* for June 5, 1865, urged support to obtain buildings for the school.

By the 1880's the state's appropriation to Oswego had increased from three thousand dollars annually to twenty-five thousand dollars; but the faculty had increased from six to fifteen. Maintenance costs climbed abruptly from 1885 to 1895, then leveled off until about 1915. Again appropriations lagged behind. The normal schools, unlike the private institutions, never had wealthy alumni to pick up the tab.

Sheldon fared better than most principals as far as real estate was concerned. From the earliest days, obtaining adequate buildings and grounds proved one of the knottiest problems of the normal schools. When the first normal at Lexington, Massachusetts, was contemplated, Horace Mann rushed into Josiah Quincy and inquired: "How would you like the highest seat in heaven?" "I would like some sort of seat there," conceded Mr. Quincy. "You can have it for one thousand five hundred dollars," replied Mann, and told him of some land that he could buy for the new normal. Mr. Quincy drew a check and thus became first donor for normal school buildings in America.[23]

Other normals were not so fortunate. They depended altogether on meager legislative appropriations. They received no land grants as the universities did. Most had to "make do" with shabby buildings, which resembled those of academies.

Sheldon was luckier. Miss Jones taught (1861–62) in the cloakroom of a "wooden school building that stood on the west side of West Fourth Street, near Bridge Street." Then the class moved to another, and better, schoolhouse. But in 1865, the Oswego Board of Education purchased the United States Hotel, on West Seneca between Sixth and Seventh Streets for the Normal's use.[24] It paid $11,500 for the building, with $14,500 for additional improvements. This building, with its wide verandas and fluted columns, was once one of Oswego's most pretentious hostelries—a product of the real estate speculation of the 1830's.

Originally, the central portion of the building was brick with wooden wings. But appropriations in 1878, and again in 1880, permitted extensive renovation, including replacement of the wooden wings with brick.[25] By 1886, the building was almost entirely new and very much enlarged. This building, accommodating 350 students, was to continue in use until 1913, after which it was razed to the ground.

As remodeled, the building had four floors. The first was devoted to shop and gymnasium, the second to recitation, library and reading rooms, the third to natural science and laboratories, and the fourth to art, literary societies and an observatory with a view of the lake.[26]

The library was relatively good for that day. Actually, libraries had been slow to achieve the central role finally accorded them. In the ten years from 1743 to 1753, the total additions to the Yale library numbered thirty-one volumes, mostly sermons. In 1782, at Rhode Island College, later Brown University, the whole library numbered between two and three hundred volumes, mostly theological and not well chosen—as the president wistfully added, "being such as our friends could best spare." For lack of attendants, the room used for a library was kept open only two hours a week.[27]

Even during Sheldon's time, most libraries were dusty, ill-heated and uninviting, and the librarian was a member of the faculty or the principal himself. The recitation method made little demand on it anyway. However, as German research methods came in, libraries became important, and books were circulated instead of hoarded. Students at Oswego not only had use of a fair library at the Normal but free access to the city library as well. "In 1869 I went over there to collect material for a debate," reminisced one student, "and Mrs. Mary Howe Smith [a faculty member] offered me her books to use, too."

Undoubtedly, such problems would have proved greater had it not been for Sheldon's generally felicitous relations with the board. In fact, only the schism of the seventies marred a perfect record. A stabilizing factor was the board's first president, Gilbert Mollison, who served in this capacity until his death in November, 1912, and who signed every diploma to that date—thirty-four hundred in all—in the history of the school.

The power of the board, either to help or hinder, dwindled with the years. Early boards had great power, but toward the end of the century, major control over the normals became focalized in the state—and thus the situation has remained.

CHAPTER 2

The Sheldon Curricula

Fʀᴏᴍ 1861 to 1865 the training course lasted one year and was purely
pedagogical, "consisting in special and thorough instruction in the
true order of the intellectual faculties and the proper methods of developing them by means of lessons on objects, animals, plants, form, size,
number, color, and drawing, together with various Physical Actions,
designed to amuse and interest the children, and cultivate taste and
ingenuity, while they afford a pleasing change, rest and physical development." [1] From two to three hours each day were devoted to theory and
methods, from three to five to observation and practice.

However, since few students possessed adequate educational background, academic training was added in 1865. Two courses were then
offered, one of which, the Elementary Preparatory and Training Course
(one term), was intended to remedy any deficiencies in elementary school
preparation. Those who showed proficiency in this area entered directly
into the advanced Preparatory Course consisting mostly of methods and
practice teaching. In 1869 the elementary preparatory and training classes
became known as the Elementary and Advanced English Courses re-
spectively. The Elementary Course provided one year of academic work
in arithmetic, algebra, grammar and composition, botany, familiar science,
rhetoric, physiology, zoology, linear drawing, history of the U.S., vocal
music, physical geography, calisthenics, declamations, essays and reading; civil government; philosophy and history of education; school law
and school economy. Graduates of this course, and those exempted from
it on the basis of manifested proficiency, entered the Advanced English
Course, comprising philosophy and history of education, geometry,
rhetoric, perspective drawing, trigonometry, bookkeeping, chemistry,
mineralogy, astronomy, geology. Elocution, being quite popular, was
often combined with lecture courses. Both courses culminated in the
awarding of diplomas which permitted teaching in the schools of New
York State without examinations. [2]

The four-year Classical Course, added in 1867, included all the require-

16

ments of the above courses, besides Latin, Greek and German. Graduates of this course received no degree, but were admitted without examination into many colleges of the country. The Kindergarten-Primary Course, added in 1881, likewise required completing the requirements of both English courses, besides an additional year of specialized kindergarten training.

Regardless of which course one took, the final year was devoted to professional work—including twenty weeks given to methods, mental and moral philosophy, science of education, objective teaching and school didactics, that is, grading of the schools, the making of a course of study, choice of suitable textbooks, correct methods of questioning, and rewards to offer pupils. The other twenty weeks of the year were spent in actual teaching. In addition, all took physical training and education.

Sheldon's last years saw several important curricular changes. Because of severe criticism for offering work on so elementary a level, the Elementary English Course was abolished in 1891, and a year added to the Advanced English Course in 1893. Mentioned earlier were the abolition of the Classical Course in 1893 and addition of manual training in 1892. Another addition in 1893 was a four-year Scientific Course. In fact, curricula everywhere about this time became so diverse as to indicate uncertainty about the normals' function.[3]

As for the practice school, two lines of work ran throughout the grades—one science, the other history and literature. These cores included all modes of expression: pantomime, symbols and signs, drawing, painting, molding, manual work, building, architecture, and oral and written speech—penmanship, spelling, reading, grammar, rhetoric, arithmetic and algebra.

The schedule of the practice school was so minutely organized, it provides some amusement today. The following is a typical morning program of the practice school in its early days:

```
 8:30 to  8:45, opening exercises.
 8:45 to  8:55, moral instruction.
 8:55 to  9:05, class 5, words and conversational exercise.
 9:05 to  9:15, class 4, phonetics and conversational exercises.
 9:15 to  9:35, class 3, primer.
 9:35 to  9:45, 1st. recess.
 9:45 to  9:55, class 5, words.
 9:55 to 10:05, class 4, phonetics.
10:05 to 10:25, class 3, primer.
10:25 to 10:40, physical actions and employment.
10:40 to 10:45, singing.
10:45 to 10:50, little children dismissed.
10:50 to 11:00, 2nd. recess.
```

11:00 to 11:20, class 1, primer.
11:20 to 11:35, lessons on Number.
11:35 to 12:00, class 1, primer.

Since Oswego itself had set the general pattern, its curriculum—except for object teaching and special offerings such as kindergarten and manual training—was typical of normals of that day. All such schools taught many subjects—especially those in the West. All had some practice teaching and some daily exercise, and the majority taught history of education.[4] All had several different curricula, differing chiefly in length. Students taking the most difficult course received diplomas for the others "en route." The reason for giving a diploma at the end of two years was to encourage students to stay that long at least. Few schools had fully organized offerings in their catalogues for the senior year; others listed courses rarely offered, largely for window dressing. In general, work required for rural, elementary and intermediate schools was shorter than that demanded for high school. Genuine differentiation of curricula by aim and content began in the nineties and became clearly accepted in the 1920's.

By 1900, almost all the normals had certain features in common— for example, all were pragmatic; they never worshiped at the altar of abstractionism nor lingered on the arid wastes of theory. They always retained whatever practices worked best. They also attached great importance to practice teaching—and consequently to their model or practice schools. Originally, some normals had both—model schools taught by the regular faculty and practice schools where students taught under critic teachers' direction. In time, however, both schools merged into one, permitting both observation and practice teaching.

Other practices emerged only after a flurry of official feathers. For example, between 1850 and 1870, schoolmen fiercely debated whether normal schools should give academic instruction. The basic issue was whether the normals should confine themselves to teacher training, since their academic offering duplicated elementary and high school instruction. The New York State and New England normals advocated purely professional training, the western schools, liberal-cultural training as well.[5] In supporting academic instruction, Dr. Wines of St. Louis said, "Any other theory seems to me far too rigid, narrow, partial, pinched, and chilling." By 1900 the western view prevailed and the normals' right to academic offerings was acknowledged. Even then, some educators believed the normals should confine themselves to professional subject matter, that is, to academic work utilized purely for the sake of reinforcing the principles of pedagogy.[6]

Other issues which caused considerable controversy had yet to be resolved. Not until the twentieth century did educators generally agree that extracurricular activities should be an integral part of teacher education, or that special critic teachers, not regular faculty members, should supervise practice teaching.

Still other issues, then current, remain controversial today. For example: should practice teaching be entirely controlled by the teacher-training institution or done in the regular school system?

The three professional constants, for most of the period, were Pestalozzian principles, object teaching and pragmatism. Oswego's program owes its own philosophical origins to Johann Pestalozzi (1746–1827), the father of elementary education, who established in 1775 a school for poor children in Switzerland, expecting support from public subscription. When he failed to get such aid, he boarded and instructed the children himself. And because money was also lacking for texts, he resorted to field trips and actual objects—finding both surprisingly effective. Such experiences proved a rich sensory background that gave abstractions meaning.

Other Pestalozzian principles were these: (1) Education's chief aim is fitness of life, in accord with highest moral and religious principles. (2) As for subject matter, facts must be reduced to their simplest terms and based on accurate perception. (3) Materials should be introduced gradually, progressively, in unified fashion. (4) Where instruction is concerned, child nature and individual differences must be respected. Children must be permitted to be active, and restrained only when social rights are endangered. (5) The best atmosphere for learning possesses qualities of "domesticity and maternalism."

These principles, with minor changes in terminology, would win approval of the most advanced education today: "In order here," writes Snygg, "we recognize such modern concepts as education for life, child and personal development, citizenship, character education, recognition of individual differences, pacing, readiness, training in scientific method, learning by doing, and need for emotional security." [7]

By 1860, Pestalozzi's theories had caught on in Germany and England but had made no headway in America. Several individuals had tried to introduce them. Warren Colburne had claimed the ideas as his own invention. Between 1839 and 1849 Henry Barnard distributed among Connecticut's teachers pamphlets on Pestalozzian methods. Swiss educators like Arnold Guyot—and Krüsi himself—were already utilizing Pestalozzian principles in this country. But it remained for E. A. Sheldon and his staff to make Pestalozzi a byword in American education.

Sheldon dressed up Pestalozzian principles and practices to suit himself. While his conclusions retained a Pestalozzian flavor, they nevertheless bore the Sheldon stamp:

Begin with the senses.

Never tell a child what he can discover for himself.

Activity is a law of childhood. Train the child not merely to listen, but to do. Educate the hand.

Love of variety is a law of childhood—change is rest.

Cultivate the faculties in their natural order. First, form the mind, then furnish it.

Reduce every subject to its elements, and present one difficulty at a time.

Proceed step by step. Be thorough. The measure of information is not what you can give, but what the child can receive.

Let every lesson have a definite point.

First develop the idea and then give the term. Cultivate language.

Proceed from the simple to the difficult, that is, from the known to the unknown, from the particular to the general, from the concrete to the abstract.

Synthesis before analysis—not the order of the subject but the order of nature.[8]

As for method, Sheldon and most of his staff practiced *object teaching*, although a few preferred *objective teaching*. Objective teaching, the creation of Pestalozzi, aimed at understanding. Objects were chiefly a means to an end. Object teaching, inspired by Miss Jones of the Colonial School, originated in the training class and was essentially a Sheldon creation. Object teaching also developed understanding but aimed chiefly at firsthand knowledge of objects. The difference was one of emphasis, rather than of fundamental purposes.

While both object teaching and objective teaching were practiced at Oswego, Krüsi, a disciple of Pestalozzi, practiced objective teaching, and actually condemned object teaching for its stilted procedures. Nevertheless, most of Sheldon's staff were coached by Miss Jones of London in object teaching.

Both versions of Pestalozzianism were tied to faculty—or "grindstone" —theory: that mind is composed of a number of powers or agencies, such as memory, will and attention, which are susceptible to training. In these terms, object teaching was intended to develop in pupils accuracy of perception and growth in reasoning power. Lessons were to be arranged according to stages in children's mental growth and designed to promote skills in written and spoken language. To these outcomes Oswegonians added ideas of relationship and sensory perception.

Object teaching was distinctive chiefly in its method of instruction. Here, in part, is Sheldon's lesson on plants:

(1) Require the children to look at some flowers and say in what they are alike. (They all have leaves; they all have stems; nearly all have the

outer leaves—that is, calyx—of a green color.) Let the children smell the flowers—they all have some kind of smell. Ask how they are produced. (From slips.) If a slip or seed be put into the ground and gets proper nourishment, what takes place? (They grow.) All flowers are grown. . . . Who made the flowers? (2) Having found out in what flowers are alike, lead the children to discover in what they differ. . . . (3) Let the children say of whom we should think when we look at flowers. . . . Why flowers are made of different colors? Whom they should thank when they gather flowers? [9]

Whatever objects were used, it was standard practice to have the children name the qualities of the objects used. Take apples, for instance. This apple is large, firm, red, wholesome, and so on. But from there the lesson might move in many directions. Children might speak of apple trees, of their roots, and thus turn to science. Or a discussion of apples could lead into horticulture—or even history. After all, according to tradition, "apples have played parts in the dramas of William Tell, of Newton, and of a notable couple in an ancient garden."

Unfortunately, some teachers carried the system to ridiculous lengths. One of Sheldon's faculty hauled a live pig to class. Another used a covered dish to teach children about Christopher Columbus. "Now what is this?" inquired the teacher as she lifted the cover from the dish. "Cover," came forth a chorus of replies.

"What kind of cover? Now remember Columbus," pressed the teacher.

"Dish-cover," replied the bright boy in the class. "Columbus dish-covered America." That was the answer, of course, that the teacher desired.

Since such farcical performances were not uncommon, object teaching came to incur considerable criticism. For example, the *Oswego Daily Palladium* for February 12, 1871, carried this satire from Dickens:

> "Girl number twenty," said Mr. Gradgrind, "Give me your definition of a horse."
>
> The girl number twenty was Sissy Jupe, who had been brought up in a circus, and knew a horse better than anything else in the world. Sissy Jupe could not define a horse. Whereupon Mr. Gradgrind—"Girl number twenty unable to define a horse. . . . Some boy's definition of a horse— Bitzer, yours?"
>
> "Quadruped; graminivorous; forty teeth; namely, twenty-four grinds, four eye teeth, and twelve incisive; sheds coat in the spring; in marshy countries, sheds hoofs, too." This and much more from Bitzer.
>
> "Now, girl number twenty," said Mr. Gradgrind with great solemnity, "You know what a horse is."

Commented the local newspaper: "Bitzer would have been marked 99 per cent in our schools."

Krüsi's own criticisms were among the most lucid. Lessons had no connection with each other, he complained. They lacked any over-all plan. There was too much crude analysis, children being asked to name the parts of the body, of a plant or perhaps of a horse. Besides, there was often only one object to work with—for example, an apple or a cube. Furthermore, object lessons often degenerated into senseless acquisitions of unfamiliar words such as *chalybeate, imbricated,* and the like.

Krüsi believed the best examples of object teaching were to be found in arithmetic or drawing, where pupils were encouraged to develop their ideas, illustrations and experiments. All sciences are based upon realities which must be observed before symbols and abstractions can be useful. But he also recognized that nature studies should lead to ideas and principles which are completely valid even though not concrete.

Nevertheless, well done object teaching cannot be written off as a wholly negative influence on American education. It left a considerable residue of positive effects. Many Pestalozzian and Sheldonian principles were firmly absorbed by American education and are still accepted today.

Sheldon, however, did not confine himself to the Pestalozzian philosophy he helped to popularize. He searched ceaselessly for better answers and was ever ready to give promising innovations a fair trial. While for many educators orthodoxy is the trademark of respectability, Sheldon viewed no system as sacrosanct, not even his own. As Hollis said: "He made systems of education as the bee transforms nectar into honey. After all, his great strength was in his sanity—his willingness to take all into account, and then risking his all to take a stand."

In consequence Sheldon developed many ideas *other* than those of Pestalozzi, many highly advanced for their day. He believed children should develop a healthy curiosity to know: "The object is not so much to impart information, as to educate the senses." Texts, furthermore, were for reference, not for slavish use. "We require the child to repeat the tables," he said, "without giving him the slightest conception as to the character of these numbers, or what they represent." On one subject, he even outdid his twentieth-century successors, the progressives. He questioned the value of compulsory school attendance. "It is very questionable, if [it] will benefit the pupils very much. The whole tendency of such a process [that is, driving the pupil] is to disgust him."

Modern educators would find little fault with the foregoing—or with the fundamental premises on which his practice teaching plans were based:

Student teachers must have a thorough preparation including exhaustive knowledge of the subjects to be taught.
Model teaching should be used in demonstrating all educational theories.

Only mature students should be admitted to the school of practice as
pupil teachers.

Assuming maturity on the part of teachers the time given to professional
training [theoretical and practical] should be not less than one year.

Observation by the student-teacher should always precede responsible
room-teaching.

The student-teacher should assume as much responsibility as will be
expected of him when given a regular appointment after graduation.

To organize, control, and instruct with complete freedom is essential.

The student-teacher should be provided with the most competent critic
obtainable.

A practice school cannot be a model school. A model or demonstration
school should be maintained in connection with the school of practice.

Actual public school conditions should prevail in the practice school.

The practice school should perform all the functions of, and be equal
to, the best organized public schools.[10]

The child and his needs remained the focal point in Sheldon's thinking. He insisted that children be given variety and change of pace:
"The children should be allowed to have two short recesses of ten
minutes each, morning and afternoon; and gymnastics and singing exercises should be frequently introduced, to give change of position and
rest to the children, and keep up an animated and pleasant state of
feeling."

Along the same vein was his concept of discipline. At first, he confesses, he was predisposed toward repression. But later he wrote:

That teacher who has to resort to forceful methods to secure order
or study is of very little value. The best work is done where there is a
warm, sympathetic relation between teacher and pupils. The children
are drawn into right doing, not driven. There is a vast difference in the
value of the two processes.[11]

Sheldon was also a prolific writer—but unfortunately, most of his
writings are buried in the voluminous files of Oswego's newspapers. He
carried the cause of education to the people, using the papers as a forum
for his views. He also wrote articles and books. The best known are his
Manual of Elementary Instruction, 1862, his *Lessons on Objects,* 1863,
and his *Series of Readers,* 1874. His readers were used widely, and Jessie
Himes, '93, '99, recalls enjoying them immensely as a child.

Certain subjects in which Oswego's contribution was particularly
distinctive command closer attention.

Heart of the program was practice teaching, copied by normals all
over the country. Oswego, at least, made no basic changes in the program

Oswego was among the pioneers to try out two gymnastic systems, the Dio Lewis and the Del Sarte. Earlier, George Winship had been an apostle of severe exercises. From 1859 until the 1870's, this gentleman toured the country, giving weight-lifting exhibitions—and his gymnasium became the sanctum sanctorum for strength-seekers. Dio Lewis, by contrast, emphasized calisthenics, not merely to impart strength of muscle but to produce grace of movement. One of his contrivances was the gymnastic crown weighing from three to one hundred pounds, which was worn to secure good carriage. He recommended use of wands, dumbbells, clubs and hand-rings. His normal school of gymnastics in Boston, founded in 1861, was the first such school to graduate a class and, by 1868, its lithesome alumni had carried the Lewis system across the country.[14] Among these alumni was Delia Lathrop, who brought the system to Oswego.

Delia's students enjoyed the exercises, but the townspeople simply sneered. Therefore, in 1868, to quell their criticism and please the students, two public performances were given, featuring exercises, fancy steps, and marching. Costumes for the occasion were black dresses with swansdown at neck and wrists, except for two students who were rigged out in red.

A few years later, in 1874, Delia Lathrop's successor, Dr. Mary V. Lee, introduced Del Sartian methods, almost two decades before they swept the country. In fact, Dr. Lee had already tried the system and found it wanting by the time it took hold elsewhere. After a decade of popularity the system died, thus vindicating her verdict.

Even greater proof of Dr. Lee's vision was her insistence on physical examinations and on exercises adapted to individual need. While physical educators generally have come to endorse this policy, they rarely practice it with the consistency required.

Any contributions by Oswego to the study of foreign language and music went unrecorded, but there is evidence of Sheldon's attempts at upgrading both areas. In 1867, for example, Sheldon invited Lowell Mason, famous hymn writer and music teacher, to conduct a dozen or so lessons at the Normal. Earlier, Mason had studied Pestalozzian methods as applied to music education in Europe where he became a close friend of Hermann Krüsi.

Mason said he would come to Oswego but only on certain conditions: that he be supplied with a musical instrument, such as a school harmonium; that he be permitted to go to bed early; that he have a good room with a wood fire and bedclothes enough "to keep me warm, or about twice as many as for another person." He also insisted on more than the dozen lessons requested by Sheldon. "A mere dozen lessons would be like pressing my new cider in a single bottle," he said.

When Mason left, after several weeks, the whole school assembled in his honor and Mary Swan, a student, presented him a gold-headed cane. Mason, utterly overcome, sank into his chair, saying, "I cannot say a word," while the copious tears rolled down his cheeks.[15]

Aside from this venture, there is little information about music at the early Normal. Generally, music had sporadic growth in the school curriculum until 1900, but thereafter—at Oswego as elsewhere—it became required.

As for foreign languages, a summer school was devoted solely to their teaching, conducted by Dr. Saveur in 1886.[16] This gentleman's system of teaching languages had gained wide recognition, and Sheldon, always avid to test important innovations, inveigled him into coming to Oswego. Saveur brought from Vermont his entire faculty, and the summer's work was pronounced a signal success.

Part of Oswego's most spectacular performance was in two new areas, kindergarten and manual training. The kindergarten idea had originated with Friedrich Froebel (1782–1852) who, in 1837, gave it its name and set the pattern.[17] Froebel studied at Jena where he was so destitute that he had to take nine weeks off to serve a jail term for inability to pay a debt of thirty shillings. Later, in 1837, he founded a school which he called a kindergarten because children grew there as did plants in a garden. And just as the plant's growth depends on removing the weeds that choke them, so do the child's natural gifts unfold in a fitting environment.[18]

The kindergarten idea was brought to the United States by German immigrants and the first private kindergarten was established in Wisconsin in 1856. After the first public kindergarten was opened in St. Louis in 1873, growth of the movement was rapid. By the time Oswego's program was established in 1881, three hundred kindergartens in all had opened.

Both Oswego and Fredonia claimed to be the first state normal to have a kindergarten training course, although Dockstader states definitely that Oswego's was first. Anyhow, Oswego was the first of the New York normals to abolish kindergarten tuition—in 1887.

Clara A. Burr, first kindergarten principal at Oswego (1882–1888) and her successor, Amanda Funnelle (1888–1911), followed the Froebelian line. They studied Froebelian texts, *The Education of Man* and *Mother Play*. They used the Froebelian "gifts" which included six balls of six standard colors, and a group of objects—sphere, cube, cylinder, and cubes differently divided. These were employed in prescribed ways to give ideas of form, color, size and dimension.

But Amanda Funnelle was no mere slave to Froebel, as Grace Allen's ('97) reminiscences show:

True, some things were prescribed, but there was considerable flexibility. It was not nearly as rigid a course as I had at Columbia later
on. . . .

The children were divided into two groups, the older being called the
connecting class. With this class we went beyond reading readiness, pressing them more than we do now. We also taught sewing, drawing, lacing,
weaving, paper cutting and paper folding. Each child also had his own
little plot in the school garden.

All of us had a lovely feeling of respect for the children, for each
other, and for the parents. We had teas and parties in the kindergarten
for the kindergarten group, and sometimes for guests. We supplied silver
from our own homes. . . .

In neither the area of kindergarten nor of manual training has Oswego's
pioneering role been fully appreciated. Manual training was a transplant
from Europe, at first along Russian lines as organized by Della Vos.
According to this system, the manual training course consisted in
a graded series of exercises or models based on an analysis of tool
processes. The Della Vos approach was well developed by 1868, pre-
dominant from then until about 1890, and standard procedure in many
shops for years thereafter.[19]

Meanwhile, in the late 1890's, another system called sloyd became
popular and was adapted by Salomon of Sweden to the elementary
grades.[20] This system called for a fixed series of useful models, each
graded on the basis of exercises or processes involved. Like the Russian
system, sloyd was concerned with accuracy, but also with utility, and
the development of sense of form and beauty.

At least three factors contributed to sloyd's growth. First were the
writings of Ruskin and Carlisle, protesting the prevailing ugliness of
manufactured products. Second was the arts and crafts movement, given
impetus by such writings. And third was the advent of the Herbartians,
whose mental discipline aims were more easily adapted to sloyd than
to Della Vos. Sloyd, said its advocates, results not only in skills, but also
in love of labor, self-reliance, industry, and mental growth. Even moral
outcomes were claimed—for example, by A. D. Mayo, speaking at
Oswego's twenty-five-year celebration. "Manual training," Mayo soberly
proclaimed, "constitutes a healthy antidote to the 'damp drift of Godless-
ness.' "[21]

Originally, from 1862 to 1886, manual training at Oswego was a
part of the regular curriculum.[22] As early as 1861 Krüsi's drawing course
included stick laying, weaving, paper cutting, color, form and *inventive*
drawing. Generally, in those days, drawing was copy-work, almost never
creative. In the fall of 1886, Sheldon established in the school's basement a workshop of sorts, the humble ancestor of today's Industrial Arts

Division. There the janitor, Cyrenius, helped students of both sexes to make apparatus for the science classes and for practice school classrooms. Today it sounds odd, but janitors often performed such functions in that day.

For opening this shop, Sheldon gave two practical reasons. First, teachers should know how to make classroom equipment. And second, instruction is more effective when teachers and children unite in constructing the materials they need.

However, Sheldon did not limit his reasons to utilitarian factors. In line with Herbartian theory, so popular in that day, he claimed for manual training a broad transfer of values. Manual training, he said, assists in acquiring sense perceptions, enhances appreciation of the beautiful, refines tastes, and enlarges vistas.

The next important move affecting manual training was passage, in 1888, of a bill, introduced by the Honorable S. M. Coon, a member of the local board of the Oswego school, legalizing manual training instruction in the state normals. The instigator of this move was undoubtedly E. A. Sheldon.

Meanwhile, Sheldon's basement project was going badly. Cyrenius' janitoring left little time for shop supervising. Besides, no special time was set aside for shop work. Students either could not or would not sharpen chisels and plane blades. Augers and gimlet bits lost their keen edges.[23]

Sheldon, undaunted, introduced a regular course in manual training in 1893 and chose Richard Piez, graduate of Baltimore Polytechnic Institute, to organize it. To make room for the new course Sheldon had discontinued ancient languages, declaring them superfluous for elementary teachers. The new course was an elective which could be substituted for geometry, trigonometry and geology, and "might prove even more practical, especially for women."

The purpose of the new course, said Sheldon, was to "train the hand to execute with readiness and accuracy the mandates of the will, to learn proper use and maintenance of tools, and to construct such simple pieces of apparatus as teachers might find needful in their work."

To remodel and equip the new shop, Sheldon wangled an appropriation of six thousand dollars which paid for remodeling the room, and for twenty double benches, each supplied with two sets of tools, including three saws, three planes, eight chisels, four gimlet bits, brace, gauges, square, rules, knife, etc. Because power was lacking, pupils had to "make do" the first year with hand-operated circular saw and grindstone. Next year an eight-horsepower gasoline engine was added in order to power lathes, power saw, and grindstone.

Originally Piez followed the Della Vos plan, stressing jobs of an exercise nature. Beginners learned to dress pieces of lumber, pare and mortise, bore holes, drive nails, lay out forms accurately and make the ubiquitous joints. However, Sheldon, while still claiming mental health virtues for manual training, increasingly stressed function and design. Gently he communicated his views to Piez, who soon acknowledged their superiority to those he formerly held.

As a result, for some years a system resembling sloyd was used—a series of useful models each involving certain essential skills. These included a bench hook, rulers, blackboard compasses, pencil block, plant press, physics apparatus, and models to illustrate solid geometry. Pupils also turned out a wonderful variety of necktie holders, ash receivers, burnt match receivers, picture frames, footstools, card tables, tool chests, pants stretchers, and whatever the pupils might find useful.

Concurrently came several important developments. While Piez retained general charge, Elizabeth Salmon assisted with drawing and color work, and Harriet Stevens with clay modeling, sewing and dressmaking. Often groups worked together on productions so interrelated as to resemble the "projects" of a later day. Sheldon also attempted to correlate manual training with other subjects. Educational philosophers had come to deplore the hodgepodge of unrelated subjects composing the curriculum. As a remedy, the Herbartians proposed relating form studies to content studies.

Sheldon's adaptation of this idea was to establish two cores, focused around nature study (the sciences) and literature (the humanities). To each of these were to be related the form subjects, that is, reading, writing, arithmetic, drawing and manual training. In essence, the plan was a combination of subject matter correlation and core curricula. Piez had little difficulty in correlating manual training with nature study, but adapting it to literature was another matter. "A third core, industry, was needed," wrote Piez in the 1930's, "but this area had yet to attain the status accorded science and the humanities."

To permit better articulation between manual training and science and to make the correlation functional, Piez was now assigned both subjects to teach. This fusion of duties brought interesting and unexpected results. Perhaps for the first time, prospective teachers learned to make physics apparatus suitable for use in the lower grades. Messrs. Hall and Bergen of Harvard had already worked out a plan for teaching physics in elementary school, without, however, showing how teachers and children might make their own apparatus. A result at Oswego was creation, in effect, of a general shop. Such a variety of objects was required in physics as to necessitate considerable shop expansion. To metal and woodworking were added glassworking and wireworking.[24]

Another momentous step was the equipment, in 1894, of a shop with twenty double benches and a full complement of tools—for boys of the grammar grades in the practice school. Three periods a week were devoted to woodwork, the remaining two to mechanical drawing.

Again there emerged a totally unforeseen result. At this time, students enrolled in the shop course did their practice teaching in the same area. This experience, coupled with Oswego's reputation at the time, made them sought after as shop teachers upon graduation—not in New York only but throughout the nation. So, just as Oswego had been famous as a center for training teachers acquainted with object teaching, now it became noted as a source of manual training instructors.[25]

The Normal women might also elect the shop course, but Campus School girls were denied shop work, and were limited to sewing instead. Cooking was not added until later when vocational preparation was no longer a term of reproach. Just why sewing should be considered less "vocational" than cooking is not clear.

It is difficult to assess Oswego's place in the history of manual training education. At least we may assume that until Sheldon's death in 1897 he continued to share abroad the fruit of Oswego's experiences within this area. On the basis of this assumption, Oswego's contributions probably were the following: (1) Oswego helped pave the way for manual training through successfully peddling Pestalozzianism to American educators—and Pestalozzi is called the "Father of Manual Training." After all, it is but a short step from objective teaching to manual training. Pestalozzi himself used furniture, tools and concrete instructional materials. "There are but two ways of instructing," said he, "either we go from words to things or from things to words. Mine is the second method." [26] The same can be said of manual training. (2) Because of his tremendous prestige and many speeches about manual training, Sheldon assisted in popularizing and legitimizing its position.[27] (3) Sheldon also helped restore the original spirit of sloyd, in contrast to the distortion of sloyd then prevailing.[28]

Devotees of the sloyd cult either had forgotten or chose to ignore the origin of sloyd itself. Sloyd had resulted from the desire to provide peasants of Sweden with useful occupations during the idle winter days and evenings and the models chosen were those adapted to peasants' tools and requirements. Most shop instructors slavishly followed the originally recommended series of models without adapting them to their own facilities or needs.

Actually, Sheldon's broad concept of manual training more nearly approximated the "manual arts" of a later day. Just as he originally applied object teaching to all subjects of the curriculum he now applied manual training to all modes of expression—even penmanship, drawing and painting. Nor did he sidestep the vocational implications of manual training, then held in low repute. After all, why deny that manual training might serve as a base for certain vocational operations?

Oswego cannot lay claim to offering the first course in manual training in this country. That distinction belongs to the Massachusetts Institute of Technology, which organized the first such course in the 1770's. Oswego can claim, however, the distinction of being the first normal school to offer such training, if Krüsi's drawing course be accepted as manual training. Certainly, though the course was not formally designated as such, its content—already indicated—justifies the claim. The first normal to offer a manual training course labeled as such—although still on an informal basis—was the state normal at Bridgewater, Massachusetts, in 1881.

Oswego was among the first normal schools, if not the first, to organize a shop for training teachers to make their own classroom equipment (1886) and among the first to introduce a shop course in elementary school.[29] The first such courses were organized about 1892 or 1893; Oswego's followed in 1894.

In the 1890's, Oswego's manual training program involved such variations as core curriculum, correlation and, ultimately, a general shop. The fact that these features lacked the names later given them made them no less authentic. "It took our scholarly successors of the next decade," said Piez, "to supply us with a vocabulary."

CHAPTER 3

A Star-Studded Faculty

SHELDON's ancestry—long-lived Puritans of sturdy New England stock—helps explain the man himself. In 1815 his father bought a farm near Perry Center, cleared about ten acres, then returned to Marlboro, Massachusetts, where he taught school in winter. In 1819 he brought his bride Eleanor to Perry in a covered wagon, the three-hundred-mile wedding trip consuming two weeks.

Their son, Edward, born October 4, 1823, felt his parents' influence keenly. From his mother, who went about the neighbors' houses with her medicinal herbs and taught Sunday School until she was ninety, he gained a sense of charity. From both his parents he gained a strong religious character.

The farm, too, left an indelible impression. There he took an active part in sheep shearing, candle-making and stuffing the sausages, with a squirt-gun type of filler—a proper prelude to a philosophy of learning by doing.

His early schooling was equally significant—at least in a negative sense. Naturally, he came to value what he himself missed—attractive school environment, motivation, and kindly discipline. The schoolyard had been an old ash-heap, and the schoolroom itself hardly less prepossessing:

> [The walls were] lined with planed, unpainted boards; and to secure greater warmth, the spaces between the posts were filled with dry, discarded tan-bark, which furnished excellent meeting-places for the mice who feasted on the scattered crumbs of many a wasted dinner. The seats—except for those for the wee pupils, which had backs—were high board benches with no backs except what were furnished by the sharp edges of the writing desks, against which we sat until the half-hour for writing came.[1]

Nor might one squirm to divert himself for a bit of relaxation. Discipline was as grim as the physical setting. Edward's tender soul

33

shriveled at the penalties administered. The culprit was sometimes required to hold some heavy object, as a book, in the hand, with the arm stretched out at full length. Once Edward himself was required to kiss his great toe—a punishment deeply resented though administered for performing the same act in fun. Ironically, present-day student initiations often involve requiring novitiates to kiss the toe of Sheldon's statue!

Utter lack of motivation completed the gloomy picture. "School life to me was one continuous holiday. I had to memorize lists of (to me) utterly meaningless words. I did study my spelling lessons one winter when a prize of one dollar was offered. . . ."

Such learning as he gained was incidental. From friends and from play he gained intellectual and spiritual growth. "This part of my early training was abundant and efficient," he said. He also exploited the school's environs to the hilt. He studied the wasp that burrowed in the ash-heap; he fished for horned dace in the stream that ran nearby. "It mattered not," he wrote, "that the rule was for a short recess. We could make it long by bringing the excuse that we did not hear the rap on the window, designed to call us in."

No wonder that the boy hated study. With tears in his eyes, he pleaded with his father to permit him to stay at home and work. His father's reply was typical of fathers the world over: "Edward, when you are older you will be sorry that you neglected your schooling."

Later school experiences were more favorable and afforded a comparison of what was with what might be. At the private academy he next attended, he met the man who awakened his ambition—C. A. Huntington. "But for him I would have died on the farm and my influence would have been circumscribed," wrote Sheldon later. In 1844, after prayers at the family altar, Edward set out for Hamilton College. However, in his sophomore year, Sheldon suffered from an attack of pleurisy "brought on from inordinate laughing," he said. Subsequent practice for an oratorical contest, "was too much for me in my enfeebled condition and brought on a mild form of bronchitis."

After recovering, Sheldon came to Oswego and became a junior partner with a Mr. Allen in a garden nursery. The young man was exuberant. "This day, September 8," he wrote, "is an important period in my life—the birthday of my manhood."

But Mr. Allen was not a good provider. He was emphatically a visionary man. As the firm began to fail Sheldon became very depressed: "It very soon became evident to me that I had embarked in a sinking ship, that the firm was practically insolvent. I have the blues so that I can accomplish little or nothing." [2]

Disillusioned, the youthful entrepreneur pulled out, redeeming what he could, and desperately sought other employment. After several days of fruitless job-seeking he wrote: "It is late at night, and the watchmen's clubs are sounding on the flagged pavements over which I have been treading all day. . . . On Sabbath morning I lay tossing to and fro with fevered head and brain . . . then got on my knees, determined to leave my case with God. . . ." [3]

During this period of suspense, Sheldon bought a five-cent notebook and set out to investigate the condition of the poor of Oswego. To his surprise, he found fifteen hundred persons, mostly children of Irish immigrants, who could neither read nor write, "as ignorant and depraved as the children of India and China." He persuaded several prominent citizens to join with him in forming the Orphan and Free School Association, to provide a home for orphans and free schooling for the poor. Such schools, called "Ragged Schools," already existed in England.

When no teacher for the school was to be found, Sheldon abandoned his plans to enter theological school that fall, and taught it himself. For this work he asked only $275 but was given $300. "Nothing could have been farther from my mind," he wrote, "than the idea of teaching school."

And so it was that, in the fall of 1848, he faced 120 "rude, untrained boys and girls," aged five to twenty-one, in the Old Tabernacle on West Second Street between Bridge and Oneida. Ironically, this building was later destroyed by fire, and still later replaced by a fire barn.

Sheldon's so-called Ragged School opened, but two teachers left because the "untamed foreigners" would not sit still. Sheldon himself had no discipline problems. A. E. Winship wrote:

When two boys got into a rough-and-tumble fight, he did not rush at them as if ready to take a hand in it, nor did he shout at them. The master merely spoke to them quietly, in a tone that the school was no place for fighting, and that if they were to fight at all they must wait until they were away from the school and from other children. More than once when several boys became restless, he sent them out to run to a certain place and back to see who could get into school first. He never punished a pupil, or spoke one scolding word to those children. He pitied them and loved them. On Saturdays, he visited their homes to see where and how they lived, and to learn what could be done to make life pleasanter and happier for them. As he went on his way to school these girls and boys swarmed about him. Some caught him by a finger, and some by his coattail, all anxious to be near him. The storekeepers stood in their doorways and laughed at the strange sight. He was happy in their devotion to him, and his school was a success. [4]

The hardest part of his job was the constant draught on his sympathies. And a glimpse at his diary easily tells why:

> Oswego, Jan. 1849. One little girl froze her cheeks. Two of the boys came today two miles, came to get warm; they cried pitiously with the cold. . . . For a coat one has but ticking.
> Feb. 3—Joseph Perkins left school for want of pants and coat. Called at Mr. Blaye's where I found three girls. . . . The mother said the children were so eager to attend school, that she made for them some cloth shoes which they wore to school until they were entirely worn out and they froze their feet; and then they were obliged to stay at home; and then the children cried to go even barefooted. . . . This widow has a boy and girl who have been at my school, bright, intelligent children. The boy had on one boot and one shoe. . . . For the boy I hope to be able to get a place. The poor widow, to show her gratitude to me for the interest I took in her, fitted me out with an umbrella, and asked me to take some punch or wine, upon which I gave her a short temperance lecture.[5]

Unfortunately, funds for his Ragged School were hard to come by. "People will open granaries, wardrobes and purses, when they hear the tales of wretchedness from distant Ireland," wrote Sheldon, "but neglect the thousands in our very midst." The Ragged School, as a result, was closed, but the seeds were already sown that would shortly result in the first free graded school system in Oswego and a permanent orphan asylum.

Meanwhile, in 1849, he had married Frances Stiles—according to Sheldon "the wisest and most provident act of my whole life." He had met his future wife during college days, when both fortuitously caught the same boat at Cuylerville. Fortunately, the craft moved sluggishly, stopping at every town, thus affording time for romance to flower. They followed up their romance with secret epistles placed in a little drawer in Mrs. Stiles's front hallway. In 1849 came the marriage and the wedding trip from Syracuse to Oswego.

Here Sheldon opened a private school, the Oswego Seminary, in the old United States Hotel.[6] When this undertaking, too, collapsed, he accepted the position of superintendent of Syracuse schools. During two brief years there (1851–53) he consolidated and graded the elementary schools, and assembled the books which became the nucleus for the present Syracuse Central Library. Oddly enough, the library possessed no record of its debt to Sheldon until furnished one by this writer in 1960.

It was during his Syracuse sojourn that Sheldon became ardently concerned for the Negro's welfare, anticipating his later interest in education of the freedmen in the South. For about this time, anti-slavery agitation was at its height, due to the passage in 1850 of the Fugitive Slave Law. Syracuse was one of the chief stations of the underground railway to Canada. Sheldon wrote, "[There] I saw this fugitive from, not justice, but injustice, dragged through the streets like a dog, every rag of clothes stripped from his back, hauled upon a cart like a dead carcass and driven away to a police office for a mock trial." [7]

Meanwhile, the free school advocates had won out in Oswego, and, at their urging, Sheldon returned in 1853 as first superintendent of city schools. A friend confided in him on arrival, "You have come to a hard place to build schools. I have tried all my life to awaken some interest in school matters, but all to no purpose." But Sheldon, undaunted by this peddler of doom, set about grading the schools, and upgrading teaching. To this end, he gave written tests to his teachers and, to insure fair evaluation, identified papers by numbers drawn from a hat. He then set the incapables adrift and replaced them with the best teachers he could find. In consequence, an agonized outcry arose against importing foreign teachers and discarding home talent. Nevertheless, Sheldon persisted.

In 1859 he instituted a system of ungraded classes, called arithmetic schools, for "uncouth, untutored, rough, overgrown boys." Students in this unclassified school were able to make up deficiencies, thus qualifying themselves to enter regular schools at a point suited to their age. "These were a new feature not only of Oswego," wrote Sheldon, "but so far as I know, of any system of graded schools." [8]

Meanwhile, Sheldon had introduced other innovations, too. He instituted regular teachers' meetings, never held in the town before. He emphasized moral training, and he stressed written examinations. In short, he dictated policy, prescribing what was taught and how to teach it. Of this period Sheldon wrote: "I carried a straight-jacket system of close classification to its highest point of perfection, accompanied by a course of study as precise, definite, and exacting as it is possible to make, tested by complete and exhaustive examinations. By looking at my watch, I could tell exactly what every teacher in the city was doing." [9]

Finally, Sheldon came to realize there was a better way. His teachers memorized their lessons; the result was too mechanical. It was his quest for better solutions that led to Sheldon's historic trip to Toronto—and his discovery of materials used in object teaching. Mary Sheldon tells how, as a child, she watched her father working with them:

> The dark shelves of the little closets opening off from the dingy office where my father worked all day was filled with wonders delightful to my childish eyes, and to his own as well. We used to talk them over— colored balls and cards, bright-colored pictures of animals, building blocks, silkworm cocoons, cotton balls, specimens of pottery and glass.[10]

Meanwhile, Sheldon had continued to live at the United States Hotel until 1856 when he bought the tract now known as Shady Shore. The next year he constructed the home which, long since remodeled, houses heads of the institution today. "It was my ideal site for a home," recorded Sheldon, "displaying a great variety of trees and flowers." There in 1858 Edward and Frances set out trees in the yard, entwining two ash saplings together, symbolic of their union. And now, in 1961, after 103 years, these two trees still cling together, while those who planted them have long since gone.

Sheldon's household continued to grow apace. Living with him much of the time was his sister Dorliska, a scholarly woman to whom Edward often turned for advice. Also there arrived five children—Mary, Charles, Frances Elizabeth (Lizzie), Anna, and Laura. All eventually graduated from the school their father founded and three—Mary, Charles, and Laura—served on its staff.

At Shady Shore Sheldon's routine was a busy one. He invariably rose at five, lit the fires and wrote or studied until a seven o'clock breakfast. Then he was off to school, taking with him his children and a cold lunch. He returned home at five or six for dinner and worked or studied for two hours or more, before retiring at ten or half-past. His studies were varied, sometimes touching on curriculum or method, often in Barnard's *Journal.* At other times he read philosophy—Hamilton, Spencer or Locke. At still others, he read Harris' *Insects Injurious to Vegetation,* a favorite of Sheldon and his daughter Mary. Of an evening both would sit in a lighted, unfurnished room in order to attract insects and compare what they caught with pictures in the book. Unfortunately, Sheldon's use of insects in zoology classes aroused persecution from those who believed such exploitation cruel and drew ridicule from those who saw no sense in such knowledge anyway.

Sheldon's life had its harsher notes, too. He was always in debt, constantly digging into his personal coffers to finance school projects. In fact, he married in debt and lived in it not too unhappily ever after. Furthermore, Shady Shore's isolation made commuting to school difficult. Anna recalls her "father's continual fight in winter with the deep snow. . . . practically every day abandoning the road and driving to school over fences and crosslots." [11]

There were also the inevitable pressures and disappointments of one who attempts much and aims for perfection. Small wonder that he broke under the strain and, in 1879, went for medical treatment to Providence, Rhode Island. "It was probably nervous exhaustion," said daughter Mary, who believed it best ignored. Sheldon was ashamed of his illness, saying he had dissipated himself in his work. He tried to resign, but the board would not hear of it, insisting instead on his taking a temporary leave with full pay.

Meanwhile, Poucher, as acting principal, and everyone on the staff distributed Sheldon's duties among themselves, nonetheless refusing Sheldon's offer of pay. After a year Sheldon resumed some of his duties, and a year later, restored by a combination of the board's vote of confidence and work among his hens and bees, he resumed the principalship again.

In 1896 came the blow which spelled the beginning of the end. His wife died, and with her a part of himself. The blow seemed to prostrate him so completely at first that his friends doubted he could return to work. Nevertheless, Sheldon struggled on, refusing to yield to grief or age. In the summer of '97 he could be found—at the age of seventy-four—enrolling as a *student* in a summer school course in Chicago to learn more about the Spear methods in arithmetic. Every day he made a hot, arduous trip from his boarding place to the school.

Courageous as it was, this venture exhausted his remaining resources of body and spirit. In the next month, August, came the end, described by his sister Dorliska:

> A few moments before his death, while his lungs were filling, and we all felt the next breath might be his last, a heavenly radiance lighting his face, he whispered, "With mother," then a moment later, "with mother and Christ." His own life had been so bound up in hers [his wife's] that when he was left alone, after she had passed away, he seemed to be leading a life of waiting. . . . Within about five minutes after these last words, he passed peacefully away.[12]

Hundreds turned out for the funeral services on August 29, 1897. That same day the Reverend Wills came on a simple woman in front of the school with head bowed, weeping audibly. Such was the love that Sheldon roused in those who knew him.

Naturally, there were many posthumous tributes to Sheldon's greatness. Most immediate was the memorial exercise held at the school on October 21, 1897. The alumni made arrangements for a marble bust but realized, to their consternation, that no model existed to go by. Richard Piez came to the rescue. He obtained permission to exhume Sheldon's body and prepared a death mask himself. Then the alumni engaged the services of the noted sculptor, Herbert Adams, who had fashioned the bronze doors of the Congressional Library in Washington. The bust was finally unveiled at a special service in 1899.

As another tribute, Sheldon's name was among those of twelve leading American educators inscribed on the face of the Cubberly School of Education Building at Stanford—along with Horace Mann, Henry Barnard, David Starr Jordan, and other all-time greats in education.[13]

The most prominent memorial, however, was arranged by the Sheldon Memorial Association, composed of educators through the state. This was a bronze statue executed by the noted sculptor John Francis Brines, and paid for by two hundred thousand school children through the state. Each was invited to contribute a penny, but one brought a dime, with a note scrawled in pencil: "Ten cents from Jack Bush because Mamma did love him so I want to contribute more." In all, $3,500 was raised, $3,000 going to the sculptor and the rest for other expenses. The statue was unveiled by Governor Theodore Roosevelt at the Capitol in Albany in 1900.[14] On it is inscribed:

Edward Austin Sheldon
Educator
1823–1897
America's Pioneer
in
Educational Methods
Erected by
Children of the Public Schools
of the
State of New York
1899
The Children's Friend

Sheldon was a mixture of Santa Claus, father and saint—but his most striking trait was his Christlike character. He was a creator without the heady vanity that sometimes comes with having created. "Innate nobleness and kindness gleamed from every feature of his fine gray head," wrote Hollis. "He was transparent as a statue of glass. He was in every respect just what he appeared to be." He was scarcely philosophical to a marked degree, nor especially analytical. His actions were governed by a simple trust in the divine and by conclusions about life mirrored in his favorite sayings: "So run that ye may obtain." "Let your conduct be such that at the close of your life, you may receive the welcome plaudit." "Well done . . . good and faithful servant." "It is better to wear out than to rust out." Also embracing important tenets of his beliefs were his two favorite chapters in the Bible, First Corinthians, Chapter 13, and Romans, Chapter 12.[15]

His daily life was a testimony to his own convictions and ideals of service. "I so revered Dr. Sheldon," wrote one, "that I was almost forgetting the fatherly spirit in him till one day I saw him stoop and tie his little daughter's shoe."

A *Star-Studded* Faculty 41
But Sheldon was neither ostentatious, sanctimonious, nor condescending. In short, there was no pontifical pretense about what he did—whether for a child or for a student. "He did not play down to us, but treated us as equals," recalls Ida Bennett, '69. One of his favorite verses was Matthew 18:3, "Except ye be converted, and become as little children, ye shall not enter into the kingdom of heaven."

However, Sheldon's humility should not be mistaken for weakness. Every question, whether minor or major, was submitted to the test, "Is it right? Is it wrong?" Having measured a question by rules of morality, nothing could swerve him from his position. When he himself made mistakes, he sometimes carried penitance to ridiculous extremes. According to Mary Sheldon Barnes:

> One day during a heavy blizzard, when Sheldon could not use his horse or sleigh, he forgot to buy a paper of needles that his wife had told him to purchase. When he struggled home through the snow at five, his wife asked, "Did you get the needles?" "No I forgot them," he replied, "but I will get them. I need the discipline that will teach me not to forget." So again he struggled to town and back—two and a half miles—to discipline himself.[16]

He also exacted high standards of those for whose moral well-being he felt responsible—notably his family and the Normalites. "A penitent might be reinstated," recalls Florence Doolittle Bean, '96, "but a rebel was expelled. His ideals brooked no tarnish. Even the familiarity of round dances was barred from our Temple of Learning."

Perhaps the measure of the man may most accurately be taken from the things he loved. "He loved his home, he loved his children, he loved his country, he loved nature, he loved God," said Frank Pierrepont Graves, commissioner of education, when the Sheldon statue was rededicated in 1922.

And he loved the rural life where he felt close to nature and God. "I have decidedly rural tastes and propensities," confessed Sheldon. He looked on the garden and the vineyard as his teachers. He read them, not as a botanist, not as a naturalist, but as a child to whom these manifestations of nature were an open revelation of a divine intelligence. "I have always remembered," wrote Helen Knowles Taylor, '96, "how Sheldon reverently looked into the face of a pansy, saying 'God loves you.'" At the National Education Association in Buffalo in 1896, some beautiful flowers were sent to the platform for him. A witness remembered: "Dr. Sheldon looked at them with that calm smile irradiating from his face and said: 'Flowers are God's own messengers of love to his children. I take these as messengers of love from you and thank you for the message.'"[17]

It is hardly surprising that one who kept his eyes so firmly fixed on life's fundamentals should sometimes be absent-minded about its trivia. Once in class Sheldon looked down and suddenly said with a smile: "Why, I forgot to button my shoes this morning." Another time Dr. Swift, pastor of the Congregational Church, spoke highly, at chapel exercises, of the moral tone of the school. After the good doctor sat down, guileless Dr. Sheldon arose and announced that someone had taken from the girl's dressing room a brown felt hat trimmed with a green feather.

Yet Sheldon, while always outwardly serene, was a deeply emotional man. He felt extremes of emotion, ranging from elation to dejection. When Lincoln was assassinated, he was overwhelmed with grief. Several times in his life he became so dejected that he withdrew for a time to gain renewed spiritual sustenance for spirit and soul. But he could also rise to peaks of happiness. "I never saw my father so hilarious as on the day of Lee's surrender," recalled Mary Sheldon Barnes. "He came home with a little flag stuck in his hat and there was nothing but festival on that day." [18]

There was something of Abe Lincoln about Sheldon, in appearance as well as in manner. His features were gentle, transparently open—almost ascetic—framed by a magnificent halo of white hair. Clear blue eyes beamed benevolently from behind gold-rimmed glasses. His bearing was erect and dignified, demanding respect while inviting trust, even from the dirtiest urchin on the street.

Against this background it is difficult to understand Sheldon's early years as administrator. According to his own testimony he was autocratic, dismissing the old district teachers, instituting a strait-jacket system of examinations, even dictating details of classroom routine. "I venture the assertion that a more perfect piece of educational machinery was never constructed," he once boasted. He also fostered intense rivalry among teachers.

Against the backdrop of the times, Sheldon's early approach is easily explained. In those days American principals and presidents were czars of the campus, in contrast to the balance of power in European schools.[19] Since medieval times, European schoolmasters had banded together and governed themselves in the manner of guilds.[20]

Other, and more commendable, traits he demonstrated throughout his career. He was a man of tremendous industry, with a busy finger in all sorts of pies. Meantime, he also had to perform the principal's usual duties —in those days many and varied. Principals always taught some classes, and often kept student records, served as secretary to the board or even acted as librarian. In short, Sheldon was no ivory-towered theorist. He was a man-in-motion and got things done.

Sheldon's greatest genius was faculty-building. He built his own brain trust; his faculty was studded with scholars. Furthermore, he was adept in maintaining their loyalties and retaining their services.

Sheldon also had a talent for keeping Oswego in touch with philosophies. His perceptive genius cut searchingly through the morass of ideas afloat and discovered uncut nuggets lying there. Many ideas he freely borrowed, giving credit where credit was due. Some he gained from outstanding persons whom he invited to Oswego to display their educational wares. One whom he brought to Oswego was the famous Dr. Mohlberg, disciple of Herbart, to "enlarge the psychological outlook of his teachers." Often he took to the road himself, even in his later years. In 1894 at the age of seventy-one he traveled through the eastern states to "gain more wisdom." Also in his last years he taught himself the new vertical writing of the time, simply to give the system a try.

Sheldon was equally eager to share his experiences with others. Oswego's peripatetic professors fanned out far and wide, lecturing and taking part in meetings. In 1891, Margaret K. Smith participated in a roundtable of psychological questions in Chicago. "She shows herself without peer," wrote Sheldon; "I am proud of her. I find no one who understands these subjects so well. She can teach them all."

Nevertheless, Sheldon was no wild-eyed iconoclast; he rejected change purely for the sake of change. "Change is not necessarily progress," he often said; "but there can be no progress without change." In short, Sheldon respected the inevitable flux of events; and he kept his ear attuned to hints of new ideas. He was an educational agnostic, testing the worthwhile, adopting the useful.

After he formed a conviction, he pursued it unswervingly. He lamented the diverse, and often conflicting, educational interests in the state. He labored long for unification of the Board of Regents and the Department of Public Instruction. He did not live to see the fruit of his labors, but undoubtedly contributed toward the unification that ultimately took place in 1904.

Finally, Sheldon was a showman—without being a show-off—with a flare for the dramatic. His very simplicity threw his more flamboyant gestures into bold relief. Yet no one has ever suggested that he sought to advertise himself. He simply believed in what he was doing and wished to share his findings with others.

Tributes to Sheldon's greatness as a principal have been many. In fact, like other prophets he was rarely without honor save within his own country. Certainly Sheldon had his foes, for several years at least. Even some of his faculty took a critical view, albeit a benevolent one. Dr. Piez believed him overrated, saying Sheldon "simply kept his eyes open, did things a bit better and had a gift for publicizing what he did." Krüsi, too, implied certain failings when he said that "in view of a life so full of labor and sacrifices a few foibles will be forgotten." These "foibles" Krüsi attributed to "an overwrought nervous condition" sometimes affected by "strict Calvinistic ideas" and "insufficient preparation" for his task.[21]

But on the national scene, Sheldon's was a familiar and highly respected figure. In his later years, the school won honors at various important exhibitions. At the Columbia Exposition in 1893 the school won the Diploma of Honor and a bronze medal. At the World's Fair in Chicago in 1893 Sheldon was made president of the Department of Professional Training of Teachers, probably the highest honor that could come to him in his chosen field. At the close of the fair, his school received the Medal of Honor and a diploma for its long and useful career under one principal. A book of children's illustrative work was sent to the St. Louis International Exposition in 1893 where it won a gold medal. The signature of one of the judges, E. Kavalefsky of Moscow, Russia, was placed on the flyleaf.

Meanwhile, he who never received a degree was awarded two honorary degrees, the first an honorary Master's by Hamilton in 1869, the second an honorary doctorate by resolution of the Board of Regents in 1875.[22] Such degrees had become common by this time. The first honorary degree awarded in America was an honorary S.T.D., bestowed on Increase Mather in 1692—perhaps so he could impress European "doctors" on his travels abroad. No other honorary doctorates were awarded for three-quarters of a century, although Ben Franklin did receive an honorary Master's in 1753.[23] By Sheldon's time, however, outstanding educators were often so honored. In fact, honorary degrees were more common than earned ones among normal school principals. Of twenty-six early principals only twelve had earned degrees.[24]

Often a person's own traits are more sharply defined by comparing him with others. Winship compared Sheldon with David Page, famous founder of the Albany Normal, calling Page a genius and Sheldon a master, adding sagely: "A genius never suffers from an experiment; a master never experiments. A genius wins admiration, a master commands it." Piez likened Sheldon to his contemporary, Lincoln: "Just as Lincoln emancipated the slaves, so did Sheldon emancipate childhood from the thralldom of mechanized . . . learning."

Most often Sheldon has been compared with Pestalozzi, the man whose philosophy he popularized in America. Both were men of vision, who gave utterance to the spirit of their age. Both taught that love, hope and faith are potent forces in education as in religion. Most important, both loved children, and helped give childhood its due importance.

Oddly enough, there were similarities in their careers. Both educated underprivileged children—Sheldon his 120 ragged boys and Pestalozzi exactly the same number of destitute orphans. And both founded schools destined to make famous an educational philosophy—Pestalozzi, objective teaching, and Sheldon, its philosophical stepchild, object teaching.

But in certain significant ways their traits diverged. Pestalozzi was an impractical dreamer, Sheldon a skilled executive, with an ample quota of common sense. Pestalozzi was at heart an urbanite, Sheldon a country boy with an almost fanatic love of fine trees. When a workman, ignoring instructions, cut down a giant elm at Shady Shore, he mourned as for a friend.[25]

Sheldon along with Krüsi, Poucher, and Cooper have been called the "Big Four" of the early Normal. Undoubtedly, the second most important of these was Krüsi, who taught at the Normal from 1862 to 1886. The assistant engineer of the program that made Oswego famous, he came by his mission naturally. For a time he studied under his father, who worked as Pestalozzi's aide, then established a school of his own.

The younger Krüsi took the doctrine of Pestalozzianism with him, first to the Home and Colonial School in London, where he met Miss Jones, and later to the normal school in Lancaster, Massachusetts. About this time he received from "a Mr. Sheldon, a man he never heard of" an offer of one thousand dollars a year to teach at Oswego, a sum which Sheldon had managed to wangle from a benevolent board. "We are on the eve of a great educational revolution in the country," wrote Sheldon prophetically on May 14, 1862, "in which Miss Jones informs me you ought to take an active part. The name Pestalozzi is to become a household word in this country." He urged Krüsi, at the very least, to come to look things over, adding: "I will gladly pay your expenses out of my own pocket."

Krüsi came, saw, and was conquered. He replied to Sheldon's invitation, saying he would pay half his expenses himself and make up for the other half in lectures to the training class. Upon arrival in Oswego, he met his old friend, Miss Jones, and lectured her class of twenty teachers, then meeting in the Fourth Ward schoolhouse. "Some of the teachers," wrote Krüsi, "looked on the class with distrust, if not derision, and considered the new system a whim of Mr. Sheldon's."

That fall, 1862, Krüsi took up his somewhat varied duties as teacher of normal methods, form and drawing, and later of geometry, philosophy of education, mental and moral philosophy, French and German.

> In class [wrote Cora Brown, '75], Krüsi was a bundle of nerves, constantly pattering around. One pupil suggested that he needed sticking plaster on his shoes to keep him in one place. . . . We always knew when it was our time to recite because an alphabetical list was closely followed. But he was as dear to his pupils as he was peculiar.[26]

Residents thought of him as the "typical absent-minded professor." But Krüsi was more than a mere eccentric. He was a great teacher and educational philosopher—far ahead of his time. He insisted on getting at meanings. In teaching languages, he taught not merely rules but the reasons for them. He questioned the current use of numbers in marking. He believed you might say a pupil was satisfactory, good or excellent, but took issue with the policy of describing a student's qualifications with a round number—say 90.

He disparaged pure reliance on book learning. He would say, "You are all for a book. I like to think within myself." Nevertheless, he recognized the value of good books as source material. At the cost of considerable effort and "great expense" he obtained from England Taite's *Philosophy of Education.*

Even more amazing was his recognition of a psychological principle that was hailed as a discovery many years later—that one perceives first the whole and then the parts. In Krüsi's words, "In looking at a dog or horse, the child does not at first scrutinize its parts and their properties but is interested in the whole animal and its doings." [27]

Krüsi wrote a great deal, but only three of his works were ever published. He had difficulty in peddling one of his books, until assisted by a student who had acted as an agent for Wilson and Hinkle. Even better known than his *Life and Works of Pestalozzi* was his *Drawing Course.* "However," records Krüsi, "the 'enlightened Board of Education of Oswego' never deigned to patronize it . . . the judgment of these men, being entirely guided by the persuasive power of book agents." His third work, a collection of his memoirs, was compiled and published posthumously.

Krüsi was acclaimed both as a person and as an educator. "Tap Krüsi where you will," said Boutwell, "and good will flow out." In 1871, he was conferred an honorary Master's by Yale; and, in 1887, the Normal held a special service in his honor. On this occasion, a portrait, made from a photograph which Krüsi especially disliked, was presented to the school. On the same occasion he was given a beautiful field glass, and the student who made the presentation was Caroline V. Sinnamon, destined to teach at the Normal even longer than Krüsi himself.

Krüsi died in California, in 1903, and his ashes were sent to the Riverside Cemetery in Oswego. On a wall of the Main Building today is a bas-relief in his honor.

Third member of the Big Four was Isaac Buchanan Poucher, who was to be connected with the institution for forty-six years, thirty years as mathematics teacher and sixteen as principal. After Poucher graduated from the Albany Normal School in 1847, he studied medicine for a time, but never completed his studies. His first teaching venture (1847–48), at Martville, paid him seventy-five cents a day and board. The next year he taught in Oswego at the school known as the Red Schoolhouse, from which he was promoted to the principalship of Oswego's Yellow Schoolhouse.

When the Oswego Normal was taken over by the state in 1865, Poucher joined the staff as head of the one-man Mathematics Department, a position he held until he succeeded Sheldon in 1897. While he was to prove merely a good principal, he was an exceptional mathematics teacher. He insisted on original demonstrations, and with his students' help, worked out a text of his own.

Students described his teaching in superlatives: "He was always helpful and appreciative of one's efforts," said Ida Bennett, '69. "One could not fail to understand his explanations, but he was never lax in his requirements." And Cora Brown, '75, recalled that:

> Dr. Poucher was keen-eyed and brisk in every movement. He loved to startle his pupils by suddenly pointing his finger at the one supposed to respond. Until I knew him better his finger frightened away whatever ideas I may have had. . . . I became very fond of him, and when I met him for the last time, after he retired, I heard the usual greeting, "Hello, Cora A!"

Additional recognition of his capabilities as a teacher came from Hamilton College which awarded him an honorary Master's in 1865.

Meanwhile, Poucher had been twice married—first to Katherine L. Allen who bore him three children, Katherine, Lucy, and Allen, the last, badly crippled. After his first wife died, he married his long-time colleague, Matilda S. Cooper, in 1890.

This final member of the original Big Four, Matilda S. Cooper, later Mrs. I. B. Poucher, was perhaps the single most proficient demonstrator of the Pestalozzian techniques. Indeed, she was the ideal teacher-in-action, a consummate artist of the classroom. "What a logical mind she had," wrote Ida Bennett, '69. . . . "I never saw a teacher accomplish so much in a given time," testified Sheldon.

Aber gives us a glimpse of her teaching technique:

> The maxims, "The idea before the word," "The concrete before the abstract," "One step at a time," "Never tell a child what he can find out for himself," were applied by her as the plumb line and tri square to test all work. Her method of inculcating principles and teaching the art of questioning was philosophical. The student was required to write logical questions and answers for drawing out the ideas to be taught; not once, but daily for twenty weeks, in a series of graduated lessons in each of the subjects taught in primary schools.[28]

The next notable figure to arrive on the scene was Mary V. Lee. Dr. Lee, according to historian Hollis, "was one of the most original, positive, and at the same time charming personalities connected with the Oswego movement." She had been a prodigy and was ever the individualist. She entered district school at the age of three. As a child she "chastised black and blue, a big girl who was unkind to small children; organized a mob against a young man who 'cracked nuts' on little boys' heads; and took on as pet protégé a beautiful olive-skinned girl nicknamed 'Nigger.'"

She began teaching at age sixteen, receiving $1.75 a week and "boarding around." She graduated from the New Britain (Connecticut) Normal in 1860, and, in spring, 1862, was chosen by the State Superintendent of Schools to go to Oswego to learn Pestalozzian methods. After a term at Oswego she and Mary A. McGonegal, '63, opened the Davenport (Iowa) Training School; and three years later she became Professor William Phelps's first assistant in the normal school at Winona, Minnesota. While there, she spent a memorable summer with the famous evangelist Dwight L. Moody instructing Sunday School teachers in Pestalozzian methods. Also while at Winona she taught grammar by the Socratic method, but concluded that this technique demanded more intellectual labor from the teacher than the pupil. Consequently, she wrote Lee and Hadley's *Grammar* (Hadley was the publisher), identical in principle with, and probably serving as the model for, Mary Sheldon Barnes's famous *Studies in Historical Method.*

In 1874, Mary V. Lee obtained her medical degree from Michigan University, which institution "agreeably disappointed her expectations." That fall she began her affiliation with Oswego Normal, which terminated with her death in 1892 and was broken only by the two years (1880–82) that she and Mary Sheldon traveled in Europe and studied at Cambridge.

There are several eyewitness descriptions of this remarkable woman:

I must confess that when with her, I continually thought of Harriet Hosmer and Rosa Bonheur and that my recent admiration for the strong, single woman revived with all its force. [Mary Sheldon to Edward Austin Sheldon, Thanksgiving, 1871]

Dr. Lee was a large and rather masculine woman, with short hair, aggressive gesture, a genial laugh—and piercing, rather restless eyes. She was a strange mixture of man and woman and she has had a large influence on my life. [Unpublished autobiography of Earl Barnes, '84]

Mary V. Lee's appearance reflected her convictions concerning women's dress. Of a woman violinist who visited the Normal she wrote: "She did not move at all except arms and hands. The rest might have been a column. I weep to think how the body is repressed." She almost despaired of progress in this area. "Very few will take off their corsets," she wrote to Minnie Watson in 1886; "but nothing good goes fast."

Dr. Lee did what she could to initiate reform, both by example and precept. She refused to wear the bustle fashionable in her time. She sold to the Normal girls, for twenty-five cents each, patterns of "sensible dresses." And Piez adds these recollections:

> She startled the fair sex of Oswego by inquiring: "Why should I go around with dragging skirts gathering up dust and filth and germs?" She then answered her own query by cutting off four inches from the bottom of her long, trailing skirt so that her heels showed as she walked the streets of Oswego. For this attitude, it seems, she was thought shockingly immodest by the local ladies of her day.
>
> But worse was yet to come, for Dr. Lee argued, "God gave me a proper skeleton to support my flesh and to protect my organs. Why, therefore, should I impose over this one an artificial skeleton?" Her answer to this ponderer was to remove her corsets; and thereafter she went about on all occasions without stays. To cap the climax, Dr. Lee next had the temerity to appear with her hair bobbed short. As someone remarked: "She was merely living before her time as she dressed then in nearly the same manner that all women now dress." [29]

Yet Mary V. Lee had a powerful personality and tremendous influence on her acquaintances. The Normal girls loved her; and the Campus School children enjoyed her games of cat and mouse with them. She held prayer meetings for Welland students and played a leading part in the Presbyterian church. When the pastor suddenly resigned, the congregation was flabbergasted, until Dr. Lee drew herself to her full height—some say six feet—and said, "I feel like an old war horse; but without a leader we can still move on to victory." The effect was electrical and the others echoed her courage.

She had her own ideas about how physical education should be taught as evidenced by the following recollections of her gymnasium classes:

> I remember the class lined up in their long skirts, bodies arched in imitation of Dr. Lee, arms gracefully extended, forefingers crooked "coaxing the little bird on a limb." [Margaret Lynch De Prosse, '89]

> We did floor exercises but did not play games. She had us show her how we walked. The girls warned me what she expected, so I strode. I strode so widely that she said it was unnecessary to take such long steps. [Eliza Allen, '94]

More outstanding was her work in science. Only recently had the theories of Huxley and Darwin rocked the intellectual world. The resultant scientific movement was communicated to Oswego by Mary V. Lee, who translated everything she taught into scientific terms. She left behind an extensive collection of specimens illustrating the subdivisions of the animal kingdom and representing the labor of hundreds of her students. Such experiences proved unforgettable, as these recollections prove:

> Zoology included dissection in class of a dog somewhat overripe by Dr. Lee; and while at home in Westford, I stewed a cat which my brother shot for me, and removed the flesh from its bones, so I could take the bones back to Oswego and mount them. In mounting them, I had the help of a cat's skeleton loaned me by another girl. [Elizabeth Allen, '94]

> Under her expert guidance, we dissected many creatures, from flies and angleworms to a lone dog. She personally took charge of the dog. We learned the wonders of animal anatomy, the function of its parts, and the animal's habitat. [Florence Doolittle Bean, '96]

Also in health classes, Dr. Lee stressed the need for temperance. She impressed the young teachers-to-be with "the importance of maintaining pure bodies, free from the tyranny of fashion, of drink, and of narcotics."

Dr. Lee died in 1892 at the age of fifty-five, and on a boulder marking her grave is chiseled simply, "Mary V. Lee, Teacher." Ironically, an error in her will defeated her intention to leave her entire estate to the school she loved. From what was redeemed, increased by gifts in her honor, there was created in her name the first loan fund in the history of the school.

Two who taught only briefly at the Normal but nevertheless left an indelible mark were Henry Straight and Mary Sheldon—who later married her student Earl Barnes. Mary Sheldon Barnes has staked a threefold claim to a special place in Oswego's history—as daughter of the founder, distinguished alumna, and outstanding faculty member. Sheldon's oldest daughter was born in 1850 in the sky parlor of the old United States Hotel, afterwards known as the Old Normal. After graduating from her father's school, she entered Michigan University in 1871, about the time when the movement for higher education for women began. She herself earnestly advocated university coeducation and was among the first women to have full privileges in a well-known university. As she had majored in science she was disappointed to be assigned Latin, Greek, botany and history when she returned to Oswego to teach. Nevertheless, she became absorbed with the idea of applying scientific method to teaching history; so, after spending the years 1876–78 teaching chemistry at Wellesley and traveling

to Europe, she again returned to Oswego as teacher of history and literature.

In 1884, she married a brilliant Oswego student, Earl Barnes, many
years her junior. Both taught for a time at Cornell, then in 1891, went to
Leland Stanford, Earl as professor of education and Mary as assistant
professor of history, a rank totally unworthy of a woman of such distinction. However, she was "the first lady to honor the teaching force of
Leland Stanford University with her membership." [30] While there, though
suffering from a "grave, permanent invalidism," she made excavations and
gathered collections for the library and museum, and published her influential *Studies in Historical Method.*

At the time she died she was preparing a general history and coauthor-
ing with her husband a history of education. She had also partially arranged the material for a popular history of the Pacific Coast.

Nothing is more revealing of her personality than this little item,
written by the Barnes's biographer, Edward Griggs:

> I was with Earl and Mary Sheldon Barnes, in London, at the time of
> the operation she did not survive. Just before going under the surgeon's
> knife, she called me in and talked to me for a half-hour. She said, "I am
> a scientist, and I think I should decide this one. If I accept it, there is
> about one chance in ten that I may come through and be restored to my
> usual measure of life and work. I think the scientific thing to do is to take
> the chance; and I want you to know that I am taking it, knowing exactly
> what it means." [31]

Mary took the chance and lost. By her own request, she was cremated
and her ashes buried in Rome near the graves of Shelley and Keats. In
1924 Ellor Carlisle Ripley, '85, wrote to Caroline Scales of visiting Mary's
grave.

> I had looked at some records supplied by a woman there who could
> not read, but still the grave was not easy to find. I began to fear that I
> should not, when the woman's son appeared. Carrying a big record book
> before him just as a choir boy would hold his hymnal, he led me to
> Shelley's grave and then to hers. Above hers are two small, simple blocks
> of stone, bearing only her name, place of birth and date of death. . . .

From earliest childhood Mary had scholarly tastes. In unpublished
recollections called *A Mind's Story—the Autobiography of a College Girl,*
Mary wrote:

> I can remember just the hour when the endless wish to know awoke—
> that divine energy which urges us to mingle with the greater world with-

out. Just a child, with mother's arm about me, I stood in the little dormer window of my room, looking up and out at the clear dome of stars, that rose from Lake Ontario to the zenith. There glimmered the softly sparkling milky way; single stars, splendid and intense, drew the gaze from point to point—but best of all, I loved groups of stars, the sister-hoods of space, and best of these, again, the three strong stars of Orion's belt. "The stars are all worlds, are all suns—like our world, like our sun," said my mother softly. "All those stars?—all worlds?" And through the infinite spaces swept an infinite life that swept my soul upward and outward with it, in an infinite longing to know the bright worlds, every one. So, in a moment, the mind awoke to its energy and joy.

She never stepped out of her natural role as a scholar. Her friend Griggs observed:

. . . no one ever talked gossip in her presence; it just could not be done. Always the conversation was on ideas. With all her warm human interest, she had the mind of a scientist. Twice I recall her correcting me for some youthfully extravagant statement; and I learned gratefully the lesson for life. Her spirit was blithe; indeed, she often reminded me of Shelley's Skylark.[32]

Fortunately, she was highly skilled at communicating what she knew. Many a visitor found his way to Mary's classroom to watch the brilliant young teacher. There she introduced students to history through tying it to local events.[33] She is best known, however, for publication of historical teaching methods. Her outlines of laboratory courses in history show how each student should build his own history through use of original dates. These books were the first in America to apply the scientific or inductive method to historical study below the college level. They helped change historical work in high schools from a "deadening cramming of dry facts" to an intelligent study of original sources.

Another intellectual giant was Henry Straight. For one who had to make his own way and died at the age of forty, Straight (1846–86) attained an astonishing reputation. Orphaned early, Straight first worked on farms, then, in his mid-teens, began teaching at a salary of thirteen dollars a month for a three-month term. He earned his own way at Oberlin, Cornell, and Harvard; assisted with biological surveys in Kentucky; then accepted the chair of natural sciences at Oswego in 1876. Four years later he also became principal of the Campus School. Three of his books were written while there: *What We Want and How to Get It, Industrial Education,* and *Guides to Laboratory Teaching.*

He also planned an excellent system of laboratories and proved the practicability of experimental work with large classes. Many of the methods he used were innovations for that period—including dissection in the biological branches, and construction by physics, chemistry and zoology classes of the apparatus they used.

> He believed that a teacher who can make a battery with twenty-five cents worth of materials is more likely to introduce his pupils to electricity than one who depends on a twenty-five-dollar battery, ready-made. Or that the teacher who can prepare the skeleton of a dog is more likely to arouse enthusiasm for physiology than the one depending on a thirty-dollar human skeleton.[34]

As for biology, Straight believed in showing plants and animals in their natural environment. He took his classes to swamps, forest, field, and lake shore, always stressing the unity of nature.

He deplored the large number of unrelated subjects then taught each day, wondering "how a child's little head could hold it all." Because geography dealt with every division of knowledge, he chose it as a core with which to correlate the other subjects—years before educators proudly unveiled the "core curriculum."

Straight, however, was neither fully understood nor appreciated at Oswego. He himself was repelled by the formality of object lessons, their pretentious vocabulary, and their lack of a central theme. "The curse of our schools," he said, "is that they are not controlled by great ideas. The object lesson system has led nowhere. There are but a few great and worthy 'bigs' in the world. These should be decomposed into the 'littles' and be so carried on . . . that by the time the child is mature he will find himself in possession of the 'bigs.' "

Naturally, this sort of attack threatened those of his colleagues who were accustomed only to object teaching. They were "wedded to object lessons and opposed nature study just as their predecessors had opposed object lessons because they were wedded to the book."

Perhaps this "conflict of interests" contributed to his leaving Oswego after seven brief years and joining the staff of Cook County Normal School. And when that school united with the University of Chicago he assumed the principalship of the University Elementary School.

When he died in 1886, his work in biology there was carried on another two years by his wife, Emma Dickerman Straight. Mrs. Straight had graduated from Oswego in 1875 and taught there the next four years. Later, from 1887 to 1890, she taught in the girls' normal school at Tokyo, then headed by Takamine, once a student of the Straights at Oswego.

There were many tributes to the quality of Henry Straight's work. All agree that he was as effective at awakening a spirit of inquiry as any scientist who ever held a test tube. The eminent educator Francis Parker attributed to Straight his own interest in correlating subject matter and said of a geography text he wrote: "I published the book, but Straight's name should be on the title page." Parker often said that the best primary work he ever saw was under Straight's direction. And the historian Good asserts that Straight was probably the outstanding elementary science teacher among the famous Agassiz' students.

Further testimony to Straight's greatness comes from Oswego's distinguished alumnus, Earl Barnes, '84:

> . . . he was more truly a scholar than any man I had met to that time. He was a genial, retiring man, with a high forehead, deep-set eyes and dark beard. He was in every sense a student, and he studied things directly. He was an inspiring teacher, rather than a formidable one.
>
> It is almost impossible for me today to realize how absolutely I was bound up in the tradition of the book at this time. I had never written a word of composition in school nor had I ever studied any real thing there. No one can imagine my consternation when Mr. Straight put me in front of a glass jar containing a frog and told me to write a description of it. He was following his great master [that is, Agassiz] but he was making it too difficult for me. I stumbled along trying my best, but it was for two or three years well nigh impossible for me to work with realities at first hand.[35]

Worthy successor to that master of science teachers was Charles Scott, who adapted elementary science to children. In more than one way, he resembled the master. He, too, was more concerned with function than with structure. Not a mere inventory of attributes but grasp of meaning was his goal for students. Also like Straight, he made extensive use of field trips for collecting specimens. "He took us by train and boat to Mud Lake," says Florence Doolittle Bean, '96, "where we studied carnivores of plant life, the sun dew, and the pitcher plant. Seeing them trap and feed on flies and insects was an exciting revelation to us."

"On students he left an indelible impression," says Jessie Himes, '93, '99. And Grace B. Turner, '99, adds: "He stopped me in the corridor one day and asked abruptly, 'Were you out last night?' 'Yes,' I replied. 'I was at church.' 'Well, what did you see on the way?' 'Orion was out,' I replied. 'Where was Orion?' he pursued. I told him, so he said that I needn't take the rest of the course."

A latecomer to Sheldon's stellar array and one of Oswego's finest all-time scholars was Dr. Margaret K. Smith, '75, many of whose contributions are cited elsewhere. For ten years she assisted in establishing new normals, then studied in Europe for two years before returning to her alma mater in 1895, as teacher of Herbartian psychology. Her last years she spent in a home for the aged, where she died in 1934.

Her techniques of teaching, described by Florence Doolittle Bean, '96, should be judged in terms of that day.

> We had to sit just so, feet on the floor—no lounging. Blood circulation must not be impeded. We must have our full powers available for concentration. She expected much but she gave much. Her logic was an art. Beneath the forbidding crust of unapproachableness, she yearned for the scholastic attainment of her pupils—with all pampering deleted.

Dr. Smith's greatest contributions were in the field of translations and writing. Besides her important translations of Herbart she was coauthor of DeGraff and Smith's *Development Lessons* and one of the translators of Lange's *Apperception*.

Another who made her mark as a psychologist was Mary E. Laing, '74, '81, who studied at the Universities of Cornell and Chicago and later in Switzerland and Germany. Her early career took her to the normal schools of St. Cloud, Minnesota, and Platteville, Wisconsin, and in 1884 she organized the Froebel Academy in Brooklyn. There she instituted a system of keeping written records of children's needs, which she and student-teachers discussed together. The reports must be read in the context of the times. The following is typical of her students' evaluations of children: "A bright, ambitious worker with a danger in the direction of physical weakness. Physical and nervous conditions very bad—must be guarded morally. Indolent, but capable; slovenly in the carriage of his body." [36]

Oswego's alumni are loud in their praise of Miss Laing. Sample comments: "She inspired students," says Anna Post, 1900, "and she was tactful. Once when a farm boy made a stupid answer she gave the student-observers a warning look not to laugh." And according to Mabel Jarvis deBeer, '99, "She had such skill that forty minutes in her class seemed like ten."

Students today think of the same Mary E. Laing in connection with a student scholarship fund. The money was raised through sale of South American bonds which Miss Laing left for this purpose.

Several other staff members should be mentioned briefly. John Armstrong, among the most brilliant and versatile of Sheldon's faculty, taught at Oswego only four years, 1865–69. Krüsi called him the most learned professor who ever taught in the Normal School. He left in 1869 to become principal of the new state normal at Fredonia.

Also making a considerable contribution, though her tenure at the school was brief (1861–64; '66–70), was Mary Howe Smith, '63. On a two-year leave (1864–66), she collaborated with Arnold Guyot in writing the well-known geography series that bore his name. She also addressed educators and geography teachers throughout the northeast on Oswego methods.

CHAPTER 4

The Nineteenth-Century Normalite's Life

THE Normal student of Sheldon's day was typically a girl or young woman, with teaching experience, and—to judge by post-graduate performance—a respectable share of gray matter. Women had become popular as teachers because their services could be had more cheaply. By 1870 women teachers were displacing men all over the country. The disproportion in the sexes was especially high in eastern normals, most of which prepared only elementary teachers. At Oswego, some of the early graduating classes contained no men at all. In fact, of all Oswego graduates prior to 1877, less than one-tenth were males.

Few of the students were upper class; the normals drew from the middle-middles or lower-middles. "State paupers," the Oswegonians scornfully called them. Contemptuous aloofness, occasionally tempered with a tinge of tolerance, was the local aristocrat's attitude toward the Normalites. In fact, for a long time, hardly any girl of the so-called genteel class dared even associate with a Normal girl. And "respectable families" rarely rented rooms to Normal boys.

The situation changed for the better after 1876. In that year, Helen Sloan, whose father had half a million, enrolled in the Normal School. Her example was followed by others of means, who no longer scorned gratis instruction.

Since the district school set no age limit on its pupils, nor did it restrict its curriculum to elementary subjects, the average entering student already had teaching experience. Many such schools were attended by young people aged nineteen or over who studied there any advanced subjects the teacher would attempt. Upon leaving the district school, these older pupils often went immediately into teaching, certified on the basis of an examination given by the county superintendent of schools. In three normals for the year 1868, 90 per cent of the entering students held teachers' certificates. Of the twenty-five hundred students entering Oswego by 1880, over a thousand had taught, each for an average of three years.

Most Oswego students, then as later, came from surrounding towns and farms. However, a considerable number came from New York City and the New England states. Eliza Allen, '94, recalls leaving her home in Westford, Vermont, in the late afternoon, spending the night in Milton, eight miles away, catching a train there at 4 A.M. and arriving at Oswego at about 6 P.M. She carried her own food for the journey.

For the most part, the students were American Caucasians. However, reminiscences give occasional mention of students of other races and nationalities:

> There was an amiable American Indian girl named Louise Crouse at the Welland in 1891. She could do a war cry and Indian dance . . . There was also a shy, quiet Negro girl. . . . And we can't forget the popular young men from the Hawaiian Islands, both of them musical and useful at entertainments. One was fair-skinned and had an American father. [Eliza Allen, '94]

> There was a Negro student in 1893; he was much respected. [Jesse Scott Himes, '93]

> The Japanese, Hideo Takamine, was sent to Oswego by the government in 1875. Until shortly before that date, Japan had shared China's hatred of foreigners. [Krüsi]

The students were fairly select, and entrance requirements no mere formality. Yet entrance into the earliest normals had been generally lax. In New York State, students had to be recommended by the school commissioner or district superintendent as "possessing adequate health, scholarship, mental ability, and moral character." A recommendation was equivalent to appointment. David Page, first normal school principal in New York State, went about with horse and wagon to examine candidates whom he rarely refused admission.

After the Civil War, most normals, including those in New York State, included among their entrance requirements good health, minimum age of sixteen to eighteen, certificate of good moral character and an examination on the common branches taught in the district schools. On the face of it, not even a grammar school education was requisite for admission. However, the normals' reluctance to deny students admission rested on logic. Some professional training was better than none and students denied admission could obtain licenses anyway.

Several factors led to improvement, however. The city training schools, which sprang up after 1885, had higher standards, hence, turned out better teachers than the normals themselves.[1] Colleges began requiring high school diplomas. Michigan was first in 1870, following the German example. Furthermore, some of the normals instituted improvements, compelling others to follow suit. For a time New York State lagged behind, but finally, in 1895, raised its requirements, thereby temporarily cutting enrollments at its normal schools.

Throughout the period, however, standards among individual normals varied greatly. While students entering the poorest two-fifths of such schools were often no more mature or better educated than our present eighth grade students, entrance requirements for the others were no mere formality. In 1878, twenty of the better normals reported rejecting 26 per cent of those desiring entrance.

Naturally, Oswego's requirements were typical of the New York State normals. The catalogue for 1888 warned that prospective students be proficient in these particulars:

Ability to spell correctly.
To read with fluency and correct expression.
To punctuate, use capitals, speak and write correctly.
To write a neat, legible hand.
In arithmetic, ability to work examples is not sufficient; to be able to analyze all processes is also necessary.
In mathematical geography, a knowledge of the earth as to form, proofs of the same, its motions, day and night, seasons and causes of the same; also political geography.[2]

To insure that students did, in fact, possess such proficiency, entrance examinations, of which the following questions are described as typical, were given. (The reader may determine whether he would have been qualified to enter the Normal.)

Decline who, he, I, sister.
Write the plural of fly, girl, Miss Jones, son-in-law, money, child, basis, focus, t, 8.
Write the following sentences with the errors corrected:
Can you learn me to write?
Them that seek wisdom shall find it.
What is the difference between .75 divided by 75 and 75 divided by .75?
A pole extended into the mud $5\frac{5}{6}$ feet; $\frac{1}{3}$ of its length was in the river and $\frac{1}{4}$ of it in the air; what was the length of the pole?
It took 9 horses to move a stick of timber weighing 12,590 lbs. How many pounds would a stick weigh which could be moved by 7 horses? Solve by proportion.
Which is the longer, the equator or a meridian circle?
Name all the seas on the east coast of Asia, beginning on the north.

State the difference between the *office* and the *rank* of an element.

Parse each *there* in *"There* will be no sorrow *there."*

Add the following: One thousand thousandths; two hundred, and twenty-five ten-thousandths; two hundred twenty-five ten-thousandths; one millionth; one billion and two billionths; twenty-four hundred hundred-thousandths.

How much is the difference between the *true* and *bank* discount of $950 for three months at 7 per cent? (Allow no days of grace.) Define true and bank discount.

If twelve tailors in seven days can make fourteen suits of clothes, how many tailors in nineteen days can make clothes for a regiment of 494 men? Solve by proportion and explain.

Punctuate and capitalize the following sentences.

when i met dr brown this morning he said to me the childrens friends have returned from france when did you see them i asked and where are they.

the teachers assistant john smith said that their latin books though much torn were still used.

johns favorite saying is economy is not disgrace it is better to live on a little than to outlive a great deal.

What powers have been particularly strengthened by your work in zoology?

Give the names of the sub-kingdoms of animals. Give briefly the characteristics of each sub-kingdom, speaking particularly of the arrangement of the circulatory, digestive and nervous systems.

What mental and moral powers has the cat? Prove it.

Name a one-toed animal, a four-toed, a five-toed.

Describe your right hand.

Name four or five causes of nervous breakdown. What is the great restorer of strength to an exhausted nervous system? How can one do hard brain work and not break down?

Name three habits liable to induce dyspepsia.

Explain the seasons of California.

How do climbing plants differ from twining plants? State your observations with reference to the means used by these plants to raise themselves.

What is an exogen? an endogen? an acrogen? a thallogen? [3]

In appearance the Normalite of the sixties was a far cry from that of the scantily clad coed of today. Attire, in those days, constituted no inconsiderable appendage to the person. When the Normal opened, hoop skirts were the fashion. In the nineties, the Normal ladies wore hats, laced-up shoes, and long, heavy sweeping skirts, lined and then faced with crinoline. Added to this weight was the "dromedary hump," commonly called the bustle. This was made of springs covered with cloth, a basket work of wire or fibers, or a bag stuffed with cotton batting.

Shortly thereafter, ferris waists instead of stays, and leg-o'-mutton sleeves, enjoyed a brief vogue. Only Dr. Mary Lee, and a few of her faithfuls, dared defy the current fashion.

On arriving in Oswego to enroll at the Normal, the provincial youth of the 1860's, no doubt, gazed wide-eyed at the splendid city. Being from the hinterland, he—or more likely she—was particularly impressed by the harbor. For here was a bustling port where schooners transferred iron to trains at the dock. Flanking the river banks were huge factories and great grain elevators. Along Water Street gaunt stone structures served as quarters for ship chandleries. Hard by, on the grass-grown wharves sat the indolent fishers, occasionally landing a pike or a salmon. In the yacht basin rowboats and sailing craft rocked gently at their moorings. And far out on the lake sunbeams played leapfrog on the waves and tiny tugs bobbled like corks. Still farther out big boats disappeared on the horizon bearing passengers for other lake ports—perhaps Detroit, for eight dollars a head, all expenses included.[4]

The residential section reflected the same picture of peaceful prosperity. Men, not women, strolled in the parks, where now-huge elms and maples were then only saplings. Along shady streets came ladies' pony-phaetons, and stately carriages drawn by sleek, well-fed horses.[5] The Civil War, then raging, seemed far away—except to a few families in mourning. No vestiges of war were visible. Despite Rebel victories, there was no fear of invasion here.

For this was a prosperous city, filling its coffers from the lumber and grain trade, and the biggest starch factory in the whole, wide world. It cherished and procured the best in culture—for example, opening a fine theater and music hall in 1861. Many eminent actors came—among them, the famous tragedienne, Mrs. MacReady, who appeared as Shylock in 1872.

Whatever was currently popular found its way to Oswego. The same year the Normal was founded saw several notable events. The spiritualists held a convention and a man named Barnes announced himself the "Angel of the Lord." Another visitor that year was the Fakir of Ava, skillful juggler and magician. There also came the learned Professor O'Leary, lecturer on physiology and phrenology, who recommended dissecting manikins in school to explain inner organs. "Future generations," averred the learned professor, "would be saved thereby from a world of misery, quackery and humbug." A few years later came a wave of spelling bees when local clubs and churches struggled with obsolete words such as snaggle, sorbile and purfle.[6]

Not all Oswegonians could afford to partake of the cream of entertainment served up. There was a caste system, a gulf between those who gave orders and those who took them. People of distinction lived on the West

Side, on a certain segment of a certain street—Fifth Street, to be exact. In fact, Fifth Street was Oswego's Fifth Avenue, society's arterial sanctum. The Fortnightly Club's chief function was to define and maintain the local Brahmin castle.[7] Even middle-class children skating in the park tended to pity the poor Normalites whom they passed.

Strangely enough, from then to now, the school's fortunes have risen and fallen with the town's though there is little or no causal connection. The town rose to its zenith between the Civil War and the 1880's. So did the school. The town began a slow decline around 1890—and so did the school. By then a succession of developments had cut deep into the heart of Oswego's prosperity—the advent of railroads, toll-free canals, changing trade routes, and the depletion of Canadian forests. The school's fortunes flagged then, too.

In two respects the city's impact on students has remained constant. For one thing, they have always sensed its historic past, with its crumbling buildings, ivy-covered fort, and Indian names to remind them. All students, sooner or later, hear the story of colonial Oswego—setting for one of Cooper's Leatherstocking Tales. Oswego, students learn, was known to white men over three hundred years ago. The Jesuit missionary, Father Simon Le Moyne first visited the site in 1654. But it was the French and Indian War that brought the young settlement fame. In 1756, the French under Montcalm captured the British fort there. But the British won it back, rebuilt it in 1759, and used it as a naval base. During the American Revolution that followed, Oswego was a British military post, gateway to the west and Canada. Finally, in 1796, after years of British rule, the settlement was turned over to the young United States. A scant thirty-two years later, Oswego incorporated as a village, in 1848 as a city—and so it remains today.

Also deeply imprinted on the memory of every student in Oswego's history are the scenic wonders surrounding it. They thrill to its kaleidoscopic sunsets. They marvel at the lake's changing hues. They swim in its cool waters in summer, and steer clear of its treacherous ice pocks in winter. In winter they photograph the evergreens, struggling beneath their snowy burden. When spring comes, and they've despaired it ever would, they rejoice in the greenest of green verdure returning.

Girl students, at least, made few sorties into this peripheral world. Their usual sphere was circumscribed by school or dwelling place—which might be one of several sorts. They might live in clubs (boarding houses), in private rooms, or at the Welland. Cost of living in the club was about $2.50 a week, besides 30¢ to 50¢ "per dozen" for washing. Students took turns waiting on tables. Sometimes a group of students went in together and rented several rooms. In fact, boys and girls who were related sometimes occupied the same suite together—with parental approval, of course.

Where cooking facilities were lacking, students sometimes "basket-boarded." Several students from the country would stay in the same house, each paying sixty-five cents for room rent. Their board they paid in food brought from the farm, such as potatoes or fruit. The woman of the house did the cooking besides filling and cleaning the lamps.

A hundred of the girls lived at the Welland, a former hotel, not to be confused with the first Welland, a local tavern. This venerable institution, built in 1850, was purchased by a syndicate for $25,000 in 1867, to provide non-profit housing for students. Dr. Poucher, who owned most of the stock, neither expected nor received any gains.

In those days, the ex-hostelry seemed pretty palatial to girls from the farm. The bathroom, located on the second floor, had several toilets with overhead water tanks and two tin-lined tubs behind screens. "To many of us inside toilets were an innovation," writes Margaret Lynch DeProsse, '89. "A lady would teach the freshmen how to flush the toilets and to knock before entering because doors had no locks." One's weekly bath also proved a problem. One had to remember to sign up in advance; or else, one had to "make do" with washbowl and pitcher filled from a pump in the backyard.

Despite such inconveniences, the authorities proclaimed the Welland a total success. "There is no dissatisfaction in any quarter," the board blandly reported.[8] If so, it is the first time in history that so many students have been quartered in perfect harmony under the same roof.

Board in 1888 cost four dollars a week, including washing. That same year, however, the charge for fuel was raised from twenty-five to thirty cents a week, and washing from twenty-five to forty cents the dozen. Students furnished their own linens and bedding. Students who did their own washing might use the laundry a half day a week, with soap and starch thrown in gratis.

Students who lived in the Little Welland, that is, the Annex, paid $2.00 to $2.50 a week for quarters, but furnished and prepared their food. Most of it came in barrels from home, the rest from neighborhood grocers. Lena Cook, '97, reports that Poucher himself introduced them to incoming students.

Boys either lived at clubs or rooming houses, sometimes eating at the Welland for three dollars a week. Still others engaged rooms and cooked for themselves. Earl Barnes, '84, describes his living arrangements in the early eighties:

> My father went first to the principal and got a list of rooms to consider for rental. Finding himself unable to decipher Sheldon's writing, he invoked aid from the letter carrier. The celerity with which that gentleman deciphered Sheldon's writing filled him with admiration. Finally,

my father engaged two rooms for us, a large front room and little bed-room, at the home of a Miss Henderson, a bonnet and hat presser. We boarded ourselves, bringing most of our supplies from home, even wood, which I chopped in the barn. . . . I can recall vividly my father's driv-ing down with the long, lumbering sleigh loaded with wood, potatoes, apples and all the things that a farm could furnish.

Students from within the state received help from the Mileage Fund created by the legislature when the normals were founded and remaining in force until 1896. This fund, which reimbursed students for travel ex-penses, helped equalize educational opportunity. Naturally, out-of-staters received no such help and had to pay twenty-four dollars tuition besides.[9]

Whether the girls lived in town or dormitory, they were expected to comport themselves like ladies. Naturally, they didn't use slang; and cer-tainly they never ventured forth alone after dark. Mostly they entertained in the parlor. They danced discreetly, girls with girls—hardly ever with the other sex. Mr. Ludlow, the local Congregational preacher, denounced round dancing, declaring, "If I saw my daughter in such a juxtaposition, as I have seen girls with their partners, I would shoot the man—and the law would excuse me." More liberal were the Krüsis, in whose house "even dancing was admitted for the sake of encouraging grace and lightness of movement as well as politeness in social intercourse."

In fact, all encounters with the other sex were strictly supervised. A girl could only go out with a boy to whom she was related or engaged. Isabel Kingsbury Hart, '07, tells this story of her parents—before they were married and both were students at the Normal in the 1880's: "My father asked for permission to take my mother on a rowboat ride. He was asked whether they were engaged and he replied, 'I hope to be before I get back.' He was given the permission he sought—and the hoped-for result transpired."

Perhaps sex transgressions occurred, but if so, we find no record of them. In fact, it was common policy to hide such incidents in that day. Morison notes that faculty minutes of Harvard in the early days never mentioned problems of illicit sex relations. Either the topic was not men-tioned in polite company, he concluded, or there was a high degree of student chastity.[10] The same could have been said of the Normal.

Originally, few restrictions were placed on women students. After all, most of them had taught several years before resuming their education. However, this sensible policy soon yielded to the inordinately repressive treatment generally accorded girls in their day. The young women re-sented the change but had no alternative but to submit. They had nothing to do with the rules that governed them.

Where government of students was concerned, there were two concepts after 1865. First was the trend toward student government in the last third of the nineteenth century. A step in this direction had occurred in 1765 at the University of Virginia, largely at the instigation of Thomas Jefferson.[11] The University had a court made up of student representatives to consider all disciplinary cases. The system failed because the students' honor code forbade informing on wrongdoers. By 1865, however, many boys' schools were making progress in this area.

The second concept, faculty control "in loco parentis," involved the ten-foot-pole relation between faculty and students. Faculty members, like papa and mama, always knew best; and the pupils, like children, must not question, but obey. This concept prevailed at Oswego, where women were concerned at least. If there were any rules whatsoever for the boys, we have no record of them. It appears ludicrous—but almost tragic too—to think that young women on the verge of graduation had to request permission to hold a class meeting without a chaperon. Mabel Jarvis de Beer, '99, recalls: "At our last class meeting before graduating the others put me up to asking the faculty to let us have our meeting without chaperons. I did, and we did. We had a blackboard there and imitated every member of the faculty. We had funny costumes and I can never forget the fun."

The school's official position on the subject, "government of the school," appeared in every catalogue—always in the same cryptic language—from Sheldon through Poucher: "The idea of self-government only is inculcated. . . . Little disposition is manifested to take advantage of the absence of teachers. Every pupil is a law unto himself. At least, this is the rule; the exceptions are rare." (Translation: Even when the cat's away, the respectable mouse won't play!)

Another antidote to student capers was the strong spiritual overtone, reflecting Sheldon's vigorous religious character and the Puritan tradition. In the ante bellum South, at Oglethorpe University in Georgia, everyone had to attend morning prayers at 6:30 A.M. And in 1797 the Yale Moral Society required its members to pledge themselves to conduct themselves according to Biblical precepts, to abstain from profanity, card playing and gambling.[12] Furthermore, the earliest printed rules of Harvard announced as the institution's chief aim, that "everyone shall consider the mayne End of his life and studyes, to know God & Jesus Christ, which is Eternall life." [13]

Sheldon placed Christ and curriculum in the same order of priority as did Harvard. "Whatever omission there may have been in the supervision of the intellectual part of the school," wrote Krüsi, "nobody will accuse [Sheldon] of neglecting the moral part. . . ."

Indeed, the Normalites' religious fare was adequate to nourish the soul. On Sundays they heard impassioned pulpiteers thunder the doom of those who sinned. On weekdays chapel was a sacred ritual. Sometimes Poucher read the scripture, especially his favorite—St. John, Chapter 2, beginning, "My little children these things write I unto you." But more often Sheldon attended the readings himself. "I remember his religious exhortations," wrote Krüsi, "uttered in a manly, earnest voice, and always impressive, because his hearers knew that his life and actions were in unison with his sentiments."

There were also prayer meetings—many of them. Every morning at the Welland, girls gathered for Bible reading and the Lord's Prayer. They conducted these meetings themselves; teachers did not attend. But on Sunday afternoons the King's Daughters held meetings in the preceptress's rooms. At one of these Dr. Lee declared: "We are all miserable sinners, aren't we, Miss Hawks?" Miss Hawks, a plump, rosy girl who lisped, said good-naturedly "I thpoth we are." Also memorable were the Saturday evening prayer meetings sometimes led by students, sometimes by teachers. "The meetings never lagged," said Cora Bennett, '69. "They were informal and very helpful to us." In short, no moral ambiguities existed. The straight and narrow path was carefully defined and few departed far from it.

The faculty concerned themselves not only with the students' spiritual well-being but with their physical health as well. Since the doctor's medical arsenal was but mediocre, emphasis was on prevention. While present-day faculty members press students to work harder, their nineteenth-century predecessors warned their charges against undue exertion.

> If you are tired and worn by overwork [the 1888 catalogue suggested to prospective students], you had better get thoroughly rested before entering. If you have become enervated by sickness or chronic disease, your first effort should be to secure vigorous health before deciding to take up a course of instruction in preparation for teaching. If the preparation does not prove too much for you, the teaching certainly will. Only those who possess strong constitutions and vigorous health are equal to such an undertaking. Nothing perhaps is more exhausting to the nervous system than teaching.
>
> The teachers endeavor to keep a careful oversight of the pupils to see that they do not undertake to carry too much work. . . . If any pupil overworks, it is palpably his own fault, and he does it in the face of the earnest protestations of his teachers.[14]

Students were also warned against "the false economy of limiting yourself as to the quality or amount of food."

It was this same concern that led to the introduction of health courses into college curricula, such as Dr. Lee's work at Oswego. Faculty members felt that something should be done to "stave off the hectic glow of consumption's hidden fire in students' faces." And students reflected their mentors' concern. One student, Hermann Von Schrenk, wrote in 1889: "The walk from my home to the school is a long one, but I think it improves my health." The student hitchhikers on the hill today seem content to forego this prophylactic advantage.

The only important school-sponsored extracurricular activity in Sheldon's day was the literary society. In fact, on college campuses generally, such societies enjoyed undisputed preëminence until well after the middle of the nineteenth century. At most colleges at least two rival societies appeared, and sometimes three. Often real rivalry resulted. At Princeton it was unheard of for a Whig to room with a Clio. One concludes that the literary societies were only semi-literary; they were also social.

There were three such societies at Oswego. All freshmen belonged to the Hall Society, established by Mary V. Lee and Ordelia Lester in 1879 and reorganized as the Keystone in 1883. This organization provided experience in public speaking and acting in short plays. Upper classmen belonged to the Avalonian, started in 1866 and reorganized as the Athenean in 1879, or to the Adelphi, begun in 1879. Students were eligible for bids to one or the other, the Adelphi being the more social of the two. The student himself had little choice. Names were placed on an eligible list from which the two societies might choose.

Each society chose a subject for study for a designated number of weeks and members read papers on various phases of the subject. The best of the papers or plays from the "privates"—held in each club's own rooms on Friday mornings from eleven to one—were chosen for the "publics," to which the student body and townspeople were invited. The following one was given by the Avalonian and Adelphi Societies, Friday evening, January 23, 1874:

> Anthem: The Lord is My Shepherd
> Salutatory: Ambition
> Debate: *Resolved,* That poetry exerts a more beneficial influence on the
>   minds of men than does history
> Tableau: Scene in a Farm House
> Essay: Gems
> Drama: That Boy Tony
> Declamation: Richter's Dream
> Valedictory: The Province of Discussion

Most of the students enjoyed the organizations, partly for lack of else to do; partly for practice in preparing talks, for experience in parliamentary law, and for stimulating contacts with other students. But Florence Doolittle Bean, '96, recalls: "Certain young ladies, however, were unappreciative of the 'feast of reason and flow of soul' and used the meetings for doing fancy work. But when the supervising faculty member detected the guilty one plying crochet hook and needle, 'corrective measures' were taken."

In such a serious atmosphere, it is not surprising that students actually studied. Study, in fact, was no side dish but a staple in the student's daily diet. Study hours, rigidly enforced, lasted from 7 to 9:40 P.M. Many times girls sneaked lamps into closets and worked on until the wee hours. "I used to put chunks of ice down my back to keep awake," says Helen Knowles Taylor, '96.

Undoubtedly, study was promoted by the rarity of outside distraction. True, church groups had socials, and sometimes the Normalites saw plays. In the sixties they saw Madame Rhea in a Shakespearean drama and Jo Jefferson in *Rip Van Winkle*. They also attended the winter lecture course to which students were given a special rate. J. B. Gouch and Wendell Phillips were among the lecturers heard.

Otherwise, entertainment was informal. In winter students went sleighing, and sometimes slush-mugging, that is, hitching a sled behind a cutter. In the autumn came Sheldon's harvest party, and in the spring maple sugar parties in the Shady Shore grove.[15] Small pails caught the sap from the trees—and boys initiated girls into the mysteries of sugar making.

In the summertime, students strolled on the breakwater and collected on the piers. They watched grain vessels unloading their cargoes in the big elevators. And sometimes they hitched rides on the tiny tugs.

Sometimes the students had parties, with imitations of the faculty a favorite feature. Student-faculty relations were formal and the take-offs a chance for emotional catharsis. At one party, Miss Angeline Fox read the roll call from a grocery list in Margaret K. Smith's best English accent: "Miss Oil! Miss Olive Oil! Is Miss Oil not present?" Angeline's rendition of the long list brought down the house and was taken in good part by Miss Smith.

There were special occasions, too, such as the centennial celebration of American independence. "I remember," said Krüsi, "how our Japanese friend Takamine [then a student], usually so solemn and dignified, entered into the spirit of fun—or celebration—by blowing a child's trumpet with all his might; while in front of our house the flags of three nations— American, Swiss, and Japanese—were displayed as a sign that our humble home was inhabited by individuals belonging to America, Europe and Asia."

There were other occasions, less festive but equally spectacular, such as the burning of the grain elevators in the early 1890's. From their vantage point near the river, wide-eyed Wellandites watched the spectacular blaze from 4 A.M. till dawn.

Most common entertainment of all was small talk. They discussed school endlessly; current philosophies occasionally; but, except during Mary V.

Lee's time, showed little interest in women's rights. Mostly they discussed their studies and their teachers, because the impact of classes and teachers was much greater then than now. For one thing, since extracurricular diversion was rare, classes assumed a more important position in the student's psychological field. Furthermore, each faculty member taught every single student. Finally, the somewhat formal teacher-student relationships tended to foster anxiety over the most trifling details whenever both parties were concerned.

Even so, faculty-student relations at Oswego reflected the general improvement in such relations in the country at large. Before the Civil War there were sometimes student brawls and town-and-gown riots. In one, Yale students bested the local fire laddies. Boots and blackjacks were sometimes hurled at professors. Andrew Dickson White, recalling his student days at Hobart and Yale in the 1850's, wrote: "I have seen a professor driven out of a room through the panel of a door, with books, boots and blackjacks hurled at his head." [16]

However, we have no records of any such shenanigans at Oswego. For one thing, outright insurrection had become rare when the Normal was founded. Besides, the Normal was primarily a "ladies' school." With a few exceptions, faculty-student relations were reasonably friendly though formal. Much about the relationship then sounds familiar today. Then as now, students had nicknames for faculty members. Students referred to "Catfish" Walters and "Limpy" Norton. Then as now they felt elated when they "put one over on" the "prof." Ida Bennett, '69, confesses that when Krüsi called on her one day she could not think of an answer.

> That dreaded zero! I could not bear that, so I rose in my place and dissembled. I said, "Before I answer, Professor Krüsi, I want to ask you about something you spoke of yesterday." Pleased, he asked what and I asked something. He stood notebook and pencil in hand. He explained and I sat down receiving a good mark. I suppose I felt the mental applause of the classmates around me, not for my answer, but for the stratagem.

Undoubtedly, hauteur often hid warm hearts, but most faculty members were stiffly formal. Mary V. Lee and "Dicky" Piez were among the exceptions. Theirs was a warm relation with students, far in advance of their day. Mrs. Krüsi, too, offered kindly guidance to students, but received "ministerial hints" that her religious views were so liberal as to have injurious effects.

Sheldon's own relation to students cannot easily be categorized. Above all, it was a paternal one; he was always ready to befriend them in trouble. "In the autumn of '98," writes Mary Alling Aber, "I was perhaps the youngest student there. I asked Dr. Sheldon if I could be excused to go home because of neuralgia in my face. Upon seeing my features twitch with pain he impulsively placed his hands on my arms and said, 'Child, go home and do the best thing for yourself that you can.' His manner was so kind that tears rolled down my face." Students often said that if he blundered it was from lack of judgment and not from lack of heart.

Naturally, entering students—often shy and insecure—were especially grateful for Sheldon's kindness. "Dr. Sheldon has been very kind to me," wrote Hermann Von Schrenk to Earl Barnes in 1889, shortly after enrolling at Oswego. "He has fixed my studies in the best way possible, and when I asked him to change certain things, he did so cheerfully and without a word." And Lillie Babcock Herrick recalled that when she took her entrance examination in Sheldon's office he offered her part of his lunch. He also let her keep her books in a corner of his desk all term whenever they were not needed.

Often he helped students with financial difficulties, too—and never lost any of the money he lent them. One former student wrote: "I shall retain some of it [the $200 that Sheldon sent] using it only in distress, for it seems to me different altogether from other money, not as mere money, but as something invested with character savoring of humanity."

Naturally, as foster father to his brood, Sheldon often opened his home to them. "The first time I ever had chicken with mushrooms," says Grace Beardsley Turner, '99, "was at Dr. Sheldon's house. They also had little biscuits with hot chicken gravy."

Sometimes he invited the entire school for fun and a frolic. "A little nonsense now and then, is relished by the wisest men," he wrote in his diary. On one such occasion, many more students came than there were seats. According to Mary Alling Aber, "He went to the cellar and brought up two grocers' boxes and placed them on end in one corner of the dining room. We then found that but one saucer and one spoon remained. To the amusement and possibly the envy of the others students I shared sugar with Dr. Sheldon."

Students recall Sheldon as an able and inspiring classroom instructor: "He led us to think for ourselves. Thinking was stressed," says Florence Doolittle Bean, '96. "I had history of education from Sheldon. We thought he was wonderful. He created a something in us," relates Grace Beardsley Turner, '99.

In both his roles, as foster-father and as instructor, Sheldon created strong loyalty. In a letter to Ellor Carlisle on May 3, 1890, Mary V. Lee wrote: "Yesterday the Normals planted seven trees in Sheldon's yard." Another indication is the liberal contribution of graduates, often from meager salaries, to memorials honoring the founder.

The importance of all other aspects of student life paled before the glory that was graduation. Such occasions were taken seriously, the lengthy programs consuming most of a day. Certain features were quite different then, for example, student demonstrations of teaching.[17] Most of the guests at these demonstrations were returning alumni; others were invited by the graduating student himself.

A second feature was the delivery of student declamations, masterpieces of supercharged superlatives—a practice dating from the first U.S. commencement of which we have a record, at Harvard in 1643. That program included "Latin and Greeke Orations, and Declamations and Hebrew Analysis Grammaticall, Logicall, and Rhetoricall of the Psalms; and Their Answers and Disputations in Logicall, Ethicall, Physicall and Metaphysicall Questions." [18]

Certain other features of the program continue, with variations, to be familiar. They had musical numbers, but more of them and more often religious than today. Diplomas were distributed, but state certification was accorded only those showing "the highest degree of success." [19]

Graduation garb was often elaborate; caps and gowns came to Oswego in the 1920's. "My graduation dress," wrote Lena Hill Severance, '73, "was of book muslin, with high neck, flowing sleeves, a polonaise with a huge bustle, a very long train behind tied back and reaching to the floor in front, trimmed with tucks and ruffles. It made quite a hit." The class of '75 was more somber. "The entire class of forty-three," wrote Cora A. Brown, "wore black grenadine over black silk. I don't remember what fiend suggested it, but it was certainly a gloomy send-off. The few males simply wore their Sunday best."

At the same time, each graduating class followed the usual traditions of such classes. They always chose a class motto, usually didactic. (Samples: "Round by round," 1873; "The Truth," '75; "The noblest motive is the public good," '99.) Sometimes they voted to have rings or pins; at other times they had neither. They also chose class colors, for instance, the red and green of the holly in 1893. And they always left some gift for the school. The class of '93 left books for the practice school library "for teachers to use."

The first to hold a class day was the class of June, 1891, numbering fifty. The main event was the burning of the criticisms passed out daily by Sara J. Walter to members of the practice class. A funeral pyre was arranged in the quadrangle, presided over by a Greek priest and priestesses. The graduates, singing the class song, deposited the criticisms on the fire as they passed. This pungent paean went as follows:

> When we first came on this campus,
> We were freshmen as green as grass.
> Now as grave and reverend seniors,
> Smile we over the verdant past.
> We're a class that will be famous,

We proclaim it with a shout,
For we've learned not to tell others
What they themselves can find out.

So away from old Oswego
With its "concentrate and drill"
We depart and, if forever,
Have these two points with us still.
Criticus, criticus, criticus, criticus,
Ah me! Criticus mortus est.
Criticus, criticus, criticus, criticus,
Heigh O! Criticus, mortus est.[20]

After graduation some went elsewhere to get degrees. Helen Williams, '69, became the first woman to graduate from the University of Michigan.[21] Most graduates, however, went directly into teaching, though many took degrees later on. In fact, of Oswego graduates to 1880, not counting those who had married or died, 98.5 per cent were teaching, in twenty-nine states and territories, including Japan, the Sandwich Islands, Nova Scotia, and Argentina.

No wonder many went far afield. In New York State in 1860 the average yearly salary of the city teacher was $384, of the rural teacher $122.[22] By 1873 salaries ranged from $260 to $2,000, $400 to $600 being most common. The differential by sex was highly discriminatory. In 1880, the average pay for "lady graduates" was $554, for gentlemen, $1,116.

Salaries elsewhere were higher. In 1877 a Mr. Thompson wrote in the *Albany Journal* that the "Normal graduates flee with joy to the West." To which statement an Oswego alumnus rejoined: "They do not flee, they are expelled . . . compelled through competition with those who teach after thirteen weeks in the 'teachers class' of a private academy." [23]

Nor had the situation improved, relatively, by the 1890's. Jessie Himes, '93, received $350 for her first year as kindergarten teacher in Utica. Of this amount she paid four dollars a week for board. Kate Hayes, '97, received her first month's pay in pennies, a two-quart pailful from a church. We infer that she was reaping the rewards of the collection plate.

To assist graduates to find suitable positions, Oswego early instituted a Teachers Bureau. To defray expenses, each student availing himself of the service had to pay fifty cents, and an additional two dollars if he accepted a position which the bureau procured for him.[24]

To sum up, the student's stay at Oswego was hardly an exuberant one. Every emotion had its inhibition. Students lived not so much dangerously —or even dully—as vicariously. However, they took a tremendous pride in their famous school, and fully appreciated its many constructive features. They spoke of Oswego then as the Harvard man perennially speaks of Harvard. In 1889 Hermann Von Schrenk spoke of his teachers as "pleasant" and the whole school as interesting. He commented on the "nicely equipped gymnasium," the "large rooms where the air is so pure."

For a time, however, scholarship apparently had something to be desired. Reputedly, "four other normals were founded to supplement what was felt to be a deficiency at Oswego." [25]

By the nineties, Oswego had regained its reputation. Alumni report that work then was difficult, thorough and respected. "It was considered one of the best normals in the East," wrote Eliza Allen, '94. "Oswego was more thorough than Dartmouth, where I attended summer school." And Grace Allen, '97, adds: "We worked hard when I was at the Normal. We respected standards."

The alumni, meanwhile, had long since organized; in fact, their first meeting was held at Normal Hall, July 9, 1867. At this time was instituted the custom of planting the ivy, a tradition followed by all except two classes which planted trees, until the building was torn down. The class of February, 1868, surmounted one small problem: "There being no gentleman in the class, the duty of planting the ivy devolved upon one of the ladies, Miss Eva Edwards, who handled the spade with as much ease and grace as any man." [26]

First branch of the alumni association was organized, at the instigation of Mary Hayes Stackpole, '86, on Long Island in 1891. Twenty-seven alumni responded, meeting at Roe's Hotel, in Patchogue, Long Island. Next came the New York branch, the well-known Oswego Boys Club, long an active organization. But from this time until the 1950's, regular alumni activity almost ceased to be.

CHAPTER 5

The Sheldon Period Evaluated

THE famous historian, Good, names Sheldon as one of the three who contributed most to improving the quality of elementary education in the nineteenth century. Horace Mann led in the creation of state systems of schools and the original founding of normal schools. Francis Parker made of Quincy an object lesson in good teaching. Sheldon spread object teaching and founded the Oswego Normal, spawning-ground of educational ideas.

More specifically, Sheldon rated three firsts in setting the pattern for structuring teacher-training institutions. He instituted the first training class for teachers in service.[1] He organized the first of the city training classes, which became so popular later on. And he founded the school which set the pattern for all the normals in New York State and for the great majority across the country.

The famous educator William Bagley, speaking at Oswego's Seventy-fifth Anniversary Celebration, called Sheldon "the father of universal education." For one thing, Sheldon had fought for free schools. He had also drawn into the educational field the overaged and incorrigibles whom others had discarded as uneducable.

Sheldon's specific emphasis in child study was also new. Froebel had founded his theory on a study of infancy, Pestalozzi on childhood, Herbart on youth, Rosenkranz on the mature man. Sheldon considered man throughout his development, from infancy onward. In contrast to medieval education which prepared people for death, Sheldon saw education as preparation for life—all of it. Unlike Rousseau, Sheldon also saw in a return to nature a return to law and order rather than to laissez-faire.

Sheldon's philosophy was an optimistic one, based on a belief in divine benevolence as manifest in nature. Children as creatures of God were to be loved and respected. They should be freed from compulsion and lifeless mechanisms in order to habituate self-activity and self-esteem.

These views concerning human development and child nature were

75

amply demonstrated at Oswego. By arranging a graded sequence from kindergarten through college, Sheldon tacitly acknowledged the importance of every life stage. He also insisted on a child's attaining proficiency at each level before proceeding to the next, thus becoming one of the earliest exponents of readiness. He arranged for making up deficiencies by means of ungraded work. At the same time, students were exempted from whatever they already knew, thus avoiding the wasteful duplication still so prevalent today. We find frequent cases of students' being excused from taking the rest of a course already begun, when the teacher found the student knew it already.

Furthermore, Sheldon classified and promoted children in such a way that bright ones might not suffer from going too slowly or dull ones forced to go too fast, sixty years before Dr. Anton Sickinger introduced his Mannheim System. Still another of Sheldon's "firsts," noted earlier, was his organization of unclassified schools, for accommodating those not properly provided for in the regular graded schools. To assist in such classification, as well as to assess progress toward objectives, he instituted a definite system of examinations. In short, Sheldon helped standardize the doctrine that individual differences should be respected.

Sheldon also improved the welfare of the teacher. By disseminating comparative information, he focused attention on teachers' salaries. He helped teachers achieve recognition by dramatizing and publicizing their achievements.

Finally, Sheldon paved the way for ultimate unification of educational control in New York State. He had begun his efforts in 1874 when feeling between the Board of Regents and the Department of Instruction was bitter. However, bill after bill failed until unification was finally voted in 1904. Sheldon had not lived to see the results of his labors, but it was he who laid the groundwork.

In short, present-day educational historians should take due cognizance of a statement by the State Superintendent's Council in 1897: "When the future historian of pedagogics shall rewrite the changes in American education, the progress in primary education and in the training of teachers, Edward Sheldon shall stand alone, the Pestalozzi of the new world."

As to the school itself, there is ample evidence of its success. Top-notch teachers turned down better positions to stay on its staff. In a day when travel was costly, students came from all over the country. At least one outstanding school superintendent, Dr. McVickar of Cleveland, came each year to choose teachers from the graduating class.[2] And the honorable David Camp testified that he had traveled widely for worthwhile ideas and would "tell with gladness what my eyes have seen and my ears have heard [at Oswego]."[3] The superintendent of schools of

Toledo called Oswego's primary schools the best in the country: "I did not notice a single instance of that listlessness and stupefaction which is inseparable from our systems of rote teaching. . . . Every eye flashed with delight, each little face was radiant. . . ." [4] Frank Pierrepont Graves, state superintendent of schools, called Oswego the "most famous school of teacher training in the United States, if not in the world." [5]

Professor M. V. O'Shea of the University of Buffalo, later of the University of Wisconsin, said the Oswego Normal had had a more beneficial influence on elementary education than any other institution in the country. President Butler of Columbia said that no school had had greater influence on the training of teachers.[6] Col. F. W. Parker, superintendent of schools in Chicago and principal of the Chicago Normal School, went even further, according Oswego first place in influence on American education.

In summary, Oswego's opinion-molding stature was so great and its graduates so widespread, that whatever it stood for had great influence. Where theory was concerned, little totally new was produced. What Oswego did was to focalize many floating ideas—for example, Pestalozzianism—and work out rational ways they might be applied to the classroom. In fact, we may say that Oswego was the first institution to wed educational theory to practice and to utilize the practice school effectively for that purpose.

Oswego stressed the importance of professional training—and plenty of it. Oswego did not originate practice teaching, but it was the first school to have the students carry on a full-time teaching program in the school of practice. Heretofore, only observation and isolated experiences in teaching lessons had been provided.

The Oswego Normal was also the first to use a true laboratory approach systematically testing ideas and theories. Anything worthwhile was tried—including systems of teaching music, language, and physical education. Especially notable was Oswego's work in the area of science which led to nature study and child study. To quote Sheldon himself:

> During the period, 1886–88, I wrote the leading educational men in the country before I had heard that any such thought existed in the mind of anybody, asking why we should not study children systematically and scientifically as we study plants. This correspondence brought out the fact that some ladies had started a movement in this direction and had sent out lists of questions for mothers to answer. Among the men addressed was G. Stanley Hall. Whether I have preserved his answer I cannot tell.
>
> When Miss M. K. Smith came to us in 1888 [after two years' study in Germany] we began work in earnest. . . . Miss Laing has taken it up

with more thoroughness but along somewhat different lines. . . . In this we have certainly led all the normal schools of this state and perhaps of other states, but as to this I do not know. . . .[7]

For several reasons it was fortunate that Oswego's own specialty was elementary education. Oswego's success began in elementary education and dramatized its cause. Oswego helped establish the principle that elementary teachers must have broad knowledge and professional skill, capable of transmitting a liberalizing general education. At the same time, expansion of the elementary school's objective necessitated a better prepared elementary school teacher. Furthermore, the study of objects required running the gamut of knowledge at least on lower levels, reaching far beyond the three R's. Hence, teachers of elementary school must have broad knowledge and better preparation. A major step was thereby taken toward establishing for elementary teachers the standards which ultimately won for them salaries equal to those of teachers in secondary school.

Oswego faculty and alumni also did much to build and foster a professional literature. Sheldon, several of his staff, and many Oswego alumni, were prolific writers. Sheldon's books had a wide sale in England and America. Hermann Krüsi, Mary V. Lee, Mary Sheldon Barnes, Jennie Stickney and Earl Barnes were all pioneers in educational methods.

Oswego, furthermore, recognized requirements of certain areas of specialization—manual training, and critic work. Oswego helped win for both these areas recognition through the country. It was the first normal to organize a manual training course;[8] the first to recognize manual training as general education; and the first to have a definite course in kindergarten methods.[9]

Another of Oswego's contributions was the initiation of a normal school tradition. The centuries of tradition that cluster about the liberal arts institutions were notably missing among these stepchildren of the state. Sheldon and his staff helped supply the color and prestige the normals sorely needed.

Oswego also deserves credit for disseminating educational ideas. Sheldon and his staff traveled extensively, taking active part in professional meetings. His students fanned out far more widely than did those in other normals. Significantly, Oswego graduates founded, or helped found, teacher-training institutions all over the country. Oswego has been called the "Mother of Normals"—and deservedly so.

Finally, we come to the contribution for which Oswego was best known and which has proved most controversial, namely, object teaching. Its detractors, who dismiss Oswego's role as interpreter of Pestalozzianism as insignificant or negative in effect, base their case on the following points:

(1) The Oswegonians were imitators, they say, and not very good ones at that. They peddled a brand of Pestalozzianism already diluted by certain British educators into a less-than-quality product. Nor was Sheldon even the first to introduce Pestalozzi to America. For that matter, object materials had already found their way to the office of the Cincinnati superintendent of schools a full year before Sheldon's historic trip to Toronto.[10]

(2) Far more important is the criticism that the object teaching method, being easily learned, encouraged a host of ignorant imitators who quickly seized upon it as a "bag of tricks." Since it was far easier to learn the method than the relatively progressive principles undergirding them, inept teachers made use of the method and ignored the underlying philosophy. They often learned rules-of-thumb, resulting in mechanical classroom procedures, often assuming grotesque and fantastic forms. In practice they reduced the system to the same verbal level as the textbook method that preceded it.[11] In fact, few teachers of the time had the knowledge or insight to use the method with maximum efficiency.

(3) Furthermore, while recognizing the worth of motivation and the need to consider individual differences, the Pestalozzians provided no adequate explanation of either. Their theory of learning rested largely on the later discredited theory of faculty psychology, making plausible the idea that subject matter is important chiefly as a means of exercising and developing hypothetical faculties of the mind. The theory implies, first, that it is more important that subject matter be difficult than useful, and second, that effective teaching depends on sufficient repetition.

By contrast, other authorities concede Oswego a highly significant role in the emergent philosophy of American education. Unlike Sheldon's detractors, their perspective is in terms of the times. Their historical frame of reference leads to these conclusions:

(1) While Sheldon was not the first to bring Pestalozzian ideas to America, Oswego publicized them and put them in a form which could be transmitted by the normals of that day. Students entering such schools were ill-prepared and the term short. Students lacked the background for a highly complex system of teaching—and the schools themselves, the monies, facilities, or scientific knowledge to organize such a course. In fact, much of the early normal's course had to be spent in making up deficits, often on the elementary school level. Little time was left, permitting only a narrow technical type of training such as object teaching. Within such limitations any attempt at broad professional training would have been so thoroughly diluted as to be confusing.

(2) The Oswego system, while relatively mechanical, constituted the first breakthrough from the textbook-recitation method. For generations children had done nothing but memorize subject matter; teachers had done nothing but hear the answers. Teachers kept school; they did not teach. Even texts were on a question-and-answer basis.[12] (For example: What is the extent of France? How is it bounded?) So long had the ship of education foundered on the shoals of the recitation method that it took a strong wind to set it free. That wind came from Oswego, wafting its way across the land and supplying the power needed.

(3) However, the change wrought by object teaching was not so drastic as to predestine its failure. For one thing, teachers still had "a method" on which to rely. They still had the security of remaining within their own limitations. Hence, object teaching served as a workable transition from completely stilted to more flexible methods.

(4) So far as psychological foundations were concerned, we must remember the limitations imposed by knowledge in that day. Actually, object teaching represented no inconsiderable advance. Even in the area of learning theory, it made a large contribution. It represented a revolt against the mere memorization of verbal symbols. It sought, at least theoretically, the enlargement of the child's field by personal experiences suited to his stage of knowledge. The inevitable consequence of these ideas was a focusing of attention on individual differences, and the introduction into the curriculum of such concrete and active subjects as industrial arts and nature study.

Such ideas radically affected the teaching of traditional subjects and practices, while helping to pave the way for new ones. The old fact-geography, sometimes called mail-clerk geography, gave way to study of one's immediate surroundings.[13] The teachers of arithmetic came to realize that numbers are simply abstractions, and began to stress objective foundations. Object lessons with plants and animals developed into nature study. Concern with "doing" laid the foundations for industrial arts. Relation of teaching to the child's personal experiences quickly revealed individual differences in development and mental ability, thus paving the way for such areas as kindergarten and classes for exceptional children.[14]

(5) Of even greater significance was the interest which object teaching awakened in the pupil as a person—for the first time in American education. In fact, in this sense, Herbartianism was to prove a step backward. The Herbartians applied to the schoolroom what was currently being found out about learning—but they forgot about children.[15]

(6) Meanwhile, object teaching also had an important effect on teaching as an occupation. Teaching acquired more dignity; it took its

first giant stride toward becoming a profession. For the first time in history a real technique of instruction was called for. Lessons must be thought out in advance. The teacher himself became emancipated from dependence on the words of a text, and able to stand before a class to answer freely. He became conscious of a new strength and a professional skill unknown in the days of textbook reciting. Simultaneously, he gained a self-respect from feeling that he possessed a skill not the common property of ordinary laymen.

(7) Oswego injected a shot of adrenalin into the normal school program, which heretofore dragged badly. The Civil War stimulated interest in education for the masses—and created at the same time, a favorable climate for establishment of more normal schools. However, had none of them come up with a method for mass-producing the needed teachers, teacher training might long have lingered in the doldrums. But Oswego popularized and dramatized the cause of teacher education and, in consequence, normal schools spread rapidly. Therefore, while the methods of object teaching would be worse than useless at present, Oswego played an effective and dramatic role in the history of education at a time in educational history when such help was sorely needed.

(8) The Oswego Normal, furthermore, left its mark on modern education. One would think from the Pestalozzian post-mortems that after the 1880's Sheldon's object teaching was dead. True, those who distorted the Oswego system temporarily discredited it, but they did not kill it. The seeds had been sown; they simply lay dormant. In the twenties and thirties, the theories of Sheldon and Pestalozzi, blended with more adequate psychological knowledge, revived in the form of progressive education.[16] Thus Pestalozzianism, as interpreted by Oswego, in the end proved more viable than the Herbartianism which displaced it. Unfortunately, however, only the perceptive few are aware that the structure of modern education owes much to object teaching.

To these points, a brief postscript should be added. Object teaching was the prescribed dish served up in every classroom, no matter how garbled the recipe. But at Oswego, fountainhead of object teaching, the system was no bag of pedagogical tricks. Sheldon, and the best of his faculty, continually sought the soundest foundations of education. It was not their fault that their imitators went astray. After all, both the other great movements in American education, Herbartianism and Progressivism, have been as thoroughly misapplied as the system they succeeded. Any system of education can be reduced to pedagogical platitudes and classroom rituals. Even today incompetents revert to the lesson-hearing of colonial days, simply because it is the easiest method of all. Nevertheless, it is no wonder that disciples of Herbartianism sought to make their own reputations by dwelling on absurdities performed in the name of the system they sought to displace.

It seems fitting to conclude treatment of the Sheldon period with a survey of the Oswego Movement, the migration by which alumni with messianic fervor spread Oswego's message abroad. For the Movement assumed fantastic proportions. "Perhaps no other school has exerted a greater impact than Oswego," wrote Hinsdale in Nicholas Murray Butler's *History of Education in the U.S.*[17] "I place the Oswego Normal as first in its influence upon the education of the country," wrote Col. Francis Parker.[18] Indeed, the school at Quincy which brought Parker fame used Oswego's methods. "Unquestionably the parent of the present system of normal instruction throughout the country," is another evaluation.[19]

Oswego made its influence felt in several ways, for example, through publications by staff and by alumni. Many were prolific writers, pouring out an endless stream of textbooks, manuals, and articles. Sheldon himself, aided by Miss Jones's notes and by his staff, supplied the standard references on object teaching. The only other authoritative reference on the topic was by Calkins, who spent some time at Oswego collecting his data.

Many came, or were sent, to Oswego, as to an educational Mecca, for inspiration. Professor Phelps, then of the state normal at Trenton, sent a teacher to Oswego to learn the methods. Others came for briefer refreshing. Widely known faculty members like Krüsi, Cooper, Lee, Straight, and Mary Sheldon saw a succession of visitors.

Oswegonians also personally peddled their wares abroad. In 1867, the whole faculty was invited to Cincinnati to lecture before the teachers' association. Krüsi, one of the five who went, described the visit thus:

> At the Institute we were struck by the great number of German teachers, whose presence was felt by the great interest they showed in the exercises. . . . Thus, for instance, the members of our Faculty were invited by the German teachers to visit with them a concert at the "Loewen-Garten." They came to our hotel in their best suits, each carrying a rose in his hand, and presenting it to the lady he had agreed to escort. I had enough of the German feeling left within me to be glad to have our American friends, mostly of the temperance order, go to such a place, and see how a German public, in spite of the beer glasses before them, can behave in an exemplary manner, and in some respects better than an American audience. . . . To judge from the comments made by the Germans on the lecturers, it would seem as if they were particularly pleased with the energetic manner and distinct utterances of our Miss Cooper, while the orthodox part of the American audience

may have particularly admired the solemn, weighty remarks of Dr. Armstrong on the wonders of Creation.[20]

Most important in the Oswego Movement were the graduates themselves who, in 1863, began the mass migration which was to continue unabated until Sheldon's death. By 1886, of the 948 graduates of the first twenty years, 485, or more than half, taught outside New York State, including every state, the District of Columbia, and six foreign countries. By 1900 hardly a normal school in the country had not counted one or more Oswego graduates among its best teachers. Testifying to the evaluation placed on Oswegonians was the pay they received. In 1877 male graduates were receiving more than two and a half times, and women more than twice, the average for their respective sexes.[21]

Perhaps the most important of the Oswegonians' functions was to help establish new normals. For this was the period of enormous growth in public teacher-training institutions, the number increasing from sixteen in 1860 to sixty-one by 1872, and eighty by 1880. Most were founded and staffed by graduates of existing normals, especially Bridgewater, Albany, Illinois Normal and Oswego. Of these, Oswegonians played the greatest part, by themselves founding twelve state normals and many city normals in this country, several in foreign countries, and assisting with the founding of a great many others. "Every normal school, so far as I know," wrote A. B. Mayo in 1886, "whether state or city, between Pittsburgh and San Francisco, has been organized on the Oswego plan; and hundreds of her graduates have been at work in them since 1865." [22]

An important by-product was reduction in prejudice against women as administrators, a reform which sadly begs reinforcement today. A. P. Hollis wrote:

> Lady graduates from Oswego have frequently been pioneers in securing recognition for their sex as school officers. One lady graduate of the first class served five years as county superintendent on the Washington Territorial Board of Education. Another lady graduate has been superintendent of public schools of Iowa City, Iowa. Still another was State Institute conductor of Minnesota. Lady graduates of Oswego have served as county superintendents in New York State, while a recent lady graduate was a member of the State Council of Nebraska.[23]

Naturally, Oswego's impact on education was greatest in New York State. The six state normals that opened between 1867 and 1871 copied their curricula after Oswego's. And when John Armstrong left to found the school at Fredonia he took with him a staff of Oswego alumnae. Even Albany, whose founding antedated Oswego's, adopted the latter's professional program in 1890. Furthermore, it was an Oswego alumna, Amanda Funnelle '62, who organized Albany's practice school.

Cornell, too, owed a debt to Oswego. That college based its work in nature study on ideas borrowed from Oswego.[24] In addition, Earl and Mary Barnes assisted with research at Cornell for a time and Eugene P. Andrews, '87, headed the Archaeology Department there for many years.

In New England and the West Oswego's influence was chiefly in the area of city training schools. The early state normals were thronged with pupils, largely from rural districts and villages, whose preparation was of the most elementary sort. The instructional emphasis was on making up the academic deficit—a deficit often so great that many normal graduates went forth with a scholarship inferior to that of grammar-grades graduates in city schools today. Even so, as late as 1860, only one Massachusetts normal even bothered with an academic department.

Oswego did much to remedy this situation—first, by originating its own city training school for teachers, the first of its kind. Thus, Oswego furnished a pattern and paved the way. Oswego also upgraded the academic standards by requiring that students make up whatever deficiencies they possessed in elementary subjects as a prerequisite to professional work.

New England, however, with characteristic independence, was slow to follow Oswego's lead.[25] Sheldon recorded his reaction after visiting what the local superintendent had designated as "the best primary school in Boston": "[The school's atmosphere] was oppressive. The children had the attitude of so many soldiers. The teacher had magnetic power. Miss Stickney said the school moved as by some automatic power."

In 1863 Boston, at least, had made an important step; it had imported Jennie H. Stickney, '63, as a pioneer missionary in the new methods. At first she found the going rough. The local teachers had agreed among themselves that they would neither speak to her nor visit her room. By the end of the year, however, she had won them over and that same fall established the highly successful Boston Training School. She attained even greater eminence, however, as author of texts in language, reading and drawing.

Another pioneer, Rebecca Jones, '67, organized and served as first principal of the Worcester, Massachusetts, Training School until it was absorbed by the Worcester Normal School, now the State Teachers College. "Her portrait in oils now hangs in my office," writes the school's present head, Eugene A. Sullivan.

Ellor Carlisle Ripley's ('85) contributions were even more varied. This versatile woman was in turn director of teacher training at the Norwich, Connecticut, Free Academy; superintendent of schools in New Haven; organizer and head of the Education Department at Wellesley; and only woman on the Boston Board of Superintendents for fifteen years.

She lived to the age of ninety-eight and left a legacy to the Mary V. Lee Scholarship Fund.

Other Oswegonians in New England were Adelaide Finch, '83, principal of the normal school at Lewiston, Maine, and William Baldwin, '84, head of the normal at Hyannis, Massachusetts.

In the central states and Midwest, Oswego graduates founded city training schools at Detroit, Philadelphia, East Saguinay, Cincinnati, Reading, Davenport, and other cities. Phelps patterned the Winona, Minnesota, school after Oswego, then staffed it with that school's alumni or those acquainted with its methods.[26] Isabel Lawrence, '73, was director of the St. Cloud, Minnesota, Normal, now the Teachers College, for forty-two years. Oswegonians were also on the original staffs of the normals at both White Water and Platteville, Wisconsin—and nine served at the Madison, South Dakota, Normal between 1887 and 1897. Longtime head of the Mathematics Department at the University of Michigan was Louis Karpinski, '97, who was in charge of the mathematics exhibit at the Chicago World's Fair in 1903. Mary Goodman, '82, taught manual training in Omaha for many years.

Oswego graduates also filtered through the normals of the West. When W. A. Norton, former Oswego faculty member, became principal of the normal at Peru, Nebraska, he reorganized its curriculum on the Oswego plan with the help of Oswego alumna, Margaret K. Smith.

Another institution owing a debt to Oswego is the University of Chicago School of Education, offspring of the Cook County Normal School. First to go there was Armada Paddock, '63—and we have already mentioned the Straights. Its famous principal, Colonel Francis Parker, often reiterated his debt to Sheldon. Another Oswegonian in Illinois was Jeannette McCool Holmes, '83, to whom the famous school at Normal erected a memorial.

In the Far West, we have already noted Mary Sheldon Barnes's contributions at Stanford. Her husband, Earl Barnes, '84, was one of fifteen men brought to Leland Stanford to inaugurate a Department of Education in that institution. Earl Barnes was one of the most versatile of the Sheldon alumni, with unusual skill as teacher, researcher and author. Alcinda Morrow Whitson, '68, after teaching eighteen years in Argentina, taught Spanish at the newly established University of California at Los Angeles. While there, she became concerned over the condition of the daughters of the Mexican workers on the South Pacific railway then under construction, most of whom were illiterate and many the victims of prostitution. She founded a school for them and once personally rescued a Mexican girl who had been seized by a bandit.

In the South, because of the southern white's suspicion of Yankees, Oswego's efforts were largely confined to helping Negro freedmen. Here is the form letter that Sheldon distributed to recruit teachers for their schools.

My Dear Friend,

Good teachers are wanted to labor among the Freedmen in the South, under the auspices of the Am. Miss. Ass. Great opportunities are here offered for doing good. If we reckon the pay only by dollars and cents, the compensation is, indeed, small; but if we calculate it by a different, and wiser estimate, it is abundant.

For subordinate positions, teachers are allowed from $15 to $20 per month and all living expenses.

If you would like to engage in this work, please inform me at your earliest convenience and oblige.

Yours truly,

E. A. Sheldon [27]

Oswego's graduates were among those recruited. After his graduation in 1875, Amos W. Farnham became principal of the Avery Normal Institute and in 1879 professor of Latin and principal of the Normal Department at Atlanta University. Later he organized the Normal Department of Claflin University in Orangeburg, South Carolina; and still later established the normal school in Orange Park, Florida. Peripatetic Margaret K. Smith, '83, also taught for a time at Atlanta University; and Sarah J. Walter, '76, was original director of training at Hampton Institute in Virginia. The present elementary school at Hampton is named for her.

One Oswegonian, Harriet Daily, '97, even penetrated into the remote mountains of Tennessee and the Carolinas. On observing the schoolmarm's modest bookshelves in the twelve-by-sixteen shack that served as a school, a primitive pioneer inquired: "Don't it hurt your heads to read so much books?"

Another alumna who bore Oswego's standard southward was Lucy Robinson Phelps, '80, who organized Charlotte, North Carolina's, first graded school and introduced Oswego methods there. Later Mrs. Phelps became the second woman in the history of New York State to be elected a village president.

Actually, Oswego cut a swath across the whole American educational scene. The foregoing survey represents a mere sampling. Oswego's alumni, usually in an important capacity, carried object teaching into every state and territory of the union. This influence was the more important because it established patterns, strands of which persist today.

Still other graduates carried Oswego's influence abroad. Below the border Fannie Snow Hamilton, '80, established a normal school for girls in Mexico City, whose graduates disseminated Oswego methods throughout the country. Maude Hill, '88, taught in Puerto Rico and Brazil.

But Oswego made its most important contribution to Latin American education in Argentina.[28] Between the years 1875 and 1883, ex-President Domingo F. Sarmiento, then minister of education, invited sixty-five American normal school graduates to establish teacher education in his country. He got the idea from a magazine article telling of six hundred teachers going by way of Cape Horn to teach in the Oregon Territory. He had in mind a thousand, but found it hard to get qualified persons. A major problem was the Victorian code dominating women's conduct in that day. An article in the *New England Journal of Education* for June, 1877, questioned the propriety of the young ladies' going so far away.

The sixty-five young women who finally went rose above the mediocre attainments generally expected of—or even permitted—their sex. During the period, 1869–98, they founded or reorganized eighteen normals and assisted in establishing others. Meanwhile, Argentine literacy rose from 20 to 50 per cent.

The schools that contributed most to this work were Oswego and Winona, Minnesota, then largely staffed with Oswego graduates. Oswego itself contributed four persons, including the most important of them all, Clara Armstrong, '68, first woman to found a normal school in South America. Assisted by Mary Gay de McMillan, '76, she opened a school for young women at Catamarca, a procedure which involved such tricks as getting prisoners to clean the building. Clara was principal and Mary head of the model school, where she also taught natural sciences, arithmetic and gymnasium. Meanwhile, the fact that Miss Armstrong was a Protestant disturbed the locals until the priest declared her a good woman —hence, harmless.

Later, both returned to the United States, Clara to recruit and take back to Argentina six other women. During her absence, the young man who had substituted for her had absconded with all the school's funds, making it seem to be her fault. She had to pay a year's salary and commit some of her personal property to pay for what "this ignoble crook" had squandered. Later the President of the Republic lifted the embargo on her property and publicly exonerated her.[29]

When her salary was cut off in 1880, in order to obtain funds to maintain herself and her work, Clara went on a sit-down strike in the administrative offices in Buenos Aires. Actually, she poured all she made into her work, paying for several talented young Argentineans' education. In Buenos Aires, she also founded the Women's Exchange to promote the welfare of women.

When she returned to the United States the Argentine Government gave her a purse of gold and paid for her passage. She was also commissioned to supervise the Argentine school exhibit at the International Exposition in Buffalo in 1901. And she was later recommended by President McKinley as director of a school for training Cuban teachers.

Next most important emissary to Argentina was Jeannette Stevens, '75, who worked for a time with her old Oswego classmate, Clara Armstrong, at Catamarca.[30] In 1884 Jeannette and her friend, Theodora Gay of Malone, set out for Jujuy to found a school, taking their own provisions. On this trip the Argentine coach driver lost his head while fording a stream but the youthful schoolmarms kept theirs and saved the day. They placed branches in the stream, thus permitting the coach to move safely across.

The young founders had to prepare their own equipment but managed to open the school by the fourth of July, a date chosen to symbolize the bond between their country and Argentina. The people of the town had a surprise fiesta for them, presenting them with banners, formed of American and Argentine flags entwined together. Boys, later added to the school, resented at first being taught by a woman. Jeannette, however, ignored their resentment and taught them baseball, tennis and other sports.

Later Jeannette left this school, entered a convent and began teaching women in a house of correction. Still later, in 1890, she opened the Cuban Annex to the normal at New Paltz. There young Cuban women were prepared for founding and teaching in normals back home.

Fourth Oswego alumna in Argentina was Alcinda Morrow, '68, who taught Latin Americans for eighteen years, first in Argentina near Rosario; and later, as noted elsewhere, in California.

All these young women achieved success despite great difficulties. For one thing, they had to go to South America by way of England, since no ships made the trip direct.[31] They had to devise materials as best they could—and there Oswego's practical education served them well. They had to break down the longstanding tradition which forbade young Argentine women to go outside their homes for schooling. Finally, they had to face raised eyebrows from homefolk who cared more for decorum than for Argentine enlightenment.

Oswegonians also influenced the education of Hawaii. First Oswegonians to teach there were Alice Haviland, '79 (later Mrs. Uldrick Thompson), and Anna Cole Hill, '80. Among the dozen or so who were there between 1880 and 1897 were Emma Adams, '91; Uldrick Thompson, '89, who became principal of the Kamehameha School; and James L. Dumas, '92, head of the newly founded Kamehameha School for Girls. Later Dumas became head of the Teacher-Training Department in

Honolulu High School which, in 1931, became the College of Education of the University of Hawaii.

The educational traffic between Hawaii and Oswego was two-way. In 1891 two Hawaiians, Samuel Y. Keliinoi and Charles E. King, received scholarships from the Hawaiian Kingdom to study at Oswego. Upon graduation both returned to Hawaii, where Keliinoi, '95, became successively grade school teacher, supervising principal of the Honolulu Normal and Training School, and member of the territorial House of Representatives. King, '95, taught four years in Hawaiian public schools, then served in various administrative capacities and later in the territorial legislature. He was most widely known, however, as a composer of Hawaiian songs, and until he died in 1950, maintained a music publishing company in New York. Later, when James Riggs retired from the principalship of the Oswego Normal, he called on King when making his round-the-world voyage in 1933–34.[32]

Oswego likewise left its mark on education in Japan. Modern education began in Japan about '72, and shortly thereafter the Japanese government sent Hideo Takamine to the United States to learn Oswego methods. Unfortunately, many details of Takamine's life and works are missing, because he himself died in 1910 and his papers were destroyed during World War II. His granddaughter now heads the Futaba College for Girls where the present Crown Prince's wife attended school.

Takamine's chief contribution has been in the area of women's teacher training in Japan. Specifically, he founded and directed the higher normal school at Tokyo, later the Tokyo University of Education, oldest normal in Japan. Incidentally, Dr. Takashi Kurasawa, professor of education of the Gakugei University in Tokyo, is presently collecting research concerning Oswego's part in the history of Japanese education.[33]

Other Oswegonians who worked in Japan were Emma Dickerman Straight, '71, as already noted; William Bishop, '91, who instructed in the government school there; and Harriet Alling, '83, who taught in a Methodist mission school.

Elsewhere in the Orient, two graduates went to the Philippines—one as a government entomologist and another to Australia. In Burma, 1879–84, Ann Barkley, '76, first trained nurse to do foreign missionary work for the Baptist Board, organized and ran a school for nurses.

Besides their contributions to normal schools, graduates rendered educational services of many kinds. Arthine A. Bush, '72, taught in the School for the Blind in New York City; Jessie Deans, '97, was instrumental in obtaining teacher welfare legislation; and Philadelphia Hallock, '81, served as editor of "The Answers to Queries Department" in *The Teacher's World and Normal Instructor*. Elizabeth Farrell, '95, initiated the program for training handicapped children in New York City and headed such classes, five hundred in all, for twenty-five years. Also in New York City Charlotte Lund, '91, initiated a program of grand opera for children. And at Washington State a building is named for Nancy Van Husen Van Doren, '68, who taught English there.

At least fifty graduates wrote books, a great many others articles, and still others performed miscellaneous roles connected with publishing. Among the most prolific writers were Mary Sheldon Barnes, '68, '69; Earl Barnes, '84; Andrew P. Hollis, '92; Adelaide Holton, '81; Jane Hoxie, '94; Sarah Sprague, '73; and Henry Saxe, '93. By far the greatest number wrote on professional topics. Others tackled a wide range of subjects, as evidenced by these titles: *Woman in Modern Society*, Earl Barnes; *American Archaeology*, Byron Cummings, '85; *Problems of Babyhood*, George Wells Fitz, M.D., '83; *Cemetery Inscriptions of Spender, New York*, Mary Frances Hall, '69, '71; *Sunday School Reform*, Mary Elizabeth Hutcheson, '81; *Hindu-Arabic Numerals*, Louis Karpinski, '97 (jointly with Professor D. E. Smith); *Skyward and Back* (science reader), Lucy M. Robinson, '80; *Soul Culture*, Sarah Elmina Sprague, '73. Helen Shaw Weller, '92, was a book illustrator, and Alfred Richardson, '79, became director of the Education Department of Macmillan Publishing Company. Lottie Blair Parker, '72, wrote *Way Down East*, a play which proved so popular that she lived on the royalties the rest of her days.

Of those who left educational work, many went into social welfare work of one kind or another. For the period that Dr. Mary V. Lee was on the staff more students entered medicine than any other non-educational field. One of them, Dr. Rebecca Stoneroad, '85, was long-time director of physical training in Washington, D.C., public schools. Even more unusual for that day, alumna Orie Storms Wyman, '80, became a lawyer. Hermann Von Schrenk became one of the most important pulp men in America. George Davis, '85, was one of the best-known engineers in the country. Among other important jobs, he helped plan the reconstruction of San Francisco after the earthquake in 1906. Other graduates became nurses, evangelists and missionaries, in China, India, Puerto Rico, and Japan. Miscellaneous occupations included: inventor, newspaper editor, secretary for the Methodist Church, naval captain, matron in a girl's reform school, matron of a Salvation Army orphanage, and street railway magnate.

Unfortunately, we can give credit to only a fraction of the numerous Sheldon alumni who achieved.

PART II

The Poucher Period

1897-1913

CHAPTER 6

Sheldon's Lieutenant Carries On

POUCHER's administration, 1897–1913, was in reality a postscript to the Sheldon period. Poucher himself had been associated with Sheldon from the school's founding. Every outstanding faculty member of the Poucher period save Bagley was either hired by Sheldon or graduated from Oswego in his time, or both. Furthermore, Poucher's avowed purpose was to continue in the Sheldon tradition. Finally, the aura of the Sheldon era hung over the school, affecting all that was done.

Nevertheless, Poucher's administration cannot be dismissed as a colorless anti-climax to the period just past. These sixteen years were marked by events and achievements of permanent significance to the school. First was the winning of a gold medal and Diploma of Honor at the Paris International Exposition in 1900. On November 9 of that year Dr. Poucher received notification of this honor from Howard J. Rogers, chief of the American Department of Education and Social Economics at the exposition. Oswego's exhibits there consisted of specimens of work done in the various departments of the school. The next year Oswego was awarded the silver medal and Diploma of Honor at the Pan American Exposition.

A second historic event was the sculpturing of Sheldon's statue by Brines, who had just completed an assignment at the new Capitol Building in Albany. In Paris Brines modeled the clay figures from which the finished statue was cast in bronze at the celebrated foundry there. After its dedication, the statue was left to stand for two decades in a badly lighted southeast corner of the Capitol.[1]

Other accomplishments related to the physical plant of the school. A triangular plot of ground, one acre in size, now part of Montcalm Park, was purchased and converted into a school garden. Encircled by an iron fence and crisscrossed with cement walks, the garden was a beauty spot, fragrant with shrubs and flowers. For nine years the garden was to serve as a laboratory for nature study and a source of aesthetic satisfaction. It was the subject of the following note in the *Minutes of the*

93

Board for March 18, 1910: "A Mr. James Fox applied for the position of laborer in the garden. He had been gardener in England for twenty-three years and one year in the Royal Gardens of the late Queen Victoria at Windsor."

Mr. James Fox obtained only temporary employment at best, because the garden was discontinued when the school moved to Ontario Heights in 1912. The plot itself became a state park commemorating the role that Fort George, which once stood on the site, had played at the time of Montcalm's conquest in 1756.

Two other acquisitions proved more lasting, the Sheldon residence and a new building. The former had been abandoned and in poor condition for some time. In fact, it had been broken into and the top of a tree sawed off and carried away. In 1908 the board voted "that Mr. Charles S. Sheldon be permitted to occupy the house free of rent, all fruit grown on the premises to be reserved by the local board." The following year, Mr. Sheldon was permitted to continue in the residence paying five dollars a month, the fruit again being reserved by the board.[2] The old homestead was part of a package deal when the twenty-seven-acre Sheldon tract was obtained as a site for the new building.

The story behind the selection of this site is an involved one. Although Sheldon himself had nourished hopes of such a project, not until 1906 was the legislature formally approached. The board argued that "if influence had not been brought to bear the Board of Health of Oswego would have declared the twenty rooms in the (present) building unfit to be occupied by human beings." Besides, added the board, "the children have no place but the public streets for recreation." When the legislature, in consequence, appropriated $25,000 for a site, the bickering began. Among sites favored by various board members were the Orphan Asylum site, the Fitzhugh Park site, the Gerritt S. Miller site, and the W. H. Kidder site. Commissioner Draper himself preferred the so-called boulevard or Sheldon site, but the board liked this one least of all. In fact, they passed a resolution unanimously rejecting this choice.

It was finally agreed in 1908 that each member of the board should write to the commissioner his preference and why. Some of their arguments sound amusing today. Mr. Stowell, for example, rejected certain sites because "they were in practically full view of the railroad tracks" and besides "there was a large turbulent hoodlum element in the vicinity." The Merrick Orchard site was rejected because it was close to the Army post.

Mr. Coon supported the Kidder site on East Seventh Street because, "Few people from that locality are found in the police courts. It is a locality pleasant and safe for young ladies to pass through either in the daytime or in the evening to attend evening lectures, concerts, etc."

Mr. Draper, however, persisted in urging the Sheldon site, for these far-seeing reasons:

It is ample in size and admirably broken in topography; in landscape possibilities, no other site approaches it. It alone commands views of both Lake Ontario and the mouth of the Oswego River. I think all this, the fact that it was the home of Dr. Sheldon is to its advantage; combined with the natural advantages which Sheldon appreciated so keenly, this is a matter of no small weight. Educational institutions are aided by sentiment as well as by other considerations. I don't wonder that this property has seemed to some of you members very distant and cold in winter, but it is practically the same distance from the center of the city as the Kidder property and no colder than other high available ground about the city. The transportation facilities are about as good as to any other site under consideration; and it must not be forgotten that such things are bound to follow the flag. I am confident that if you can think well to join me in approving the Sheldon site another generation will be disposed to say that it was the best thing it came our way to do for the Oswego Normal School.[3]

After this tempest-in-a-teapot, the board in April, 1908, concurred in Mr. Draper's choice of the Sheldon site and decided to offer $15,000 for it. Shortly thereafter, Assemblyman Lewis introduced a bill asking an appropriation of $300,000 for construction of the building. However, since both the Albany and New Paltz buildings had recently been consumed by fire, their needs took precedence. Professional courtesy demanded that Oswego's request be temporarily withdrawn.

Next year (1909), however, the legislature appropriated $340,000 for a new building, "exclusive of furniture and equipment." The cornerstone was finally laid as a feature of the Semi-centennial Celebration which began June 29, 1911. Engraved invitations were sent to every living graduate and many came from all over the country. Most of this celebration was devoted to speeches, and at the close of one by Mary E. Laing, motion was made that October 4, Sheldon's birthday, should henceforth be celebrated as Founder's Day. A less solemn feature was a dance, which the local paper reported as follows:

In the evening, the alumni attended a dance which was held in the New Armory on West First Street. Favreau's orchestra furnished the music. The younger members of the group did most of the dancing; while the older ones enjoyed each other's company and looked on until the Grand March began at ten o'clock in which all took part. Oswego men and boys, who were not members of the alumni, were not allowed to attend. They must have gained some satisfaction from learning . . . that the absence of many men distracted from the pleasure of some of the young ladies.[4]

Finally, came the culminating feature, on October 31, 1911, the laying of the cornerstone. In it was placed a "sealed copper box containing the following—the Holy Bible, copies of the *Oswego Daily Times* and *Oswego Palladium*, address of the Honorable P. W. Cullinan, a catalogue of the Oswego Normal and Training School, a small silk American flag, copy of *Redbook* presented by Frederick Clark, program of the semi-centennial exercises, and finally, a scroll signed by all members of the current graduating class.[5]

After the cornerstone had been laid, a group of five hundred children sang "America," and by the time they had finished many in the crowd had joined them. Among the crowd was Dr. Mary Walker, clad in her Sunday-best and carrying a large umbrella. Dr. Mary—local celebrity, feminist, and only woman doctor to serve in the Civil War—always dressed in straw hat, topcoat and tails, to dramatize the need for change in women's dress.

The new building, completed in 1913 and costing $400,000, was an impressive structure of tapestry brick with blue Indiana limestone, terra cotta, and marble for trimmings. Actually, the building was to have been occupied a year earlier. In fact, the 1912 graduating class assembled in front of the old building and sang a song of farewell.

The move to the building came none too soon. About the only facility recalled by Poucher alumni as available and adequate was the science laboratory, of which the school was very proud. In general, facilities which present-day students take for granted were missing. Halls in late evening were dark; students of 1900 often taught by gaslight. There were no lockers; no places to study. The only study hall was around a large table at the end of a corridor, a nook hardly conducive to concentration.

Worse still, library facilities were limited, according to Isabel Kingsbury Hart, '07.

Lack of funds necessitated many shortcuts, especially in the library, which was open for only a few hours a day. There was no librarian; faculty members rotated this function among themselves. . . . My own memories are restricted to the reference shelves which were always accessible, and to the periodical room which was just plain funny. One big piece of equipment stood in the center of the room—a long, narrow desk, perhaps ten feet long and thirty inches wide, like those of the old-style English accounting rooms at which clerks stood. A superstructure ran above the middle of the desk similar to a modern clothes rack, from which hung strong but fine steel chains. Each chain, in turn, was attached to a current issue of a magazine. A student could read the magazine only as long as he could endure standing. Possibly the chains were long enough to permit sitting, had there been any chairs.

Nor were students trained to use such facilities as existed. "I came from a high school which had no library," recalls Frances Gaffney, '07, "and I was let loose in the one at Oswego with no more idea how to use it than a babe. The catalogue was Greek to me. I was too proud to ask so I just foundered."

Notwithstanding such evidence one finds this item in the school catalogue for 1910–12:

PEDAGOGICAL LIBRARY: This is very complete, containing many of the most valuable works published in the English language on psychology, pedagogy, and the history of education. It also contains many of the most valuable German publications on these subjects, and is being largely added to each year.

Fortunately, curricular revision, unlike building improvements, moved ahead, especially in the area of manual training. Dr. Piez taught manual training until 1900 and Earl Burchell simply pursued the same program until 1903. Meanwhile, however, certain developments precipitated radical modifications. First was the interest in demand for teachers of handcrafts, and second, the discovery that only half the normal schools had conformed to the statute of 1889 requiring teaching of manual training.[6]

The resultant reorganization left in full charge Joe Park, who then proceeded to organize the Special Drawing and Manual Training Course in connection with the four-year English curriculum. In addition to work required for the regular two-year normal school diploma, persons electing this course took the following: Manual Training I, including joinery and cabinet making, 150 hours; Manual Training II, including carpentry, pattern making and wood turning, 150 hours; Manual Training III (molding, concrete work and art metal), 150 hours, and drawing (mostly mechanical), a total of 850 hours. Graduates of this curriculum earned the regular normal school diploma as well as a "special Drawing and Manual Training Certificate," and usually found good jobs after graduation.[7]

The manual training program for the period 1902–11 may be appraised in terms of aims, and employability of graduates. Aims were somewhat confused, reflecting both vocational emphasis and Herbartianism. Herbartian influence was apparent in the linkage of manual training aims with the study of man. Students were told that "their hands met God's when materials were simplified, combined or changed with man's intelligence." Furthermore, correlation was the order of the day. Gertrude Miller, '06, recalls a "room-around frieze, inspired and executed entirely by students, correlating manual training with social studies."

At one stage, boys were apparently required to take sewing along with the girls. Ben Van Oot, 1902–05, reports that he had no such training, but Don McGuire, 1904–07, recalls that both sexes took both needlework and manual training: "I recall spending a semester with the needle. One item was a seven-gored skirt. . . . Meanwhile, the girls learned to use rip and crosscut saws in a definitely masculine manner."

Meanwhile, the State Department's interest in industrial education had a strong influence on Oswego's program. Third Assistant Commissioner of Education James E. Finnegan emphasized the twin needs for laying foundations for industrial education in elementary school and preparing teachers capable of harmonizing prevocational objectives with general education. Also supporting this view was Commissioner of Education Draper, whose efforts culminated in legislation (1908) for creating a system of industrial and trade schools. Within three brief years the number of such schools had grown to 37 and enrolled 3,947 boys and girls.

About the same time, the country began to feel the impact of a new philosophy of industrial arts. Charles Russell Richards, James Earl Russell and Frederick G. Bonser began to talk of industrial arts as a broad orientation to the world of contemporary work.

The generally increased interest in both these areas was reflected at Oswego in improved staff, facilities and curriculum. Before 1910 Joe Park handled all instruction himself with the aid of one or two student assistants. In this year he obtained a full-time assistant, a second in 1912, and still a third in 1916. Total equipment, including benches, tools, and machines, represented an outlay of ten thousand dollars.

Meantime, the curriculum was again sharply revised. In 1911 the New York State Education Department abolished the old manual training and drawing course and established a two-year course including 650 hours of instruction in general education; 700 hours in professional education; and 1,050 hours in technical courses, including joinery, cabinet making, wood turning, pattern making, art metal, machine shop, printing, bookbinding, molding and forging. This curriculum was to continue unchanged until 1921 when a revised two-year curriculum was established.

Three special achievements marking this period deserve special mention. In 1912 a printing press was added; the same year publication of the *Vocationist* was begun. Even more significant was institution in 1912 of what was probably the first full-time, off-campus cadet teaching in the country.

Graduates of the new curriculum in the years following 1911 often included two or three women students. Nevertheless, girls were not encouraged. Before 1918 they were permitted to take the course by special dispensation; after that, for about two decades, not at all.

In other courses major curriculum changes occurred in both 1900 and

1905. The first followed a two-year study (1898–1900) by a committee of normal school principals and involved several important modifications: [8]

(1) With the exception of the kindergarten and kindergarten-primary courses, the normal school courses of instruction were abolished.[9]

(2) In line with national trends in normal schools a wide elective offering permitted preparation for more specialized subjects or positions. The following substitutions were allowed: Greek, Roman, and English history for general history; a course in manual training or its equivalent, for any two academic subjects—if approved by the principal.[10]

Admission continued for a time to be by limited examination on elementary subjects. Normally, the student attended common school eight or nine years, normal school or high school for four years and a college or university four years. This state of affairs was not uncommon. Writing about 1900, President Harper of the University of Chicago estimated that at least one quarter of the colleges then chartered in the U.S. were doing work of a character little different from a high school or academy.[11]

New York shortly undertook radical upgrading of standards, however, following unification of the State Department of Education in 1904. The 1900 revision had been viewed as tentative and the period 1900–'05 transitional. The 1905 changes were more radical and lasted for fifteen years. Features of the new curriculum were as follows:

(1) Admissions standards were sharply raised, the candidate henceforth being required to possess a high school diploma of seventy-two regents' counts. Thus, entrance requirements became much the same as today.

(2) Several factors argued for such a change. First was the desire to improve teacher training. Second, the increasing number of high schools made it feasible to require high school graduation for entrance. Nevertheless, to permit admission to persons without such qualification, the high school department was re-established.

(3) A further change was the increased professionalization of the curriculum. This change, urged by Commissioner Draper, was forced by pressure from private colleges which resented competition from state supported schools.[12] The New York normals were becoming exclusively professional at a time when normal schools in other states were devoting increasing emphasis to content courses.

(4) Three general curricula were established—the manual training program already described; the normal; and the kindergarten-primary, each leading to state certification for life in the area concerned. The normal course consisted of the following:

> Besides psychology, principles and history of education, school economy and logic, observation and practice, there were methods courses in

language, grammar, composition, literature, primary reading, spelling, phonics, arithmetic, algebra, American history, geography, nature study, elementary science, vocal music, penmanship, drawing, and elementary handwork, manual training or household arts, and physical training.[13]

About one-quarter of the total time was devoted to observation or professional subjects and one-fifth to the activity subjects. The remainder of the time was distributed over methods in all the elementary school subjects. The kindergarten, kindergarten-primary course was similar with certain additions, including: songs and games, mother play, gifts, occupations, and kindergarten procedure.

(5) Another radical departure was the decision that ten of the normal schools—including Oswego—should be limited to training elementary teachers.[14]

Relative popularity of the three curricula is revealed in numbers graduating from each. In 1908 five graduated from the classical course including one male; fifty-eight from the normal course (one male); twelve from the kindergarten course (no males) and three from manual training (one female). By contrast, in June, 1912, ninety girls and ten boys were graduated from the normal course, three girls from the kindergarten course, ten girls from the kindergarten-primary, nine boys and one girl from drawing and manual training, two girls from the critic course.[15]

At least three other important curricular developments—one state-wide—occurred before Dr. Poucher retired. In 1910 the commissioner of education, whose office had been created in 1904, became empowered to prescribe the courses of study for the normal schools. Henceforth, the local boards would have no control over curricula. The fact is that few had exercised any such prerogative anyway. After 1869 curricula had been prescribed by the principals with the approval of the state superintendent of public instruction, or the commissioner of education after 1904.[16]

A purely local development involved integrating the kindergarten with the rest of the training school in order to remove friction and special regulations covering this department. After 1911 the superintendent of the training school had charge over all departments from kindergarten through high school.[17]

Despite these charges, Commissioner Draper remained dissatisfied. "There is too much wandering around in the tall grass," he said. He deplored that "nothing in the common schools leads to a trade, and that there is too much emphasis on method." [18]

Between 1897 and 1913, heyday of Herbartianism, principals of the practice school were Grant Karr, William Bagley and David Gibbs.

Amanda Funnelle continued to supervise the kindergarten, which functioned separately from the rest of the school; Harriet Stevens, the primary school; Mary O'Geran, the intermediate school; and Caroline V. Sinnamon, the high school. The high school was taught by subject-matter specialists alone, aided by a few paid student assistants; lower grades were taught by cadets under the supervision of division heads and subject-matter specialists. In general, teachers of methods supervised their respective specialties in the practice school. Classes were small, numbering about twelve to twenty, and each was in the full charge of one or two cadets for a period of twenty weeks.

Method generally suffered from being overemphasized as such—a pedagogical blunder to persist in New York State for some years to come. Normals in other states were already beginning to break away and introduce more content. "I have felt strongly," writes Fanny Gaffney, '07, "that we should have had more content and less stress on lesson plans. We had fine courses in literature but basic English grammar was neglected. I have suffered from this neglect all my life."

Method was stilted, and formality still the rule. Students were addressed as "Mr." and "Miss," and children always had to sit in the same seat. Teachers made a fetish of clean blackboards. The question-and-answer method was the one most commonly used and lesson plans were a sacred ritual, a mistake more clear-sighted critics perceived even then:

> A general lesson plan was written and every lesson somehow forced into it. The lesson plan became one of the early hobbies of the normal schools.[19]

> The average normal graduate seems imbued with the idea that a rigid adherence to methods is the only road to success.[20]

However, if any such prophetic soul lurked in Oswego's classrooms we have no record of him. "If we didn't keep to our schedule," recalls one of a group of graduates, "we didn't get a good mark. We would write down 'ideal answers' on the plans and then angle for the 'correct' answers." Students who strayed did so at their own risk, as Nellie Trout Hogue's ('03) experience proves:

> My plan for a Practice School demonstration, teaching how to make small baskets, was O.K.'d but after launching into my introduction I grew enthusiastic. I expanded into sources of raffia, basketry methods, Indians and Aztecs, etc. The children and I were having a wonderful time hurling questions and answers at each other. But the supervisors said I needed an extra term to bring me down to earth in my teaching. "You overteach," they said. Some years later, in a private school, I had

no set curriculum, no textbooks, but the children passed the Regents with flying colors. They did work more intensively and extensively than required, building their own texts, reading widely and effectively. My "no limit" philosophy finally bore fruit.

The underlying philosophy at Oswego was by now a strange blending of Pestalozzi, Froebel, Herbart, and Dewey—the special blend in each instructor's case depending on his own background and vintage. Sheldon's spirit and philosophy still hallowed the halls over which he so long presided. There even lingered degenerate traces of object teaching in materials sent to the St. Louis Exposition of 1904. And in the kindergarten Miss Funnelle still worshiped at the twin shrines of Pestalozzi and Froebel.

Remnants of the early emphasis are evident in these recollections of work at Oswego.

> The objective method was very prominent in 1902–05. We often used apparatus for teaching in the Practice School; and we planted, cultivated, sprayed and harvested whatever the neighborhood children left in the school garden. [Ben Van Oot, '05]

> We used much more equipment than was the usual practice in the areas of handwork and science. The term object teaching was not used, but we were fully aware that Oswego stressed interest rather than the purely academic approach. However, our "background work," for example, in literature and Latin, was strongly academic. [Don McGuire, '07]

Herbartian influence was clearly evident in local slavery to formal lesson planning. Oswego was not alone in its subjugation. When object teaching waned, the normal schools eagerly seized upon neatly packaged lesson plans to take their place. Anything for simplification! Herbart, as translated in McMurry's *Text on General Method*, was followed as slavishly in many classrooms as object teaching ever was. While emphasis on children's interests was a constructive derivative of Herbartianism, insistence on formal steps was a distorted one.

Meanwhile, permeating, and gradually gaining ground upon, these philosophies were the teachings of John Dewey, G. Stanley Hall and William Wundt. Already Dewey's *School and Society* had appeared but was slow to catch on. An occasional Oswego teacher—notably John Karr —talked of children's needs and child-centered classrooms. Furthermore, as superintendent of the practice school he forbade corporal punishment. However, at least one student teacher, Anna Post, '00, discovered that "pressure on a child offender's shoulders worked wonders." Child study received a shot in the arm from the publication of G. Stanley Hall's monumental work on adolescence in 1904.

Ruth Park Harder's own experiences in the Campus School kindergarten in the early 1900's illustrate the strange mixture of philosophies on the way out and those on the way in.

> We learned everything by drill and flash cards. In reading we learned words first and put them into sentences. But we had a lot of fun. We all felt it a privilege to attend the practice school because we did things differently there. We went in groups of six to the garden. We had nature walks that we loved. We put on special programs in the auditorium, including dramatic skits.

In summary, one may say that pedagogy and philosophy were generally formal, but over-all teaching excellent. Teachers were dedicated, scholarly, and efficient; and students gave them full credit for it. Graduates heatedly deny that Oswego's instructors could be indicted on charges commonly leveled at teaching in those days: "Teaching techniques of the period," wrote Henry Seidel Canby, "are of three types: (1) Come and get it or stay away. I have it. (2) Indifference, meeting boredom with boredom. (3) Factual, cramming the student."

As principal, I. B. Poucher was destined to serve another sixteen years, until he retired in 1913. He had originally intended retiring in 1911 but decided to remain until the new building was ready. Then he told the board that his children wished him to resign from active duty. "Besides," he added, "I have been blessed in continuing my labors for a period of sixteen years longer than the scriptural time allotted me to live." [21] Actually, he was allotted seven more years, when he was "recalled, at the ripe age of ninety-three, from the scene of his earthly labors."

"In appearance," recalls Clara Stowell Peters, '06, "this handsome man with piercing black eyes was an impressive figure. With his finely tailored suits, low-cut vest and large expanse of white shirt, and pince-nez tied to a heavy black cord, and often wearing a carnation, he was the picture of sartorial elegance."

Although he was seventy when he became principal, his posture was still erect and his deportment vigorous. "The fact that he was an old man never occurred to the students," says one alumna. "Several of the present faculty look paler and more flabby than Dr. Poucher ever looked."

In private life Dr. Poucher was a Presbyterian and a Democrat. His family gave away their politics when they named him Buchanan. His loyalty to the party and personal friendship with Grover Cleveland accounted for his appointment to the position of collector of customs for the Port of Oswego.

In personality he was serious but had a fine sense of humor, was aloof but nevertheless approachable. His concern for spirituality was evidenced by his emphasis on Christian background in writing student recommendations.

"These and other traits," asserts Bertha Jenne, '04, "served him well as an administrator. He made decisions quickly, easily, never seeming to become ruffled. He took over the reins with apparent ease and held them lightly but firmly."

His relations with faculty and students were excellent. He never imposed his views on his staff; he believed differences of opinion should be respected. "This is a great institution," he would say upon reporting faculty differences to students; "we can still disagree and respect each other."

It is not easy to assess Dr. Poucher's contribution. As mathematics teacher he was outstanding; as the "Colonel House" to Dr. Sheldon, an invaluable assistant. As principal he ran a sound, well-ordered school, and was accorded various personal honors, among them an honorary Doctor of Pedagogy degree by Syracuse University in 1902.

However, one wonders to what extent honors accorded the school of the early 1900's were a tribute to its earlier fame. Poucher had three major handicaps to making a name for himself as principal. First, he followed a man of such reputation as to dim his own achievements. Second, he was now an old man, in the twilight of his career. And third, he had no secretarial help or administrative assistance except that provided by Allen, his capable but crippled son. Even at that, he had more of such help than did Sheldon.

Rivaling Poucher in prestige was Caroline L. G. Scales, a leading contender for the title, "best teacher in the history of the Normal School." Caroline Scales was educated at Oswego State Normal, '99, and later at Wellesley, Radcliffe, and the University of Chicago. Miss Scales, whom the students privately called "Glorianna," taught English and history at Oswego from 1884 until her death in 1926, and was preceptress at the Welland from 1887 to 1906.

In appearance, personality and ability Miss Scales was outstanding. She was tall and handsome, with beautiful brown eyes. Until she turned gray —when she adopted blue—she always wore brown.

On the one hand she has been described as dignified, austere, "down-East" and formidable; on the other, as sweet, gentle, gracious and appealing. "She made me think of Chaucer's 'dayntee nonne,'" wrote Florence

Doolittle Bean, '96. Students were in awe of her, but everyone respected her. Some feared her; many loved her, albeit remotely. Sometimes fear changed to affection as one came to know her better. Apparently her metallic expression was a façade for a warm interior.

As mistress of the Welland, Miss Scales was strict but fair, always ready to give help and advice, and often entertained the girls in her rooms. "Late Sunday afternoons," wrote Mabel Jarvis de Beer, '99, and Nellie Trout Hogue, '03, "she invited us to her room for culture and cookies. She would read to us from Browning, Emerson, Marcus Aurelius, Tennyson and others, while we sat on sofa pillows on the floor."

As a teacher, Miss Scales was "brilliant—all intellect and brain." As a literature teacher she was superb. She never tolerated slipshod standards. She demanded much of her students, but no less of herself. "We were expected to know the pedigree and all that was fit to print about the archangels of Milton and all the Greek gods and goddesses," says Isabel Kingsbury Hart, '07, "and woe betide those who skimped their preparation. Nor was she any less thorough in teaching composition. No one completed her course without learning how to study, parse words and analyze sentences." "Amusingly enough, however," recalls Maye Lighthall Russell, '00, "students often found a word on their papers which could not be deciphered. Upon asking Miss Scales what it was, she confessed that its translation was 'penmanship.'"

Perhaps the students slaved over their work but they also learned to love it. "She made Shakespeare and Chaucer live," says one. "She instilled such a love of the classical in me," adds Grace Beardsley Turner, '99, "that my boy friend, who later became my husband, bought me a statue of the Goddess Athena that I had admired. It stood in my living room for many years, until my housekeeper complained of its immodesty and I removed it to my bedroom."

Miss Scales also taught girls to speak with poise; one-minute speeches were a specialty of hers. She was a woman of many talents. Her work in drama was also prominent; she often wrote and directed plays. She had no less stature as a history teacher. "She enthralled me in Greek and Roman history," says Jessie Himes, '99. "She used source materials a great deal. Another effective technique was placing big maps in the room with little pictures on them." In fact, Miss Scales's room was more like a living room than a classroom, according to Irene Mackin Chapman, '11. Windows held growing plants and were draped with brown or gold. On the board she wrote quotations, while classic statuary graced every nook. Miss Scales was ever the same, the dedicated classicist, capable of sparking a love-match between the undergraduate and Grecian tragedy.

Only a single recollection suggests that Miss Scales had even the tiniest spark of humor. On one occasion, when the faculty were supposed to perform, Miss Scales gave a "speech" using nothing but the ABC's, dramatically repeating them over and over as though they constituted the most important message on earth.

Equaling Miss Scales in prestige if not in teaching ability, was Richard K. Piez, already introduced in the Sheldon chapters. Under Poucher, Piez's sun was to rise even higher, not to set for many years. He spent the year 1900 at New York University, where he received the Doctor of Pedagogy degree, then studied four months in German schools. Upon returning to Oswego he took charge of psychology, history of education, and drawing.

"In those days Piez was debonair but gangling, hands and arms seeming too long for the rest of him," says Grace Allen, '97. "His manner was alternately warm and severe," adds Rena Clark Pettibone, '08, "so that one was filled with fear and trembling one minute, love and admiration the next."

"The young bachelor had personality plus, in those days," recalls Florence Doolittle Bean, '96, "and was most acceptable to aspiring young maidens." Piez himself had a yen for Margaret K. Smith, peculiar-looking but brilliant, and much older than he. When the two went walking on the pier, students would gleefully poke each other. But nothing came of it; Piez finally married an army officer's daughter and Margaret K. retained her spinster-status.

Until 1902 Piez taught manual training and encouraged females to take it. Jessie Deans requested of Dr. Poucher permission to substitute manual training for mathematics, "because I can't learn math, but I can do anything with my hands." "If Dr. Piez will take you," decreed Dr. Poucher, and Dr. Piez did.

For most of the Poucher period Piez taught psychology and drawing but was better known then for the latter. He used no textbook in psychology, simply lecturing in well-modulated voice tinged with German accent, and sometimes raising questions:

> I remember my first day [says Helen Kelly, '06]. I had on a pink dress and a big pink taffeta ribbon in my hair. I was so scared the ribbon was dancing. Dr. Piez's first question was: "What does one mean by teaching?" We all sat there speechless. Finally, I raised my hand and said, "To make others believe and understand what we ourselves believe and understand." He said, "Let's change the word 'make' to 'lead.'" And he wrote the revised definition on the board.

At least one student was greatly impressed by Piez's manner of conducting class discussion:

When I did my practice teaching I resolved to emulate his skill. I was teaching sixth grade drawing and using paper which was rough on one side and smooth on the other. The first day I handed one sheet to each pupil and then said, in my best pedagogical manner, "Now children, you notice that this paper has two sides." "Marvelous," said Henry Rappleye, the precocious son of our math professor. I realized my mistake and tried to correct it. "What I mean," I began again, "is that this paper has two different sides." "Still more marvelous!" said Henry. [Ben Van Oot, '05]

However, most of Piez's early students found his psychology teaching vague—a judgment commonly made of this subject in those days:

In one study, questions were sent to graduates of normal schools of Massachusetts, New York, Pennsylvania and the Northwest for the period 1897–1905. These individuals reported their psychology work to be generally indefinite and unproductive. Sample opinion; "It began nowhere and ended in the same place." [22]

Piez's art teaching was more impressive and students enjoyed their trips to the river to sketch. "He was highly sensitive to perfection in art," says Florence Doolittle Bean, '96. "My memories of art at Oswego are delightful," adds Nellie Trout Hogue, '03. "I had work in pencil, ink, charcoal, watercolor, mechanical and architectural drawing—and how I loved it. Now in my later years I am painting in oils, selling and giving away some creditable things. This interest, started at Oswego, is enriching my later years."

Nevertheless, many report Piez's practice of laughing at less artistic efforts. "You left a leaf off, Miss Nutting," he told a girl who was drawing a tree. And he strode to her desk laughing out loud. Another student, when copying a guinea hen, was asked, "Did you ever see a guinea hen?" "No," was the reply. "Well, that explains it," answered Dickie.

More sensitive souls underwent considerable misery. "I was awfully sensitive," says one; "when he criticized, I didn't dare look up." "I thought I'd done a pretty good job of copying an opossum perched on a branch," says still another, "but Dr. Piez asked, 'Did you ever see a pig climbing a tree?' Then he brought the opossum to life with a few strokes of charcoal."

One might also criticize Piez's art teaching as formal and uncreative, merely requiring exact reproduction of models. After paying him high tribute, one alumna wrote to Dr. Piez, "One thing should weigh on your pedagogical conscience. You undoubtedly discouraged a great surrealist when you habitually flunked me in water colors. My technique was simply thirty years too soon." In Dr. Piez's defense, his methods were those accepted in his day.

Besides teaching, Dr. Piez was known as an agitator, chiefly for professional and civic improvements. He was largely instrumental in obtaining for Oswego city playgrounds and a municipal water supply. "A city system is needed to combat our typhoid epidemic," he argued. "There's no epidemic," an opponent replied. "We've had only forty cases this season, and that's about normal." Also successful were his efforts as head of a Teachers' Alliance (1906–07), to raise teachers' salaries. Heretofore, the maximum for grade teachers had been $375 per year.

Naturally, some of his efforts were on his own behalf. In 1898 he sought a year's leave for study abroad with sixty dollars a month pay for himself and one hundred dollars for his substitute, promising to leave a year's supply of lesson plans. For precedent he cited the full salary paid Sheldon while the latter was on leave for two and a half years. Poucher and a teachers' committee approved Piez's request, but the State Superintendent turned it down. "It would be establishing a precedent which I do not believe we can justify," declared that gentleman firmly. "Normal and training schools are state institutions and the interests of the public must be considered." He dismissed the mention of Sheldon's dispensation as a "very special case," justified by his unique achievements.

Amanda Funnelle, who "reigned" over the kindergarten from 1888 until her retirement in 1911, also spread Oswego's gospel at the Albany State Normal and at city training schools in Indianapolis and Detroit.

Miss Funnelle's appearance was hardly prepossessing. "She was of medium height, thin and wiry with gray hair, parted and combed close to her head, never a hair out of place," recalls Mary McCormack, '08. Her immaculate white shirtwaist, with high collar and proper bow, added to her severe dignity. "Austere, unapproachable, but wonderful," sums up Grace Allen, '97. "A whimsy old lady with high color who walked on soft, kitten feet."

Her standards were as severe as her demeanor. "Even the best froze in their tracks when she spoke," according to Madeline Rose Jeffrey, '06. Jessie Himes, '93, '99, recalls seeing a girl whom Miss Funnelle had reprimanded weeping. "I said to myself there must be some other way. I resolved I'd never break a pupil's heart."

On the other hand, Miss Funnelle dedicated her life to helping her students, who did their practice teaching in the morning and met with her in the afternoon. "We sat around little tables," writes Clara Taylor Cornish, '08; "and Miss Funnelle began by asking a student to state the lesson for the day. Woe to all of us, especially the offender, if it was not stated correctly."

Froebel was Miss Funnelle's religion, but Froebel was currently interpreted in various ways. By now liberals had abandoned Froebelian "gifts" and symbolism; but students of German fundamentalists continued to follow the party line. The struggle so affected the kindergarten that John Dewey, after 1896, did not want to admit that his University School had a kindergarten at all.

Miss Funnelle's own interpretation was now a strange mixture of traditional and progressive. She retained Froebel's gifts and symbols, and overemphasized petty detail. Girls *must* close doors quietly; they should *complete* their toilet before leaving their rooms.

In practice, however, her interpretation of Froebel was flexible. "She felt that Froebel intended freedom, not rigid compliance," explains Grace Allen, '97. "I was shocked to discover later how slavishly others followed his teachings."

Even by today's standards, Miss Funnelle's practices were fundamentally sound. For one thing she encouraged love of the beautiful; her room was always attractive. "There was a tall blue bowl on her desk," says Jessie Himes, '93, '99, "which often held beautiful lemon lilies. I decided I'd always make my room attractive, too." Even more deeply affected was another:

> Miss Funnelle came into my life with a bang. She entered the dining room holding a gone-to-seed dandelion in a slender Rockwood vase. Setting it carefully on the table, she said, "See what a lovely thing God has made. He loves beauty." Just an old dandelion opened a new world for me. In a few years it became my privilege to open the eyes of city children to God's beauty in Central Park and on the Palisades. [Nellie Trout Hogue, '03]

Students were also expected to become keen observers and to encourage the same habit in children. "On our very first day she asked us to write a description of our homes, gardens and other details," recalls Helen Knowles Taylor, '96. "She also emphasized creative imagination. I remember being asked to pantomime picking a bunch of violets in such manner that the others could guess what I was doing. No one could see my violets and I could feel the sympathy of my classmates."

According to Ruth Park Harder, "Handcrafts were stressed, too. As kindergarteners in 1902 we sat in tiny chairs around long tables and wove colored strips."

Undoubtedly, Miss Funnelle made great impact on students. "First in my memory will always live Miss Funnelle," testifies Rena Clark Pettibone, '08. "I would not have missed her leadership for a great deal," adds Helen Taylor, '96. "She was one of the great educators of her time." In short, kindergarten alumni are unanimous in acknowledging their debt to this small martinet.

Like Miss Funnelle, Dr. Amos Farnham had already attained prominence under Sheldon, having arrived in 1894, and finally retiring nineteen years later. This beloved professor began his career as a nurse to Union soldiers in the South but a fever cut short his work. He graduated from Oswego Normal in 1875 and was later awarded an honorary Master's from Claflin University, a school for Negro freedmen where he taught. He went abroad in 1912 to observe stream erosion in France and to study glacial streams in Switzerland. Still later he was awarded an honorary doctorate by the University of the State of New York.

Amos Farnham was tall and slight in stature, with handsome, severe features. He was "ethereal, delicate and gracious; meticulous but absent-minded." He was so precise in dotting his i's and crossing his t's that students of one era called him "Miss Mary."

As a teacher he was highly respected but something of a "character." "I can still see his gestures in 'Methods of Geography,' as he described a plateau," writes Don McGuire, '07. "A high [slowly raising his hands from desk level to eye level] and nearly level [hands moving evenly sidewise] extent [hands continuing to move outward] of land."

Once he left a note on Anna Post's desk after observing her student teaching. "I see you're going to have discipline," it said. It was the practice then for supervisors to leave such notes for students whom they observed.

Farnham's own teaching methods were progressive. He used pictures for illustration; he taught local as well as world geography. Students made drawings of schoolroom, tables and yard to scale.

Farnham's influence was widely felt. He was well-known for his text *Oswego Methods in Geography* and articles dealing with geography method, most of them in the *Journal of Geography*. His teacher's "Litany" was quoted in papers from coast to coast.[23]

Another alumnus of the Sheldon faculty was the founder's only son, Charles, who taught nature study at Oswego from 1893 until 1914, when he retired. Before returning to his alma mater, Charles Sheldon had a colorful career. He was assistant to the state geologist in Albany 1875–76, studied natural history at Cornell, 1876–80, and taught natural and physical science at the state normal in Kirksville, Missouri, 1883–93. Several summers during this period he did special botanical work for the federal government.

His courses at Oswego had several memorable features. Many recall the school garden which Campus School children and Normal students planted spring and fall. "Each of us in the Campus School had a small patch," says Ruth Park Harder, "which we worked until there wasn't a single weed or stone."

Another project was collecting natural specimens—leaves to be pressed, and insects to be mounted under glass. Graduates recall their "bugging" experiences with amusement. By day they went in groups to the country, armed with cyanide bottles, glass-covered boxes and nets for butterflies. "We chased moths in the evening," says Grace Beardsley Turner, '99, "and amused passersby would pause to watch us leaping about with our wire nets."

The female insect-catchers found snaring fun; however, at least one male reports having felt silly:

> It was embarrassing to me, a rather awkward, husky guy, chasing around the neighborhood catching butterflies while my former playmates, by now factory workers, cast jeers and sarcasm at my pedagogical endeavors. I must admit that I was more interested in the feminine bipeds at the school than I was in the Crustacea, Lepidoptera or any dipteron of the neighborhood.

While boys made less avid bug-catchers than girls, with dissection the opposite was true. For this ritual, boys stalked, stole and chloroformed many a hapless frog and cat. The more conscientious settled for felines that nobody wanted. "In collecting specimens," affirms Helen Kelly, '06, "not a stone was left unturned—literally. We even skinned a snake."

Reactions to this unpalatable task varied. Most of the girls experienced some squeamishness. "I had continuous conniptions," confesses Nellie Trout Hogue, '03, "even though I wore cotton gloves under rubber gloves. Finally, I got a classmate to do my carving for me and subsequently obtained my knowledge of a cat's internal anatomy by hearsay, not sight."

Better suited temperamentally to the task was Martha Gaines Fine, '05, elected by the six girls with whom she worked to do the cat-carving. All went well and at the end of the project one of the boys cured the skin and presented it to her.

Sometimes these avid students-of-nature ranged farther afield. "One spring we went to Sodus Point," recalls one, "in a little steamboat. This was my one sail on Lake Ontario." "And who can forget Charlie Sheldon's bugology trip to Fair Haven in 1904?" asks another. "We went there by boat and returned by train."

Two of the best-remembered principals of the practice school belong to this period—namely Grant Karr and William C. Bagley. The former graduated from Jena University, Germany, and taught at Oswego from 1899 to 1906. In 1940, Dr. James O'Gorman, '07, for many years chairman of psychology at Hunter College, gives Karr chief credit for introducing Dewey to Oswego.

"He was in a class by himself," asserts one alumna. "A charming personality, hail-fellow-well-met, one of the best beloved and most influential members of the faculty," adds another.

Opinions of his teaching are more variable. "He was vague, just wandered around," recalls Anna Post, '00. "He taught methods, but we got no methods," affirms Helen Kelly, '06.

Perhaps confusion stemmed partially from his unorthodox teaching. One alumnus commented:

> He always used polysyllabic words when words of one syllable would have sufficed. In philosophy of education he soared into the realm of theology, metapsychology, and metaphysics and lost no opportunity to display his knowledge of Homer, Pythagoras, Pericles, Aristotle, Socrates, Euclid . . . and, of course, Karr.

Van Oot, at least, found Karr's methods effective. He refers to Karr's

> . . . extensive knowledge of things pedagogical and the clever and subtle manner in which he sought to correct teachers' errors. I vividly recall his asking me to read Dewey's pamphlet on "Interest as Related to Will" and to suggest ways that his philosophy could be improved. Later, when I studied under Dewey, that assignment had its effect, but I'm not saying what it was. . . . Dr. Karr's method had proved effective and awakened my otherwise passive interest in principles of teaching.

In contrast to Dewey's philosophy was that of William C. Bagley, superintendent of the practice school from 1906 to 1908, later to become one of the outstanding educators of his time. A man of medium height with thick graying hair, narrow face, and piercing black eyes behind rimless pince-nez, Bagley had an unassuming but dynamic personality. As principal he urged teachers to get degrees. As teacher he wasted neither time nor words. He meant business but was never unfair or demanding. He seemed to know what his students were doing and how much they knew.

His philosophy is somewhat outmoded today. He said teachers should stress the "how" with the little child, and the "why" when he becomes more mature. After "how" becomes a habit the child should know the reasons.

As a disciplinarian, he was traditionalist. "Maintain discipline and permit no exceptions" was his watchword.

After several bouts with a youthful recidivist, a student teacher received this note from Bagley. "Miss Button, This is Jack's last trial. Please hold him to strict account. W.C.B."

Isabel Kingsbury Hart recalls a similar case: "When I was a student teacher, a big boy insisted on cutting capers in the hall. Unable to find a faculty member, I ejected him bodily from the building. A friend warned me of the seriousness of my behavior, whereupon I went to Dr. Bagley and confessed. After I had left, Dr. Bagley called the boy to his office and thrashed him."

"As a result of his teaching," says Fanny Gaffney, '07, "I went out to teach determined that no little charge of mine should ever whisper or giggle, regardless of what he might or might not learn. I simply took Dr. Bagley's dictum too seriously. Now I have seen the pendulum swing too far the other way."

Certainly, Bagley's practices at Oswego were in harmony with the philosophy for which he later became famous. In the depression of the thirties progressivism was to come under fire. Critics of progressivism, called Essentialists and led by Dr. Bagley, demanded return to firm discipline and serious intellectualism. Bagley's major contribution was to alert educators to the absurdities which had clung to the progressive movement, like barnacles to a ship.

Lydia Phoenix was less influential than the foregoing, nevertheless well-remembered. A graduate of Oberlin and the Boston School of Oratory, she taught music and physical education. "She was an odd-looking character," recalls Clara Stowell Peters, '06, "gray-haired, bright-eyed, small and not robust. More positive attributes were perfect poise, a serene expression and a charming voice." Helen Quigley Ziel, '20, describes her as a "typical matron-in-an-orphanage-type, prim and sedate, but very efficient." She was serious, even solemn, but not cold.

For teaching music she was ill-prepared, but in those days one was often drafted for uncongenial chores. Her direction of music in chapel was dignified and dramatic, but notably lacking in skill. "For theory," says Helen Kelly, '06, "She used a little textbook, *A Primer of Vocal Music* by Eleanor Smith, the only textbook I remember using at the Normal School."

In physical education Miss Phoenix felt more at home and was fairly effective, despite poor facilities. "Once a week we took calisthenics in the auditorium," relates one student, "where Miss Phoenix and a pianist put us through our paces. We stood between the seats or marched through the rows, while counting lightly in time with the music." "We were put through a system of breathing, stooping and stretching, in the Emerson method," adds Ben Van Oot, '05, "a system applicable to training actors and orators but hardly appreciated by the men in the school."

I can still see Louis Karpinski [writes Bertha Jenne, '04] with his large hands and long arms, waving them around and bending his tall body over to touch the floor with his hands. To say that his motions were slightly exaggerated is putting it mildly. If Miss Phoenix ever saw him, she gave no sign.

As often the case when instructors take their work very seriously, the simplest episodes became a source of amusement, as Clara Taylor Cornish, '08, relates:

> One time Miss Phoenix was giving directions such as "right arm up, over head, 1–2–3–4; down, 1–2–3–4," when by mistake she said, "Left foot up, over head, 1–2–3–4," causing great merriment among the students, and embarrassment to poor Miss P. . . . On another occasion she was asking students to assume certain poses, one being that of the famous statue, "The Thinker." The students were trying desperately but futilely, not knowing of such a statue. Mary Elizabeth Bloomfield had an urge to sneeze, and not wishing to disturb the class, pressed her finger against her nose. To her amazement she heard Miss Phoenix say, "Only one has assumed the attitude of 'The Thinker' and that is Miss Bloomfield." The others complimented Miss Bloomfield on being so bright.

Where health theory was concerned, Miss Phoenix attempted to compensate for current omissions in health teaching. "She had a calorie complex," tells Helen Quigley Ziel, '20. "She was a missionary on foods. She had us sell calorie charts to the townspeople, explaining to them what they meant." She even dared attempt sex education, a hush-hush subject in those pre-Freudian days. "You could mention every bone in your body, the digestive process, and where the muscles were placed, but there was no mention of sex," explains Grace Beardsley Turner, '99. Notwithstanding the common taboo, Miss Phoenix evicted the boys one day and proceeded to unfold for the girls the "facts of life." Townspeople were shocked and one more curricular innovation indefinitely doomed.

In her earlier days, Miss Phoenix taught aesthetic dancing according to the del Sartian pattern. These reminiscences yield glimpses of the methods she used: "We would blow soap bubbles and bounce them to music with small felt-covered rackets," relates an ex-pupil. "On one occasion," adds another, "we private pupils were to dance as wood nymphs, barefoot and costumed in gauze. However, Miss Scales heard of it and we had to wear shoes."

Still other staff members deserve recognition. There was the Latin teacher, lovely Laura Alexander. "I was more interested in her pretty clothes and perfect grooming than I was in Gaul but I managed to pass, thanks to my admiration for her as a person," writes Clara Stowell Peters, '06.

Remembered for her kindness to students is Lina Loveridge, '98, Miss Scales's handsome young satellite, and teacher of "Literature and Story Method" until her untimely death in 1908. Her relation with students was a healthy one.

Walker Rappleye, the energetic teacher of mathematics, used no texts but was quite effective. "Rap" sang spirituals and had a delightful sense of humor. When students came late to class he always recited, "A-dillar, a-dollar, a ten-o'clock scholar," to the embarrassment of the late arrival.

Also beloved was Mary McElroy who taught at the Normal from 1884 until 1914, a "quiet, unassuming lady who called attention to the favorable aspects of one's teaching, only mentioning incidentally the unfavorable."

Head of modern languages was a big-hearted Frenchwoman, Madame Grossen, who also spoke Spanish, Dutch and German. "All the English she knew she had acquired from books," reports Madame Grossen's daughter, Jeanne; "hence, English idiom was her bete noir."

Then there was Chester Tether, who taught physics and chemistry. "All I remember from his course," says Helen Kelly, '06, "is that liquid should be poured from a bottle opposite the label, lest the legend become stained and illegible." Still others recall Tether's early morning bird walks.

Another member of the staff, not a faculty member but very highly respected, was Mr. Cyrenius, the aged janitor who had been with the school for many years. However unsatisfactory the school facilities might have been, this conscientious gentleman kept them shining.

What shall be our evaluation of the Poucher faculty as a whole? Normal school teachers of the day are generally portrayed as miserably prepared. Thirty per cent of all instructors, according to one study, had received no training in advance of the school in which they were teaching. Such data, however, must be kept in proper perspective.[24] It is remarkable that 70 per cent *did* have additional training, despite their low pay. In 1911, Oswego's total annual budget was a mere $40,000, permitting only $29,390 for twenty-five teachers' salaries. The average salary of all state normal teachers was $990.70 in 1904 and still only $1,172.32 in 1912.[25]

Furthermore, fringe benefits were notably missing. Not even the principal could afford a car, although a few local citizens drove them by then. Apparently, faculty members were encouraged to take leaves to study on their own but they received no pay and had to arrange for a suitable substitute.[26] Despite these difficulties, almost all the Poucher staff had studied in several colleges, often abroad, though rarely seeking a higher degree. And the majority were graduates of the currently best normal school in the country, namely Oswego. Finally, teaching ability is hardly in direct proportion to length of preparation. "There were some awfully good teachers in those days," says Anna Post, '99. Further confirmation comes from Ben Van Oot, '05, who recalls "the professional sincerity of the faculty members, their definite objectives and thorough knowledge of subjects taught; the friendly faculty-student relations and the utter lack of need for disciplinary action."

Decline in Oswego's national reputation stemmed from other causes. For one thing, Poucher's faculty were less prolific writers than Sheldon's. Poucher himself did little to spread Oswego's reputation abroad or to encourage innovations at home. Experimentation was now the exception and not the rule. While certain staff members were undoubtedly great, no one came forward to coordinate their efforts. Furthermore, general improvement of the nation's normal schools made Oswego's achievements less conspicuous.

Others credit Oswego's decline to a "backward look." With the aroma of past greatness in their nostrils, they failed to breathe the fresh air of the present. As a result, Oswego's fame became frayed at the edges. For years to come, the school seemed to rest on its laurels, suffering from a stalemate of success.

CHAPTER 7

Student Life as a New Century Dawns

THE typical student of the early 1900's differed little from her counterpart of Sheldon's day. She was still a female from a nearby farm or rural community, ranging from lower-middle to middle-middle class, and somewhat unsophisticated. There were the same exceptions as formerly, a tiny fraction being male, well-to-do, and downstate or out-of-state. Actually, there were fewer downstaters and out-of-staters than in earlier days. For one thing, the school's prestige had declined. Besides, out-of-staters found no welcome mat, as this item shows:

> Non-residents of the state are not solicited nor encouraged to enter our normal schools, but in exceptional cases, such persons who specially desire to do so and who comply with the requirements for admission may be admitted by special appointment of the State Superintendent, upon paying in advance to the treasurer of the local board a tuition fee of $20 per term of nineteen weeks. The application for appointment should be made some weeks in advance in order to allow for investigation of the candidate's qualifications.[1]

It is hardly surprising that very few persisted in running the gantlet of this imposing array of stipulations.

As for the rarity of the socially elite, teaching was hardly more respectable for the upper class than in the earlier days. In fact, an upper-class graduate of 1899 was urged by her father not to teach lest she should "take the bread and butter out of the mouth of some less affluent girl."

Among the few male students there were at least six Filipinos, sent by the United States government so that they might provide educational leadership in their country. Unfortunately, boys in a normal school were then looked on as sissies; and the boys themselves felt awkward at first.

117

"I was scared stiff," said one, "at being enrolled in what Henry Alexander called a 'female seminary, a petticoat college where there were forty girls to every boy.' "

The new arrival in 1900 closely resembled the one disembarking at the Oswego depot forty years before. Clothing was still cumbersome, and dressing no mean task—for the girl at least. Her pompadour was elaborately undergirded by "rats" constructed of matting. Her back hair was combed into a psyche knot, or three rolls held by fancy wire or bone pins. A flat bow of velvet or satin often perched atop this structure.

School dress was simple, outwardly at least. The standard classroom uniform was white shirtwaist, with high, closed collar and four-in-hand tie; and plain wool skirt, straight and tight, or bell-shaped. Sleeves were long, cuffs stiff, and held together with links donated by doting parents or admirers. Impending dress reform was heralded by solemn faculty decision to permit practice teachers to wear short sleeves, *if* they came beneath the elbow. Hardly visible—and it is just as well—were black stockings, held up by a ferris waist or tiny corset. Pinch waists and padded hips were the vogue. Clara Taylor Cornish, '08, reports that she wore her first pair of silk stockings on graduation day.

Dress-up clothes were even more elaborate. Evening dresses were of flowered chiffon or a delicate plain blue or pink. The more daring girl might wear short sleeves, and low-cut dresses showing three or four inches of neck. Every decent girl wore embroidery-edged, close-fitting panties, a ruffled—for front curve when necessary—corset-cover, and two starched cotton petticoats.

In bad weather, the girl's fashionable array called for still further embellishment, requiring considerable persistence to put on. She wore heavy woolen leggings coming to just above the knee, lined with fleece, like glorified spats. Or she could settle for black knit heavy leggings with a strap just under the instep, of stretchy material with no zipper or buttons.

Sports apparel was the same as for everyday. Three or four petticoats were standard equipment, even for skiing and sleighing. Gymnasium apparel was equally as modest as outdoor gear.

> My gym apparel [writes Nellie Trout Hogue, '03] covered me from head to heels. Bloomers, long sleeves, sailor collar, long cotton stockings, and full skirt were proper. Years later at the University of Chicago I was bawled out by the swimming instructor for refusing to appear without stockings in the women's pool. Now in Florida in my old age I never wear stockings. Such is progress.

At least, once she was dressed the girl of the early 1900's was done. There was no masquerade with rouge or lipstick, which simply were *not* in those days. However, more imaginative girls wet the roses on their quilts to rub the color on their lips. Nor was bathing a problem. Only the very fastidious bathed more than once a week.

As for the boys, there was no standard attire for everyday. "On special occasions," said one, "we did not own a tux or tails; a dark suit served all functions. We wore starched 'boiled bosom' shirts; attached collars and cuffs were coming in. Collars were separate and stiff, cuffs detachable and generally double (reversible). During the period after President McKinley even youth my own age, myself included, wore black armbands."

When the students of the early 1900's arrived at Oswego what did they find? They found a town which, like the school they came to attend, basked in the glory of another day. Trappings of prosperity obscured hints of less prosperous times to come. Local society was still sharply divided into rich and poor. A very few of the rich even had cars and the first one reached Oswego in 1900. At the other extreme were the Italian immigrants who came between 1900 and 1905 and the Poles who followed them.

At long last, there began to be heard voices of women urging reforms in behalf of their sex. One notes in the *Daily Times* for May 12, 1910, advertisements of talks on corsets, dress reform, and suffrage. But the Normal girl had no part in this effort. Her world was bounded by the walls of the school or the Welland, or in some cases a room in town.

Students of both sexes spent most of their day in school, which lasted until five in the afternoon. The only breaks were lunch and assembly—attendance still required. During opening days of the term, local pastors addressed the students in turn. For the rest of the year faculty members took turns presiding and reading the Bible. Special features of these exercises were musical numbers by the students' favorite soloists, Walker Rappleye, a tenor, and Charles Sheldon, whose baritone easily plumbed to the low notes of his favorite song, "Out of the Depths."

After school, students returned to their living quarters. All boys, plus local girls and a few out-of-towners, lived in private homes or clubs. A club was merely a boarding house for several students. Boys' rooming facilities were somewhat more variable in quality than the girls'; one enterprising male "coed" even lived in a bank.

The remainder still roomed at the Welland, now described by one ex-inmate as a "rambling, shabby wooden firetrap" and by another as "balconied, vine-covered and pretty." Anyhow, by 1910 the school catalogue could claim proudly that "every part of the building is heated by steam and lighted by electricity." Nevertheless, Dr. Poucher threatened that "if the young ladies were not more careful about turning off lights when not in use, power would be turned off and oil lamps returned."

Furthermore, proclaimed the catalogue, "efforts are made to make this a pleasant home. . . . Dictionaries, gazetteers, daily papers, periodicals, encyclopedias, and the best magazines of the day are found in the reading room." A piano in the parlor and a lone telephone also contributed to the girls' welfare.

Certain other facilities were adapted by the Wellandites to purposes for which they had not been designed. According to one student:

> Windows on the first floor were understood to have been used after hours to permit entrance to the building. Also handy was the heavy rope fastened to some of the windows for a fire escape. However, one "lady student" who tried it reports that "half way down, the loop of rope around my leg came undone and I arrived at the bottom with torn stockings and bloody hands."

Meals at the Welland were rather formal affairs. Breakfast was served at seven-thirty, dinner at noon and supper at six. Every girl must sit quietly at her place until Miss Scales, the directress, was seated. While the food was good, it was routine.

Despite such reports institutional food had improved greatly since the early nineteenth century. At Harvard in those days the cold bread served for dinner was said to have the "consistency of wool." At Yale, "the breakfast consisted of ollapodrida hashed up from the remains of yesterday's dinner and fried into a compound known as slum."

Little wonder that food was often a source of discontent at college. The earliest recorded rebellion at Harvard occurred in 1766 over bad butter.[2] The Wellandites, however, took out their distaste in mild grumbling.

After supper there was time for a brief stroll by the lake, but doors were locked promptly at 7 P.M. and woe betide you if "C.L.G.S." as Miss Scales was known, had to unlock to let you in. Apparently, these rules had been relaxed for a time, for we find this item from the local paper for November 19, 1909: "Students of the Normal School are not to entertain company of either sex after 7:30 P.M. Mondays through Thursdays, and not after 10:30 P.M. the other nights, according to new, stricter regulations imposed by Dr. Poucher. The regulation is not popular, to say the least."

In any case, high jinks after "lights out" at ten were common. Mattress parties were a specialty of the house. Several mattresses were dragged into the same room, after which the girls first stuffed the keyhole and then stuffed themselves.

Another stunt was cooking in the closet, by the light of a tiny china lamp, over small alcohol stoves permitted the girls. "All this," confesses one, "with four or five girls in a clothes-filled closet. When Miss Scales's cultivated nose brought her to the door, we fled down the fire escape, often losing on the way such garments as corset and shoes. It was an ordeal to have to go to Miss Scales to claim items of intimate apparel."

While partying, girls entertained themselves playing whist, euchre, dominoes and tiddlywinks. Or they embroidered bureau scarves, made fancy pillows out of cigar ribbons, stitched nainsook shirtwaists, tatted, or just talked.

As for more serious violations, there are few to record. In fact, acts considered serious in those days would often be dismissed as schoolboy pranks today. Two boys who shot into a girls' room in the Welland just to "stir up excitement" were expelled. On another occasion certain young men, on vacation from Yale and Cornell, broke into the Normal and painted the statuary. They were adjudged as tinged with vandalism instead of endowed with healthy animal spirit.

Actually, most of the boys were quite well-behaved, despite a total lack of school-inflicted restrictions. "No scandals," recalls one, "are among my souvenirs! I do recall, however, that I met Mrs. McElroy, the upper-grade principal, just after I had taken a mouthful of honey glycerine and whiskey 'cough-cure-all.' I felt that she smelled something, but no comments were made." By contrast, the school continued its restrictive regulations on women students. For them, the Victorian era experienced a lengthy hangover. Drinking and smoking were unheard of; even slang was whispered in cloakrooms and suppressed in corridors.

Nor were the faculty members derelict in performing their custodial duties. Girls from the Welland were severely cautioned when C.L.G.S. detected them eating in the park. Public eating simply was not done, nor was public primping. On one occasion Miss Scales observed a young lady powdering her nose at an upstairs window. Weren't there more private places where that sort of thing was done? she demanded to know.

Problems, too, were much the same as in Sheldon's day—study, finance, and health. The Poucher students, like their nineteenth-century counterparts, were students in more than name only. For one thing, many had been sent to school at great personal sacrifice to their parents, a fact calculated to make them take their work seriously. For another, teachers themselves maintained high standards; neither homework nor critical comment was missing. "An icy remark from Miss Scales about misspelled word or misplaced comma," asserts Isabel Kingsbury Hart, '07, "was all any sensitive soul needed." Furthermore, these students had a sense of purpose: they had come to school to learn to teach. Finally, Oswego had an enviable reputation, which inspired students to maintain it.

The financial problem, too, remained much the same as in Sheldon's day. Students had little money, but a little went a long way. Total expenditures for the three years were less than one year costs these days. Depending on whether one lived at the Little Welland, in the Welland proper, or in town, the total cost for three years might range from $650 to $1,000.

Those who boarded in town paid $3.50 to $4.00 a week for room and board, with another 25¢ for laundry. The Welland itself was a non-profit concern operated by Dr. Poucher, who received rent and laundry money in the second-floor office every Saturday morning. Such charges rose little in the sixty years of the Welland's operation. Weekly rates were listed in the 1910–12 catalogue as follows: room rent, 65¢ to 85¢; fuel 30¢; light 10¢; towels and bedding including "laundering of same," 15¢, all paid in advance.

Girls in the Welland Annex or Little Welland still prepared their own food, and rumor had it that they half starved themselves. The only resource was the Mary V. Lee Fund, adequate for helping only a few.

The practice of basket-boarding continued, as these reminiscences show:

> Each week I took a cake, a pie, a loaf of bread, two quarts of milk, one quart of canned fruit, besides potatoes, butter, fruits, vegetables, and occasionally meat and egg. In addition I paid a dollar a week and took care of my own room. We also furnished the fuel for our kerosene heating stove. [Blanche Hall Darling, '06]

Fortunately, incidental expenses were slight. Hacks were available, but the Normal students rarely used them. Textbooks were free and doctors' calls a bargain at a half-dollar each. Most students got by on fifty cents to a dollar a week, which paid for paper, pens, and some recreation. The more thrifty could manage occasional rental of horse and buggy, at two dollars for four for a whole afternoon. Of course there were a few extras, for example, graduation dresses and senior pins, whose emblems were sometimes designed in drawing class.

The male student's situation was somewhat different and more difficult. The girl who had no funds simply had to forego higher education. The boy, however, often tried to make his own way, defraying expenses with any kind of jobs he could obtain. Some sold books or stereopticon outfits during the summer; others sold aluminum house utensils; still others acted as janitors in public buildings or private homes. Spading gardens in summer and shoveling snow in winter afforded welcome, if less steady, work. A visible monument to several young men's industry is the Country Club Golf Links constructed in the early 1900's.

Nor was their work paid at union rates, as one odd-jobber's reminiscences show:

> I was most fortunate in finding yardwork, various types of housework, and stable work at a nearby household, the fringe benefit being the availability of horse and buggy or cutter and saddle for special activities, courting included. On Saturdays I worked in a hand laundry where the hourly rate of five cents had risen to ten before I left the school. Fortunately, there were no serious activity costs in those days. [Don McGuire, '07]

With this background, it is small wonder that the morale of some of the men was affected when several Filipinos arrived at the school, all expenses paid by the U.S. government. At a time when no government subsidies and no privately endowed scholarships were available, these boys had everything handed them on a silver platter. "We did not object to the government's plan to educate them to lead education in the Philippines," writes one graduate, "but we felt the money should be a loan, not a gift." The same graduate when solicited for a contribution to a memorial for the Filipinos—or pensionados as they were called—questioned the "appropriateness of a gesture prompted only by sentiment and not by achievements."

> Shortly after returning to the Philippines it was reported that one of these men, suffering an exalted opinion of his own importance, disowned and denounced his own parents. . . . Besides, the [American] students had to perform menial jobs about town to keep themselves in school, even washing out bathtubs and spittoons at the railroad Y.M.C.A. They resented the fact that they, as American citizens, had to perform these menial tasks while the Filipinos sat in the lap of luxury and attended school at government expense. The fact that the government sent these men to school in New York and paid all their expenses hardly justifies a memorial of any kind.[3]

Oddly enough, the writer has run across no other alumnus who harbors such feelings. Anyhow, this letter indicates no resentment of the Filipinos as such, but merely of their favored status at the Normal. One observes that two Negro students of the same period aroused no resentment at all. In fact, the socially homogeneous student body was generally democratic with rare exceptions. Several girls of well-off families in town were both scorned as snobs and envied, and formed a clique of their own.

Another problem, almost as acute as in Sheldon's time, was health. Serious illness among young people occurred on a scale unknown today.

Edna Jones Ryon, '06, recalls three or four deaths while she was there. According to then current diagnoses, one girl caught a cold and died of pneumonia, another died of stoppage of the bowels, and a third died of smoking too much.

Students reporting illness were attended in the school "hospital" described in the school catalogue (1910–12) as a room furnished with "easy chairs and lounges." While any pupil was free to go to the hospital, "no books, papers or periodicals were to be taken there."

Another problem-of-sorts was making one's own fun; for apart from capers cut in the Welland, opportunities were limited. There were no movies, no choruses, no band concerts—for Wellandites, at least. There was no bike-riding, a sport ill-adapted to unpaved streets and ankle-length skirts.

Stock companies and minstrel shows (sample offering: "She Couldn't Marry Three") came to town, but after 1909 the Normalites could not go. "The authorities at the Welland have taken a stand," noted the local paper, "against musical comedies. The Normalites were shut in last night and prevented from getting to the Richardson to see 'The Stubborn Cinderella.' " [4]

The only town affairs now permitted the girls were lectures and entertainments at the churches. The churches gave receptions for the students in October, stiff affairs, well attended only because of lack of something better.

More fortunate girls profited by acquaintances in town. Some managed to attend local dances in this way. Others even rated invitations to the Yacht Club, the gathering place for the society of Oswego of that day. [5]

The students themselves showed considerable ingenuity in devising their own amusement. The most common diversion was walking, probably because it was cheapest. Favorite walks were in Kingsford Woods, and to the town cemetery. It was fun to read the quaint couplets on the gravestones. In the springtime students liked to stroll along the canal or on the breakwater, occasionally stooping to hurl stones in the lake. Also at this season came picnics and weiner roasts. Just before school closed each year, the Welland cooks prepared a picnic supper which was held at Sheldon Point. There the girls sat around a big fire, eating and singing.

Not always did students seek diversion afoot; sometimes they took trolley or buggy rides. One might go by trolley to Fulton or to Syracuse or to a refreshment stand on the hill. And in the summer there were carnivals at the end of the trolley line out on the beach.

Slightly more expensive but even more fun, were the buggy rides, which, at least once, ended in disgrace:

Occasionally, we would coax the livery stable boy to let us take Fanny, the pride of the stable, who could travel fast and make the trip to Fulton in an hour. One day all went well until Fanny insisted on racing down a stony hill, thereby falling and skinning her beautiful knees. Crestfallen and apologetic we returned Fanny, subdued and limping, to her owner, who never let us have her again. [Rena Clark Pettibone, '08]

Nellie Trout Hogue, '03, recalls another disastrous trip:

We hired a horse and surrey to go out Fruit Valley way for a day's jaunt and a foot-wetting in the lake. All went well until our horse got colic. He wobbled into town, leaning on the shafts, with his head held up by two of the girls. We finally propped him against a tree and went for the liveryman. This irate gentleman threatened to sue the school because we had let his animal eat wet grass. Alas! There were no more buggy rides to the country. Anyway, we had enjoyed the experience, including wading in Lake Ontario and buying hot custard pies from farmers.

About the only coeducational activities permitted, though never actively encouraged, were walking together or dating at the Welland. Not just any boy was admitted to this sanctum sanctorum; he must be of impeccable reputation. Among the ineligibles were the Filipinos, whom the girls were "warned not to date or dance with at any time." Apparently, the taboo stemmed from racial discrimination, although the girls themselves found the boys romantic and dated them on occasion.

Dates, in fact, were special achievements because males were a rarity, hard to come by. In fact, a state of cold war existed between the Normalites and local belles over the available supply. The town girls resented outsiders coming in and taking "their boys," especially the more sophisticated youths on vacation from Yale or Cornell. Nevertheless, the town girls had the better of it. They could entertain in their private parlors; they could even stage "pillow parties," which involved throwing pillows at each other to decide whom to kiss.

The boy who actually braved the Welland to date a girl was viewed as a hero. More frequent callers agreed among themselves on a system of bell-ringing, to notify girls which date had arrived. Once inside, dates sat in the same parlor, but only till the stroke of twelve. Then, like Cinderella at a signal, the fair damsels had to disappear.

Apart from these stilted rendezvous, coeducational activities were generally missing. This sad item found its way into the local paper in 1910:

The girls at the Welland went on a sleigh ride Saturday night beneath a young moon, with Venus hanging low in the sky. The only trouble was that there were no boys present, and one fetching miss described the meeting as "like coffee without sugar or cream." The next time the manual training class will be invited.[6]

The sexes were segregated even at dances. At social meetings of the literary societies and the Normal Christian Association, girls danced with girls and boys with boys. Before one class party, Dr. Amos Farnham solemnly warned: "Young ladies and gentlemen may engage in *square* dancing together, but in *round* dancing—no!" The sexes were permitted to dance together for the first time at graduation in 1905.

Nevertheless, Jeanne Grossen Ashley, '07, recalls that some of the young men found a way around the dictum, as illustrated here:

Since we were not permitted to dance with the boys, we girls met once a week for old-fashioned waltzes and two-steps. We danced sedately, while one girl played the piano. On one occasion, however, a grinning male looked in upon us and, noting no teacher present, entered and began dancing with a pretty blonde.

Shortly, someone called: "Miss Phoenix is coming! Watch out!" The gentleman was equal to the emergency. He seized a scarf from the top of the piano, tied it around his waist and continued dancing with a flapping skirt.

Miss Phoenix stepped into the room, noted the masquerade and smiled, but her eyes gazed relentlessly at the offender. The latter understood, and with a graceful bow to his lady-friend, left the room, the scarf still trailing behind him.

In view of such restrictions, the male students finally decided to boycott the dances altogether:

Instead, the men would select their favorite lady and go for a sleigh ride in the country or organize a corn-roasting party at a farmhouse. Those who could afford it went to the Connolly dancing hall in the town. Some of us were called "on the carpet" before Dr. Poucher, but no disciplinary action was taken when he learned the reason for the boycott. One of the men stated during the interview: "I am very tall and thin and when I dance with one of the short round men I look like a tangent to a big circle."

Once in a great while coed dancing was allowed, but only under the eagle-eyed supervision of ubiquitous chaperons. Fraternity dances at the high school became taboo for Normalites after the Normal faculty ceased to chaperon them.[7]

It was harder to coerce students who lived with their families in town; their presence in "public halls" caused dismay. Finally, Dr. Poucher unbent and offered the use of the gymnasium where "proper chaperonage can be arranged." According to reports, the girls "didn't think much of the idea of having a lot of nosey old fussbudgets interfering with their flirting." [8]

The school did no more than in Sheldon's day to fill the gap partly created by its own edicts. There were receptions with faculty members in the receiving lines. These were formal affairs, calling for evening clothes and tails. Also "dress-up" were the twice-a-year dances in the dining room, to which town girls, but no boys, could be invited.

Less formal activities still included the literary societies, religious association, orchestra, and for the first time, regular interschool sports. Actually, major sports in colleges had developed rapidly since 1850, but deficiency of male students retarded their growth at Oswego. Hence, before 1900, boys' sports were limited to informally organized basketball teams, baseball teams and lawn tennis.[9] There was even a football-team-of-sorts, generally considered an "indifferent source of news, unless someone happened to be killed."

By 1910 when the first Oswego–Cortland gridiron classic occurred, the team was considerably improved. In fact, Oswego triumphed over their now traditional foes 10 to 0, rounding out a four-game schedule without a single defeat. According to the *Oswego Daily-Times*, however:

> . . . it took two sets of officials to complete the contest, which the press of the time refers to as a debate. [Finally], the Oswego team put in their own referee, Henry Alexander. . . .
>
> At the game all the color and enthusiasm of big college football was present with the 24th Infantry Band livening things up, and, what is somewhat difficult for present Normal students to believe, three hundred Normal girls attended in a body and whooped it up. The only thing that saved the other spectators from ennui during the disputes was the fact that the girls did a few barn dances on the gridiron.
>
> Somebody suggested that [Oswego's] only fault was a tendency to tackle high, and somebody else—never mind who—retorted that it was probably due to the fact that they attended a coeducational institution.[10]

Incidentally, it has been the contention of sports followers who viewed local athletic events at the turn of the century that it was not always necessary to be enrolled at the Normal to play on its football team.

The first basketball team to represent the school was composed of six of the dozen or so male students of 1903–05. According to one of the players, Ben Van Oot, '05:

. . . the initiative in organizing this team was taken by a student, Theodore Breckheimer. The school had no funds for uniforms or equipment so we provided our own. We bought them from the Spalding Company in Syracuse. The basketball uniforms were all alike, green body and white band about the middle, the letters *O N S* green on white. There were no dressing rooms or showers. Mr. Cyrenius, the school custodian, took compassion on us, and rigged up a shower bath behind the boiler room in the basement. This makeshift served for a year until Dr. Poucher had a dressing room with showers installed in one of the basement classrooms. The gym where we played was adequate so far as floor area was concerned, but the ceiling was low and was supported by six iron posts which interfered considerably with our playing. The team was reasonably successful and the publicity gained was partly responsible for the enrollment of some twenty-five additional men the following year.

Nevertheless, this team could not compare with the Wonder Team of 1909–11, the best-known athletic team in the annals of the school. Among its victims were Yale, Colgate, C.C.N.Y., and the Buffalo Germans, who were considered invincible in those days. After progressing several rounds in the National Scholastic Championship Tournament in Chicago, the Wonder Boys finally lost to St. John's. Several of the boys said that big universities tried to lure them away from Oswego with offers of free tuition. Back home, so many people called to inquire how the team was making out, that the telephone company lacked enough operators to handle the calls.

The girl students played basketball, too, and by the same rules as the boys—as well as working out with wands and Indian clubs. Both sexes also enjoyed tobogganing, slush-mugging and skating, but skiing was not then locally in vogue. Coasting downhill to the river on a sled accommodating ten or twelve was another favorite. In 1903, however, a group ventured onto the frozen Welland Canal and had to be rescued by the police. Meanwhile, the school catalogue declared that "each student is encouraged to attend regularly the exercises in at least two forms of athletics."

Much more important than sports were the literary societies which constituted the only organized social life in the school. The societies also retained the same general pattern as before, though subjects of study often reflected the times. "While I was at Oswego, from 1910–12," writes Ethel Leadley Hughes, "we held a 'public' on the peace movement. One feature was a debate whose winners proved conclusively that there would never be another major war."

At least two other organizations are worthy of note, the school orchestra and the Normal Christian Association. The orchestra was organized in 1904 by Frank Plunkett, a student. Frank himself played the cornet, Brad Joyce the bass viol, Harry Robbins the piano, Don McGuire the drums, Oom Paul Froelich the clarinet, Walter Dowdle and Ramon Ochoa the violin. The following year Professor Ernst Favreau, a local music teacher, organist and orchestra leader, was engaged to direct the students' instrumental efforts; and in 1911 Mrs. Charlotte Waterman took charge.

The Christian Association held Saturday evening prayer meetings with an average of about 25 attending out of approximately 325 students. All faiths were welcome to attend. Each fall the Association held a reception in order to get acquainted with new arrivals and during the year engaged in social work. Eight students, 1898–99, taught mission Sunday School; others collected food and clothing for the poor and conducted Sunday morning services at the jail.[11]

Certainly none of the foregoing sounds highly exciting. Fortunately, institutional routines were sometimes broken by special events, including important occasions and "acts of fate." Among the latter were Big Snows, when students crept through deep, narrow tunnels or snowshoed along the lake. The assassination of President McKinley in 1901 stunned the student body. Of more local concern were two spectacular fires, the first at the starch factory on the river in 1905. "We all gathered on the bridge," writes Martha Gaines Fine, '05, "and saw the air filled with bursting, burning corn, like a continuous Roman candle." Even more exciting, to the Normalites at least, was the fire at the Welland which occurred about 1 A.M. Easter Sunday night, 1907:

When the fire alarm sounded [writes Rena Clark Pettibone, '08] we took to fire escape and ropes, leaving the rooms dark, because of Dr. Poucher's constant admonitions to save electricity. Unfortunately, in this case, the fireman had difficulty determining whether there were sleepers still inside. . . . This being Easter Sunday, I had worn a new black voile over taffeta of which I was proud, since it meant the fulfillment of a long-standing wish. Girls seldom wore black in those days; black was for older and for more sophisticated women. My first thought was to save that dress, so I hastily donned it. Then I thought if we had to go home, I must have a suit in which to travel, so I slipped that on over my new dress. Thus encumbered, I had some difficulty negotiating the fire escape, especially since skirts were ankle-length plus. My appearance was no funnier though than seeing Miss Holmes, with her hair hanging and clad in a red flannel robe—and looking as though she had lost a fortune. "All I could save was my curlers," she mourned sadly. We stood there together watching the girls come down the ropes with various prizes they had "saved," one with her window curtains under her arm, another with a T-square and triangle. Fortunately, the fire was confined to the laundry and extinguished. No one was hurt and no possessions were lost, the only souvenir of the fire being the odor of smoke and amusing memories.

Incidentally, the main fire escape had been installed only a few years before and thoroughly tested. The circular tower, however, was a hazard to anyone who hesitated even a second to let go and slide. In such case the one from a higher story would knock those below so the latter might come out head first. Some of the students liked the morning test so well, that they continued the fun all afternoon.

Also exciting were visiting celebrities who sometimes wended their way to the remote outpost of Oswego, though less frequently than in earlier days. One visitor was Jane Addams of Hull House in Chicago; another Willian Dean Howells, who delivered an address on the subject of novels.

Still another diversion for the Normal pupils was Dr. Mary Walker. The sedate Normal School officially ignored her, but students sometimes called at her home. As Mildred Button Conant, '09, recalls:

> Seven or eight of us went to her house and were given crackers and buttermilk. Dr. Mary then showed us the wonderful relics in her attic, while explaining the evil effects of women's clothing on their health. Noting my heavy skirt, she remarked that if I had suspenders to hold it up, I'd be better off. All clothing should hang from the shoulders, not the waist, she said.

Also noteworthy were "special days," for example, May Day, when all the students visited Dr. Poucher's home and held a Maypole Dance. Of course, the culminating feature was Graduation Day, finally relieved of the reading of student essays in June, 1900. However, graduates continued to do demonstration teaching in the practice school before returning alumni to permit the latter to compare current practices with those of their day.[12] From that date at least until 1910, the program also consisted of class songs, prophecies, and class poems of which this sample is typical:

> When I was chosen class poet to be
> Fear clutched my heart, my mind was at sea.
> Which of these poems should I imitate
> Evangeline or the Poor Minstrel's fate?
> At last a solution, however, I did find—
> Our class and its splendors came to mind.
> A class which like ours all others surpasses
> In wit, and numbers, and beautiful lasses.
> A theme indeed, it were easy to take
> So I'll give you the reasons our class is so great. . . .[13]

There was until 1910 no school song, though the present school colors, green and gold, were already being used. Decorations for at least one graduation day carried out the green-and-gold motif, using vases of buttercups and daisies gathered from fields just outside town.

By 1910 speakers addressing the graduating class dispensed tidbits of advice for a sane and successful future. In one unique address, Dr. Sherman Williams warned the class of 1910 not to be peculiar.[14] Nor is the topic of graduation complete without mentioning the garden parties to which Dr. Poucher invited graduates.

Graduates for the period had no trouble finding jobs. On March 22, 1910, Poucher could report that all but one of the twenty-nine graduates had already been placed in good positions. And that one, said Poucher, "didn't know much, therefore couldn't expect to get a decent job." The beginning salary for women was around $400, for men somewhat more.

As to alumni attainments after Sheldon's time, we have only meager records. Of the few we have been able to trace, several have achieved distinction in education. Ben Van Oot, '05, was for many years state supervisor of trade and technical education in Virginia; Austin Edwards, '06, became head of psychology at the University of Georgia and James O'Gorman, '07, at Hunter. Jean Betzner, '09, taught at Columbia for many years. Bradley Joyce, '06, was principal of the Western Pennsylvania School for the Blind; and Ernie Lonis, '05, was a member of the Board of Visitors of his alma mater.

Among those who made contributions outside the field of education were the well-known poet, Leslie Savage Clark, '11, and Georgia King Pearson, '01, a major contributor to the Planetarium and Hudson River Museum in Yonkers. Louise Dillon Aiken, '09, who suffered a false accusation against her character while at Oswego, later helped others in trouble as matron of the largest jail in Maryland. Marion McCormack Tubbs, '11, wrote poems and a children's book called *Puckerty Dolls*.

Poucher graduates also made contributions outside the country. May Whiffen, '98, was missionary in the Dominican Republic; Florence Thayer, '99, taught in Puerto Rico; and Sabra Hayden, '01, had charge of a girls' boarding school in Brazil, where she taught mixed groups of Americans and Brazilians.

In the Pacific, Emma E. Winslow taught for many years in Hawaii; but Poucher alumni's chief overseas activity was in the Philippines. Several of the pensionados, sent by the government to Oswego, made significant contributions upon return to their homeland. Alejandro Santos, '07, served as principal of the Pasig Central School, assistant supervisor for Rizal Province, and for three years as president of the Rizal Teachers Association. Cenon Monasterial, '07, was a division superintendent; Francisco Llamado, academic supervisor for the Division of Cavite and one-time staff member of José Rizal College. José Batungbacal wrote many books, among them *Great Architects of Filipino Nationality; Moral Training of the Filipino People;* and *Our Fighters for Freedom from Mactan to Bataan.* W. A. Sutherland's *Not By Might* describes the postgraduate contributions of the pensionados, including those at Oswego.

More important were the subtle, long-term effects, clearly apparent in graduate testimonials like these:

> I believe the Normal students assimilated the "spirit of the institution," which led to desire to progress and excel in one's chosen field, a habit of extending oneself, a desire to hustle, an interest in youth, and a realization of the service one might render—a realization that teaching is good work, a vocation replete with challenge that can be fun. [Don McGuire, '07]

> Early in my sojourn at Oswego I became aware of a spirit of freedom, a challenge to think through, to be observant, to be generous with those who disagreed with me. We all developed a sense of humor and good will together. I became conscious of eternally modern educational truths, the goals for fruitful living. At Columbia in 1909, at Chicago in 1911, at Penn State in 1942, I found my educational philosophy up-to-date and acceptable. I hope to continue this quest for truth, for creative goals, for a workable philosophy, for deepening religious convictions. This has been the reward of fifty-nine years of living as an Oswego graduate. [Nellie Trout Hogue, '03]

PART

The Eggs A

191

PART III

The Riggs Administration

1913-33

CHAPTER 8

Milestones of the Riggs Administration

IN 1912, Riggs wrote, "For fifty years the two principal products of Oswego have been starch and teachers. They have both gone to the ends of the earth and carried the name Oswego with them. If you want starch in London you ask for a pint of Oswego." But neither Oswego's starch nor teachers flourished in the two decades that followed. The starch factory expired and the college came close to it. Not that James G. Riggs or his faculty were personally to blame. New York lagged where teacher education was concerned while other states forged ahead. Normals elsewhere had long since become teachers colleges, had improved their facilities and built fine residence halls.

Alumni continued to support the school, but their loyalty was defensive, not the confident pride of earlier days. And those who went on to obtain degrees at other schools almost always preferred to think of the higher-status school as their alma mater.

Truly, this period was Oswego's darkest hour, and not until the mid-thirties did a somnolent institution begin the slow struggle upward again. Nevertheless, these years did see certain important developments and events; the first was the dedication of the new building in 1914. After the banquet, all repaired to Dr. Sheldon's old homestead where they saw a drama, "The Olden Time and the New," written by C. L. G. Scales and portraying the history of the school. According to Finegan:

> In dramatic tone and action it was a presentation of high order and was witnessed by an audience of three thousand delighted people. In the evening, at the Pontiac, a reception was tendered by the faculty to the visiting alumni and guests of honor.[1]

No sooner had the school removed to its new home on the hill, than the building's deficiencies began to be felt. Its exposed position led

135

to the construction, in 1914, of a covered passageway from the streetcar tracks to the building at a cost of $250. This convenient but unsightly device was put up each year in November and taken down in March until replaced in 1919 by the present pergola, which was to become a symbol of the college itself. In 1959–61, when time had taken its toll and the structure began to crumble, alumni, students and friends rallied and voted funds to pay for its restoration. The library, too, got a face-lifting, being furnished and remodeled by vocational students after World War I. The inadequate recreation area was remedied somewhat by purchase in 1914 of the thirteen-acre Clark Athletic Field, bringing the total school acreage to forty.

The housing problem led a group to form in 1923 to raise money for a dormitory. This group, chartered in 1927, under the name of Sheldon Hall, Incorporated, sold shares of stock, promising reimbursement of 10 per cent interest. For a time the project flourished, chiefly through the efforts of alumni, who dug deep into their pockets to buy shares. Benefits were held, including a faculty play called "Rollo's Wild Oats." On July 2, 1924, Lena Hill Severance, '73, wrote that half the money had been raised and "the committee is very sanguine." Uldrick Thompson, '80, hand-carved a mahogany clock, especially for the projected hall. Roughly thirty thousand dollars had been raised and an architect paid nine thousand dollars, when a combination of economic depression and mismanagement caused serious depletion of funds.

Shop facilities fared better. In fact, Riggs's single greatest achievement was securing the Industrial Arts Building. Since students in this division had increased from 20 to 116 within the ten-year period, 1915–25, the Regents were urged to appropriate money from a recent bond issue for a wing to the main building to be used for vocational training. Fortunately, the Regents refused, because the 1930 legislature voted $300,000 for a separate building, besides $50,000 for equipment.[2] Preliminary drawings, approved August 19, 1930, were revised almost immediately, because of scientific developments in automobile, aircraft, electrical and mechanical industries.[3]

The cornerstone laying was a hastily contrived affair. Upon learning that Governor Franklin D. Roosevelt was coming up the canal on an inspection trip, Riggs seized the opportunity to interest him in the school by asking him to lay the stone. The Governor accepted and the scramble to get things ready began. "Riggs called me in," said Harry Karcher, "and asked, 'Can you make a box to put in the cornerstone?' Then we picked a spot on the lawn, though we didn't know just where the building would go. Finally, we built a corner, and left a hole for the box."

At the ceremony, held August 18, 1930, Roosevelt made it plain that he had approved the appropriation for the building, not to add to capacity but to improve teaching. Afterwards, the Governor showed that he was thoroughly familiar with the art of cornerstone laying. "Give me a little mortar on this trowel," he directed a workman, "and I might add that I have a union card in my pocket." Then he handed the trowel to Riggs, saying, "I want you to put it in a glass case in the building." Riggs nodded assent—and one finds the historic tool thus displayed today.

Actual excavation, a short distance from the original cornerstone, was delayed to permit the transplanting of 220 spruce trees. Not quite two years later the building—one of the finest of its kind—was completed, and, on June 16, 1932, it was dedicated by Frank P. Graves, commissioner of education.

An amusing postscript to these events deserves recording. Franklin D. Roosevelt, pausing briefly at Oswego the following year, inspected the new building. "By some miracle," he observed, "I see that the present site is a hundred feet from where I laid the cornerstone last year." [4]

The Riggs period was marked by three tragic events: war, an influenza epidemic, and the stock market crash. The war, especially, had a strong impact on campus life:

> One of my most vivid memories [says Gertrude Lake Ennis, '17] was the special assembly called that April morning in 1917 when Wilson declared war on Germany. Mrs. Waterman led us in singing "The Battle Hymn of the Republic" and "America." Dr. Riggs made the official announcement in a solemn manner. We were all deeply impressed. Our beloved teacher, Dr. Richard Piez, related the events leading to the declaration, emphasizing the importance of international relations.

Even before America entered the war, ten students had "joined up"; others rapidly followed suit. The school's enrollment shrank by a total of 40 per cent.[5] Only ten men students remained in the industrial arts course. Women students were drafted into woodworking classes to help instructors hold their jobs.

Those on the home front made their contribution, too. The men of the faculty, who were overaged or involved in teaching army cadets, had military drill, sometimes carrying sticks in lieu of rifles. Women faculty and students served and knitted at the state armory. They also collected books for soldiers and sailors, but 175 were discarded as "unsuitable." Some of the Normal girls volunteered to work on farms that were short of help.[6] Campus School youngsters collected fruit pits, string, and tin foil and formed units of the Junior Red Cross.[7]

A senior chapter on the college level made sling bandages, garments, and comfort bags for the boys. These bags contained a toothbrush, tube of toothpaste, face cloth, cake of toilet soap, three cigarettes, a roll of gauze, and two pounds of sugar.

But the school's major contribution to the war effort was providing housing and training for a detachment of the Army Corps. The first detachment of two hundred soldiers arrived July 15, 1918, the second October 15, leaving December 15. Each stayed three months. The Campus School wing became their dormitory, the cafeteria their mess hall, and the regular shop rooms their laboratories. The government supplied most of the equipment, and the doughboys themselves constructed wooden buildings for blacksmithing and auto mechanics. These young men, half of them under twenty-one, received instruction in machine shop, electricity, carpentry, woodwork, blacksmithing, gas engine repairs, sheet metal, and concrete work.[8]

Theirs was a full life. At six-thirty reveille sounded and the men formed in the front of the main building for the flag raising. Classes taught by the industrial arts faculty were held until 10:30 A.M. when there was drill, then classes again.

The soldiers were housed on the ground floor of the main building and regulations forbade them to go upstairs. They also had orders to bathe at least twice a week. For amusement, on pleasant days the boys would wheel a piano out on the lawn and sing their favorites, especially military songs.

From the war interlude the school profited in at least two ways. At a time when enrollment was seriously depleted, the Army provided students and made it possible to keep many of its instructors. And when they left, the school was richer by two wooden buildings and much shop equipment, both parting gifts from Uncle Sam.

It was during this same interim, October–November, 1918, that a major flu epidemic broke out. The school closed but turned over the Welland to the Red Cross for use as an emergency hospital. Faculty volunteers cooked there and tended the sick. Oddly enough, not a single case broke out among the soldiers themselves.

The great struggle also found its way into the programs of the Normal literary societies. In 1918 Adelphi had a program on feeding Europe; sub-topics were "Herbert Hoover" and "The Acorn as a Food."

Meanwhile, there were assorted patriotic programs. First there was the special flag-raising program, October 21, 1917. Noted the *Oswego Palladium-Times*:

> The most inspiring patriotic exercises ever held in this city took place yesterday afternoon on the campus of the Oswego State Normal School when the new steel flagpole was dedicated by raising to its peak a monster American flag, 38 by 20 feet. A service flag also flew in front

of the school with eight stars representing the students in service. There
was a big parade to the college, including new hospital units at the fort
that the Normal girls cheered as they passed.[9]

Next came the memorial service, November 8, 1918, for Merle Hewitt,
Oswego's first student to die in the war and the person for whom the
student union is named. Finally, came the Armistice parades in 1918, the
first one on November 7, after a false alarm that war was ended. "When
the real parade came," relates Helen Quigley Ziel, '20, "we had another
parade and a dance." Later in the spring Dr. Riggs had beautiful maple
trees planted along Washington Boulevard, each named for a Normalite
in the service.

The third disaster of the period was the stock market crash of 1929.
Several faculty members owned stock. Mr. Jay Rudolph became so excited when he heard the news that he simply walked out on his class
to obtain information. For several days thereafter few classes were
taught. As for the students, they became harder than ever to recruit.

Happier events occurred, too, beginning with the dedication of the
new building in July 1, 1914.

> Exercises were held in Normal Hall, the stage prettily decorated with
> daisies, roses and summer flowers. The twelve members of the graduat-
> ing class of Normal High, discontinued after this year, escorted the
> seniors.
>
> The menu of the alumni banquet that followed was as follows: Rose
> Leaf Cocktail, Consommé Japonnaise, Bread Sticks, Olives, Baked White
> Fish, Dressed Cucumbers, Creamed Chicken and Mushrooms, Stuffed
> Lamb, Potato Rosettes, Green Peas, Pickled Pears, Rolls, Butter, Tomato
> and Cherry Salad, Crisped Wafers, Strawberry and Pineapple Sherbet,
> Coconut Lily Cakes, Black Coffee, Mints, Salted Peanuts, Charged Deep
> Rock Water.

Graduation days, too, were gala affairs. The 1916 commencement was
held in the grove, but a strong wind constantly blew the speaker's notes.
Thereafter, commencement wisely retreated indoors again. Certain com-
mencements were distinguished by the manner of the graduates' attire.
In 1920 women graduates for the first time wore "handsome white gowns
with corsages" and the men dark blue coats and blue trousers.

Another solemn but gala occasion occurred October 4, 1922, when
Sheldon's statue was removed to Oswego from the dark hole to which it
had been relegated in the Capitol Building in Albany. The statue was
placed in the front hall of the main building and dedicated for a second
time. "It is a signal distinction," wrote Dr. Skinner, "when the same
statue is to be twice dedicated. But you will agree with me that if any

statue ever deserved a double dedication the statue of Dr. Sheldon is worthy of that honor." But Sheldon's statue had not yet found its final resting place. The statue overwhelmed the small lobby where it stood and was removed to the front lawn, where it still stands.

As for education events of wider scope, Oswego's participation had all but ceased, except for get-togethers with others of the New York normal family. Oswego's exhibition of the Normal catalogue and the *Vocationist* at the Bohemian exhibit in Prague stands out solely for this reason.

Meanwhile, the curriculum was undergoing significant changes. The two-year general elementary curriculum, adopted in 1911 before Poucher retired, when a third year was added, lasted until 1922. Agitation for modifications, both in content and in length, had begun in 1912 but bogged down because of the war. Critics pointed out that the current curriculum offered only a smattering of method, while cultural enrichment was largely ignored. Whatever cultural content there was, was largely a duplication of the offering in high school. Two years, they argued, had proved insufficient for doing both well.

Another strong argument for a three-year program was the new teacher-certification law which, in effect, would require better preparation for those preparing to teach. Background for this action goes back to 1875. From then until 1841, power to examine and license teachers was in the hands of local school commissioners. Then in 1895, an important statute of the state of New York stipulated that every teacher appointed anywhere in the state of New York be "trained." However, twenty-four different standards were used through the state, and the resultant confusion finally led to the establishment of a State Department of Certification. Finally, better trained elementary teachers would strengthen the hand of those at that time fighting for a single schedule for elementary and high-school teachers.

By 1920, a committee of principals and department heads was engaged in making a new curriculum. This was the first time in New York State that anyone other than principals and the State Department had participated in curricula-making. William Bagley of Columbia, formerly of Oswego, also contributed advice.[10]

Aside from being one year longer, the 1922 curriculum differed little from the 1911 version. The same curricular classifications were offered—kindergarten, intermediate, and industrial arts. Content was still largely a review of high school work. By 1915 the idea that teacher-training institutions should limit themselves to professional content was gone,[11] but at Oswego, the emphasis remained professional, though comparatively less so than before. Not that number of hours in education ever actually declined. The ratio of professional to cultural courses simply became less when the third year was added. Professionalization of courses other than education, however, began to diminish.

The curriculum also remained subject-matter centered, and the subject matter itself fragmented. For example, the offering in history might be made up of unrelated tidbits called "The Reformation," "The Renaissance," "French Revolution," and the like, providing no real understanding of the sweep of events.[12]

The child-centered curriculum was yet to come. Content and vocabulary were often beyond children's comprehension. "A sentence in one geography book," says Isabel Kingsbury Hart, "read this way: 'Buffalo became a busy port because it had a large basin and many slips.' Now I ask you, what is a fifth grader's concept of a slip? Is it the slip his mother wears, or the kind she grows in a tomato can in the kitchen window? You see why I became a devotee of the lantern slide."

Methods had changed no more than curriculum. These comments concern certain methods classes: "Our drawing teacher would give us a picture of a mother feeding her children and say, 'Draw it.'" "In arithmetic we'd be told to turn to page 47 and do the problems. They never taught me how to teach them." "Many taught by question and answer."

Professional training, too, remained substantially unchanged. There was the same vertical organization. The same teacher who taught a subject on the normal school level supervised its teaching in the Campus School. She also gave occasional demonstrations in the Campus School, but the classes were regularly taught by the practice teachers themselves. Said one young woman: "Except for these demonstrations, we never saw live teaching ourselves." Two girls were assigned to a grade and took over the entire day's work. "We were simply on our own," recalls another. "Our only guidance consisted in comments on our lesson plans, and two or three visits a year from our supervisor."

Perhaps one reason for the stalemate in methods and curriculum was the failure to develop a consistent, integrated philosophy on which to base modifications. True, philosophical changes occurred but they refused to jell. Whatever philosophy there was, was a mixture of Herbart, Thorndike, and any other "newism" that came along. Object teaching was gone, but Froebel still lingered in the kindergarten in 1913, as Hazel Hewitt's reminiscences show:

> We would sit in a ring on the floor. Once we had a dove. We washed it and spread its wings. We did weaving, actually on too difficult a level. We also wove a hammock for a doll. We still used Froebel's gifts, little blocks of different sizes. We would all go through rituals with them doing the same thing at the same time.

Consonant with the persistence of Herbartianism, Dr. Ida B. Earhart, '95, in her book, *Types of Teaching*, 1915, suggested ways to build lessons on Herbart's five formal steps, at the same time warning that they were not suited to all types of lessons.[13]

Diluting, and finally gaining precedence over, these earlier philosophies was Thorndike's associationism. This was the era when Thorndike of Columbia and Judd of Chicago were at loggerheads. Thorndike's theories tended to popularize drill and teaching of specific details while another educational giant, C. H. Judd of Chicago (1873–1949), stressed basic principles and generalizations.

Oswegonians, most of whom had either attended Columbia or been exposed to its influence, preferred Thorndike, but followed no one philosophy consistently. Many of the faculty had been educated in an earlier day, but had latched onto recent ideas. The problem with at least some of them was to dress up the old offering so that it would have the New Look.

As for method, the shibboleth of the hour was the project or unit. An early example was a twenty-five-foot motorboat, built by the seventh and eighth grade boys in 1914 and dubbed *The Caroline* in honor of Caroline V. Sinnamon, their principal. The boys worked after school and on Saturdays in gangs of eight and ten.

In spring, 1915, many classroom activities were integrated around preparation for the May Festival, designed to emulate an old English May Day. The pupils selected their own May Queen, and Lord of the May, and designed their own costumes, including emblems for shields, helmets, bows and arrows. A fifth-grade pupil composed one of the dances and taught it to the others.[14]

Later projects embraced a broader range of subject matter. In 1931, a kindergarten child dramatized train play by pushing two pieces of wood about the room making the sound of the engine as he played along. The train interest spread to the larger group and involved trips to the library, to the station, a ride on the train, and highly organized play with trains made of packing boxes. Simple experiments cleared up the difference between smoke and steam.[15]

Another well-integrated activity was conducted by Garson Rockoff. His class was studying the League of Nations and the World Court. The Art Department colored the flag; the Industrial Arts Division helped in building staffs; health and physical education classes assisted with folk dances; and the English Department helped with writing the sketch prepared for final dramatization.

As for the various subjects taught in the Normal School, English was emphasized, especially speech. Physical education underwent considerable change, under the direction of Sarah Oldstead, Max Ziel, and Marion

Angel. All three taught girls' physical education and, after 1921, Ziel also taught boys' physical education. Until then boys and girls took it together. The program consisted mainly of calisthenics, Swedish and American marching, and folk dances.

One area of curricular activity was eliminated and three others were added during the period. On July 1, 1914, the High School Department was abandoned. There was neither sufficient space nor staff to accommodate any area not contributing to the fundamental purposes of the school.

Meanwhile, in 1913, Oswego had latched onto a current fad, the open-air school.[16] According to the catalogue, it was for "teaching frailer children who didn't look rugged." Such schools were generally intended for anemic children with a tendency to tubercular troubles. The first were organized in New York City and Berlin about 1910. Two hundred others appeared by 1913. Children were provided with Eskimo suits, double wool blankets, and sleeping bags and were taught while sitting swaddled in robes with the windows of the room wide open. Attention was also given to diet. At Oswego as elsewhere the experiment lasted only a few years.

More important than the open-air school and destined to last two decades, was the department, established in 1916, for training teachers of retarded children. Basic to this development were research studies by Binet and Goddard, which had created interest in the welfare of the mentally retarded. As a consequence, the former unclassified schools, which lumped together all cases of retardation, were replaced by special classes, established on the basis of mental tests.

New York State reacted to this development by passing a law requiring that school districts having at least ten children retarded three or more years in mental development establish a special class. To satisfy the need for teachers of such classes, special classes were created at Oneonta and Oswego.

Reasons for the establishment of the class were recorded in the Minutes of the Board: "Mental defectives are likely to wander about and become thieves, firebugs, and murderers. The girls may become worse because they are likely to be succeeded by a brood of their own kind." [17]

Oswego was a pioneer in this work. Hitherto, no regular course anywhere had been established to furnish such teachers. The nearest approach had been a six-week period of observations and lectures in a few institutions for the feeble-minded. Several universities had offered courses related to the topic, but they were not sequential.

To conduct the program, Riggs first employed Helen Gray, who left after two years to institute similar work at Albany. The program was then headed by Flora Otis, assisted by Adelaide Fitch, both trained at the famous Vineland Training School under Goddard, the top specialist in the field. Later they were assisted by one of their own graduates, Garson Rockoff, who subsequently headed the program himself.

The program included a year of theory, observation and practice. In addition, students observed at the Syracuse Institute for Mental Defectives. As for facilities, there was a shop for boys; whereas for the girls:

> There is a cozy little flat on the third floor . . . where [children in the special department] learn care of the home. Each day the children have a different duty about on the same schedule as their mothers at home. Monday is wash day and Friday is cleaning day. There is a parlor dining room, vestibule, kitchen, bedroom. Children also cook, and prepare their own luncheons.[18]

The cost of the program was high and the total number trained comparatively small. As many as seventy-five took the work in the summer. Regular term students numbered thirty-six, with about a dozen graduates a year. Graduates received a special diploma authorizing them to organize and supervise subnormal classes.

Meanwhile, in 1916, the Normal severed its remaining ties with the Oswego city schools. To this date, the city had furnished teachers for the training school. Henceforth, such teachers were to be employed by the state; and the city was to pay a lump sum of $2,500 a year for teaching not more than 350 city children.[19]

The summer of 1919 was the first regular summer school session at Oswego; the only previous ones were the music school in Sheldon's time and the private summer school taught by Piez and Park from 1913 through 1918.

The first summer school session was given in 1839 by Henry Barnard, who brought together twenty-six young men and gave them instruction for six weeks. But the modern version of the summer school, as we know it, originated about 1872. The first regular summer session instituted in the New York normal schools came somewhat later, at Oneonta in 1912.

The most popular feature of early summer schools at Oswego was Camp Shady Shore, a tent colony begun in the summer of 1919, when a few students pitched their tents by the lake. In 1920 there were four tents, and, in 1921, thirty additional tents were obtained from the state militia.[20] By the 1930's there were twenty-one cabins, six tents, and a large trailer area. Furniture, iceboxes and cots were furnished as well as electricity.

When Riggs came, library facilities were very poor. As late as 1915–16, fiction and non-fiction were still placed indiscriminately together. But

Caroline Hahner, the first librarian, instituted many improvements. A card catalogue was begun in the early twenties, and in 1927 came the first interlibrary loan. The next year, in 1928, the Children's Library was opened. But not until Helen Hagger took charge in 1945 was the library to become the highly efficient service area it is today.

As for industrial arts, the 1911 curriculum was in force when Riggs took the reins. Courses in psychology, history of education, English and science methods were the same as those taken by the elementary students. The former Special Drawing and Manual Training Curriculum had been abolished, and instituted in its place was the two-year Industrial Arts Teacher Training Curriculum—largely because the term "manual training" had fallen into disrepute. Actually, the new curriculum was industrial arts in little more than name only. Work was still of the formal disciplinary type. It was based on the theory that there were certain fundamental skills in every trade which could be taught through set exercises. True, more attention was paid to design and utility of projects, but little attention was paid to interpreting an industrial civilization. Perhaps at this point we could say that Oswego was in the process of graduating from *manual training* to *manual arts,* but had a long way to go to become *industrial arts.*

The major factor which held back the achievement of a true industrial arts program, at Oswego as elsewhere, was lack of instructors to interpret it. Most of the instructors were tradesmen and craftsmen with little sympathy for the new idea, which they scorned as "skimming the surface." Nevertheless, they reflected still-prevalent practices of their times. Besides, they probably obtained better results with methods which they understood than they could have with a new philosophy foreign to their experience.

This situation persisted until 1917, when passage of the Smith–Hughes Act constituted a coup d'état for advocates of vocational education. The natural result was a general upsurge in vocational education and concomitant demand for qualified trade teachers. New York State got on the bandwagon. It accepted Smith–Hughes provisions on May 21, 1917— thus qualifying for grants in aid from the federal government, and the feeble interest in industrial arts at Oswego almost died, to be revived again three years later. Current shop programs at Oswego and Buffalo were scuttled in favor of training teachers for general industrial shopwork.

Philosophical implications of the about-face were radical. After all, industrial arts education and vocational education are poles apart. Vocational education stems from the history of apprenticeship, industrial arts education from educational theories of the Renaissance and Reformation. Pedagogically, industrial arts was founded on the assumption of the need for development of basic skills instead of specific trade training, as a preparation for industrial vocations. Secondly, industrial arts education is concerned with laying a foundation for all industrial vocations; vocational education purports to train youth who have already chosen an occupation. Obviously, industrial arts may well be an integral part of education on all levels, while vocational education is more properly confined to secondary and adult education.

Leaders of industrial vocations in the state had their own ideas as to how to implement their program. They favored teaching "the small community industrial worker" skills and knowledges in a number of trades. The industrial arts teacher was frequently expected to give instruction in all building and metal trades to boys who planned to become industrial workers. This theory was to prove fallacious, because it satisfied neither the purposes of industrial arts nor of vocational education. On the one hand, boys failed to gain the philosophical background required to integrate their training in various skills; on the other, they gained only a smattering of several trades without the depth of skill needed for any specific vocation.

Naturally, these views were reflected in the new vocational education practices at Oswego. The school began preparing teachers for service in the general industrial school, a vocational school with courses suited to the needs of young people living in communities of less than twenty-five thousand.

Other innovations in the new program were these: mature persons, though not graduates, could be admitted; time allotment for shop work and mathematics was drastically increased; and twenty weeks of specified types of employment were required during summer vacations.

However, exclusive preoccupation with vocational education proved unwise; therefore, in 1921, industrial arts education was resumed. The new curriculum, adopted that year, was different in several important ways from the one it displaced. Plumbing and concrete work were eliminated; but electrical work was added, as well as a ten-credit-hour elective shop course designed to permit specialization in the student's major field of interest.

This curriculum lasted until 1925, when certain minor changes were made. No longer was a high school diploma by itself adequate for admission; specified credits were required. Nor would trade experience now be acceptable in lieu of a high school diploma. Since 1920 special courses had been established in several major cities through the state to meet the demand for teachers of specific trade subjects.

At the same time, to lighten the strenuous load on faculty and students, total credit hours for the two-year program were reduced from eighty-three to seventy-four. The program formerly required 6¾ clock hours a day in shop and classrooms. The industrial arts staff of Dr. Park, five instructors, and several part-time assistants could hardly absorb the load. The problem was simply one of overstuffed curriculum and understaffed faculty.

Curricular changes of a fundamental nature were yet to come. For one thing, it was hard to shake off firmly fixed vocational objectives. Two years would support nothing but a narrow program anyhow. However, after 1925, Arthur Hauler completely overhauled the practice teaching program. He arranged for teaching at off-campus centers to which he gave close personal supervision.

The first really significant changes since 1911, except for the vocational interlude, came with the institution of the three-year program in 1929. Factors accounting for the third year were long-standing discontent with the two-year program, coupled with increasing demand for better trained industrial arts teachers.

The character of the 1929 curriculum may be summarized as follows: (1) Shop work was increased nearly 50 per cent, culminating in a course known as Composite Shop Work. Lack of such a course had seriously handicapped graduates going into the single shop laboratories. (2) Practice teaching was lengthened from six to ten weeks, and removed almost exclusively to off-campus centers. Such an environment generally approximated the one in which the practice teacher would ultimately find himself employed. (3) Industrial arts objectives received substantially greater recognition than before. (4) Greater emphasis was laid on general education, design, and range of shop experience. (5) The candidate admitted to this course must be a high school graduate, at least eighteen years old. In addition, he must offer three units of shop work and mechanical or architectural drawing, or six months of approved trade experience.

A natural outcome of the growing interest in industrial arts was the institution of the general shop. After all, a complex industrial culture can only be interpreted in a shop permitting demonstration of the integration of a wide range of processes and skills. Actually Russell in 1909 and Bonser in 1910 had the general shop idea when they developed elementary school programs around food, clothing, shelter, utensils and machines. In fact, general shop got its start from these men and their students, as they fanned out over the country. Also contributing to development of the general shop was growth of the junior high school, which became the champion of pupil exploration.

For a long time, however, general shops—like the industrial arts philosophy they reflected—existed largely in name only. Experimentation and planning were overlooked. Projects simply meant bigger and better birdhouses. The general shop itself was simply an aggregate of unit shops. In fact, even today the unit shop emphasizing wood and metal prevails.

Nor did general shop catch on immediately at Oswego. Gene Essex in industrial arts and Lucile Allard in the Campus School, however, led the way—and general shop at Oswego became a fact as well as a name. Concurrent with this development, Roy Fales of the State Department of Vocational and Industrial Education, and Art Hauler and his cadets from Oswego, carried the idea of general shops throughout the state. In effect, Oswego graduates composed a state-wide lobby for general shop.

Both industrial arts education and the general shop were manifestations of larger currents of educational and psychological thought. They harmonized with the increasingly popular concepts of correlation, integration, and basic understanding. In consequence, classroom programs became centered around activities rather than subjects. The industrial arts man, for example, might be called upon to assist with a unit on colonial life, embracing broad concepts related to food, clothing and shelter. He had to be versatile enough to build a colonial home and to equip it with utensils. Or in an Indian unit, pottery would be required.

A concomitant result was expansion in the areas with which the general shop was concerned. How could an industrial civilization be interpreted without taking cognizance of all basic industries? Hence, to wood and metal were added electricity and printing, and still later textiles and ceramics.

These years saw a great expansion in number of I.A. students. Before the war, only a handful had graduated each year, and during the war itself the program dwindled to almost nothing. In the twenties, several factors led to expansion: more shop work for girls in public schools; more for boys not good in academic subjects; and modern theories of education which stressed dynamic, constructive learning as contrasted with passive learning.

Most of Oswego's industrial arts boys were just that—boys, straight from high school. When vocational training was accepted in lieu of a high school diploma, however, there was an increase of older men with experience in carpentry, machine shop, electricity, plastering, shipbuilding, and printing. Actually, their effect was a salutary one. "They livened up the classes by relating their practical experiences," says Robert Dicke, '30.

Industrial arts was now the male's exclusive domain. In the early days, there had always been girls in the program. However, as time wore on, they faced increasing discrimination. By 1914–16, they were still admitted, but not really assimilated, as Gertrude Lake Ennis' experience (1914–17) reveals:

The manual arts course was not very old and developed from the early sloyd plan of handwork, which girls had been trained to teach. Under Dr. Joseph C. Park the course was greatly expanded. Letitia Beebe from Long Island and I were the only girls in our class and the last who were allowed to take it, partly I think because machines were introduced and became important in training students. We were very young and eager to try and so Dr. Park, with an amused twinkle in his eye, gave us permission. Having taken a college entrance course in high school, there were some conditions to work out, such as drawing and physics. That part we handled nicely. But the shop work was another thing.

At first the boys were reluctant to concede that we should be there at all. They stood around and watched our first struggles with planes and saws; but as we persisted, they soon helped us and accepted us. Mr. Early who taught the woodworking was very patient and painstaking. One of our first class projects was building some bleachers back of the building to use on the football field. All sports at that time were very amateur in character; not much time or coaching was given. Of course we two went along and the boys bet on how many times we would hit the nails on the head. We disappointed them and made out pretty well. We took a lot of kidding but it was fun. As I look back they were really very decent because we were clumsy and ignorant. Most of them thought we would not last.

The print shop was very popular. We met our boy friends there and while we set type we had some fun, too.

With the vocational education interlude, 1917 to 1920, came complete exclusion of women from industrial arts; yet no one seriously protested.

Throughout the period, the industrial arts program operated under severe limitations. All classes and laboratories were located in the basement of the main building. Some of the noisier classes were limited to late afternoon so as not to disturb those above them. Another problem was getting the kind of faculty desired. It was difficult to compete with industry for qualified help, and even harder to find persons both imbued with the industrial arts philosophy and capable of communicating it to students.

The Industrial Arts Department of the Riggs period also left its monuments and traditions. The concrete and bricklaying class of 1922 drew designs for an ornamental gate in the rear of the building which was constructed with field stones from the lake shore.

Another permanent "monument" to the Riggs period was inauguration, in 1930, of the annual Spring Conference, destined to become an important feature of the industrial arts activity program.

The industrial arts curriculum for the period largely neglected the humanities. Not even extension to three years permitted more than a fraction of the time needed for liberal education. Such cultural offerings as existed were diluted with professionalization. "We had shop math, and even shop English," says Harry Karcher. "There was a halo around the shop program." All teachers were supposed to adapt their subjects to the special needs and interests of industrial arts students, as though their cultural needs differed somehow from those of people generally. Few industrial arts men believed that shopkeeping and Socrates belonged together anyway.

Under such circumstances the expected happened. Faculty members, attempting to adapt materials to a course they themselves did not understand, often failed. One instructor suggested to the industrial arts fellows that they pick the poetry they would like to study. When the men responded that they had no ideas on the subject, the instructor decided that "Snowbound" would fill the bill. Finding themselves somewhat less than enthralled with the poet's efforts, the students amused themselves by throwing pennies to the front of the room. Kate Hayes also tried. "She asked me for electricity problems to use in math," says Harry Karcher, "but she did not understand them herself."

Marian Mahar's approach was somewhat better. As shop speech teacher, she attempted to make the work practical, without tying it specifically to shop. She had the boys pretend they were making speeches at banquets, talking to trustees, and the like.

The Oswego Story
in Pictures

The first Normal School Building, which occupied the remodeled
United States Hotel from 1866 to 1879

Second Normal School Building, occupied 1879–1913

Edward Austin Sheldon,
his wife, Frances (seated), and his sister, Dorliska

Mary Sheldon Barnes,
daughter of the founder, alumna,
faculty member and writer

Hermann Krüsi,
member of Oswego's faculty
1862–86

An English class of Caroline L. G. Scales, about 1893

Kindergarten methods, 1893

Physical science laboratory in the second Normal School Building

Caroline Scales reading classics to students in her room at the Welland about 1893

Normal School workshop, 1893, where students learned to use tools
and to make simple scientific apparatus

Normalites put on a play, February 5, 1892

Dr. Mary V. Lee reading to a group of students, 1888

Members of the Class of 1889 hold objects pertaining to their classroom program

Students Kate B. Osterhout and Gertrude Odel having tea in their room
at the Welland, May, 1895

Class of 1891

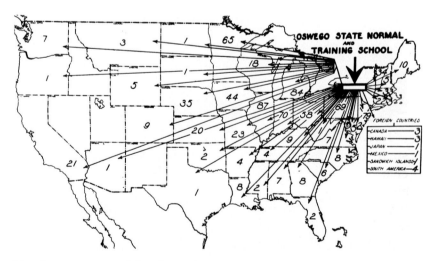

Map showing numerical distribution by states of Oswego Normal School graduates
from 1861 to 1866

Diploma awarded
Oswego at the World's
Columbian Exposition
in Chicago, 1893

1. Joe is playing that he is a stage-driver. He has an easy-chair for his stage, and two other chairs for his horses.

2. How he does use the whip!

3. It is well that his horses can not feel the pain. But if Joe's horses were alive, I think he would not whip them so.

A page from one of Sheldon's famous readers

The Normal School faculty, 1902–03: bottom row, left to right, Joseph C. Park, manual training, civics; Mary O'Geran, penmanship, intermediate supervision, sewing; Grant Karr, director of training, education; I. B. Poucher, principal; Amos W. Farnham, geography methods, English; Harriet Stevens, primary principal; Jeanne Grossen, French, German. Second row, Louis Karpinski, science, mathematics; Richard K. Piez, psychology, drawing; Lina L. Loveridge, history methods, grade supervision; Caroline Scales, English; Herbert J. Smith, Latin, Greek, logic; Kate Hayes, mathematics methods, grade supervision. Top row, Mary MacElroy, grammar school principal; Lydia Phoenix, music, physical education, dramatic reading; Amanda Funnelle, kindergarten methods; Mary Rainey, kindergarten assistant; Charles Sheldon, botany, zoology. (Not shown: Walker G. Rappleye, Caroline V. Sinnamon.)

Amanda Funnelle and
Caroline L. G. Scales, 1910

Richard Piez, preparing coffee
at fall cookout in 1900

Normal School Song
Air - Die Lorelei
To Edward Austin Sheldon.

1 O blue are Ontario's waters,
And fair in the sunset glow;
But fairer, O Alma Mater,
Is the name thy children know

Chorus.
Then hail, all hail to Oswego,
To our Normal School so dear;
Roam we the wide world over,
Our hearts, our hearts, they are here.

2. And the name, the fame of our founder,
Through the changing years it stands;
For he built as they build over yonder,
The house not made with hands.

3. Of wisdom and love he builded
In the willing hearts of youth;
Fair temples of loving service,
Fair shrines to beauty and truth.

4 He carved and wrought the temple
With the love that never tires;
Help we the altars kindle,
Guard we the sacred fires!

Oswego, N.Y. 1910.   C. L. J. S.

Original of the first
alma mater, written by
Caroline Scales, 1910

Saturday

Morning — Nine O'clock

Prayer	Reverend Richmond H. Gesner
Hymn, Dear Lord, I Thank Thee	Maker
The Greatest Need of Our Schools	Dr. Lewis H. Jones, '68
Five-Minute Talks	

PART I

Dr. Margaret K. Smith, '83   M. Harriet Bishop, '91
William A. Baldwin, '84   George A. Lewis, '77
Anna W. Booth, '89   S. R. Shear
Jennie E. Dennehy, '91

Normal Orchestra

PART II

Amelia B. Myers, '79   Edith M. Tufts, '96
Jessie S. Himes, '93   Harriet J. Brown, '75
Dr. Leroy D. Farnham, '72

Honor to Whom Honor Is Due	Anna B. Herrig, '90
Vocal Solo, Recessional	DeKoven
Arthur L. Perry	
To Lina Lyman Loveridge, '98	Bertha W. Fuller, '04
"Others first, self afterward."	
"A pard-like spirit, beautiful and swift."	
Dr. Sheldon's Favorite Hymn	Calm Me, My God
Founder's Day for Oswego	Mary E. Laing, '74
School Song	O Blue Are Ontario's Waters
Recitation, A Noble Life and True	E. Nesbit
Mrs. Luella Phillips Pierce, '88	

Greetings from
The New York Oswego Alumni Association
President, A. W. Richardson, '79
Ordelia A. Lester, '71
The New England Alumni Association
The New York Boys' Association, Charles C. Stimets, '72

Election of Officers

[16]

Page of a student's
program of Semi-Centennial
Exercises, 1911

Dr. Mary Walker (in straw hat) at cornerstone laying of present Main Building,
October 31, 1911

Note written by Campus School Principal W. C. Bagley
to a practice school teacher, 1908

The Snowshoe Club of 1912

The Oswego city trolley, used for Normalites' excursions, pauses
at E. First and Bridge Streets

Normal School faculty, 1919–20: front row, Lucy Norton, Charlotte Waterman, Florence Bunker, Harriet Stevens, Flora E. Otis, Lydia Phoenix. Second row, Laura Harden, Leslie Savage, Mary O'Geran, Caroline Sinnamon, Caroline Hahner, Joe Park, Marguerite Heaton, Jay Rudolph, Adelaide Fitch. Third row, John Park, Arthur Brock, George Brinkerhoff, Lawrence Van der Berg, James Riggs, Chester Tether. Back row, Amelia Myers, Frank Wagg, Ransom Libby, Kate Hayes.

Jay Rudolph's print shop in the early 1920's

The first general shop, under Gene Essex, instructor

School orchestra, 1914: left to right, Harry Olmstead, Jess Laughton, DeForest
Lavoy, Susie Donovon, Ellen Drumm, Laura Kerr, Hazel Breeze, Louis Baker,
Sid Parr, Ellen Footherape, Mrs. Charlotte Waterman (director)

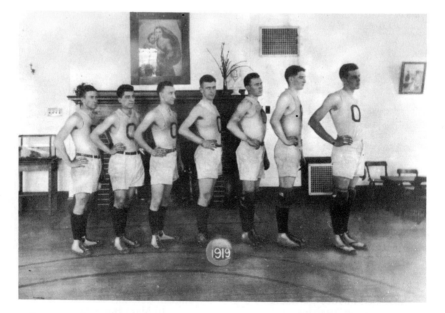

The Normal School basketball team, 1919: left to right, Gilbert Allen, Albert
Bougie, Francis Kinney, Nelson Allen, Ed Louden, Ned Colbert, Fletcher Miller

Letter written by
Principal Riggs to
Psi Phi boys requesting
return of purloined
signs, 1930

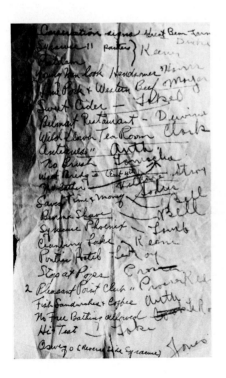

List of signs stolen
with name of Psi Phi boy
who took each

An Army detachment trained at Oswego Normal during World War I

Assisting Red Cross work, World War I (in headdresses, Leslie Savage, left, and Mary O'Geran of the faculty)

Campus School garden, World War I, on site of Lida Penfield Library

Camp director in tent at Camp Shady Shore, 1922

Summer school students' living quarters at Camp Shady Shore in early 1920's

Open-air class, Campus School, during World War I

Summer school, 1926: Allen Cook (front center) broke eastern endurance flight record for model planes of this type. Albert Adams (left) and Frank Schneider (right) supervised activities.

Ceremonies at dedication of new building, July 1, 1914

Parade celebrating authorization of Industrial Arts Building, 1930. Jay Rudolph, Leo Cribben and Harry Karcher, left to right, are in lead car.

The Swetman faculty, 1944: front row, Jay Rudolph, Charles Turner, William McGarvey, George Pitluga, Mrs. Florence Chambers Bailey, Marian Angel, Elizabeth Lopez, Leo Cribben, Matilda Wordelman. Second row, Gene Essex, Frank Schneider, Beulah Counts, Mrs. Ann Galbraith, Florence Mohr, Mrs. Harriet Simon, Seward Salisbury, Mercedes Erro, Irene Eisele. Third row, Harry Karcher, James Moreland, Charles Wells, Mrs. Esther Hibbard, Mrs. Isabel Hart, Mrs. Caroline Hahner, Gordon Wilber, Carey Salander. Fourth row, Wadsor Scoville, Marian Mahar, Mrs. Mary Hennessey, Aulus Saunders, Frances Reynolds, Roland Burton, Ralph Swetman, Eric Brunger. Fifth row, Charles Yager, Golden Romney, Marjorie Culver, Harold Alford, Dorothy Wright, Don Tower, Donald Snygg.

STATE UNIVERSITY OF NEW YORK

COLLEGE AT OSWEGO

The State University College
at Oswego is this year observing
the One-Hundredth Anniversary of
the founding of the institution by
Dr. Edward Austin Sheldon in 1861.

As a part of the Centennial
observance Dr. Dorothy Rogers,
Professor of Psychology, has written
a history of the college, Oswego:
Fountainhead of Teacher Education.

Since students in your school
of education may find the account
of the growth and development of the
Oswego College and its contribution to
education interesting and informative,
we are sending you this complimentary
copy of the book. We hope you will
add it to your collection on the
history of education.

Sincerely yours,

Charles F. Wells, Chairman
Centennial Committee

Ralph Swetman chatting with students in the early 1940's

The old Sheldon homestead

The Sheldon homestead (side view) after being remodeled

First Campus Clean-up Day. Faculty members and wives, left to right, are, Ralph and Alice Swetman, Golden and Zel Romney.

Lida Penfield, English teacher, for whom the new library is named

Richard K. Piez, on the faculty from 1892 to 1937, shown during the 1930's

English teacher
James Moreland,
better known as
"Jimmy"

Mrs. Eleanor Roosevelt
arriving to address
student body,
September, 1944

After the fire swept the school auditorium, January 18, 1941

Operation Clean-up after the fire, January 19, 1941

Debate Club, 1940–41: back row, David Crump, John Blann, Joe Dahlstrom, Dorothy Carroll, Raymond Green, Garfield Burnham, Philip Benevento, Dr. Charles Wells. Front row, Dolores Lavenburg, Marshall Schmitt, Nina Livacarri, Dorothy McNeil, Nancy Moore, Stanley Drazek.

Cleaning Romney's Pond for skating

Student Recreation Association Halloween Dance, 1940

Ann Post, member of Board of Visitors, and President Harvey Rice
at ground-breaking for first dormitory

Cartoons illustrating pitfalls caused by construction program of the 1950's

Certain prominent faculty members of recent years. Top row, left to right: McCool Snyder, Vernon Rank, Kermit Kuntz. Center row: Joseph Shoenfelt, Gordon Wilber. Bottom row: Charles Yager, George Pitluga, Harry Porter, recently appointed provost of State University. Drawn by M. D. Hartmann and William McGarvey.

Presiding at the graduation exercises of 1949: left to right, Dean Thomas Miller; President Harvey Rice; Mr. Sidney F. Foster, speaker, presiding justice, Appellate Division, State Supreme Court; Chairman of the Board of Visitors E. M. Waterbury; Dr. Aulus W. Saunders, who presented the College with the portrait of former president Ralph Swetman

Class of '51 disinterring time capsule of Class of '40 and burying another. Presiding is Robert Burnside; president Harvey Rice holds scroll.

Fred Finkleday, recipient of Oswego's outstanding teacher award, 1950, is congratulated by Governor Thomas E. Dewey, right, and President Harvey Rice, center

President Hamilton of the State University of New York (second from right) meeting with former Dean Harold Alford (left), Dr. Harold O. Powers, chairman of the Science Department (second left), and Melvina Svec, associate professor of geography (right), on a visit to the campus

The Hon. Frank Moore, former Lieutenant Governor of New York State and current chairman of the State University Board of Trustees, addressing the college's graduating class on June 9, 1958

Dr. Thomas H. Hamilton, president,
State University of New York

Dr. Hermann Cooper, executive dean,
State University of New York

President Foster Brown (rear left) and Executive Dean of Teacher Education
for State University Hermann Cooper (rear right) with the College Council:
standing, left to right, James Lanigan (chairman), Clarence Leighton, George
Penny, Sam Castaldo, John Aylward. Seated, Mrs. Dorothy Barclay, Mrs.
Marian Steele, Mrs. Margaret Richardson, Miss Marian Mackin.

The Instructional Council, 1961 (except for Maurice Boyd and Robert Mc-Manus): back row, left to right, Aulus Saunders, Theodore Moss, Gardner Wells, Charles Wells, Donald Snygg, Stuart Tosh, Harold Powers, George Kopp, James Hastings, Seward Salisbury, Virginio Piucci. Middle row, Melvina Svec, Charles Turner, Louise Ostberg, Frank Robinson, Helen Hagger, Arthur Hauler, Emmet Stopher. Front, Norman Whitten, Sherwood Dunham, Paul DeVore.

Dr. Hermann Cooper, executive dean for Teacher Education of State University, breaks the ground for Lakeside Dining Hall near the construction of Johnson Hall. Looking on from the front row (from left) are former Dean Harold D. Alford; Robert Raby, representing Raby Construction Company; James E. Lanigan, chairman of the College Council; Miss Marian Mackin and Mrs. Thelma Barclay, College Council members; Mrs. Hilda G. Bohall, Alumni Association president (behind Dr. Cooper); Theodore H. Beers, associate professor of Audio-Visual Education; Carolyn Godden and Kenneth Purcell, student representatives, and Dr. Foster S. Brown.

Dr. Brown, on a trip to Indonesia to evaluate the State University–Ford Foundation project, talks with Prof. M. Sadarjoen Siswomartojo, dean of the project (left), and Dr. Roger Bancroft, former State University project director (right)

Robert Helsby, alumnus, former director of the Industrial Arts Division, now Deputy Commissioner of Labor of the state of New York

Dean Charles Turner entertaining prominent educators from India

Torchlight Ceremony, 1957: seated left, Hilda Bohall. Behind rostrum, Foster
Brown, Herbert Van Schaack, Charles Wells. Seated directly to right of ros-
trum, oldest graduate present, Dr. Mary Robinson Pierce, '97. Behind Dr.
Robinson, Isabel Kingsbury Hart.

Arthur Hauler, center, receiving award of the Industrial Arts Steering Committee of the New York State Vocational and Practical Arts Association from
alumnus Richard Enders, 1959

Alumni Banquet, 1954: left to right, Mrs. John Cullinan, 1905; Mrs. Grace
Beardsley Turner, 1899; Mrs. Raymond Cady, 1901; Mrs. Margaret Gleason,
1885; Miss Emma Dashley (oldest living graduate), 1884

The President's family: left to right, Sue, Wallace, Celia, Irving, Ruth, Mrs. Brown

Faculty Wives Dance, January 14, 1960: left to right, Mr. and Mrs. Richard Benjamin, portraying President and Mrs. Lincoln; Mr. and Mrs. Robert De-Lancey, portraying Gen. and Mrs. U. S. Grant; Dr. and Mrs. J. Sherwood Dunham, portraying Dr. and Mrs. Sheldon

Professor Donald Snygg instructing industrial arts students in psychology, 1956

An art class sketching by the lake shore

Professor George Pitluga conducting a
tour of the college observatory

Seward Salisbury's class in comparative
religion visits the Jewish synagogue

Textiles laboratory

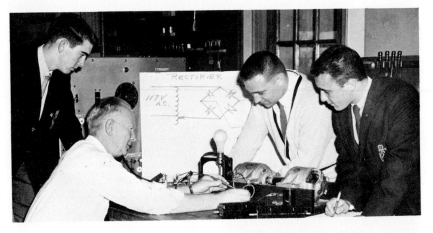

Donald Shutts demonstrating equipment in electricity lab

Blind student taking part in a pilot study workshop co-sponsored by the federal Department of Health, Education and Welfare, Office of Vocational Rehabilitation, and the American Foundation for the Blind, summer, 1960

Industrial Arts Spring Conference, 1960

Freshman Orientation

The Student Union Snack Bar

A typical room of the College Union

Aerial view of Fallbrook Farm

The Symphonic Choir, directed by Maurice O. Boyd

Members of the Alpha Sigma Sorority invited to sing at the Nixon-Lodge
Republican Rally, New York City, November 2, 1960

Men's sports at Oswego: upper left, Ron Davis, Oswego's all-time highest basketball scorer, sinks a basket against Brockport. Upper right, coach Max Ziel (now retired) instructs the baseball team, 1953. Middle, goalie Lou Villar makes spectacular save in traditional Oswego-Brockport soccer game, fall, 1959. Bottom, students participate in track, a traditional intramural sport.

Students using the
electric ski tow at Fallbrook,
winter, 1959

Unique indoor riding arena at Fallbrook, the college recreation headquarters

Fallbrook Snack Bar

Finale of Catalina Club show, "Catalina Christmas," December, 1960

Archery range, Lee Hall

Tennis courts

Girls' physical education activities: top, trampoline; second from top, volleyball; second from bottom, badminton; bottom, modern dance

"Object Teaching," 1961 style; culmination of unit on dairies, summer school primary group

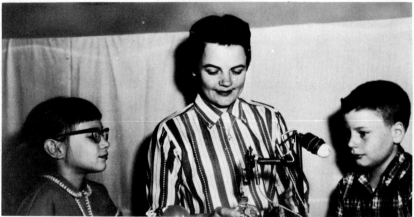

Christine Campbell and Terry Kowalski, fourth grade, watch a demonstration of a thermostat

Mark Piucci and Scott Tosh, kindergarten, exhibit leaves

for placing through the state many tablets commemorating significant events.

Because he was so smooth in his dealing with others, he was known as a politician; human relations were his forte. "After more difficult board meetings, he was simply wrung out," says Anna Post. "He did whatever he could to avoid controversy." He wanted everything to run pleasantly, with no fuss or feathers. "I'm just the oil can around here," he told Frank Schneider.

Toward students, Riggs's manner was friendly but formal. He would stand in his doorway in his frock coat and shake hands with students as they entered the building. He said little to them about scholarship—believing that area the province of instructors—but plenty about manners and morals. There was to be no loud laughter in the corridors. Nor were boys and girls to stroll through the halls together. "Once, when I stopped to chat briefly with a boy in the lower corridor about the football team," recalls one student, "I was dragged before my supervisor to explain why I had stopped to talk with him."

In short, Riggs believed ladies must be protected from the more predatory elements of their world. One of his first acts on taking office was to clamp down on the girls at the Welland, rendering the archaic rules more archaic still, as recorded in this item from the local paper:

Dr. James G. Riggs, who became principal officially yesterday was blamed for the new rules. Among them:

No young woman student shall appear in West Bridge Street without a hat and at all times the hair must be decorously dressed.

No gum chewing will be permitted on any street, and the eating of ice cream cones and candy on the streets is conduct unbecoming a future teacher, and is moreover a bad example.

A rule causing considerable trouble is that prohibiting, "riding in automobiles or carriages from the new school to the boarding house or vice versa." The school is more than a mile from the Welland. There has been considerable transportation by "gallant young men" who are the owners of automobiles or "fancy runabouts." The girls say the ruling is ridiculous but must refrain from riding or face expulsion.

Another rule reads that no walks on the lake bank or around Shady Shore, the home of Dr. Sheldon, shall be taken either during or after school hours. Shady Shore is a portion of the thirty-acre campus and is thickly wooded.

Last night, Halloween, many of the young women planned to attend parties and social affairs around town but at seven o'clock the preceptress announced that no permission would be extended and that hereafter the doors of the Welland would be locked at seven-thirty every evening except Saturday, when two hours later would be the rule. She also stated that evenings are for study periods and there will be no more parties. Most of the girls have paid their board up to the first of the

year, when they claim they will leave and get quarters in private families
where the rules will not be as strict and where they will be able to enjoy
life just a little bit.[1]

Of course, there were rebels who defied the rules—girls who could
handle a cigarette with the virtuosity of a sleight-of-hand performer, or
girls who sneaked cider at sorority meetings. But most of the girls were
models of unemancipation, their initiative driven underground.

Restrictions on boys were fewer, but more strictly enforced than before. One boy, now an eminent geologist on the staff of the University of
Seattle, was expelled for going in swimming on the first of March on a
dare. In brief, the Spirit of the Jazz Age hardly penetrated the staid halls
of the Normal School.

Where his staff was concerned, Riggs held the reins of authority
lightly, in a day when the principal's word was law. To his largely feminine faculty of about thirty-five, he was like a kind father, or elder
brother, depending on the age or personality of the person involved. He
never attempted to subdue the strong personalities on the staff. There
was no administrative council in those days, but something of a clique.
He also relied heavily on his secretary, Lillian House.

At his first faculty meeting he said, "My door is open to you at any
time. I am never too busy." And he meant it. He never interfered with
his staff where their teaching was concerned. He appreciated their
strengths and tolerated their weaknesses. He relied on them and created
an atmosphere where everyone felt comfortable and relaxed. Nor did
he place pressure on them to take part in community activities.

Riggs set firm standards for faculty members' personal and social
lives. He strongly opposed smoking. He finally permitted the men to
have a smoking room, but forbade women to smoke at all—anywhere.
On various occasions he called women staff members in and asked them
whether they smoked. "If you do, I'll have to ask you not to," he would
say. Some did surreptitiously, but not on campus or in public.

His emphasis on decorum extended to dress. Marjorie Culver recalls
an incident when the faculty were at Lake Placid Club together. "Dr.
Riggs called me aside," said Marjorie, and said to me: 'Miss Culver, I
noticed that you entered the lobby without a hat.' It never occurred to
me to wear a hat up there in the woods."

Riggs also took it upon himself to insist that faculty members travel.
To Marian Mahar he said, "You must be aware, Miss Mahar, of things
beyond the horizon." And he guaranteed a thousand-dollar loan so that
Marjorie Culver would have no excuse to give up a trip to Europe. "You
want to do these things while you are young," he told her.

The Riggs period saw a succession of faculty social functions. Once
he asked Grace Badger to arrange a cakewalk. Another time he initiated

a dance and decreed all should attend in colonial dress. "I turned my coat inside out and wore a plumed hat," reminisces Harry Karcher. "And we all danced the Virginia reel. A couple of people with know-how taught us. All of us in those days had to buy full dress, swallowtail."

Another time, the summer school faculty put on a mock play called *Conquest of the Skunk.* "Walter Schiebel," said *The Camp Shady Shore News,* "knows more about skunkiovissimus smellorum than he dares to admit."

On October 9, 1919, the men entertained the faculty. Festivities "jest fer wimmen" included "tarjet praktis, weel bara weelin, three leggit rase, aple eten corntest, and the soda kracker wissul." Rules for the occasion were: "None of your darn bettin or cussin if ya get xsited; no sassin the Ofishell; try your darndest, there's going to be prises."

The social climate even extended to faculty meetings, lending a holiday atmosphere. "We always had tea and sandwiches," says Harry Karcher. "And often Dr. Riggs would pass a plate of grapes, pears or tangerines, while the meeting went on. We felt we belonged to a family." It should be added that local emphasis on having a good time was a reflection of the generally light atmosphere of the twenties.

Riggs's small faculty, like their boss, were of the old school. Relations among them were formal but friendly. They never addressed one another by first name, but joined in various projects together. Frank Wagg and Caroline Scales jointly adopted a French war orphan. Richard Piez, Caroline Scales and Ned Dearborn read Robinson's *Mind in the Making* together and discussed it. Many faculty members joined informally in fishing, boating and going to the movies or Yacht Club.

The same relationship existed among different divisions of the school. "G.E.s" and "I.A.s" (as the students of the General Elementary and Industrial Arts Divisions were called) got along well, although the general elementary faculty resented the salary differential. There was no difference in status between the Campus School and Normal faculties because the same persons served in both capacities.

Most of the faculty had given many years of service to the institution, and had been educated in a day when degrees were not too important. True, standards had improved since 1900 as shown in the following comparison.[2]

	Degrees in New York Normal Schools, 1871–82	Degrees at Oswego, 1926–27
Doctor's degrees, all kinds	3.33%	8.82%
Master's	21.67%	25.53%
Bachelor's	1.67%	17.64%
Without degrees	73.33%	50.00%

It is also true that Oswego's progress compared favorably with that of other New York normal schools, but not with the country-at-large. By 1930, about one in three at Oswego had a Master's against 60 per cent for teacher-training institutions in the whole country.[3]

Of course, figures may conceal as much as they reveal. The Riggs staff were passionately committed to the teaching cause. Many of them were widely traveled. Some had studied in foreign schools. A surprising number of the industrial arts men had worked at a trade. Many were graduates of the best normal school of their own day, namely, Oswego under Sheldon. Many had taken summer school work, though not always toward a degree. The majority had taken courses from Columbia, then deemed the "fount of knowledge." Some took local extension courses offered by Syracuse after that school decided to get its share of the extension kitty. Finally, several persons of distinction were brought in as visiting teachers in the summer session, such as May Rogers Lane (1872–1932), Oswego alumna, who wrote several books on vocational guidance while residing on Lake Ontario's shore.

As for faculty income, Lena Severance wrote in 1926 that "salaries are almost as fixed as the state boundaries." However, a new salary schedule adopted in 1917 compared favorably with those elsewhere. Critic teachers received $1,000 with increments to $1,500; departmental assistants, $1,400 increasing to $2,000; and heads of departments, $2,000 increasing to $3,000. The summer session faculty all earned $300, including distinguished visiting professors. "Outstanding persons," wrote the Commissioner of Education to normal school principals, "should be advanced without regard for academic preparation but only when qualifications are sent to the Commissioner of Education."[4]

Teachers might, of course, retire on a meager pension at age seventy. However, where faculty welfare was concerned, no association existed to safeguard their rights or secure them benefits. There was no official sick leave. True, there was a retirement law, but otherwise, faculty welfare depended on local initiative.

The Oswego faculty were fortunate in this regard. For example, Riggs requested a leave with pay for Grace Badger, who was absent several months on account of illness. Riggs wrote, in pleading her case; "I feel hope is a strong factor in her recovery." He personally conveyed to her the good news, while she sat on the beach under a large umbrella.

Because of complaints that she received a teacher's salary while actually serving as secretary, Mrs. Baxter, Riggs's capable secretary, finally returned to teaching. After that, Allen Poucher was Riggs's assistant. When playing football in his youth, Poucher had been permanently lamed.

First regular librarian was Caroline Hahner. Before her day, such services were variously performed by the principal, instructional staff, or students—if at all. Actually, self-service had been the rule.

Piez's power continued as strong as ever. By now he was a married man and a not-very-successful farmer. His stock of cows and milk business were troublesome. By now, too, he wore a black glove on his right hand, crushed in an accident.

"He could teach almost anything anyone else could teach and do it better," asserts Frank Schneider, "but after hurting his hand he gave up art, and concentrated on psychology." He lacked training in that field, but compelled his listeners by the power of his personality. "Mark Hopkins on one end of a log and a student on the other," was his instructional ideal. As in earlier years, a favorite technique was confounding students with questions; nor did he have patience with shallow answers. "Now here is a child who plays hookey; he's never played it before. What are you going to do about it?" is a question that Hazel Hewitt recalls.

Where theory was concerned, graduates remember his telling about environment and heredity—and Thorndike's experiments with dogs and mice. Motivation and learning theory were neglected, and principles were acquired indirectly.

Piez also did considerable writing; his efforts included articles in the *Vocationist,* as well as the beloved "My Creed" and "Teacher's Pledge." The Pledge he administered himself to every graduating class from 1926 to 1938, but after that time the tradition was abandoned.

Since Sheldon's day Piez's role with students had altered. The once debonair bachelor was now oracle, father, counselor, and friend.

One graduate wrote Dr. Piez, "The older I grow the more I am convinced that education stands or falls on personalities. Hundreds of us know that you have always been the cornerstone of the Oswego Normal."

Piez's teaching was honeycombed with his own philosophy. "He introduced us to *The Prophet*," says Hilda Guy Bohall, '27, "and never a day passes that I do not think of something he said." The Piez method undoubtedly made its impact on many students. "Long before Al Smith popularized the phrase, 'Look at the Record,' you taught us to look beneath the surface for facts," wrote Grace Lynch, '13, later a winner of Oswego's Outstanding Teacher Award.

Miss Scales, too, remained a pillar of the institution—until she died. "She was old now, but her mind was still clear," said Ned Dearborn of her in 1921. Nor did she ever cease to be a scholar. "She lived in a room," says Max Ziel, "that had neither electricity nor heat. Yet she'd sit there until one or two in the morning, wrapped in a coat, and studying by the light of a kerosene lamp." Strangely enough, with all of her love of the classics and the arts, she hated music, declaring its influence baleful.

In 1926, Caroline L. G. Scales died in her sleep, and thus ended the life of another of the all-time greats of the institution. She left behind her two special contributions. She wrote the old alma mater, "O Blue Ontario's Waters." And she was largely responsible for the College Club in Oswego which later became the local branch of the American Association of University Women.

Another of the greats was Caroline V. Sinnamon ('88, '94), who taught at her alma mater for thirty-seven years, and is best remembered as principal of the Senior Department of the practice school. Carrie Sinnamon was tall and stunning, always looking as though she had just stepped from the bandbox. She always wore stiff white shirtwaists and black tie, a style of dress emulated by her students.

In manner she was poised but somewhat aloof. She believed teachers must stay on their pedestal. Once when a student offered to walk with her across the river, she politely explained that such familiarity between faculty member and student was improper.

Many were in awe of her, some even feared her, all greatly respected her—and most adored her. "I was terrified of her at first," said Marian Mahar, "but we all respected her because of her character. She demanded good work and she got it."

Aside from a surface coldness, Carrie Sinnamon was a superb teacher. "When I described the ideal teacher in my book, it was Miss Sinnamon I had in mind," says Ned Dearborn. "She was thorough, stimulated interest and directed student teachers with insight and understanding. She was a perfectionist inspiring her students to achieve high moral and professional standards." However, her very presence so completely forestalled discipline problems that student teachers sometimes had problems when they went out on their own.

Younger than the Big Three just described was Kate Hayes, '97, last teacher employed by Sheldon. As Dearborn describes her, "She was a vigorous Irish gal, proud of teaching and capable of instilling the same pride in others." She had great common sense and was well liked by the students.

Many amusing tales about Kate Hayes have come down through the years. Her morning conferences with practice teachers were interesting and varied. She would give a stern pep talk on arithmetic methods, then an equally stiff lecture on the importance of grooming. "See that your seams are straight and that your slip is not showing," she would admonish the young ladies.

Also on the staff were several elderly ladies-of-the-old-school, alumnae of the early Normal, who gave many years of service to the institution. Among them were Mary McElroy, Lydia Phoenix, and Harriet Stevens—who taught continuously at Oswego for fifty-five years, for many years as principal of the Primary Department, and retired in 1927. "Whatever success I attained in twenty years of teaching reading, I owe Miss Stevens," says Martha Gaines Fine, '05.

Also influential was Charlotte Waterman, who was hired by Poucher in 1911 and who retired twenty-two years later. For all that time she was head of music and for the last year, she also served as first dean of women. "She had a brisk, sharp tongue, and a keen sense of humor," says Ruth Harder Park. "All told," wrote Isabel Hart, "she was highly respected and a 'powerhouse.'"

Among those whom Riggs himself employed was gentle and soft-spoken Frank Wagg, who started the bookstore, of which Mrs. Gene Essex took charge. He constantly stirred up student activity, encouraging them, for example, to send large gifts of canned milk to the Middle East.

One of the strongest women on Riggs's staff was Lucy Norton, head of the History Department from 1921 to 1934. She had a broad background of experience, having taught in Korea and studied in Germany. As a teacher she was steeped in her subject, interesting, and strict but fair. "She flunked me once," says Garson Rockoff, '22, "but I earned it. When I took the course over, I made an A."

She was one of the founders of the present City Women's Clubs, and gave unstintingly of her energy to civic work. She gave talks which shocked the local townspeople on such topics as birth control and the advantage of public power—then opposed by influential persons in Oswego.

Still head of industrial arts was Joe Park, who laid the foundation for industrial arts at Oswego. Park began his career as principal of Cherokee Baptist Academy, in the Indian Territory. From 1902 until his retirement in 1939 he taught manual training and industrial arts at Oswego, and was head of the department since its organization in 1908.

Park's leadership in his field was widely acknowledged. In 1905 he was offered a position in Michigan promising eighteen hundred dollars within two years, but a raise to fourteen hundred dollars at Oswego induced him to stay. In 1926 he was chosen by Near East Relief to go to the Middle East, Greece and the Holy Land to initiate programs in industrial arts. Six years later, in 1932, an honorary doctorate was conferred on him by Alfred University. The same year he was among the hundred selected as most outstanding in the field of industrial arts in a nation-wide survey of college professors and state directors. By this time his department was recognized as one of the best in the country.

Park was a fine-looking man with a wonderful personality. He was slightly built but stately, with blue eyes, prematurely gray hair and a pink-cheeked complexion.

In personality he was modest, gentle and unassuming. Rare flashes of temper faded quickly. He had a gift for concentration, and was able to "carry on" in his office at one end of the old shop. "As a husband and father, he was ideal," says his daughter Ruth. "He never disciplined us. He simply had a way of making us want to do the right thing." Park's integrity did not permit him to show his children favoritism in school. "I had mechanical drawing from my father," says Ruth, "and he demanded perfection. I thought my drawing of a trunk at an angle was good, but it was returned marked 'Rejected' with the initials 'JCP' at the bottom."

Park's contributions were manifold. As an administrator he converted a one-man position into one of the best-known industrial arts departments in the country. As an interpreter of Oswego's program he wrote a textbook and numerous articles for the *Vocationist*. He also strongly influenced industrial arts students. He insisted that they have a sideline as well as a specialty to permit flexibility in obtaining jobs. He affected their personal philosophies besides. Arthur L. Perry, director of research of the Rahway, N.J., public schools wrote to Dr. Park (April 4, 1931), "With you I learned to do each day's work as though it was the only day I had before me and make it my best. One other quality I learned, which you taught by example, was to maintain wise silence."

Other stalwarts of the Industrial Arts Division were several ex-tradesmen, who served the school long and well: Gene Essex, general shop (1927–58); Jay Rudolph, printshop (1918–53); Harry Karcher, electricity (1921–57); Ransom Libby, machine shop (1917–33); Wadsor Scoville, drawing (1920–52); and Chester Tether, science (1904–33). "I am not sure whether Tether finished high school or not," says Harry Karcher, "but he did a good job." Tether was also known for his absent-mindedness, especially in the way he handled his Model-T.

Noted for the same trait was the beloved Wadsor Scoville, in whose class students enrolled a "Scottie Dog." "Scoville could not hear well, and someone always answered for the dog," says Clarence Ridgeway, '27. For half a semester the students got away with turning in plates under the dog's fictitious name. Wadsor, always a good sport, appreciated the joke as much as anyone.

Frank Schneider, one-time draftsman of naval vessels, in charge of woodshop from 1926–57, was best known for designing model speedboats. During World War II Schneider taught courses in aircraft woodworking and glider construction at Cornell.

In 1925, on the heels of these craftsmen, came Art Hauler, always highly influential in industrial arts—at first locally, later across the state.

Despite their short stay here, certain persons deserve mention because of some special distinction. Ned Dearborn, head of the practice school from 1921–23, left to become first head of teacher certification in the state. For many years he was head of the National Safety Council.

George Gombarts and Valee Wieselthier rate mention for supplying a dash of color to an otherwise somewhat conventional faculty. Gombarts was an artist, complete with cane and spats. Valee Wieselthier became something of a legend. As Don Shutts, '31, tells it, "Male students and staff went out of their way to pass the ceramics shop to watch this glamorous creature. There she sat, cigarette dangling from her mouth, clad in slacks, with legs crossed, revealing painted toenails through open-toed shoes. Riggs, who abhorred unpleasant confrontations, announced that no one must smoke in the building. Whereupon Valee sat on the window sill, letting the cigarette smoke trail outside." "Riggs tried again," adds Frank Schneider. "He explained that the building was not fireproof. Valee simply pointed to the kiln and said, 'Compare my little cigarette with that.'" Valee's defiance quickly reverberated through the staid corridors, providing a heady stimulant for those growing weary of arid convention. Not surprisingly, her tenure was brief. Later, she was a sculptor for the New York World's Fair.

During this period, students remained about the same. Boys were still rare in the elementary division, but the industrial arts delegation was rapidly increasing. Students were largely home grown or from nearby communities—a very few from farther afield. In fall, 1920, several superintendents of schools from Newfoundland arrived for a year at Oswego. Back home these men conducted schools in coastal villages, traveling in fishing boats from one place to another. Two years later ten student nurses came from the Crouse-Irving Hospital in Syracuse.

In appearance, students changed little until after World War I. Already, however, Queen Victoria's shadow was lengthening. Even in the wake of the radical style reforms that followed, Normal girls had to retain the "schoolteacher look." "Once when I was practice teaching," recalls Peg Mansfield Richardson, '29, "Miss Brewer came to where I was standing in front of the room and said, 'You must go home and change your dress. It is too short.' Another girl was expelled for having her hair cut boy-style."

Until after the war, many women students continued for a time to live at the Welland, where parents were assured of "supervision by faculty members who have the young ladies' interests at heart." Furthermore, "arrangements are made for social intercourse under usages to which people of culture are accustomed."

To the end, the young ladies persisted in adding to the unladylike legend of the Welland. One of its last "inmates" tells the following story:

> One night one of the girls wanted to stay out for a dance later than allowed. So her roommate slept on a cot on the porch with a string tied

to her wrist which was fastened to a pop bottle hanging over the railing. When Helen returned she pulled too hard on the bottle and the string broke, but did not awaken the sleeper. We crept down through the dark hall stairs to let her in. Halfway down, we became convulsed with laughter and the preceptress peered out of her door. We were amused, because her head was covered with curlers; but we were scared, too. She did not see us and closed the door. We then let poor Helen in by slipping the spring lock.

After 1918 such tales were no more. For fifty-one years the Welland had lasted, though it had never paid its way. After Poucher died, no one remained to underwrite its losses.

With the Welland's closing, agitation for a dormitory increased. Miss Scales's English class of 1923 wrote themes on the subject. Here is a sample:

> [Oswego's] out-of-town students are scattered throughout the city. Many of them after eating a scanty breakfast in one swallow or two— if they eat at all—have to walk one or two miles to school every morning or else increase their living expenses by paying carfare—often on an overcrowded streetcar. . . . Many girls live in rooms poorly lighted and much too cold or ill-ventilated for effective study.[5]

For the time being, however, the legislature made no move to fill the need. Some persons attributed this policy to several disastrous fires in the first dormitories the state attempted. Others blamed the powerful private colleges, accusing them of obstructing anything that might place the normals in better position to compete for students.

For two more decades, therefore, students continued to resort to unsatisfactory living arrangements. Some still lived in clubs, the best known being the Normal Club at 30 West Fifth Street. Here several girls washed dishes and cleaned the dining room to pay their board. Other students roomed in "approved" houses. For such housing each girl was to pay $2.50 a week, besides $5.00 extra for two meals a day.

Still other students—senior girls or boys of any class—could live in apartments. To save money, as many as twelve students sometimes shared the same suite of rooms.

It was during this period, too, that Greek organizations began to have their own houses, or at least to rent them. Not until the late thirties, however, did they occupy these houses in considerable numbers.

Until Oswego became a college, student schedules resembled those in high school. Classes lasted from nine to twelve and from one to four, five days a week. Assembly attendance was still required, but hardly appreciated. In its "Last Will" the Class of 1926 left to the school "large pillows and ear muffs for general assembly." Programs contained plenty of music. "Music hath charms . . ." quoted Riggs, whose own favorite hymn was "Spacious Firmament on High."

There were few signs that students were aware of the larger world. True, one class assumed charge of an Armenian orphan girl through Near East Relief. To help pay for it, each class member was charged with selling twenty-four bars of candy.

Meanwhile, recreation assumed greater importance, though it was still as informal and cheap as in former days. In winter, students went sleighing and snowshoeing; in summer, hikes often terminated in weiner roasts or snacks at an eating place on Perry Hill. Also popular were hare-and-hounds races and trolley rides. In the mid-twenties proms and costume parties were the rage. In 1926 a backwards party, a pirate party, and a valentine party were given. Dances were rare and saturated with supervision. On November 22, 1918, the faculty arranged a dance for the army cadets. The Normal girls, properly labeled, were led to the gymnasium by faculty members, in groups of eight.[6] "At the dances you went out and bowed to each faculty sponsor in turn," recalls Peg Mansfield Richardson, '29.

Commercial amusements were scarce. There were the movies, an ice cream parlor, and Haresign's refreshment stand at the corner of Washington and Sheldon. There were also certain places where fellows went for homebrew, spaghetti, and a session with the one-armed bandits. Close to the campus, in the late twenties, were a miniature golf course and an archery range.

The boys had a good time. After all, they had a bumper crop of girls to pick from and they came and went as they pleased. But girls were hamstrung with rigid regulations. Mrs. Waterman went so far as to compile a blacklist of men whom women students were not to date. "There was nothing normal about the life of the Normal girl," says one alumna, "It was so dull that I was glad when it was over. When I got my diploma, I said to myself, 'Well, you can't take it away from me now.'"

The most marked change in student life was the upsurge of organized activity after 1920. Until then the literary societies flourished wih programs for war years being developed around patriotic and social questions: "America in the New Era," "What the New Voter Should Know," and "Children Who Toil." Student programs were liberally sprinkled with songs like "Tipperary Days" and "When the Boys Come Home."

Other organizations of a quasi-curricular nature were started, among them the new honor societies. Professional societies had long since taken hold in the country at large, beginning with Phi Beta Kappa in 1776. First at Oswego were the Sheldon Forum, organized in June, 1922, and the Sheldonian Society, organized in 1923. Sheldon Forum was composed of fifteen boys chosen by the student body on the basis of scholastic standing and recommendations by the English Department. The avowed purpose was to promote discussion and debates on current topics. Members of its feminine counterpart, the Sheldonian Society, were chosen by the student body on the basis of their "scholastic, moral and social standing." Just how one's "moral standing" was determined is not recorded. The purpose of this organization was threefold—literary, fraternal, and social.

Still another postwar trend was the attempt to bridge the gap between academic and non-academic life. This effort took the form of organizations sponsored by various academic departments—especially music, English, education and social studies. Mrs. Waterman, head of music, took over the orchestra, begun in 1911, and began a glee club in 1914. Every student was required to take part in one or the other: "I got a notice from Mrs. Waterman to appear in the Glee Club, "writes Peg Mansfield Richardson, '29. "I could not sing a note, but that did not matter. I had to be in it, and was placed in the front row when the Club entertained."

Less formidable and in keeping with the spirit of the Roaring Twenties, was the Jazz Orchestra, which was added in 1927.

The English Department was active in encouraging drama, debates, and school publications. The school yearbook, the *Oshwakee*, was started in 1919. Its strange name gave way to *The Normalian* in 1922, and, in 1927, to *The Ontarian*, the title it has since retained. As for drama, plays were nothing new at Oswego, but there was no dramatic club until Adelaide Fitch organized one in 1927. Intercollegiate debates began in 1927, forty-six years after the first one was held in this country in 1881.

Out of the History Department came the League of Women Voters, founded in 1926 by Lucy Norton. Women were neophytes in this field, having received the vote only seven years before. Programs for 1927 included "Child Labor" and "the Forty-eight-Hour Work Week for Women in Industry."

The professional departments sponsored several other new organizations: the Industrial Teachers Club was established in 1920; the Kindergarten Club, 1927; and the Child Study Club, 1930.

By 1930, not counting social clubs, there was a total of sixty-six organizations in all, including twenty-three interest and avocation clubs, sixteen subject matter clubs, eight music organizations, eight public speaking or literary type clubs, and eight athletic organizations. One could now say of Oswego what Wilson said of colleges generally in 1919: "The side shows are so numerous, so diverting, that they have swallowed up the circus." [7]

More purely social activities, collectively known as Campus Life, also appeared. In this respect, too, Oswego had lagged behind. Elsewhere, the "college life world," was already on the way to dominating the curriculum world. Canby called the prevailing pattern "strenuous idleness," and the typical college "a place where two philosophies of life (curricular and extra-curricular) salute in passing and sometimes even stop for a chat." [8]

Partially accounting for this development were the mental hygienists, psychologists and progressive educators. They dwelt on the importance of the whole person, and of good mental health.

At Oswego, social activities passed under the control of the Greeks. For one brief period the independents organized but soon fell apart. Oswego was a latecomer to Greek affairs, reflecting a tardy interest in the student's social life. In fact, fraternities had arisen in the late nineteenth century, though their real beginnings date from the 1820's. In the early days these "coteries of campus covenants" were opposed on the ground of their secrecy. One youth, so the story goes, was murdered to prevent his revealing secrets. Opposition subsided after 1865, when the fraternities abandoned some of their secrecy and agreed to watch their scholarship.[9] By the end of the century the fraternity had definitely displaced the literary society as the rallying point in American college campus life.[10]

Even after this time some opposition continued, especially after fraternity fires and certain initiations and scandals. The Greeks, however, had obtained too firm a foothold to be dislodged.

The first fraternity at Oswego was Psi Phi, organized by Ransom Libby and Max Ziel in 1924–25. There were only four charter members, but by 1927, the organization had grown sufficiently to buy its own house. From the first, Psi Phi was a strong organization, managing to snare the top athletes and campus personalities. For a time, no Jews were admitted, and several boys, in consequence, were deeply hurt. Fortunately, the rule forbidding Jews was booted out at the 1930 Psi Phi convention.

Meanwhile, another fraternity had formed, the Kappa Kappa Kappa. Since KKK might easily be confused with a still better known organization, its name was soon changed to Delta Kappa Delta.

Typical of life in both houses is Robert Dicke's sketch of life at Psi Phi from 1928 to 1930:

> The free and easy life was evident in the fraternities more so than the sororities. The girls were in private homes and the owner of the home who was also the house mother kept pretty close tabs on the girls, particularly on school nights.
>
> There was no ban on automobiles. At Psi Phi we had three cars: Nels Bush had a Cadillac, Harold Steinfeld had a Ford coupe, and I had a Ford touring car. Later Frank Bertsche had a Ford roadster. None of these, you understand, was new.
>
> We had house rules and a house mother. However, the house mother,

"Mother Whalen," had a back room and didn't know when we came or went. Her main responsibility was cooking. In fact, most of the time she was never in the house but at her own home. I might add that no one was expelled from school or the fraternity for misconduct.

Our living expenses by today's standards were rather low but we did have some serious discussions when the fellow running the kitchen wanted to raise the price of the food by fifty cents a week. To forestall this, we set up a series of fines for leaving food on one's plate, twenty-five cents for butter, ten cents for bread, etc. It worked! We didn't have to raise the price.

As I remember, we paid $3.50 a room and $4.50 for board for the week. Depending upon the size we had two, three or four boys in a room. These were left unlocked at all times and were used for dressing purposes, clothes storage, and study. We all used the unfinished attic with cots for our beds. The choice spot was the cupola which housed three cots. In winter it was cold, in summer it was hot.

House rules, fortified in some cases by a fine, were set up to put the house on a self-sustaining basis, meaning that no outside authority was needed to keep us in line. In essence we cleaned up after ourselves, making it easier to do the common chores such as dusting and sweeping the living room.

Our house rules concerning parties and alcoholic beverages were simple: no parties without a chaperon and no alcoholic beverages. To my knowledge those two rules were never violated although it seems rather strange.

We did have to refurnish, such as painting, plastering, wallpapering, carpentry. This we did ourselves—when I don't know—but it got done. The one thing that was a crisis, however, was the heating system. That we didn't have time for, so had to go "in hock" for it.

I think we all got wonderful training in living and leadership. We had the full responsibility of taking care of ourselves. The mortgage had to be paid; the old house had to be maintained as well as feeding ourselves. In 1930 we had to negotiate the mortgage again. We had difficulty meeting payments just as others did at the time. I believe it was rather easy as the bank had no prospects for our house at that time.

One reason for the wholesome atmosphere was the interest shown by the advisers. "They were advisers in every sense of the word," said one. "They often came to the fraternity houses and attended the meetings."

True, fraternity life was often lively, but it rarely got out of hand. The idea was simply to be daring. "Sometimes we had difficulty getting into new places because of our ages, but managed never to be turned away," said one. "At other places Dago Red was readily available. And there were 'reports' that several boys earned pin money driving cars with contraband as cargo."

When the going got dull, someone would contrive something special. In March, 1930, the Psi Phi fellows went on a jag of purloining signs from public places. "The police showed up," writes Robert Dicke, '30, "and demanded the signs. We refused to admit them without a search warrant in order to give ourselves a chance to hide the loot. Dr. Riggs got in the act, however, and wrote us the following note:

Psi Phi,

The charges of yesterday are sustained by complete evidence. It is a culmination of a series of acts running back for some time. The new element is the disclosure by officers of the law.

You have admitted the charges. You do not excuse the acts nor justify your position. The faculty agree with you that it was a foolish prank. They cannot protect you from the consequences of such foolishness. They believe they have a right to expect more from you in conduct than from college students because you are to be teachers.

Our advice is to do the manly thing by admitting your wrong doing, restoring fully the property and by offering a gentleman's apology for a thoughtless and culpable act.

I feel the unfortunate effect of the occurrence at the time when we are pressing hard for a new Industrial Arts building.

J. G. Riggs

"Our reaction to Dr. Riggs's note [continues Dick] was to get busy and return the signs, for which we demanded, and received, receipts. Nevertheless, our act of retribution did not save us from a severe reprimand by the judge."

The first women's Greek organization on campus, Clio, was organized in 1923. Others followed swiftly after: Arethusa, founded at Brockport in 1870, was first organized at Oswego as Sigma Pi Beta in 1924. Agonian Society, first called Pi Rho, was established in 1925. There were eight charter members in Ago, and Sally Olmstead was sponsor. Alpha Delta came in 1925, organized by Lucy Norton.

Sorority initiations were childish but innocuous affairs. Typical was Arethusa's initiation in 1925. The two new members with long hair were obliged to wear it in many beribboned pigtails. Others ran hobby-horse races, scrubbed steps, and ushered in the chapel.

The most important sorority function of the period was an Alpha Delta convocation, arranged by Lucy Norton, at the D.A.R. house in 1926. "We had a ball," says Hazel Hewitt, '29, "and for once were permitted to come in late."

With the influx of the Greek societies came greater interest in varsity sports. Interschool sports in the United States—lagging behind England—began in the 1850's with boat-racing. For a long time competition was relatively casual, and 1880 is taken as the dividing line between the informal competition before that date and the rise of highly organized big-time athletics. By the turn of the century, coaching had become a paid profession, and by the twenties, called the Golden Age of Sports, interschool sports were a firmly entrenched institution. Concomitantly there arose the plague of Spectatoritis; most undergraduates were content to sit on the sidelines rendering their lungs in common cause.

At Oswego, as far back as the nineties, men students had informally organized athletic teams and arranged off-campus games. But it was not until the twenties, after the industrial arts program brought larger numbers of men to campus, that varsity sports became firmly established. The basketball team, organized in 1918, received a shot in the arm in 1921 with the appointment of Max Ziel as first regular basketball coach.

Max's first year was hardly auspicious, marked by four victories and nine losses. Only 209 points were scored all season, 115 by Captain Matthews, the team's rangy center. Next high scorer was Skillen with 26 points. Scores in those days were low, nothing like the scores piled up nowadays. Succeeding years were more successful and basketball became Oswego's Number One sport.

Regularly scheduled football came to Oswego in 1920, just two years after basketball, and fifty-one years after the first intercollegiate game in the United States between Rutgers and Princeton. A night game played at Fort Ontario in 1930 was among the first night games to be played in the Northeast.

From the first, football at Oswego had its troubles:

> We had no regular playing field [recalls Robert Dicke, '30]. We practiced on the lawn of the main building, and only when we had a home game did we have our practice at the Fort. But the number one problem was lack of material both as to quality and depth. The coach was lucky if he could get enough men out to hold a practice scrimmage. To illustrate the greenishness of his material they even drafted me, a veteran of two sandlot games. In fact, I was a line replacement the first year and a regular the second.

The twenties also saw establishment of golf, track and baseball, long after these sports had won their spurs generally. In fact, baseball began to be popular during the Civil War, track and field between 1865 and 1875, and golf in the 1890's.[11] At Oswego, the track team was originally directed by a student, and entered only one meet a year—against Cortland. Dick Elton, now on the staff at Brockport State, set a record in one meet that stood for eight or nine years.

In all these sports, Ziel, and whatever assistants he managed to muster, faced many problems. One was transportation to games. The school once owned a ramshackle affair called the Normal Ford. Otherwise, private cars had to be used. The "Just Imagine" column of the 1926 *Ontarian* contained this item: "Just imagine the football team having a bus to make a trip in."

In summary, funds and staff were inadequate; the record of wins was spotty. Most of the players were drawn from the Industrial Arts Division, only a two-year program until 1929. Schedules naturally had to be modified accordingly. Until 1925 Oswego only played high schools, then normal schools, and finally college teams.

Certain traditions were established but the most colorful element was the coach himself, known to all and sundry as Maxie. An early tradition was the Block-N banquet, now the Block-O, for honoring athletes and awarding them letters. A tradition which refused to become firmly established was a name for the team. Sportswriters alternately dubbed the players Normalites and Zielmen.

Also established then was the rivalry with Cortland, a real Hatfield-McCoy affair. "What started the feud?" Max Ziel was asked. "We made it that way," he replied. "In those days we had a two-year course, and they had a three-year course. That made them feel superior; they thought they were 'It.' Naturally, that made us want to knock them off. We gave them quite a lesson in playing basketball till the war. Once we were playing at Fort Ontario—I think it was in 1928. By the fourth quarter we had them 24–0, so they wouldn't finish. They went home."

Intramural sports, meanwhile, languished. Intershop basketball and baseball were played in 1928–29, but otherwise little was done. At least once, in 1927, a game was arranged between men and women students.

Women's varsity also languished—and then died. Intermittently, through the early years of the century, women students had played basketball off-campus. When they played at Mexico High in 1921, they ran into a sleet storm and spent the night in a farmhouse. The next year, 1922, several of the players contracted scarlet fever, and the team's record suffered accordingly. The 1923 season went better but had to be cancelled when the meager funds allotted women's sports ran out.

Until 1923, when Marian Angel came, women's basketball teams were coached by men and played men's rules. "We had a wonderful time," recalls Max Ziel. "I used to play with them myself and one of them really gave me a bad time. They protect girls too much."

With Marian Angel came an abrupt about-face in policy. She discontinued boys' rules and gradually displaced interschool games with intramural competition. By 1929, all games were played on campus. Women's teams that year were called the Basketeers, Raccoons, Live Wires, and Sans Noms. "The Sans Noms," reported the *Ontarian*, "tried to make a name for themselves but dropped their game to the Live Wires."

Already, in 1925, Miss Angel had organized the Women's Athletic Association. Unfortunately, however, the organization was severely handicapped for lack of funds. From the pittance allotted them, the association managed a modest annual banquet where girls were awarded cheap trophies on the basis of points amassed in various sports.

Funds for all sports, men's and women's, came from the Students' Athletic Association, in which membership was voluntary. Tickets cost $1.50 and entitled the holder to all games and permission to join in hikes, sleigh rides and snowshoeing. The Country Club was used for many activities.

With the general increase in student activity it is hardly surprising that students should have desired more control over their affairs. In 1920, therefore, student government came to Oswego, though originally with more limited functions than in most institutions. The general pattern was set by the Harvard College Laws of 1642. Harvard's organization was borrowed from the seventeenth-century Latin school residential regulations. Every possible aspect of student life was regulated—promptness, dressing, gunning, swearing, ad infinitum. But at Oswego the faculty retained considerable control. Riggs was honorary president of student government, and appointed a faculty member as treasurer. Amendments to the constitution had to be not only ratified by the student body but approved by the faculty.

Most important single function of student government at Oswego, then called "G.O." for General Organization, was determining distribution of funds. In 1923, each student paid $2.50, of which the athletic association received 50 per cent; Treble Clef, Glee Club and Orchestra combined, 10 per cent; Sheldon Forum, 2 per cent; Industrial Teachers Club, 10 per cent; Senior class, 10 per cent; Junior class, 5 per cent; Freshman class, 3 per cent; and 10 per cent, miscellaneous. There was no Sophomore class in those days.

Even by 1922–23 the administration pronounced the experiment in student government successful.

> Realizing the changing conditions of our democratic life and the early responsibilities for which our young teachers are preparing, the faculty agreed to a trial of student management for the activities which concern their school life and which previously had been entirely under faculty control. Up to date the trial has been successful.[12]

As time went on, student government's activities and responsibilities expanded, and students assumed the offices held in the beginning by faculty members, as this thumbnail sketch by S. J. Clough, General Organization president from 1931 to 1932, shows:

> Officers were nominated from the floor, with fraternities vying for offices of president and treasurer, and sororities for those of vice-president and secretary. There wasn't much in the way of pre-election campaigns —no posters or rallies. When I was elected, Psi Phi promoted my campaign by holding open house for each sorority, complete with dancing and refreshments, for the express purpose of selling its favorite son, a Freshman. During the entertainment period I was prevailed upon to give a highly melodramatic rendition of "Casey At the Bat."

Officers were formally installed at a special student assembly, jointly conducted by Riggs and the outgoing G.O. president.

The relation between G.O. and the faculty was a wholesome one. Dr. Riggs and the main G.O. adviser, Mrs. Waterman, dean of women, in no way dominated the organization. Instead, they helped make it a meaningful part of normal school life. S. J. Clough continues:

> Illustrative of this relationship was an event that occurred in the year I was G.O. president. The principal suspended two students for taking books from the library without proper check-out. However, he asked the G.O. Executive Council to review the case. He accepted their unanimous recommendation that the students be given another chance.

G.O. in those days had certain regular duties as well as responsibilities to assume on special occasions. In 1930–32, the G.O. president served on the faculty assembly committee and was charged specifically with handling such preliminaries as the prayer, responsive reading, and features presented by students.

In 1931–32, the G.O. renovated the school gymnasium in order to glamorize school dances. The dingy floor was sanded, the steel work painted, and a large multicolored cheesecloth canopy purchased. Whenever there was a dance, it took several students most of the day to install the canopy.

Each year the G.O. president and president of the Women's Athletic Association were sent to a thirteen-state meeting of student government representatives from teacher-training institutions. This conference lasted three days and was concerned with making student government more meaningful in the student representatives' respective schools.

Student government was a symptom of a friendlier, though still formal, relation between faculty and students. The sun was finally setting on the Victorian era but another day was yet to dawn. "We would not think of hitching rides from instructors," said one. "When I was doing my practice teaching under Art Hauler," said another, "I simply didn't think of leaving the building before he did, often at six o'clock."

Formality first began to break down among industrial arts students, who were often older and had prior work experience. By the early thirties, industrial arts faculty members sometimes chatted with students as they ate their lunches in their cars.

Faculty members also befriended students in helping them to find jobs, especially after the financial crash of 1929. "We left no stone unturned," says Marjorie Culver, who drove one girl all the way to Connecticut for an interview. "For several years no principals came here for teachers."

"There were two jobs when I graduated," says Taylor Harter, '33. "The first I failed to get because I was too young. The second was in New York and paid seven dollars a week." Don Shutts had better luck: "I was the only 1931 industrial arts graduate, so I had the whole state to pick from. There were two jobs. One fell through, and I got the other."

As for students' over-all morale, the picture is confusing. Typical of more favorable alumni reactions are these: "We didn't feel inferior," says Don Shutts. "We simply resented it that liberal arts graduates could teach with so little professional preparation." "And I found out," says Peg Mansfield Richardson, '29, "that, just because we graduated from Oswego, administrators assumed we were educated and knew how to teach—and they still do."

Still other alumni, while casting no stones, hand out no bouquets either. Certainly, the status of the school had changed. It was the end of an epoch. Furthermore, most of the New York normals were now in low repute. Because of the pressure for better high school teachers, normals across the country were raising standards and rapidly attaining the status of teachers colleges. However, nine of the New York normals felt no such pressure because of their exclusive concern with the elementary level.

PART IV

The Swetman Administration

1933-47

CHAPTER 10

A Period of Improvements and Crises

THE administration that followed, 1933–47, was a turbulent period of striving and stress. Ralph W. Swetman inherited a school morale suffering from several decades in the doldrums. In short order he became obsessed with a mission of urgency; he inaugurated his own Operation Bootstrap.

An asset in the operation was Hermann Cooper, appointed to the newly created office of assistant commissioner of education in 1933. Cooper was—and is—a man of incomparable fearlessness, energy and dedication to teacher training.

Cooper was also the first to provide leadership in state-wide discussions of curriculum. He initiated discussions of a four-year curriculum, the distinguishing feature of which, the professional sequence, has persisted to this day. He also instituted annual intrastate meetings, where staffs of the teacher-training units might pool their ideas. Finally, he traveled over the state, talking to faculties, encouraging progress. "The fellow was spitting fire and brimstone," said one faculty member. "He was building a fire under everybody. He intended to lift the whole teacher-training program."

Both Cooper and Swetman were seriously impeded by events in the years ahead, first the depression and then the war. In addition, Swetman had to cope with special local problems. Distress signals at Oswego were constantly flying. Nevertheless, these two great leaders, Cooper and Swetman, succeeded in laying the essential groundwork for progress in the more prosperous times to follow.

Swetman's attempts to raise standards extended to every area of the college and its program, including students, faculty, methods, curriculum, building and grounds. For evaluating students, psychological tests, first popularized in World War I, now came into regular use at Oswego. Entrance requirements for 1939 included both a high school average of 72 and satisfactory performance on selective admissions tests. Students already enrolled were sometimes given comprehensive examinations. Remarked the *Oswegonian* for May 14, 1940: "We still wonder what the color of the eyes of the third generation of fruit flies springing from a line of red and purple eyed parents has to do with general culture."

Swetman also stressed improving classroom teaching. The Riggs faculty often taught very large classes, but the Swetman staff came to complain at enrollments of thirty-five. Meanwhile, Swetman himself visited classes and encouraged faculty members to do the same.

For several reasons, Swetman showed even greater concern over staff. For one thing, the American Association of Teachers Colleges had adopted higher standards in 1926, by which normal schools were rated. In consequence, many teacher-training institutions now rivaled liberal arts colleges in faculty preparation, though the New York normals lagged behind.[1] Swetman himself inherited a staff who possessed only one earned doctorate among them, and 55 per cent had no degrees at all. Furthermore, he was specifically mandated by Albany to raise the level of the institution. Finally, Ralph Swetman himself was no man to tolerate low standards.

The new broom, in Swetman's case, swept very clean. In 1934, the board announced that "faculty members were to be encouraged through leaves of absence to secure Master's degrees by September 1, 1936." Swetman went the board one better. He issued an ultimatum, stating that no one would stay after 1935 who failed to get a Master's degree.

The faculty were electrified and the scramble began. Some of them got Bachelor's and Master's degrees, "catch as catch can." "Colleges were generous about interpreting extension then," recalls Harry Karcher. Several admittedly made a lark of it, selecting snap courses and piling up credits as fast as they could. Still others simply resigned. None of the old-timers felt secure. The banks would not O.K. loans and the list of resignations steadily grew.

Not everyone who left at this time was "led" to resign. Swetman highly respected Lucy Norton, who undoubtedly left of her own volition. So did Park and Piez, who resigned because of age. They may have been a bit out-of-date, but Swetman valued them in their role as institutional stalwarts.

For whatever reasons the old guard left, this period was one of the saddest pages in Oswego's history. Different people would write it in different ways. Some record these acts as necessary, unavoidable; others decry them as cruel and unforgivable. The old guard were bitter, and so were their friends.

Swetman's detractors made a strong case. Surely, some of the older faculty lacked degrees, but degrees had only recently become the sine qua non of professional respectability. Most of them had traveled, and taken numerous courses, though not toward a degree. All had worked at low pay; most had "given their all" to the school for many years. Now, still a few years from retirement, several were encouraged to resign, some to suffer real deprivation.

Admittedly, they were given a chance to get degrees. It was hard, however, for the more elderly, some with failing health and eyes, to work on a degree, competing with students many years their junior.

Others were avid in Swetman's support. Speaking at a faculty dinner, board member Edwin Waterbury said that "some of the more sedate members of the community believe Dr. Swetman is running roughshod over certain ladies and gentlemen of the faculty. But Swetman is acting on order of Commissioner of Education Frank P. Graves to upgrade the faculty enough to become a teacher college." [2]

Furthermore, say others, the school was simply so run-down, and many of the faculty so out-of-date, that drastic measures were necessary. The record does indeed seem impressive enough to justify Swetman's action. By October 27, 1936, the *Palladium-Times* could report that "nine Oswego normals" had doctorates, against one when Swetman came. Where faculty preparation was concerned, by June 5, 1941, the school ranked among the highest 19 per cent of normal schools and teachers colleges belonging to the association. And by 1944, of 106 faculty members, 44 had Bachelor's, 39 Master's, 18 doctorates and 5 others had degrees nearing completion. Median age of the faculty was 41 years. [3]

Some persons held mixed views. "He did what he had to do," admits Hermann Cooper, "but he moved too fast." "It seemed reasonable to me at first," says one faculty member, "but when I became acquainted with some of the 'victims' I found the wholesale firing inhuman. Nevertheless, we who were brought here by Swetman identified with him, believed in him, and thought him a great leader." "They seemed effete and incompetent," said another, "because they belonged to another age. They had surrendered to the rule of orthodoxy because they were bound up in their own tradition."

Swetman made a fetish of rebuilding his faculty; he had definite ideas about the kind of faculty he wanted. He sought creative people with ideas. He liked to maintain firm control but his faculty were no figureheads. He was sufficiently self-confident to assemble strong personalities about him without feeling threatened. He wanted top-flight universities represented, and a few foreign schools. He also wanted representatives of every part of the country. On special occasions, most importantly when visitors were present, he liked to have faculty members stand up and tell where they were from. He thus cut down on inbreeding, a common practice previously.

Some of the local Oswegonians, who supported jobs for local talent, were less than enthralled with this practice. One year when six out of seven new faculty members came from the West, a mimeographed sheet, called the *Oswego Valley News,* referred to the influx as "the parade of the ten-gallon hats."

Swetman also wanted more men than formerly on the staff—here, too, following a trend. Many voices demanded emancipation from petti-coat rule in normal schools. "There is too much femininity in the saddle," asserted Dr. Charles R. McClare at a state meeting of school superin-tendents in Syracuse, to which Oswego was the only normal school in-vited.[4] As so often is the case, the pendulum was to swing just as far in the other direction.

Most greatly affected in this regard was the Campus School. Begin-ning with a lone male grade teacher in the 1930's, this area came to have an increasingly greater male representation.

Swetman had certain trump cards in getting the staff he sought: rela-tively good salaries and fringe benefits such as sabbaticals, sick leave and retirement. Nor did he spare his own efforts. He scouted the coun-try—and his screening method was unique. To potential candidates he sent personal letters outlining the requirements of the job. This is an excerpt from a letter to Aulus Saunders, then a prospective applicant for his present position as head of the Art Department:

> You could count on complete administrative support within the limit of our not too great resources. You would find very stimulating associates. We are assembling a group of comparatively young people on the fac-ulty who are all interested in doing distinctive work.
>
> Sometime early in the fall, we would expect you to spend about a week visiting children's art classes in some of our particularly good schools in New York and New Jersey. I would especially recommend that you spend at least two days observing the work carried on by Miss Louise Nabor of East Orange, New Jersey. This would have to be done at your expense.
>
> The Oswego State Normal School has had a great history. We are not satisfied with what is termed, "good, substantial work." We want something that is distinctive, outstanding, and which indicates leader-ship. In extending this invitation to you, we should understand that you would have at least two years to show what you can do. At any time, we would try to give you a frank appraisal of your progress. . . .

The application blank accompanying such letters required that one outline his philosophy, name the books that had the greatest influence on him, and numerous other things. One apocryphal story tells of a potential applicant who did not bother. He simply returned the applica-tion with this line red-penciled across the front: "You won't find the man you are seeking. Jesus Christ died two thousand years ago."

Candidates were interviewed by a panel composed of Swetman and all persons who would be working with them directly. After all prospects had been interviewed, the panel cast secret ballots. This procedure worked well and assured the newcomer support by his colleagues who had helped to hire him. This was simply one example of how the rich personalities Swetman employed rubbed together and regenerated a spirit of growth which cut through the stagnation.

With Swetman also came an abrupt about-face in educational philosophy. His house-cleaning extended to this area, too. Long-standing tenets of the professional program were replaced by others. He sounded out prospective faculty members to determine what they believed. And he encouraged those already employed to keep abreast the times." "Give me teachers to match my children," was a favorite saying of his.

An important plank in Swetman's philosophical platform was belief in the normal curve. "The better the teacher, the broader the distribution of grades," he stated. "But," protested Garson Rockoff, head of the program for training teachers of exceptional children, "my students are so few in number and so highly selected that the normal curve does not apply." But Garson argued in vain.

Swetman's guiding principle, or educational ideal, was Hamilton College, which gave him his start in life. There the poor farm boy became president of his Senior class and a three-letter man. Oswego, he told himself, must be the teachers college version of Hamilton.

The over-all school philosophy was progressivism, finally flourishing after taking years to catch on. Its leader, John Dewey, had attacked Herbartianism back in 1896 with a plea for pragmatism. "Man is a psychophysical organism striving to preserve itself against his environment," said he. Such philosophical fustian gained little headway until Kilpatrick came along and made it intelligible. "What he really means," said Kilpatrick, "is that knowledge must be applicable to the solution of man's problems." In short, content must satisfy needs.

But needs cannot be satisfied without taking into account the nature of the child and how he learns. Formerly, teachers taught subject matter and children were incidental. Oswego's Orilla Miner, for example, had interpreted classical art to those children whose limited backgrounds permitted no appreciation of it. Actually, her attitude had been typical of her time. The new emphasis in all subjects was on development of the child as a person, not merely as a pupil.

The progressives' ideas about learning were based on the recently popularized psychological field theories. Teachers must operate from general principles, not according to packaged rituals. Children learn by wholes and not by parts, pronounced the enlightened ones. Methods, though bootlegged in by many, became a naughty word.

A related principle was "learning by doing." The child learns by experimenting; and the problem-project method was the response. At Oswego, for instance, the third grade organized activities around constructing a hollow canoe.

The progressive creed began to catch on in the twenties, then spread like wildfire. Academic abstraction gave way to problem-solving, philosophical indecision to confident certainty. Like searchers at the end of a treasure hunt, the educators shrieked, "Eureka! The classroom philosophy to cure all ills!" Soon progressivist clichés were afloat in most American classrooms, including those at Oswego.

The shift in philosophy brought a radically altered curriculum—the result of progressivism, Swetman's personal beliefs, and two opposing forces which influenced teacher-training institutions generally. One was the scorn and criticism of those who disparaged professional teacher education. The other was any immediate requirement of the teachers college's chief customer, the public school. Hence, while aping the liberal arts colleges enough to lend an aura of academic respectability, teachers college curricula were essentially pragmatic, coordinated with emergent needs of public schools.

The more fundamental curricular changes at Oswego were these:

(1) A trend, long apparent in the country as a whole, finally caught up with Oswego—that is, de-professionalization of subject matter. The normal schools were concerned about how they looked in the eyes of colleges and universities.[5] Hence, they took a step deemed by many as necessary for academic respectability; they divorced content courses from method. In consequence, at Oswego, the Education Department was now recognized as such and reorganized by Emmett Betts.

(2) A second trend was displacement of individual chairs of instruction by subject-matter departments. Over the years subjects had broadened and subdivided into narrow spheres of specialization within the same general field. No longer could one individual cope with the breadth and depth involved in a major subject-matter discipline. Many colleges began to face this fact around 1900, but Oswego lagged until the thirties. Then Swetman, with customary dispatch, adopted the departmental set-up.

(3) Another change aimed at achieving academic respectability was the increase in ratio of liberal-cultural to professional courses. At Oswego all courses to this date had had their professional component; after 1934, liberal-cultural courses accounted for 61 per cent of the total. The four-year curriculum reduced professional work still further from 39 to 30 per cent.

(4) As to choice of course content, new criteria now applied. Materials chosen must be broad, comprising all the basic facts of knowledge which

everyone should know. They should concentrate on problems of contemporary life instead of the past. Teachers must, therefore, understand social, economic, and political processes, interpreting the present in terms of the past, while not dwelling upon it.

Furthermore, content must be tied together. The accidental hodgepodge of courses must have a theme. Balance must replace the lopsided imbalance of the twenties, when professionalism overshadowed general education. Students must not be bombarded with little pellets of subject matter; content must be correlated.

Content must also be useful; mental discipline was tossed out the window. A learning task was not merely a form of intellectual gymnastics. Something should be accomplished by it—instrumentalism, the Deweyites called it.

Nor can one simply guess what works; one must know. Hence, the bulwark of pragmatism was the laboratory, and all kinds of laboratories were established as proving grounds for the curriculum. At Oswego, in the early thirties, a general science laboratory was established under the direction of Professor Guy Wagner. One of its features was a vivarium, showing assorted animals, including snakes and turtles, in their natural habitat. There were also a social studies laboratory and a reading clinic, the latter being one of the first in the state. Finally, in 1939, a curriculum laboratory absorbed these separate laboratories, besides adding other functions. This work, writes Wagner, constituted the foundation for his later, widely known laboratory work at Iowa State.

Consistency naturally demanded modifications in program, too. In the liberal-cultural area greater stress was placed on "academically respectable" subjects like English, languages and social studies. However, the dispensers of these disciplines hardly had a chance to glory. A countertrend toward electives and liberalization soon made inroads into their newly won gains.

Following the pattern of the state-wide curricular organization of the professional area in 1939, Harold Alford integrated the potpourri of methods courses into four broad areas—child development, child and curriculum, student teaching, and seminar in education. Especially successful innovations were participation, and the placement of practice teaching in the Junior year. Participation consisted of performing meaningful tasks in classroom management.

The placement of practice teaching in the Junior year brought several gains. Returning students had a final year for strengthening weaknesses which had been revealed during student teaching. The plan also permitted Seniors to be on campus, thus facilitating their placement and providing leadership to underclassmen.

The professional work was arranged according to a four-year sequence, professional and liberal elements paralleling each other. This plan differed from the usual one which devoted the first two years to liberal education and concentrated the professional courses in the last two years. The Oswego plan had several merits. For one thing, liberal courses should not be confined to one's less mature years. For another, the concentration of cultural and professional courses into mutually exclusive periods sacrifices whatever values may accrue to broadly distributed learning.

Practice teaching, too, underwent considerable reform. To date, practice teaching in the General Elementary Division had been haphazard, scheduled irregularly, a few hours at a time. Harold Alford introduced a full semester of practice teaching, and each student was to have both urban and rural experience. Jobs were hard to come by in those days and a student needed to be prepared for either type of situation; yet the same preparation would hardly do for both. There was a greater gap between socio-cultural pattern of farm and of city than today. Besides, the depression had retarded centralization and reduced many of the remaining rural schools to having a single teacher for eight grades. And all too many teachers had gone to rural areas with only the flimsiest preparation for the problems they would face. Harold Alford was imported from Arkansas for the express purpose of doing something about this problem. He combed the countryside for centers where students could obtain a teaching experience simulating rural conditions; and in the summer he set up a one-teacher school in a tent on Camp Shady Shore. Children of summer school campers were the pupils.

Despite such attractions, the summer school limped along after the depression. Few teachers could afford to come; and Oswego could provide little in the way of special inducements. The chief lures were the lake and the climate, which helped attract visiting professors of distinction.

By contrast, Oswego's off-campus services were gradually expanding. Teachers were called upon to participate in community programs, both to render service and to advertise the college.

Also in this period the school's first extension service was initiated, well over a century after Benjamin Silliman had offered the first such course at Yale in 1808. Such offerings became general after 1890, but were rare in the area of pedagogy until 1910.[6]

Another innovation, a Works Progress Administration Nursery School, came in 1935. However, this and other additions were offset by certain deletions. To save expenses, Swetman dropped the program for preparing special class teachers and suspended the kindergarten from 1934 to 1946.[7]

Progress in industrial arts was handicapped by at least three factors. The first was lack of funds.

To gain some idea of the tightness of Oswego money at that time, [recalls Lee Hornbake] I had three hundred dollars to equip a new laboratory for elementary school industrial arts. There was not an additional cent for anything else; I had the complete capital expenditure budget for the year. With the generous help of the small maintenance crew—Mack Howland, "Pop" Shufelt and "Smitty"—we did reasonably well.

A second problem was the lack of respectability for the industrial arts. In the early thirties industrial arts was still looked down on by men in vocational education. In fact, for some time, industrial arts existed in little more than name only. Lacking clearly defined concepts, industrial arts men often continued to pattern their curriculum after vocational education. Furthermore, it was difficult to obtain instructors capable of translating the industrial arts philosophy into practice. "Many shop teachers," explains Arthur Hauler, "good at helping children make pretty things, gained a reputation as outstanding teachers, and within a few years were on a teachers college staff training other young men how to help children make pretty things."

These first two problems were faced by Park. War, the third factor retarding progress in industrial arts, was faced by Wilber. For a time, everyone made model airplanes for the Navy. Instruction of pre-flight Air Corps trainees at the College diverted attention of faculty members and consumed their energies. Enrollment fell off rapidly, corrupting the morale of students and the faculty alike. Only nineteen industrial arts students graduated in 1943 and a mere fourteen in 1944.

However, where long-term goals were concerned, the war gave impetus to both vocational education and industrial arts. By June, 1945, the war was over and a reversal in enrollment soon was underway. Forty received I.A. degrees at Oswego in that year and sixty-seven the next.

Despite obstacles, Park's last seven years, 1933–40, were marked by certain significant developments. First was occupation of the new building in 1933, then considered one of the best of its kind and deemed adequate for the next quarter-century at least. This expansion came none too soon. Next year the three-year program was extended to four, requiring correspondingly greater facilities.

The four-year program was less fortunate, however, in another respect. Both Oswego's and Buffalo's requirements were now almost identical, but Buffalo was permitted the degree-granting privilege which Oswego was denied. Naturally, Oswego was placed in an awkward position, making it difficult to compete for students at a time when students were hard to come by.

Curricular developments kept pace with expanded facilities, thus paving the way for the four-year program, and then the degree. In 1933, the

I.A. curriculum was largely methods. The new one, which took effect in September, 1935, was better balanced, providing twenty-nine to thirty-two hours of professional work, thirty-nine technical, and fifty-seven to sixty liberal-cultural. Meanwhile, the student-teaching program was greatly expanded by Art Hauler. Hauler took Juniors to visit school shops in order to orient them for what lay ahead, and in 1936, he introduced a seminar course for industrial arts teachers in the field.[8] By now, women students had invaded the shops again, but on a far lesser scale than in earlier times. In the summer of 1935, two women enrolled in general metals and auto mechanics. They refused to wear coveralls but donned slacks instead.[9] That same fall, for the first time in years, a woman was permitted to register for a major in industrial arts. Ironically, permission had to be obtained from Albany.[10]

Another innovation was provision for industrial arts specialists to come to Campus School classrooms to help children correlate projects with classroom work. A group of children might make replicas of a post office or a store they had visited. In addition, Gene Essex's general shop class operated closely with the Campus School, thus learning how they could fit into an elementary program.

Industrial Arts at Oswego took a leap ahead upon the appointment of Gordon Wilber as director in 1940. The aging Park's leadership had weakened, and the industrial arts men had gone their various philosophical ways. Wilber himself initiated new ideas and modified old ones. He stressed student planning, created the Department of Industrial Arts laboratories subsequently developed by William Huss, and greatly expanded offerings and facilities. But his major contribution was concurrent development of an industrial arts philosophy and a curriculum to implement it.

To assess the status of industrial arts at Oswego during this period, progress was steady, but spotty. Not all the staff holdovers from manual training days could easily adapt. Shining examples of the new philosophy were, however, increasing in number. In 1942 activities in the general shop were organized around air-age activities. William McGarvey, in the newly organized transportation shop, insisted upon a concept of transportation in the broad sense of the word. Students were expected to study every kind of modern transportation—pipelines, airlines, automobiles, etc.—and the functions they played in the social order.

The industrial arts concept found an especially friendly reception in the Campus School shop, under Virgil Nestrick, followed in succession by Lee Hornbake, William McGarvey, and Frank Robinson. Hornbake's aims were admirably demonstrated in a year-long project involving the whole Campus School in 1940–41.[11] Working with classroom teachers, Hornbake organized twenty-one activities sequentially, but not rigidly so, for all grades. Many projects were carried on as major enterprises in the classroom. In the eighth grade, photography, letterpress printing, and bookbinding were combined in the production of class yearbooks. The three most important by-products of the year's project, according to Hornbake, were the development of manipulative skills; discovering the talented and guiding them into crafts and mechanical arts; and the development of creativity.

William McGarvey, who followed Hornbake, used a dual plan of scheduled classes in shop as well as special periods devoted to projects climaxing classroom activities. Even little children were permitted use of machine tools. Yet not a single serious accident occurred during McGarvey's years in the elementary school shop.

This same instructor was among the first elementary shop teachers to focus on the child instead of the processes involved. One child, with his jigsaw, cut one wooden pistol after another. "His mother was an alcoholic, and his father a borderline case," explains McGarvey, "and the boy was simply working off tensions." Old-timers questioned this philosophy, but McGarvey viewed the shop as a place for children to solve their problems.

To sum up, Oswego's undergraduate industrial arts program continued, despite crises, to be the best in the country. And Gordon Wilber, through writing and speeches, spread Oswego's reputation even farther abroad. His book, *Industrial Arts in General Education,* has been one of the most widely used textbooks in the country.

Underlying all the foregoing changes was Swetman's desire to earn the right to grant degrees, a practice which arose in the Middle Ages. They arose then as a form of professional license, with both church and state exercising authority in the field.

Normal schools began to grant degrees in the 1890's; New York's first degrees were granted by Albany in 1890. Degrees were necessary to give teachers recognition as a learned class, besides motivating them to extend their professional qualifications.

After 1900 there developed a squeeze; for some time thereafter, few additional normals granted degrees. Powerful colleges and universities, jealous of their own prestige, led the opposition. They feared that extending the privilege to the lowly normals would cheapen degrees generally, including their own. The criticism was also a reaction to the great increase in number of specialized degrees offered prior to World War I. David Starr Jordan suggested the degree of B.S. (or Bachelor of Surfaces).

Despite the one breakthrough at Albany, these deterrents proved generally effective in New York State until the thirties, when the normal school principals took up the fight. Swetman threw himself into the thick of it, his tactics midway between gentlemanly maneuvering and bare-knuckles brawl. After a brief but thorough period of stringent improvement, he asserted Oswego's right to a degree. "We were ready for it," writes Lee Hornbake, "and longer delay was unfair to all concerned. Admissions standards were high, the curriculum reasonably well-balanced, and faculty qualifications excellent."

However, Oswego had to bide its time; the Regents preferred considering all the state normals at once. In 1935, the Regents appointed a commission to determine their status. Three years later, the commission, chaired by Dr. Charles Judd of Chicago, visited all the normals and submitted a highly critical report, excerpts from which follow.

> Up to 1895 the normal schools of the U.S. were little more than secondary schools offering short methods courses in the elementary school subjects. Only in 1934 did New York close its training school for rural teachers and in 1935 began requiring all elementary teachers to have three years of post secondary education. New York State has been slow to achieve four-year curricula. The reason for the trend toward four years is the enrichment of curriculums of public schools. Besides, modern civilization is expanding. . . .
>
> New York adheres more closely than many other states to the tradition that teacher-preparing institutions should administer a strictly professional curriculum. . . .
>
> The faculties of teachers college and normal schools in the U.S. were found by a national survey of the education of teachers to be made up largely of women, to be older and have less academic training than other types of institutions. . . .
>
> New York teachers have exceedingly heavy instructional loads. Very little outside the college at Albany is done that may be remotely classified as scholarly production. . . . .
>
> Lack of dormitories is a major handicap. Many students come from homes with limited social training and need social life, especially to be teachers. . . . The impression the visitor gets of normal schools in New York State is that "they belong to an earlier generation . . . distinctly not suited to present-day teacher-preparing programs." . . .
>
> At Oswego the I.A. Building is modern and well-equipped. In contrast . . . the shabby old building used for general normal school classes is strikingly behind the times. . . .
>
> The normal school at Oswego cannot fill its quota and it is located in a part of the state diminishing in commercial and industrial importance. There does not seem any large promise that numbers will increase. . . .
>
> The normal schools' program is not comprehensive enough for school in modern society. Emphasis on "the child" and "observation and participation" is excessive, sends into schools highly specialized young people who cannot cope with problems of adjustment of schools. Even more emphatically is this true of special curriculums (including manual arts at Oswego).

Much instruction is of a "subcollegiate grade," a "chaotic mixture"
of the traditional and the new. Many instructors are "bewildered." [12]

From the awesome pinnacle of their liberal arts background, the committee obviously looked on New York's pedagogues as inhabitants of
the academic hinterland. They hinted that only by semantic generosity
could these schools be endowed with the college label.

Apparently, New York's Board of Regents failed to take this report
very seriously. Already, in 1937, the Regents had authorized a four-year
curriculum, and on May 20, 1938, the four-year course became standard
for all normals. About this time the committee's report was released,
and hardly had a decent interval elapsed before degrees were permitted.
Certainly there had been insufficient time for radical improvements.

Oswego might have won the industrial arts degree even earlier had
it not been that all the New York normals offering specialized departments were waging the same battle. Those schools weakest in qualifications hurt the case of the others. Nevertheless, success finally greeted
their collective effort, and at the Convocation of the Board of Regents of
the University of the State of New York in October, 1939, the degree-
granting privilege was extended to all special departments of the state
normal schools.

News of the industrial arts degree came when most of the faculty
were at a conference in Albany. The entire Oswego delegation, except
Isabel Hart and Lida Penfield, gathered at the bar of the Hotel Clinton
and celebrated. When the G.E.'s attained the same privilege, students
and faculty responded with a spontaneous parade down Bridge Street
and all over town.

An immediate problem was to determine what type of degree to give,
the traditional arts degree or a strictly professional one. Many felt the
arts degree possessed greater prestige. Others considered the traditional
degree colorless, with no special significance. The professional degree
won out, partly as a concession to the strong private colleges that opposed contamination by the normals of the liberal arts degrees.

Naturally, an interval elapsed before degrees were actually given.
The first industrial arts degrees were conferred at Oswego in June, 1940,
and the first to receive a diploma, by reason of his position at the head of
the class, was Robert Helsby, later director of industrial arts. The first
general elementary degrees were conferred two years later, in 1942.

That same year, 1942, Oswego changed from a normal school to teachers college. Elsewhere the changeover had begun decades before; four
normals had made the move by 1900 and over 150 by 1930.

The shift occurred for several reasons. The normals were associated
with low standards and overemphasis on methods, which had fallen into
disrepute. Furthermore, university requirements had forced the standardi-

zation and accreditation of high schools, thus requiring employment of college trained teachers. Besides, the twentieth century's complexity and consequent expansion of the school's function dictated more than a purely professional higher education.

Normal school graduates were from lower social strata, hence, less effective with the legislature. But the normals fought on, their very existence at stake. And it goes without saying, Swetman was in the thick of the fray. Every legislator who exposed a chink in his armor was attacked by a barrage of letters from Oswego. Every time a relevant bill was introduced, a local delegation led by Ralph Waldo himself hot-footed it to Albany, coattails flying.

The normals won their case for several reasons. For one thing, the New York normals, like last year's Easter bonnets, looked sadly out of date. Other states had made the move. Why not New York? Besides, there were schoolmen who preferred professionally trained teachers to converted liberal arts graduates. Anyway, when the din of battle cleared away, the teachers college advocates emerged as victors. A legislative act (1942) changed the names of the state normals (except those at Buffalo and Albany, which were already "Colleges for Teachers") to teachers colleges, and it became the duty of the commissioner of education to prescribe courses of study.

The same bill decreed that faculty members, henceforth, should be known as president, dean, director of training, dean of women, professor, assistant professor, instructor and assistant instructor.

Let the accomplishments of the normals stand as their epitaph. They helped disabuse Americans of the idea that any fairly intelligent person can be a good teacher.[13] It was their influence that led universities and liberal arts colleges to install college departments and colleges of education. Besides, as Bagley pointed out, the normals provided the environment that helped students fit into the life of the community: close student-teacher relations, a simpler style of living, and absence of social distinctions.

Facilities at Oswego, meanwhile, showed no visible progress. Visitors to the campus were hardly impressed by what they saw; or rather they were impressed—adversely. One faculty recruit wrote home, "It's like a big barn surrounded by backhouses built during the depth of the depression." Another confided to his diary: "My first impression is not a good one . . . the dreary front entrance, the poorly kept lawn, the dark halls, the worn piece of cork covering the main hall floor, the gloomy old framed photographs of men with beards on the walls. . . ."

"Poucher's Pride" had indeed deteriorated. Swetman's office looked like an old bank, says Garson Rockoff. The wooden shacks erected in World War I to house army cadets still stood, housing supplies instead.

The cafeteria, aptly labeled "Mongeon's Dungeon" was a small, dimly lit basement room, cluttered with rickety tables pock-marked with peeling paint. Occasionally there rose above the din of voices the rattle of dishes, and the loud barks of Swetman's dog, "Supe" (for Superman), that wandered among the tables nudging diners and snatching tidbits from the unwary ones' plates. One prim faculty lady, thus nudged, turned around, and "told off" a male faculty member standing hard by, wrongly attributing to him the nudge sustained by her posterior.

In the matter of facilities, Swetman labored mightily, but largely in vain. He launched his own space project long before Sputnik was heard of. He carved up what space there was into a complex network of partitions, frequently altering their design.

His plan for permanent construction, calling for gymnasium, heating plant, practice school, and extension to the Industrial Arts Building, was shelved during the war, but finally approved by the State Public Works Postwar Planning Commission in 1945. However, since Swetman soon after resigned, to his successors fell the task of implementing expansion.

Those were the lean years, and the school was bound fast in the strait jacket of poverty. Nevertheless, Swetman wrung from the legislature nine thousand dollars to face Sheldon's old homestead with stone. The local paper had urged such restoration years before:

> Should not the city fathers and the people of the community take an interest in this birthplace of the country's primary educational system? Just as George Washington was the father of his country, so is Edward Austin Sheldon the founder and father of our present system of primary education. The home of Washington at Mount Vernon is maintained in its original state as a shrine to the memory of this great man, but for years and years the old homestead of Dr. Sheldon has been neglected and it is the sentiment of a large number of the local citizens that steps should be taken to preserve it and make it a place of public interest, for it is immortal in the history of the nation as well as Oswego.[14]

So they face-lifted the homestead and thereby displeased Alice Swetman. "They took it out of character," she complained. "They made it colonial when it was meant to be Victorian. It also possessed the distinction of being the first stucco house in the country. The Portland cement people denied the claim, saying Horace Greeley's was first. However, Greeley's house was really a converted stable, so my claim still stands."

Swetman's next undertaking was to talk Sheldon Hall, Incorporated, into underwriting purchase of the sixteen-acre Baylis tract. But Governor Lehman vetoed a bill, urged by Swetman, to purchase fifty additional acres of the same tract.

It was equally difficult to get money for supplies. Jay Rudolph super-vised the book store and anything non-profit was against Jay's religion. Occasionally the financially starving institution gingerly extended its lean hand into the coffers of this "non-profit" enterprise for a loan, often to purchase coal, a perennial problem. "Apparently," writes Lee Horn-bake, "whoever decided how much coal we needed was thinking in terms of Key West."

But the sixty-four-dollar question was what to do about housing stu-dents. All sorts of makeshift quarters were used. Former army barracks were reconverted into family apartments for G.I.'s. Male veterans were accommodated at Fort Ontario. In 1946 the Federal Works Administra-tion constructed "temporary" wooden buildings to be used for shop, science, art classrooms and dining hall. This bleak assemblage of ram-shackle structures became known as Siberia—although Frank Hulme preferred to call it Outer Mongolia.

The remainder lived in town, many in shabby apartments, doing their own cooking. Some of the boys obtained free rooms by performing various chores such as clearing snow, mowing the lawn, and firing the furnace.

Incentives to rent rooms were tempting—and the landlord's obliga-tions simple. Rooms must be cleaned and beds changed once a week. One bulb, of at least forty watts, must be supplied near the work table. And, for obvious reasons, the shades must be "proper and workable." Heat as registered by a thermometer must be sixty to seventy degrees—no place for those inclined to chill.[15]

No wonder that a few landlords, recognizing a good thing when they saw it, cleaned up. Several bought old firetraps, chinked the holes, painted them and packed in the students. At $4.50 a head per week, four in a room, in cheap bunk beds, they had a gold mine. Hence, a modestly furnished room often netted the landlord nearly eighty dollars a month.

Nevertheless, the housing shortage continued and required more stringent measures. The college offered to furnish any vacant rooms available—and still there were not enough.[16] So, on the first day of school, September, 1946, Swetman cut up a telephone book and doled out to each faculty member a half page of numbers to call. New faculty members who were unacquainted with the town, indiscriminately called taverns, run-down dwellings, and even houses of not-so-fine repute, politely requesting rooms for students.

As a final measure, girls were required to follow a formal set of rules called "Standards for Student Relations with Landladies." (Anything to keep householders happy and in a mood to rent rooms!)

Nevertheless, the desperate housing situation continued. Funds of Sheldon Hall, Incorporated, had continued shrinking in value; hence, the project never got off—or above—the ground. In 1936 a sixteen-acre site was purchased, but funds fell far short the amount needed for building.

Some of the original investors became disgruntled. Lena Hill Severance, alumna and former faculty member, wrote to Swetman, explaining that her savings had diminished since her husband's death and asking to withdraw her funds. Obtaining no immediate reply, she wrote to Dr. Piez. However, he wrote that he was unable to obtain a list of stockholders or even to find out the name of the present president.[17]

Instead of attempting to arrange legal withdrawal of Mrs. Severance's funds, Swetman made financial pleas in her behalf. She was outraged. "I object to having an appeal made for me as an act of charity," she wrote Swetman on September 13, 1940. "I placed funds in Sheldon Hall, Incorporated, as an investment, not as a gift."

For several years the question of what to do about the remaining $28,000 in the Sheldon Hall Fund remained in the air. At one time Swetman favored a cottage plan, putting up units as funds became available. Others proposed that the funds be used for a recreation hall or for educating Sheldon's grandchildren.[18] What actually did happen was this: The investors or their heirs were induced to surrender their claims and the controversial funds were turned over to the school in 1944.[19]

Paralleling the foregoing developments came crises with the regularity of a heartbeat—one a serious fire. At 11:12 P.M., January 18, 1941, an excited call came to the Oswego Fire Department from a restaurant at the foot of Normal Hill. The Normal was on fire. By the time two pumpers and a ladder truck skidded there over icy roads, the auditorium was a sheet of flame, fanned by a brisk southwest wind. Swetman, just recovering from a serious illness, bustled into the building to rescue various treasures. Aulus Saunders made a gallant but futile attempt to save certain paintings. Harold Alford tried to save some records, pushing water out of his office with a broom. Lloyd Sunderman emerged victoriously clutching his diploma. Still others lost their way amidst the dense smoke and falling plaster and had to be rescued—gasping and choking, and with streaming eyes.

Jimmy Moreland accosted a fireman, anxiously inquiring whether the auditorium seats could be saved. "Impossible!" replied the dumbfounded fireman. "Not even one?" pressed Jimmy. "Not even one," said the fireman. "Thank God!" sighed Jimmy in relief, glad to see—or feel—the last of those uncomfortable seats.[20]

In the beginning, the fireman had broken through the massive front doors. The clock had stopped at 11:18 but the lights burned on, aiding the fight. By midnight the flames were under control and by 4 A.M. the last spark snuffed out.

What caused the blaze no one knew. There was no night watchman.

It could have been a defective wire, which was supposedly repaired the day before. Anyhow, the next morning, Sunday, revealed a shambles. A full-sized stuffed alligator, relic of bygone biology classes, had been dislodged, and the stuffed peacock which once perched in Jimmy Riggs's office was knocked through a skylight and decapitated amidst broken glass. A chunk was broken from the forehead of Sheldon's bust, executed by the noted sculptor Herbert Adams. Auditorium seats lay in twisted ruins. The sixteen-hundred-dollar Hammond organ was destroyed, soon to be replaced by the same anonymous donor. The concert piano had vanished, with not a trace of it ever to be found. The Wilmarth collection, painted by alumna Grace Wilmarth's mother from masterpieces at the Corcoran in Washington, was no more.

But the Swetman faculty were specialists at crisis-handling. Next morning Operation Mop-up began. They and their students formed a brigade and scrubbed the place down, only to discover that that was a poor way to impress insurance adjustors. In true Swetman spirit, mimeographed sheets had already been passed out proclaiming classes-as-usual for next morning.[21]

Two positive benefits emerged. A night watchman was added to the staff and emergency funds for repairs were voted by the legislature.

Another crisis arose in 1942 when the Commissioner of Teacher Education threatened to discontinue the General Elementary Division at Oswego and industrial arts at Buffalo so that all industrial arts would be focused henceforth at Oswego. Reasons given were several. For one thing Oswego's enrollment had fallen off drastically. Hence, proponents of the plan saw it as a way to save Oswego; opponents saw it as a lamentable scheme to make it a trade school.

The latter rallied fast. Harold B. Johnson, chairman of the board was displeased—and Swetman came from his lair like a roaring lion. Neither man bothered to alibi; the justice of their cause was its chief defense. To close down G.E. was an uncontemplatable calamity, a betrayal of the Sheldon tradition. Through the years, these men argued, Oswego had played a key role in elementary education. The I.A.'s needed to have opportunities for observation and practice teaching. The G.E.–I.A. combination provided a healthy social situation for students. In fact, argued Swetman, after a thorough search of the law, the school charter actually forbade such a change.

Finally, in 1942, a veritable barrage of reasons, ranging from plausible to dubious, smacking of reason spiced with desperation, was ferreted out and crammed into a booklet with the formidable title: "Summary and Digest of Statements Presented by the Board of Visitors, Administration, and Faculty of the State Teachers College at Oswego at a Hearing Conducted by the Teachers Education Committee of the Regents of the

State of New York and the Commissioner of Education on the Proposal That the General Elementary Division Be Discontinued."

That did it. Who could argue with anything as imposing as that? Elementary education emerged from the fray bloody but unbowed.

Hardly had the school had time to struggle to its feet than it sustained another blow—this time from war. Quota-hungry draft boards hurriedly gobbled up men who had specialized in industrial arts. The once-proud school had to fight for its life. Again Swetman saved the day. He encouraged 4-F's and wives to enroll. He pulled strings and got assigned to the College the 324th College Training Detachment of pre-flight cadets. The young men came, in installments of three hundred, taking classes at the College and flight instruction at the Volney Airport in Fulton. They were housed on the ground floor of the main building and forbidden to go above it.

A staff of non-commissioned officers controlled drill and flight training; the regular faculty taught the rest. Among others, Charles Wells and George Pitluga taught physics, and Bill McGarvey, mathematics. There was considerable undercover maneuvering to get these plums by those to whom the jobs meant extra pay.

The effort to make the cadets' academic training respectable was difficult but successful. In all, 978 cadets had been trained by the time the last ones left on May 30, 1944. And on the basis of comparative comprehensive examinations, the cadets of the 324th Detachment stood in the highest 20 per cent in competition with cadets from the several hundred pre-flight college training units over the country.[22]

The College had benefited in several ways. The cadets had kept a core of male faculty members on campus. They temporarily plugged the gap in the reduced student body. The government spent heavily for remodeling and repairs. And faculty members, compelled to produce results in a hurry, gained valuable teaching experience.

Meanwhile, the rest of the faculty and student body aided the war effort in various ways. At the very first, the Commander at the fort pleaded with the boys to stay in college—but they were called up anyway. One boy, whose mouth was besmudged with lipstick from goodbye kisses from the coeds, said: "If I'd known it would be this much fun, I'd have signed up long ago."

Finally, a total of 556 Oswego alumni and former students served in various branches as follows: Army, 392, Navy, 120, Marines, 20, Coast Guard, 4, Wacs, 7, Waves, 8. A strapping 30 per cent received commissions. Twenty-four men were killed in action, or reported missing; ten were captured, but later liberated.

The faculty did their share, too. Aside from the pre-flight instructors, 25 per cent of the faculty men obtained leaves to participate directly in the war effort. Others taught evening courses to war plant workers in such specialties as electronics, metal skills, aircraft model construction, and glider construction. James Moreland was chief air raid warden, William McGarvey, an airplane spotter. Arthur Hauler instructed key craftsmen in local industries in the techniques of teaching their own skills to others.

Faculty and students shared in certain projects together. They sold bonds and collected scrap metal—eighteen tons of it. In 1941 they helped entertain the soldiers at the fort with a Blackfriars' presentation of *East Lynne*. On the appointed evening, the cast cooled their heels for three hours waiting for the soldiers to appear. A call to the Commander revealed he had forgotten about the affair. He immediately dispatched a Negro contingent who marched into the auditorium in formation at 11 P.M. The Blackfriars lived up to the age-old theatrical tradition: "The show must go on."

The school also assisted at the War Relocation Center at Fort Ontario, where one thousand refugees were temporarily housed as wards of the federal government (1944–46) pending determining their place of permanent residence. The College provided instruction in English to the refugee children entering the schools of Oswego and admitted twenty-two of them to the Campus School. Several refugees entered the College as special students.

Charles Snyder, assisted by Marian Mahar and Seward Salisbury, organized a "Live in America" forum, teaching the refugees English as well as American manners and mores. Oswegonians resented the way these people would go into eating places, order a Coke and then pull out a lunch they had brought with them. They disliked the refugees' habit of handling food in the stores and haggling over prices.

The refugees, in their turn, presented music and dramatic programs before the College assembly and taught German and French to College students. Meanwhile a distinguished visitor to the shelter in September, 1944, had been Mrs. Roosevelt, who later addressed the student body. She admonished them to have tolerance of other people and of their convictions.

Not all that occurred was crisis; milder, but still memorable events took place. In 1935 certain prominent persons, among them Payson Smith, commissioner of education, Dean Harry S. Ganders of Syracuse, and Ned Dearborn, director of education at New York University, tried unsuccessfully to get Sheldon into the Hall of Fame. Three years later, in 1938, Aulus Saunders presented to the school a portrait he had painted of Dr. Park.

During the same period, many distinguished visitors came to the campus, among them David Snedden, the Columbia professor who pioneered industrial arts, and Edwin Markham, the poet. One of the Psi Phi boys had a double thrill, for, being a skillful barber, he shaved Markham and acted as his valet the morning of the program.

Another visitor was Uldrick Thompson, donor of the hand-carved clock which now stands in the Industrial Arts Building. It took "some doing" to dig up the clock and put it in working order before Thompson arrived.

Other noteworthy events concerned college tradition. In 1947 Dawn Allen, first grade teacher in Minetto, was presented by Dr. Harold Alford with the first in a series of annual awards for "significant service in advancing the cause of public school work in the schools of New York State." Her certificate read: "This is to certify that Miss Dawn Allen has received this citation of honor awarded in 1947 by Oswego State Teachers College for meritorious service in the field of elementary and teacher education." Other graduates of the Elementary Division to receive this award have been Estelle Suits (1949), Pascal Goodness (1951), Ethel Costello (1953), Agnes Meyer (1955), Elizabeth Rhodes (1956), Grace Lynch (1957), Ethel Van Wie (1958), Alice Freeman (1959), and Emelie Carroll (1960). Members of the Industrial Arts Division to receive the same award have been Emerson Neuhardt (1948), Fred Finkelday (1950), Jack Lillie (1952), Carl Neuscheler (1954), Earl Spaar (1956), Richard Enders (1957), Weldon Sheppard (1958), Norm Nichols (1959), and Ivan Beams (1960). Since 1956 the award has been given each year to alumni from both divisions.

Another tradition, the Torchlight Ceremony, was born in 1936, at the seventy-fifth anniversary of the founding and repeated annually during Alumni Week. In this ceremony inspired by Isabel Hart, composed by Lida S. Penfield, and first organized by Florence Chambers, the torch-bearer walks beside the College president to his place in front of Sheldon's statue and hands the torch to the president. The president then hands it to the oldest graduate, and so on around the circle. Finally the torch is returned to its standard where it stands lighted while the carillon plays both alma maters.

The next year, on June 12, 1937, a half-century alumni club was organized, with all those graduated fifty years ago or earlier eligible for membership. Another tradition, the first alma mater, sustained a body blow. Sunderman, head of the Music Department, disliked what he called the whine in Miss Scales's song, sung to the tune of the Lorelei. He wanted something with more zip. Swetman, too, favored the change. Therefore, to the chagrin of many alumni, a second alma mater came into use.

CHAPTER 11

Swetman Transforms Staff
and Student Body

R ALPH WALDO SWETMAN was born in 1886, in the wilderness near Camden, New York.[1] The family sold milk and eggs but could afford to keep none for themselves. After his Junior year at Hamilton he taught school in Puerto Rico, though when he arrived he knew no Spanish and his pupils knew no English. He learned Spanish, however, and after returning to Hamilton he also taught himself Latin, managing to read Cicero after two weeks, and Virgil after two more. Meanwhile, he made Phi Beta Kappa and, by playing his violin, the Hamilton Glee Club. During his Senior year he was elected president of his class on a reform ticket. He later attended Colgate, Columbia and Stanford—where he obtained his doctorate. There he was Cubberly's teaching fellow and compiled a book on California school law, adopted by most of the colleges of the state. Then he won a job teaching in Tempe, Arizona, because a board member said "it took a man of character to drive that ancient Lincoln."

By this time, Swetman had also acquired a wife, a woman of no less strength and individuality than himself. Alice Swetman, in her earlier days, had teamed up with Katherine Hepburn's mother, among others, to fight for women's suffrage. After her marriage, she was her husband's rear guard, backing him in all his undertakings. Once, with a baby on the way and no money in the bank, Ralph had to choose between principle and position. Trapped by circumstance, he sought his wife's advice. Alice hesitated not a moment. "Give up the job," she said.

Swetman arrived in Oswego in 1933. During the years that followed arduous labors were to take their toll. In July 22, 1938, he suffered a general breakdown for a time, but was on the job again in the fall. Eight years later—on November 3, 1946—he was suddenly stricken with coronary thrombosis. Nevertheless, he insisted that a party scheduled at his home for new faculty that night go on—and it did. The "Freshman faculty"

196

frolicked—somewhat soberly to be sure—while Swetman lay prostrate beneath the same roof.

Still flat on his back, he was driven non-stop by Golden Romney to Florida to recuperate, while Dean Thomas Miller took over as acting president. It became necessary, however, for him to apply for disability retirement, effective June 31, 1947.[2] Swetman was appalled at his own decision, necessary though it was. "I can't leave Oswego now," he told Alice. "You'd be surprised," she answered. "You can." Swetman rallied sufficiently under Florida's sun to run on a reform ticket for mayor of Boca Raton. Despite powerful opposition, he lost by a mere margin— then turned to travel.

His death a few years later was a blow to his devoted wife, but Alice was no soldier to lay down her arms. Now in the 1960's, after more years than her features show, she is a living inspiration for oldsters. Constantly, she treks about the world, including Iron Curtain countries, as intellectually curious as ever.

Swetman occupies a unique place in the annals of the institution, contrasting sharply with the man he succeeded. Riggs was reserved and gentlemanly, Swetman informal and lacking in polish. Something of the farmboy lingered in him. "I remember Dr. Swetman at chapel," recalls Earl Spaar, '48. "There he stood, with baggy trousers, one pants leg caught in his sock halfway up to his knees, saying that at Oswego we'd always have a friendly spirit."

The humble background that explained Swetman's dislike of formality accounted for his lack of humor. Years of struggle produced a serious outlook. When students did a "take-off" on him, he was not amused.

Administratively, Swetman was a man of many talents. He was a brilliant strategist, martialing his faculty force like a general planning a campaign. He was a commander-in-a-hurry, sparing neither himself nor others. He was single-minded in purpose, and his cause was teacher training. In 1933 he was offered the presidency of a state university, but he refused to be diverted. Instead he came to New York, where two normals sought him as head. "Which school is the greater challenge?" Swetman inquired of a friend. "Oswego," came the reply and so Oswego was chosen.

So engrossed did he become in the college that he had little time left for the town at the foot of the hill. The townspeople, in turn, irritated by his neglect and his ouster of certain old-timers, had little fondness for him. Town-gown relations plunged to an all-time low.

Not one of his critics, however, ventured to question his motives. Character was stamped on every feature. "Another Abe Lincoln," says Golden Romney, "one of the greatest men I ever knew."

Certainly, he had Lincoln's strength of conviction and persistence in pursuing objectives. "Builders use positives," was his watchword; he was never one to concede defeat. For example, he tried again and again to make seaworthy an old tub-of-a-boat that should have been scuttled. This awkward craft, weighing about sixteen tons, reputedly had been a rum-runner in prohibition days. Before that, it was on the deck of Dewey's flagship in Manila harbor. When Swetman bought it, it was beginning to rot; but it was rendered usable by adding a bilge pump. Once, while he was ashore, his boat drifted away, with his wife on it. Another time he and his party became seasick. The boat went aground on an island whence the forlorn marooners were rescued by the Coast Guard. Swetman, nevertheless, continued to patch up his craft until it ran aground off the coast of Carolina. He left for a time, then returned, to find that a family had set up housekeeping on it. Generously, he left them in possession, glad to be rid of the thing without conceding defeat.

Swetman, without doubt, is among the great men in Oswego's history. He stands out as a rich personality and one of the institution's significant benefactors. He jolted the school out of its complacency and improved its sagging fortunes. He preserved it from stagnation at a time when such help was sorely needed.

One of Swetman's accomplishments was the development of student responsibility. He spent hours working with the student council, going over policies affecting student affairs. On one occasion, he summoned to his office the president of the student body, Bill Haessig, and the *Oswegonian* editor, Doris Brown, to wait with him for the call announcing the elementary degree. Afterwards, Bill and Doris rushed out, alerted the students, and called a mass celebration in assembly.

Swetman also made a point of friendliness to students, a friendliness without familiarity. He shook hands with them in registration line. And because little money was available for assisting students, he often lent them money.

Swetman never sacrified principle for popularity. A long-time tradition among seniors had been an all-night dinner dance at the Mexico Point Club, ending with church the next morning, still in full dress. Swetman forbade the dance, citing especially the wearing of formals to church. The students decided to have the party anyway and wore buttons to indicate they were in on the secret. Upon finding out, Swetman stated emphatically that any seniors attending would be deprived of their diplomas. The students who felt uneasy were actually relieved to have been found out.

Swetman's relations with faculty members paralleled those with students. He viewed the faculty as a team, and drew them into the business of running the College.

Faculty meetings were sacred and, as one faculty member said, "he prepared for them as though for a Broadway production." Every subject affecting the institution was discussed and voted upon. "We even deliberated on whether to delay the firing of the furnaces until some late date in October and use the money to wash the windows, or whether to be warm earlier and put up with dirty windows," recalls Don Tower. Whenever there was a lull, Leo Cribben introduced motions for adjournment—but to no avail. Finally, all matters of importance were put to a vote, but if it came out "wrong," that is, against Swetman's wishes, the "boss" advanced further arguments till votes had changed. Hard seats often proved a more cogent reason for changing ballots than did Swetman's logic.

Reactions to "Swetman democracy" were conflicting. Some persons claimed that Swetman, in essence, gave orders, thinly cloaked with a veneer of democracy. He somehow "led" the faculty to vote predetermined pledges to the Community Chest. He "caused" the women on his staff to vote against their own right to smoke on campus or anywhere in public. Others opposed "Swetman democracy" simply because they found it boring. "We'd have welcomed an ultimatum from the office," says Marian Sortore; "we tired of discussing minor matters."

Still others take a more kindly view. "He welcomed opposing opinions," assert George Pitluga and William McGarvey, "and never thought the less of dissidents." "He believed he was democratic whether he was or not," say others—and Alice Swetman agrees. "He went to endless trouble to arrive at right answers," says Alice, "and he was usually right. After so careful an appraisal it simply did not occur to him that he could be wrong. He tried hard to win others to his point of view, but if he did not succeed, he felt compelled to follow his convictions."

Where staff leadership was concerned, Swetman had one signal advantage. It is unusual for a college president to have a faculty so largely hired by himself. After a brief time fewer than a dozen had been employed by his predecessors. There was no place for elder statesmen on a campus run by a man whose goal was to break with a sterile past.

Among the handful of holdovers who remained were Penfield, Rudolph, Cribben, Ziel, Hauler, Schneider, Karcher, Scoville, Angel and Culver. Survivors of the shakeup, these men and women remained influential within the school.

The rest of the staff were hand-picked, and the record testifies to Swetman's genius as a faculty builder. Among those he employed, several went on to higher positions. Two became college presidents, Don Tower and Harry Porter. Tower succeeded Betts as director of training, but left to become president of Brockport State Teachers College. And Porter, who taught social studies at Oswego (1941–47), became head of the Teachers College at Fredonia. Two others became deans—Lee Hornbake, who taught industrial arts in the Campus School, is now dean of the University of Maryland, and Golden Romney is dean of the School of Physical Education at Washington State. Lucian Kinney became professor of education and, for a time, acting dean at Stanford University. Tony Marinaccio, Oswego alumnus and principal of the Campus School from 1946 to 1949, is now superintendent of schools in Davenport, Iowa. And Lloyd Sunderman, then chairman of Oswego's Music Department holds a similar position at the University of Toledo. Finally, Gordon Wilber became director of the Industrial Arts Division and, upon retirement, director of a program for improving industrial arts teacher education in the Philippines.

All these men made significant contributions during their stay at Oswego. Tower was a master administrator and an inspiring teacher. "He made me feel that teaching was a wonderful thing," says an alumna. "I took his philosophy so seriously that I accepted a job at eight hundred dollars a year, simply because it posed a special challenge. Because of his influence, I went forth with the bright light shining in my eyes and won a recommendation that would get me into heaven."

Other Swetman employees remained to become key figures in later administrations. In fact, many of the present administrative personnel were Swetman appointees: Dean Turner; Director of Admissions Mott; Financial Secretary Salander; and five departmental chairmen: Saunders, Salisbury, C. Wells, Snygg, and Ostberg.

Several faculty members, though employed by Riggs, probably reached their professional peak under Swetman—Leo Cribben, Marietta Odell, Isabel Hart, and Marian Mahar.

With hair flying, and fired with enthusiasm, Marian Mahar, holding forth in a classroom, was a wonder to behold. "A thrilling teacher," recalls an alumna. "We couldn't help soaking up some of that spirit." In fact, her absorption with her task was so complete, that her absent-mindedness was legend. Once she came to school wearing pink bedroom slippers; another time she invited guests to lunch, only to forget all about them, and spend the lunch hour shopping. Another time she accidentally sewed up a small kitchen towel in a turkey, which she later carved for some guests. Marian was no clown, however. Others took her as seriously as she took herself. She was a scholar to her finger tips, often dashing to Europe for a breath of the historical atmosphere she tried to recreate in her classroom.

Another individualist was Leo Cribben, gruff in manner but warm in heart, who brought a year's supply of razors and other incidentals when he first came. He had been warned that Oswego was at the end of nowhere—but it never occurred to him to bring overshoes.

Leo taught many subjects before he settled down as head of mathematics and dean of men. Regardless of what he did, he did it with dispatch. "I took history from him," recalls Bob Helsby, "and he polished off the Roman Empire in fifteen minutes flat." And in mathematics he led students nimbly but skillfully through a tangled mass of theorems and equations.

Another unorthodox but powerful personality was the chairman of physical education, Golden Romney, closer perhaps than anyone to "the boss." This handsome giant was well-nigh worshiped by many of the maintenance personnel, students, and members of his staff. And like the present director of physical education, Gardner Wells, he showed an unusual appreciation of both women's and men's phases of the program.

Also beloved was James Moreland, known as "Jimmy," a short, balding ex-reporter whose trademark was a friendly slap on the back. "Every institution needs a Jimmy," declared Maxine Stroud, a faculty wife. Jimmy was a master of student relations, of classroom teaching, and assorted other skills. "He had a photographic memory," says a Moreland fan. "He knew everything from who won the Kentucky Derby to the name of the present Secretary of State's wife and all her in-laws. He was alive, vivid, and full of love. Often he gave neighborhood children money for carfare." But even the greatest have their weaknesses. Jimmy was sensitive about his lack of a doctorate and, to avoid displaying his status, often ducked academic processions.

Then there was Lida Penfield, a dainty, beautiful, cultured lady, who joined the faculty in 1917 and replaced Carrie V. Sinnamon as head of the English Department in 1932, and retired ten years later. She was an authority on local history, wrote a small volume called *Stories of Old Oswego*, and directed a two-hundred-year pageant of white man's activity in the area, but her real distinction was her personal influence. "She set a tone of culture," asserts her successor, Charles Wells, "that no one else can ever beat."

Just as Lida Penfield was dedicated to culture, so was Isabel Hart dedicated to the College. Aside from Sheldon himself, no one has ever been more closely bound to the school. In the 1880's her parents met and married at the old Normal, from which she herself graduated in 1907. Her daughter, too, became an alumna, and now a granddaughter is there.

Mrs. Hart served as first executive secretary of the Alumni Association and first dean of women, but made her most significant contribution as geography teacher. She made extensive use of visual aids, long before they came into general use. She insisted on diligent preparation and precise thinking. She also stressed understanding. "Do you understand?" she would ask. If the student said yes, she would counter with "*What* do you understand?" Once she asked on a test: "What are the most important concepts you have gained in this course?" "I've gained a concept of what a concept is," wrote one student. To reinforce theory, Mrs. Hart conducted study tours throughout eastern Canada and the United States. And she was author or co-author of numerous children's geography texts and workbooks.

One of Mrs. Hart's co-authors on the social studies series, *Home and Helpers*, was Marietta Odell, well-known reading expert and supervisor of student teaching who taught at Oswego for almost thirty years. She was also a collector of old children's texts and picture books—a collection now owned by the College. Mrs. Odell was killed in an automobile accident in California while on sabbatical leave in 1949.

Among those who left their mark on the Campus School, and then left, were Irene Eisele, apostle of Progressivism; Mike Auletta, only male grade teacher; Marian Sortore, called by an alumna "a composite of someone you could like and admire, but who made you work"; and vivacious Annette Brigham. Only three persons then in the Campus School remain on the staff today: Matilda Wordelman; William McGarvey, now in psychology; and Mabel Hawkinson, now in education.

One may wonder how Swetman was able to retain so much talent. The fact is, he managed to imbue his faculty with the feeling that they were partners in a significant undertaking—restoring the greatness of Oswego. Besides, many deemed it a privilege to work under his leadership.

Another factor was progress in matters affecting faculty morale. Salaries began climbing slowly, ranging from $2,800 to $6,000 in 1947, excellent pay for the times. The industrial arts staff received an additional five hundred dollars, because of industry's competition for men with such skills. Department heads received more money than others, and there were several one-man departments. This situation led Leo Cribben to comment: "I don't know whether I am real head of a theoretical department or theoretical head of a real department."

Swetman also cut teaching loads of twenty to thirty semester hours to fifteen semester hours a week—a step long overdue. The deleterious effect of excessive load began receiving general recognition as early as 1910.

Social demands on faculty members likewise diminished. The only "musts" were a fall reception, a spring dinner, and an original skit by the new faculty. The 1941 neophytes did a take-off on progressive education, which incensed certain persons present.

Also formed in Swetman's time were the Faculty Wives Club and the local chapter of the American Association of University Professors. Faculty Wives was initiated by Alice Swetman, and the A.A.U.P. was sparked by Aulus Saunders, George Pitluga, Don Snygg, and William McGarvey.

Faculty relations were good, with minor exceptions. G.E.'s continued to grumble about the salary differential favoring I.A.'s. Yet faculty members for the most part were bound together by a sense of common cause, namely, whatever the current crisis.

The make-up of the student body remained substantially the same with some variations. The majority still hailed from nearby towns or down the hill, with a growing delegation from New York City. The result was a slight but detectable increase in cosmopolitanism and sophistication.

Lack of funds, however, dictated simple habits. One fraternity possessed only three cars—or clunks—among them. Clothing was whatever a student could muster. A hundred or so of the needier students had fifteen-dollar-a-month jobs with the National Youth Administration, as assistants in the library, offices, buildings, and on grounds.

Financial assistance, however, was scarce, and higher education a luxury few families could afford. Student bodies shrank, and colleges fought for their lives. The New York normals vied among themselves, seeking to snare recruits, but after skirmishing for tactical advantage, they reached a gentleman's agreement. They carved the state into spheres of influence, each agreeing to respect the private precinct of the other. Only in New York City were staked-out claims forbidden. On that happiest hunting ground of all, Swetman turned loose his prize recruiters, Jimmy Moreland, Golden Romney, and Art Hauler. Faculty members chipped in to help pay expenses. "To help save your jobs," was Swetman's tactful tool of persuasion.

While there were quite specific standards for admission, the impression was sometimes the reverse. Harry Karcher, who was also sent recruiting, recalls, "The administration told us in effect, 'If you can get them to the front door, we'll grab 'em and pull 'em in.'" An alumnus adds: "If you were warm, they took you."

Legend has it that Messrs. Romney and Moreland promised prospective students the moon. "What you want—Oswego's got it!" was their watchword. One student was interested in an art school. "But Oswego *is* an art school," said Golden, "forgetting" to add, "industrial arts." Moreland even promised a flying fortress for industrial arts boys to work on. "They weren't liars," says one faculty member, "just supreme optimists." Anyhow, no one belittles the job they did. They brought in the students— by hook and perhaps some crook—and kept Oswego open.

Once drawn to Oswego, frosh underwent a brief orientation of sorts, actually a summary of can-do's and can't's, and a several weeks' initiation. In 1937, novitiates were required to get down on all fours in front of Sheldon's statue and praise the founder. "Sheldon was praised more than Allah ever was," recalls one alumnus. "Noonday activities included kissing Sheldon's right foot." [3] Concluding the 1938 initiation was Turnabout Day when the lowly frosh put their erstwhile tormenters through their paces.

Male upper-classmen were required to wear shirts and coats backwards and trousers above their knees. Women had to wear pigtails and no cosmetics.[4] The usual tribal rituals of a college campus!

The rules learned during orientation were now a mixture of late Victorian and modern. Thumbing rides was still deemed unladylike. So were extreme styles of dress. In 1934 Marietta Odell posted this notice on the bulletin board: "Sunback dresses are for the beach, not the classroom." Hard liquor was out of economic reach; but wine and home-brew were sampled on the sly.

In colonial times, alcoholic sociability was an accepted part of all social relations. Colleges put restrictions on hard liquors, but none at all on beer or wine. In the early nineteenth century, however, many colleges, under the influence of the temperance movement, banned drinking altogether.[5] However, after prohibition ended, Oswego, like many colleges, began to permit limited drinking at social functions.

Rules were reinforced by other incentives to encourage high moral standards. Swetman often talked in chapel stressing points like "P.A." for professional attitude. Once he lectured the girls alone, after one of them was observed sitting on the lap of an Air Force cadet. "He wants us to climb off their laps and back on our pedestals," a student was later heard to remark.

Once upon a time such admonitions were solemnly heard and obeyed. Now students began to assert themselves, especially after the war. These youth had cut their teeth on Dewey's philosophy, not "the child shall be seen but not heard" dictum of another day. The growing number of men and the postwar influx of veterans speeded the process. Besides, Swetman himself encouraged student participation. One result was stronger student government, respected by faculty and students alike. When a lens was stolen, student pressure caused it to be returned.

Naturally, gears did not always mesh smoothly. Several issues arose, for example, over smoking. In 1941, after much haggling, men faculty and students were provided smoking rooms, but women students and faculty were forbidden to smoke either on campus or in public places. To support this policy, Swetman, in 1941, sent questionnaires to superintendents and found they preferred non-smoking women. An outraged *Oswegonian* columnist took issue: "The rule encourages untruthfulness. Let girls smoke, too, or cut it out altogether."

Another bone of contention was required attendance at assembly, compulsory ever since the school's founding. Elsewhere, required chapel had been attacked in the wake of the secularism that followed the Civil War, but for many years after, the rule continued to prevail. Stephen Vincent Benet tells how, in the early 1900's, the "whole sleepy college [Yale] congregated together in early morning's dim, irreligious light." [6]

By 1913, twenty-eight out of sixty institutions questioned had abandoned the requirement.[7] Swetman managed to hold the line into the 1940's, but his successor finally succumbed.

A third topic at issue was grading. In 1938–39, the students recommended trial of a SU (satisfactory-unsatisfactory) marking system for a year. Swetman, champion of the normal curve, was drastically opposed to any such bimodal distribution. A survey sent to presidents of student bodies through the country obligingly indicated general preferences for the time-honored system, and the students' crusade collapsed.[8]

Students began to assume more responsibility in other areas as well. Each time the faculty attended the biennial convention of the Association of New York State Teachers College Faculties, the students took over classes under the watchful eye of Swetman. Students even made the graduation addresses in '42 and '43, something never done at Oswego before or since.

Students also began to sponsor activities, such as, in 1938, a program of art exhibitions. Once they borrowed paintings from the Metropolitan Museum of Art; on another occasion they exhibited photographs by Stanley Emerick and Nelson B. Hall of Oswego.

Growing student initiative testified to the drastic shift in faculty-student relations. Gone were the old guard, and with them the formally correct atmosphere of a ladies' finishing school. No longer were students expected to keep their distance. Classes were smaller and faculty members began calling students by their first names. Ann Galbraith, the physical education instructor, even wrote a note of apology to student Doris Brown: "Dear Doris, I hereby relinquish to you our bone of contention," she wrote. "You were right." "Hi, Doc," meanwhile, became the undergraduate's greeting to faculty Ph.D.'s of both sexes. "It was like a big happy family," says one alumnus. And Harry Porter adds, "Faculty members even knew the students' grandmothers."

Students also joined with faculty members in various campus projects. According to the *Palladium-Times* "twenty students and five doctors of philosophy constructed Romney Skating Rink in true pioneering style." [9] Later, also under Romney's supervision, they built a lodge by the lake to be used for student recreation.

The friendly staff-student relationship paved the way for assigning each faculty member a group of student advisees. As early as 1918, psychologists were loudly vaunting the virtues of "wholeness." Then, in the new age of mass enrollments, coupled with concern for development of the whole person, general orientation devices proved insufficient. In fact, by 1918, individual counseling became the order of the day.[10] Swetman, always alert to innovations, lost little time latching onto this one.

Relations among the students themselves also underwent change. As industrial arts students grew in number they became a power on campus. Concurrently, their relations with G.E.'s crystallized into a pattern.

> We didn't want to be classed with plain school teachers [says one I.A. alumnus], and looked on G.E. men as sissies. We were a close-knit group, an all-male corporation.
>
> Once a girl was permitted to register, but she barely lasted a semester. We eased her out gracefully. Twice some new and innocent registrar tried to combine, for academic courses, the I.A. and G.E. groups, but that never lasted either. I suspect we felt the school was run for our benefit, with the G.E.'s tolerated to provide us with dates. A very pleasant arrangement.

Also leavening student relations, at least temporarily, were the vets. "It was hard to compete with them," says one graduate. "But we benefited from their seriousness. Some of it rubbed off on us."

The growing numbers of males and cars brought closer contact with the town—like the school the victim of the general economic depression. Formerly famous businesses had closed, and carcass-like buildings stood rotting. Once famous for starch and shipping, Oswego now attained a distinction of sorts through having lost its claims to distinction. In 1943, newsreels round the world portrayed it as the typical small American city.[11]

Mediocre or not, the town was exploited for all it was worth. Conzone's, Buck's and the Snake Pit were favored for food, beer, and jukebox; Psi Phi beach for romantic rendezvous. "There was some discreet petting there," reminisces an alumnus, "but the moral climate was almost 100 per cent high."

On-campus activities were varied. A survey by Charles Wells in 1940 revealed photography to be the chief student hobby, with woodwork second. Favorite hobbies of Sophomore elementary students were music, knitting, reading and stamp collecting. One group learned sleight of hand from Romney; another participated in a hospitality program conducted by Mrs. Hart. On Saturday nights dances were held for all students in the gym. One student, now a New York City school principal, attended a costume affair as Adam, wearing only a fig leaf—or so the story goes. For summer, special features were added—in 1935 a camp sing, forum discussions and "weekly bridge for ladies." In 1937 was instituted the "annual" boat trip to Canada, repeated several times thereafter.

Other annual events were the May Day festival and Christmas caroling, a custom still persisting. In 1936 the carolers serenaded the city hospital, orphanages and retired faculty members. Achievement Day, later discontinued, was for recognizing students who excelled in extracurricular activities.

More highly organized activities of the period fall under these general heads: clubs, publications and sports. Varsity athletics, at least, sustained a setback. Golden Romney, who headed the Department of Health and Physical Education, de-emphasized varsity in favor of intramural sports and was supported by Swetman. Since funds were limited, they felt the interests of the many should supersede those of the few.

This policy was manifested in several ways. Aside from adding golf as a varsity sport in 1942, the program was curtailed. Basketball and baseball schedules were trimmed. Varsity participation was not allowed practice teachers, thus placing Ziel's teams at a disadvantage. Even more drastic was the move to discontinue football. For two years the controversy raged, rousing nation-wide interest and causing press associations to carry the discussions from coast to coast.

Local opponents of football cited the danger of injuries, expenses, time taken from classes, and ignominious scores. William Chatfield, '38, re-calls Oswego's defeat by Kutztown, Pennsylvania, 59 to 0. Maxie himself was commissioned by Swetman to sell these arguments to students. "It was hard to do," he reminisces. "I'd been playing football myself since I was eight years old." To Maxie, football was youth's highroad to grit, gumption, and assorted other virtues. Finally, on February 13, 1936, students voted out the sport, 229 to 115, but periodically ever since, groups have attempted its revival.

Women's activities, directed by Ann Galbraith from 1934 to 1945, were varied. Rifle practice was held in the attic of the main building and archery practice on the lawn. Tap dancing was added in 1935. Another sport, tried in 1934, survived only briefly.

> A group of avid roller skaters got permission to take over the corridor in the basement of the main building. Nights after school the thunder from a dozen pairs of skates was carried upward to the library. The noise was deafening and Mrs. Hahner was about to lose her mind. When one of the skaters failed to negotiate the turn at the end of the corridor, crashed through the glass in a door and cut her wrist, our skating was brought to an abrupt end and peace was restored in the library.

Playdays, when teams from several colleges met together for friendly games, were held several times a year. The *Oswegonian* for January 15, 1940, featured this item: "Playday a Huge Success: Mrs. Galbraith and Her 31 Lovely Ladies Travel to Cortland."

For recreation, most students depended less on sports than on clubs, which had proliferated. The Greeks by now were riding high; and the social hierarchy was rigid. Swetman encouraged organization of several non-Greek social clubs as well, the most successful being the Sons of the Wilted Wallet. This organization was formed on November 10, 1939, on the principle "that lasting college friendships could be preserved in a social group of moderate means." "It's not the dollars but the sense that counts," was their motto. On February 11, 1947, appeared a similar but unrelated organization, the Daughters of the Wilted Wallet, but it folded a few years later. Social status, such as provided by sororities, is more important to girls than to boys, who have much broader opportunities to gain recognition.

Other organizations rapidly increased—among them two unusual organizations, since expired—the Longfellows Club, composed of six-footers, and a date bureau. An *Oswegonian* editorial for December 20, 1935, complained, however, of the bureau's initiation fee. Prewar boys liked to date two girls—a sorority member to insure admission to dances and a town girl to get an occasional free meal.

Religious organizations of the period were the Canterbury Club (Episcopal), Hillel (Jewish), Newman (Catholic), and O.P.Y.O. (Oswego Protestant Youth Organization).

Also of a more serious nature were the honorary scholastic organizations such as the Sheldon Forum for boys, and Sigma Pi Rho for Girls. The latter organization, taking its name from S for Sheldon, P for Poucher, and R for Riggs, was absorbed in 1942 by Kappa Delta Pi when Harold Alford sponsored the establishment of a chapter on campus. Sheldon Forum merged with Epsilon Pi Tau, which established an Oswego branch in 1940. "An accomplishment I'll admit I'm proud of," confesses Gordon Wilber, whose efforts underwrote the move.

Regular student periodicals finally appeared, a development long overdue. Since the early 1800's, American colleges had had their organs of student opinion—generally in the form of literary magazines until 1865, then newspapers thereafter.

Oswego's first periodic publication—aside from the catalogue—was *The Vocationist*, produced intermittently by the industrial arts faculty, from 1910 until 1935.

The yearbook, which made its debut in 1919, until the forties was largely a record of the senior class, including activities, will, nicknames, and prophecy; after that it became a directory of the college as a whole. A frosh annual, *The Green Cap*, was added in 1937, but survived only briefly.

Not until 1935 did the first student newspaper appear, originating with a summer session weekly produced by William D. Taylor's news-writing class. That same fall it resumed publication as Volume 2. Special issues during ensuing years included an all-girl edition (1941) and, annually since 1939, an April Fool's edition, called the *Offwegoagin*. A mock editorial in the issue for 1939 states that "we have complete freedom of the press," thereby creating at least some doubt whether such freedom existed.

Opinions differ as to the effect on academic atmosphere of recurring crisis and social whirl. Some alumni question its quality. (Sample comments: "Kids were grade-conscious, but academic atmosphere was lacking." "Students were serious, but administrative emphasis was on keeping them happy.")

Conflicting views were these: "Students were academically-minded because it was the beginning of the four-year program. Besides we had better screening." "We worked harder in those days than students do now." Don Tower supports the more positive view: "Students I knew were well-qualified and diligent." And Lee Hornbake says, "We flunked students who couldn't make the grade."

Regardless of which view was right, the postwar trend was in the more serious direction. "Suddenly we weren't happy-go-lucky teen-agers anymore," testifies one alumna. "The war helped mature us."

PART V
The Rice Administration
1947-52

CHAPTER 12

A Short But Eventful Period

THE acting president from Swetman's collapse in November, 1946, until fall, 1947, and again from Rice's resignation in December, 1951, until Foster Brown came in September, 1952, was Dean Thomas Miller. Miller, a native of Pennsylvania, obtained his doctorate from Syracuse University. He served as grade teacher and principal in public schools, as instructor of education at Syracuse University, and as director of off-campus teaching at Potsdam before coming to Oswego in 1944.[1] For some time Swetman had had his eye on Miller, who had made a name for himself in the realm of recruitment, a crucial question for student-starved institutions.

Miller was a handsome "family man" and a vigorous administrator. He was built like a football player, had straight black hair, and a flashing smile. He was deeply devoted to his charming, unassuming wife, Marion, and his two children, Thomas Jr., and Celia.

As administrator he was a man of principle, refusing to lower admissions standards in a day when students were hard to come by. But his chief contribution was in helping expedite the program for expansion. And in his brief, but effective performances as "chief executive," the institutional wheels turned smoothly, harmony prevailed, and crises obligingly abated.

In fact, Miller was so effective as acting president that several faculty members surreptitiously plotted to install him for good. The board, however, pointed to the unwritten law that the "chief executive" must come from the outside and invited the faculty to draw up a list of qualifications to guide them.

Faculty members themselves showed something less than enthusiasm for the meeting devoted to this assignment. Their attention was at least partially diverted by a crucial World Series game being played that same afternoon. One fan sneaked from the room several times to bring back the score. At one point Maxie Ziel leaped to his feet and said he had decided

213

to declare his own candidacy for the position. The faculty seemed really concerned about only one qualification, that the candidate be familiar with the problems of teacher education.

Their plea was respected and led to the appointment, on July 15, 1947, of Harvey Mitchell Rice, the first of Oswego's chief administrators born in the twentieth century and the first *not* to hold a degree from Hamilton College. To give more dignity to the office, the tall, handsome young President was formally inaugurated on October 24, 1947. Some of the faculty jokingly referred to the event as "the coronation of H.M. [His Majesty] Rice."

Oswego's new President was born in West Virginia in 1907 and received his doctorate from Ohio State University. During World War II he was head of a special services division of the Office of Research and Inventions that improved methods of training aviation cadets, thereby reducing the number of crashes of trainees. Before coming to Oswego he was vice-principal of a high school; instructed at Ohio State, where he conducted a radio program called "This Week in History," and served as head of the History Department of Albany State Teachers College. He was also author of historical articles and books.

Harvey Rice and his young wife, Dorothy, were a striking couple and wonderful parents. He was tall, gray-haired and distinguished, his wife, slender, blond, and charming. They taught their two boys, John Dillard and Bryan, to swim in the treacherous waters of Shady Shore; they led them exploring the ice caves in winter. But they were firm with their children, too; and they urged Campus School teachers to show them no special favors.

The young couple were good sports, well equipped with a sense of humor. Dorothy Rice took it lightly when she sprained her ankle while taking modern dance from Joyse Sanders. Her husband joined the students in laughs at his own expense when he arrived at a sorority "open house" on the wrong day.

Another of Rice's characteristics was ingenuity. Once when the Rices were marooned by a heavy snow he got the big plow and dug a path to his door. A neighbor, Jessie Rudolph, saw the plow and motioned frantically for it to clear her road, too. Rice drove the plow over and Jessie almost fainted when she saw whose help she had commandeered. Jessie's husband was a faculty member.

As administrator, Rice was a man of tremendous energy, with keen concern for civic and educational affairs locally and across the state. He was president of the New York State Teachers Association and active in the state Parent-Teacher Association. On-campus he compressed into four brief years a considerable array of achievements before he left to become

president of the State College for Teachers in Buffalo, and later of Mac-
alester College in St. Paul, Minnesota.

The major development in curriculum was increased interest in general,
as opposed to liberal, education. For a long time liberal education had
been in vogue but now educators became concerned over general education. The two were said to differ essentially in that liberal education draws
on the heritage by studying it as an end in itself while general education
utilizes the heritage as a means for understanding the problems of modern
living. In other words, liberal education is distilled from the world's culture through the ages; while general education attempts to rescue students from the sloughs of impracticality and specialization.

Unfortunately, however, concepts as to what general education should
include and how it should be implemented were so varied and often
nebulous as to invite confusion. Nor could anyone claim that the endless
discussions of the topic at Oswego yielded significant results.

Concurrently came a trend toward more electives; the test of a department head's generosity was the number of hours he was willing to pitch
into the common pot. Departments sat themselves down and thought up
all sorts of electives, many of them based on general education objectives,
some of them never actually taught.

The most notable development in industrial arts was further diversifica-
tion. New shops were added, including textiles, elementary industrial
arts, ceramics, and transportation. Driver education was introduced in
October, 1947, and the Elementary Education Industrial Arts program
in September, 1951. This expansion was the natural outcome of an industrial arts philosophy which calls for interpretation of the society, however complex that society may become.

Certain important administrative and organizational changes were
made, too. The director of training, Harold Alford, now became the
first director of the Division of Elementary Education, a position created
to parallel that of the director of Industrial Arts Education. Meanwhile,
an Audio-Visual Department was added—and the size of the Campus
School was increased to permit two groups in each grade. This proliferation of administrative offices represented a trend across the country, as
non-instructional staff personnel increased from 17 per cent in 1883 to 34
per cent a half-century later.[2]

The foregoing developments were accompanied by a series of important
events. One was the creation in 1948 of the State University of New York,
of which Oswego became one unit. This institution is not to be confused
with the University of the State of New York, created in 1784. The latter,
the first of its kind, was actually no university at all, but a governing body,

established with power to inspect educational institutions and to grant charters and degrees. Thus, while New York was the first state to centralize control of higher education, it was the last to create a state university.

The new university, headed by Alvin C. Eurich, was something of an innovation. Possessing no central campus, it was a sprawling decentralized institution of forty-two units, including teachers colleges, community and technical colleges. With a total enrollment of forty-two thousand students, the infant university immediately became third largest in the nation.

Naturally, the creation of State University out of already existing institutions brought certain changes in its wake. The state teachers colleges now became State University of New York Teachers Colleges. The state seal continued to be used until 1950, when the University adopted one of its own. During the two-year interval faculty and students had been urged to suggest a motto. The one finally chosen was highly appropriate for a state populated by so diverse a collection of races, creeds and socioeconomic levels: "Let each become all he is capable of being."

Another boost in Oswego's status came with the graduate program, which grew from fairly recent tradition. Not always had advanced degrees possessed any special prestige. As late as 1825 the Master of Arts degree was awarded to any holder of a Harvard Bachelor's degree after a lapse of three years and the payment of a fee. It was often remarked that "all a Harvard man has to do for his Master's is to pay five dollars and stay out of jail." [3] The Master's was transformed into an earned degree in the 1870's, but not until 1887 at New York University was graduate work in pedagogy begun.

By the time Oswego undertook to offer such a degree, considerable planning always preceded inauguration of the program itself. During 1947–48, Rice, Miller and others conferred with numerous administrators, alumni and public school teachers to determine what graduates needed. The program got under way two years later and in June, 1950, the first degrees were granted. On that date seven proud candidates became the first to earn the right to wear the green-and-gold hood of Oswego.

Oswego made another bid for status in 1950, when it sought institutional accreditation. Moves toward standardizing teacher education were first undertaken in the eighties when the normal presidents of the Middle West met to discuss standards and reported to the National Education Association. This organization in 1915 established a Committee on Surveys and Standards. Not until 1926, however, when standards were adopted by the American Association of Teachers Colleges, did the actual accreditation of institutions begin.

By Rice's time accreditation had become essential for institutional status. And so it was that Oswego applied for, and gained, accreditation from the Commission on Accrediting Institutions of Higher Education of the Middle States Association of Colleges and Secondary Schools, the Dun & Bradstreet for teacher-training institutions in this section.

A more tangible evidence of progress lay in the acquisition of buildings and grounds. Lands acquired included the tract where the College Union now stands and the old camp at the north beach between Mentro Avenue and Shady Shore.

Building expansion involved both permanent and temporary structures. At Oswego as elsewhere during World War II, army barracks were erected as homes for married vets. This project, locally called "Splinter Village," was completed in 1947.

In January, 1948, five additional barracks arrived, to serve as classrooms, cafeteria and gymnasium. "The gymnasium," wrote President Rice in his Annual Report for 1948–49, "is so fragile that thrown basketballs or hard-running players go right through it."

Later that year, on June 1, 1948, the Dormitory Authority authorized a temporary residence hall for seventy-two women, to be housed eight in a room, at $4.50 each a week. Since the girls arrived before the dormitory was ready, they were all bunked temporarily in the gym, where less-than-enthusiastic faculty women supervised. One unwilling draftee immediately got in bed, pulled the covers over her head, went sound asleep, and consigned her charges to fate.

A permanent addition, due largely to the efforts of Swetman and Miller, was Sheldon Hall, purchased in 1947 by the Oswego College Foundation, successor to the now defunct Sheldon Hall, Incorporated. This beautiful structure, an eighty-year-old showplace overlooking Oswego harbor, was originally named Lakeside, and later Rushwood Hall. A plate on the wall was brought over by A. G. Cook's forbears from England.[4]

The year 1951 saw two other permanent acquisitions, two fifty-foot additions to the Industrial Arts Building and, at long last, the student union and dormitory, a form of structure with a long tradition. English concepts of the proper housing of students were planted in America by the colonial college. However, even before the Civil War, dormitory life was seriously criticized as being an outmoded remnant of medievalism. The Reverend Manasseh Cutler called such halls "the secret nurseries of every vice and the cages of unclean birds." And German-trained professors, common in nineteenth-century America, felt money might better be spent on libraries, laboratories and faculty salaries. For a time, therefore, dormitories fell into disuse, until concern for student life and a rash of private off-campus housing ventures led to on-campus residence halls. Once they caught on, however, they multiplied, and there were many luxurious ones by 1900.

For various reasons New York State lagged behind until parental pressures and serious student housing shortages brought action. It was a long overdue event, therefore, when Governor Thomas Dewey applied the mortar to the cornerstone of Oswego's first dormitory in June, 1950. Subsequent construction, under State Architect Lorimer Rich, was marked by tragedy when a workman "fell or was thrown" from a scaffolding and died.[5] The new dormitory-student union was finally occupied in the fall of 1951, complete with soft pastel shades, kitchen, modern blond furniture, and snack bar. Each wing had its own recreation room, music rooms, and business offices. Room and meals cost $17.50 a week.

Also of significance for students was creation of a Department of Personnel Services directed by a dean of students (Victor Ricks) and an associate dean of students (Dorothy Mott). As early as the First World War, many persons had felt something should be done about the "sideshow of extra-curriculum." In fact, in the years that followed, personnel problems grew even more complex as colleges drew from a broader range of social classes. Out of this concern came the personnel movement intended to link student activities with the basic purposes of the colleges. Critics, however, branded the counselors as dispensers of sweet reasonableness dedicated to killing student initiative and high-handedly parceling out students' time.

One outcome at Oswego was the now-elaborate freshman orientation contrasting sharply with the lone speech of a few years before. In 1950, for example, the frosh had to hide a turkey on campus for twenty-four hours and, at a girls' softball game, unveiled a female Bobby Feller. Other features were a cookout, block dance, picnic, welcome dance and vesper service.

An event specifically affecting the faculty was creation in 1949 of a Faculty Council, designed to act in all matters relating to their welfare. Representatives were elected from the Industrial Arts Division, the Elementary Division, the Campus School, and the faculty at large.

Traditionally, administration of the teachers colleges was strongly centralized in the president. Faculty participation in policy-making had been neither sought nor welcome.[6] However, of recent years faculties had come to insist on a greater voice in questions relating to them. The major expression of this trend was the growth of the American Association of University Professors, sometimes supplemented by organizations like Oswego's Faculty Council, concerned exclusively with local matters.

An event of quite different nature involved Swetman's portrait, painted after his retirement at a cost of fourteen hundred dollars contributed by faculty, students and friends. On the evening of June 30, 1950, a passing motorist reported smoke coming from the library. The recently hung portrait had been taken down, placed on a neat pile of torn books, and set afire. Simultaneously, fires were set in the lounge furniture in the browsing area. Arson investigators and city police attempted to break the case. Everyone had his conjecture as to "who-dun-it." "Yet, so far as I know," says Harvey Rice, "the mystery was never solved."

The most distinctive change in the student body during this period was the influx of veterans. In fact, Oswego had 450, the highest number of any of the teachers colleges. Many of these veterans, either because of high school index or lack of money, would not ordinarily have gone to college. Nevertheless, the vast majority, here as elsewhere, made better-than-average grades. Maturity and seriousness of purpose counteracted whatever other handicaps they may have had.

The vets were a close in-group; older than the others, they mingled little in the social life on campus. Many had families, and "made do" with small incomes, living in trailers or veteran housing. "In basic training," wrote one student veteran, "the motto was, 'If it moves, salute it; if it is still, pick it up; if you can't budge it, paint it.' Revised version for the college vet: 'If it cries, change it; if it has wheels, buy it; if it is hollow, rent it.'"

A second change was in numbers. The growth of student body created a housing problem. Pending completion of the dormitory, students lived six in a room in old army barracks. Many continued to live in town, under slightly revised housing provisions.

> Approved houses must have no more than 8 per bath, hygienically clean. The lights in the hall must be left burning after 11 at night. Windows must be well screened. There must be a single bed, desk, easy chair, good mirror, dresser, individual towel racks, removable covers for mattresses, temperature between 65–70 degrees, until 11 on weekdays, and 12:30 on Saturdays and Sundays. One-hundred-watt study bulbs are to be permitted in study lamps if requested. Hot water must be provided for daily baths. Boys and girls must not be roomed in the same house.

Meanwhile, students' expenses were climbing while the dollar was losing its value. By 1949 the average annual cost for the school term was five to seven hundred dollars, exclusive of laundry, clothing, and personal expenses. These students, like their predecessors, saved money by dressing simply. "A fellow who wore a coat and tie was someone to be suspicious of," says one alumnus. Dungarees, sweatshirts and khakis were the current vogue for men, sweaters and skirts for women. Skirts were longer in 1947, reminding senior Al Godden of "potato sacks." [7]

Manners and morals, like students' clothes, were slightly more casual than before. One reason was the times, another the generally more liberal philosophy of Associate Dean of Women Dorothy Mott. A new device was the "automatic campus." A girl was simply notified through the mail if discovered violating rules pertaining to signing out, securing permission for weekends or staying out after hours.[8]

One temptation to stay out overtime was the current popularity of certain town hangouts, chiefly Herbie's, McCarthy's and a place nicknamed "Bucket of Blood." The *Oswegonian* for March 6, 1951, described McCarthy's:

> Cars of all sorts, sizes and shapes adorned the front yard. Inside was one small demanding TV set. Blurred eyes gazed upward to watch the crazy antics of a video star. Fists clenched new ten-cent beer glasses, and nicotine was evident on many finger tips. . . . The older, more uninhibited habitués of the place were perched contentedly on their stools around the bar. . . . In the other room a jukebox blared incessantly, unheard by its many contributors. . . . If there were only three or four around one table, they were miserably outweighed by the table with six or seven.

But the so-called Bucket of Blood was the real center of interest, complete with Negro band and hint of intrigue. "Where the beatniks of our generation ended up," says one alum. "Supposed to be the front for subversive activities, but more impression than fact," says another. At any rate, the faculty felt some concern while the place lasted, and relief when it closed.

On-campus, the glut of social activity continued. Students collected club memberships like scalps, to add to their personal prestige. "It labeled you as a VIP to be able to say, 'Well, I must go now. Another committee meeting, you know,'" recalls Connie Bond, '51.

In the Greek organizations hazing was as harmless as ever. In 1949 frosh had to learn to spell Blimpy (Nunzio) Spiridigliozzi's last name; Blimpy was a popular upperclassman on campus. And for one day sorority rushees must have no social contact with non-sorority members and were permitted only the common courtesies of greeting.

Intramural sports, meanwhile, thrived and two new sports appeared. Wrestling was organized as a major sport in 1947 under the direction of George Pitluga; and a trampoline club was organized in 1951, with Louise Ostberg as sponsor.

Emphasis on varsity was still relatively slight; and losing teams did little to foster enthusiasm. "Budgets were inadequate," complains Max Ziel, "and cooperation in recruiting athletes missing." Max himself, however, continued as popular as ever and a constructive influence in the lives of the boys.

Perhaps varsity in Rice's time will be best remembered for certain unusual events, the first a basketball game with Niagara University, November 29, 1949. Here is the account in Ziel's own words.

Many coaches didn't like me because I played zone defense, which I brought into New York State in 1921. Because of it we defeated many teams we had no right to beat. The Niagara team was too strong for us, but we scheduled them because of the large guarantee. For the same reason we scheduled Canisius and St. Bonaventure. Although these games meant three defeats we netted enough money from them to finance our other games.

Anyway, at Niagara, we threw a zone defense at Taps Gallagher's team. They got the ball, took it to mid-court and held it there. My boys wanted to go out after them but I wouldn't let them. The crowd began yelling at me. Action was paralyzed. At half-time I told the boys, "We are still playing zone." The game resumed, but the same thing happened. Then the crowd got mad at Taps. They'd paid $1.75 to see a game, but they saw no playing. The game made big news.

Another interesting development was the use of hypnosis by the track team. "The coaches weren't in on it," says Don Snygg. "It was simply worked out by the boys, a council of desperation." At any rate, hypnosis did not hurt—or help—matters. The track remained where it was, in last place.

The only totally new aspect of student activity was concern for political affairs. Traditionally, American college students have taken little interest in such things, in sharp contrast with youth in other countries. For one thing, college administrators, especially publicly controlled ones, discourage political activities, perhaps because of unfavorable publicity.[9]

Nevertheless, because of the war and the influx of veterans on campus, Oswego students, like those elsewhere, became more politically minded. An International Relations Club was formed, and an Intergroup Council arranged programs concerning minority groups. In 1948 a mock presidential election was held, with Harold Stassen coming out first, with Thomas Dewey second.[10] Also organized were a campus discussion group and a chapter of the National Association for Advancement of Colored People, including members of both racial groups.

About the same time, students running for office became more thoughtful in preparing their platforms. Miles Borden, running for student body president in 1949, promised to work for a school bus, unified control of student organizations and funds, and individual mailboxes. Miles was elected and most of these things came to pass. The first school bus, for example, was acquired in 1951.

Most intriguing feature of student political activities was rumor of subversive groups on campus (1948–50). Focal points of this activity were reputedly a certain basketball team and the Bucket of Blood. Such rumors, we should add, were commonplace in those days. Everyone with a tinge of liberalism was suspect, and any favorable comment about Russia a sure sign of being a Red.

The more serious attitude was also reflected in a higher quality student newspaper and more editorial matter. As a result, Columbia Scholastic Press Association in New York City awarded the paper first place honors in 1949 and its highest award, the Medalist, in 1951. And in 1950 the *Pen and Brush* appeared. Composed of stories, poems, photographs and drawings, this publication was intended to encourage literary and artistic talent.

Despite these advances, student morale was only mediocre. Colleges were bursting at the seams and students went where they could. At Oswego, for example, students had outrun facilities. Science laboratories were outmoded; and almost everything on campus was in need of repair. Swetman and Rice had laid the groundwork for improvements, but it would take time to put them into effect.

The creation of State University aroused only passing interest. Most students ignored this development altogether. Even the school's early fame was all but forgotten. "We knew who Sheldon was," said one, "but that was as far as it went."

Where alumni affairs were concerned, there was significant progress and one noteworthy event. The association obtained a half-time executive secretary, Robert Helsby, an office and secretarial help. Within two years' time, Helsby and Alumni President Hilda Bohall had established fourteen local chapters through the state.

The "special event" occurred in spring, 1950, when the class of '40 dug up the time capsule they had buried ten years before. "It had been punctured by a post from a snow fence," says Bob Helsby, '40, "and smelled like a cross between a garbage dump and a sewage disposal plant. But Helsby's rat trap and Tom Moore's ice skates were still in good condition." At the same time the class of 1950 buried another capsule to replace the one disinterred.

PART VI

First Years of Foster Brown's Administration

1952-61

CHAPTER 13

The Present-Day Staff

S TATE UNIVERSITY, created in 1948 for the development of state-supported higher education, offers four-year programs in liberal arts, science and engineering, home economics, industrial and labor relations, veterinary medicine, ceramics, agriculture, forestry, maritime service, medicine and teacher preparation as well as two-year programs in agriculture, industrial, health, technical and service areas. Oswego is one of the eleven units designed to prepare public school teachers for the state. These units, called Colleges of Education since 1959, are supervised by Executive Dean Hermann Cooper, assisted by Dr. Frank Lane.

To administer State University the Governor appoints a Board of Trustees presently chaired by Frank C. Moore, which in turn chooses a president. The first president, Alvin Eurich, was succeeded in turn by William S. Carlson and by Thomas Hale Hamilton. Each local unit has its own council appointed by the Governor, and a president appointed by the State Board of Trustees on the recommendation of the president of State University and the local College Council. Present administrative officers within the local college itself are the president, dean, associate dean, director of the Division of Elementary and Secondary Education, director of the Division of Industrial Arts, principal of the Campus School, dean of students, and financial secretary. Collectively, these men compose the Administrative Council, which acts in an advisory capacity to the president. The policy-making group for the instructional program is the Instructional Council chaired by the dean and consisting of directors of divisions, chairmen of departments and others concerned with instruction, such as the coordinator of student teaching and librarian.

Representing the faculties of all the units of State University collectively is the Faculty Senate; of the Colleges of Education specifically, the Association of New York State Colleges of Education Faculties. Locally, faculty members share in reaction to policy-making through department heads and faculty committees—especially the Faculty Council and Pro-

225

motions Committee. The Promotions Committee, created in 1957, is composed of the dean, the directors of divisions, principal of the Campus School, and elected representatives of the faculty.

Two figures in State University have had an important influence on the fortunes of the local College, Thomas Hale Hamilton and Hermann Cooper. Hamilton, a youthfully handsome career educator, was an officer in the Navy during World War II, did considerable writing, and served as vice-president of academic affairs at Michigan State immediately before becoming president of State University of New York in 1959. In the brief period he has been here, he has already won great respect from the teacher-education members of his institutional family.

His colorful lieutenant, Hermann Cooper, has already been around long enough to become an institution. This former athlete, collector of china, musician, and long-time educational leader could well qualify for the title "Mr. Teacher Education" in New York State. He is a familiar figure on College of Education campuses, all of which are second homes to Hermann Cooper.

Administrative advisers on the local level form the College Council, formerly the Board of Visitors. This group has had only five chairmen in its long history—Gilbert Mollison, E. B. Mott, Harold Johnson, E. M. Waterbury, and now James Lanigan. The first women to become members of the board (in 1918) were Anna Post and Mrs. Virginia Kingsford Higgins.

The present chairman, James Lanigan, is a magna cum laude graduate of Syracuse University, retired executive of the Niagara Mohawk Power Corporation, past president of the New York School Board Association, president of the Fulton Board of Education, and one of the most popular speakers in upstate New York.

Three of the council's members are Oswego alumni: Samuel Castaldo, former naval officer and commanding officer of the Naval Reserve Center, now vice-president of Castaldo Homes, Incorporated; Margaret Mansfield Richardson, well-known classroom teacher and effervescent personality; and Marian Mackin, civic leader and power in the Democratic party. Miss Mackin was also executive secretary of the Red Cross during World War II, chairman of the local Housing Authority, and organizer of the Women's Auxiliary of the Oswego Hospital.

Others on the council are Marian Steele, John Aylward, Clarence Leighton, George Penney, and Dorothy Barclay. Marian Steele is a graduate of Boston University, an active community worker, and the wife of R. Frank Steele, president and manager of the Adams Electric Light Company. Her hobbies are fishing and deer hunting. John Aylward (A.B. Brooklyn College; LL.B. Columbia) is a member of the law firm of Scanlon, Weight, Willmott and Aylward, and village police justice of Black River. Clarence Leighton (A.B., U. of Rochester; B.L., Pulitzer School of Journalism at Columbia) is the oldest living past president of the New York State Society of Newspaper Editors; president of the *Oswego Palladium-Times;* and a director of the Oswego County Savings Bank. George Penney (Albany Law School) is former president of Oswego City Savings Bank; president of Oswego Hospital Board; and former surrogate of Oswego County. Finally, Dorothy Barclay (Adelphi College) is a world traveler, former Republican committeewoman, civic leader, "gentlewoman farmer," orchid fancier, and breeder of show horses, which she has flown to meets all over the country.

The person most important in Oswego's destiny since July 1, 1952, is President Foster Brown, who was born at Leyden, New York, and received his Bachelor's and Master's degrees at St. Lawrence, where he was captain of the track team and took first place in the pole vault at the New York State Intercollegiate Conference. As president of the student body he represented his college at a conference at Stanford University, going by way of the Panama Canal.

His early professional experience admirably equipped him for his present position. He was teaching principal at Coeymans and Hillsdale, superintendent of schools at Suffern, dean of the State Teachers College at Cortland, and part-time research associate in the State Department—all in the state of New York. Meanwhile, he found time to win his doctorate at Columbia and to write articles for such well-known magazines as *School Executive, Education Digest,* and *Nation's Schools.* During this same period he married a teacher in one of his schools, Catherine Packard, and now they have five children, Ruth, Susan, Wallace, Celia, and Irving.

Brown is a handsome man of wiry build with light brown hair and hazel eyes. He has the modulated, yet firm speech of the business executive; the coordination of the athlete; and the youthful appearance of the catalyst who shoulders responsibilities without absorbing them.

His chief concerns are his family and education—and in both areas he has achieved success. Each member of his family possesses a rare composite of popularity, intelligence and leadership. Catherine Packard Brown is acclaimed for her qualities as mother and wife—quiet yet warmly human, unassuming but self-assured, efficient without seeming to hurry.

To his role as administrator, Foster Brown brings a wholesome philosophy and a thorough dedication. "We should be proud of what we are doing," he told the local chapter of the A.A.U.P. in 1954. "There are those who would look down on us, but there is no reason why we should get down so they can do so." He likes to quote Lincoln who said that education is the most important single thing we can be engaged in.

Brown perceives his own special role as "that of co-laborer, who has specialized in a particular area, responsible for such organization and facilities as will permit efficient operation of the education process." To that end, he places high priority on superior facilities and faculty, as well as on wholesome relationships among all parties concerned.

Where facilities at Oswego are involved, he has proved the right man in the right place, a "natural" for an era of expansion. He appreciates the value of buildings and grounds, and he has the vision to develop them. "It used to make a bad impression when a parent dropped a son by Colgate, with its fine buildings, then found so much poorer buildings when they left their daughter here. It created the impression that the preparation of teachers was somehow less important." "He has had the foresight to see what this campus could be," says a College Council member. "He can envision the possibilities," adds his wife. "We have sometimes walked together through deep snow and brush, but to him it was not rough land. In his mind's eye he already saw a developed campus."

An even more essential ingredient in the education compound than buildings, believes Foster Brown, is staff. For he places great emphasis on faculty morale—the subject he chose for his own doctoral dissertation. In fact, he himself initiated participation of staff representatives in making promotions.

Brown also believes in the larger view appropriate to a growing school. He expects quality production but provides the facilities and the support for doing the job. "If he says something, you can bank on it," says one of his assistants. "You won't suddenly have the rug pulled out from under you."

Despite all these concerns, Brown finds time for community relations. "Oswegonians never fully realized what the school means to the city until this administration," said a member of the College Council. Wherever feasible, he makes available college services and facilities to the people in the area. Nor does he fail to do his personal share, performing activities as varied as washing cars for the polio drive and speaking on Laymen's Day at the church. In addition, he has served on various boards, is vice-president and trustee of the City Savings Bank, and has been active in the Red Cross, Presbyterian Church, the Rotary, and the Fortnightly Club.

In short, Foster Brown possesses traits well befitting him for his present role. First of all, he has tremendous drive. "He likes a challenge, something he can sink his teeth into," says his wife. He also has the courage of his beliefs. While no radical reconstructionist, he is ever ready to entertain a promising idea and give it a chance to justify itself. Brown himself says: "An administrator's mistakes affect so many people it is best to have patience." He shows an excellent sense of timing, knowing when to go ahead, when to stop, and when to change his course. "He keeps his mind open and reversible," says Don Snygg. "He has enough confidence to change his mind."

Furthermore, he is a confirmed optimist, concentrating on the positive aspects of any situation. He is the rare man who can dream dreams and balance a budget. "He is the man with the forward look, the man who can see beyond," said John D. Ackley, a prominent citizen and school board chairman from Hillsdale, New York. And this mood he has succeeded in communicating to the college.

Despite his relative youth and brief career as president, important honors have already begun to come his way. In 1952, his alma mater, St. Lawrence, awarded him a distinguished service citation and, a year later, named him trustee. In 1958, he served as executive secretary of the committee which selected Hamilton as second president of State University and was among the officials to speak at his inauguration. The next year he was sent to Indonesia to evaluate the education projects conducted jointly by the State University of New York and the Ford Foundation. And just last year he was presented a certificate of merit by the local Chamber of Commerce for his vision in directing the program of expansion at the College.

Obviously the president's job is a many-sided one—and for this reason certain assistants have been added. Present administrative assistant to the president is Charles Coward—ex-construction engineer, aircraft jig-maker, infantry captain, student counselor, and alumnus (B.S. magna cum laude and M.S.) of Oswego. Director of Public Information Harry Charlton is a graduate of Syracuse University and a veteran newspaper-man.

Second in command until June, 1960, was Harold Alford, native of Arkansas and a key figure in New York State education since 1934. He was educated at Hendrix College, where he played football and majored in chemistry, the University of Chicago, and Columbia, where he was elected president of the graduate school students. Also, before becoming dean in 1954, he served as high school principal and as district school principal in Arkansas, and as head of the Education Department and director of the Division of Elementary Education at Oswego.

Harold Alford's contributions are manifold. He originated the present Campus School Parent-Teacher Association, organized the Epsilon Omega Chapter of Kappa Delta Pi, developed the rural education program in the thirties, and instituted student teaching practices copied over the country.

As a man, Alford is warm, outgoing, gracious, and modest. He is widely traveled, an avid reader, highly versatile, and an expert at photography. His wife, Ruth, is a strong personality with unusual creative talent and a rare sense of humor.

As a dean, he showed himself a master of establishing harmony and of coordinating a smooth-running instructional program. His forte was creating the sort of climate in which each faculty member could realize his own best potential, an assertion borne out by statements like these:

> When you go to see Harold about something he tries to figure out a way to do what you want to do. He frees people to work.

> He is a steadying influence. One of his greatest assets is his accessibility. People can communicate their needs.

It is hardly surprising that Alford was chosen to assume the very responsible position which he presently holds in Bandung, Indonesia. There he is directing a team of faculty members from many units of State University in their efforts to assist the Indonesians in building a program in teacher education.

Closely paralleling Harold Alford's career is that of Charles Turner, present dean of the College. Both are from the West; both are career educators; both have climbed the same professional ladder; and both are admirably suited by education and experience for their tasks.

"Charlie" Turner was educated at Northeast Missouri State Teachers College, University of Missouri, Teachers College, Columbia, and the University of Chicago. As a Missouri schoolman, he was, in turn, rural teacher, assistant to the superintendent of schools, and superintendent of schools. He came to Oswego in 1941, and, in 1954, became director of the Elementary Education Division and, in 1958, of the Secondary Division as well.

Turner's contributions are as broad as his background. At Oswego he has played the key role in reorganizing the educational sequence for elementary education and a major role in reorganizing the secondary curriculum. He has directed the preparation of many professional booklets and handbooks, doing much of the writing and editing himself. Among the most important was a bulletin entitled *Professional Preparation of Elementary Teachers in the State University of New York*. In addition he is active in the New York State Teachers Association and is first vice-president of the Central Zone. As evidence of his effectiveness as a liaison man between professional field and college program he originated the idea of close cooperation between public schools and college through the National Commission of Teacher Education on Professional Standards program.

Charlie, as he is known to his colleagues, is liked, admired, and respected. Like the man whom he succeeded as dean, Charlie Turner is consistent and dependable, never appears ruffled, and keeps his head in any crisis. He has a solid quality that has a stabilizing effect on any group he leads. He is also a prodigious worker, performing the hardest chores related to any project he is directing, never expecting of others more than he is willing to do himself. "Every institution needs a Charlie Turner," says Tom Miller, president of the State Teachers College at Edinboro, Pennsylvania.

Undoubtedly a major factor in Dr. Turner's progress has been his wife Evelyn, also a native of Missouri and a teacher, who shares her husband's active interest in education.

First to occupy the post of associate dean at Oswego is Stewart Tosh, who worked for General Electric Corporation for three years and then earned his way through college as an electric welder. He won his A.B. degree and a Phi Beta Kappa key from Union College. He later earned his doctorate from Syracuse University, where he was awarded a fellowship. During World War II he ran communications schools overseas. As a schoolman he was chairman of the Social Studies Department and elementary principal at Little Falls before coming to Oswego.

Other top personnel in the professional program include Virginio (Dit) Piucci, George Kopp, and Sherwood (Sherry) Dunham. "Sherry" Dunham, director of the Education Division, was already demonstrating leadership qualities in college, where he was chosen president of the Senior class and king of Homecoming activities. As an aviator in the war he won three air medals. In education he won his spurs as public school teacher and administrator. At Oswego Sherry has proved himself a skilled administrator and a master of human relations—"a good guy to work with," as one colleague put it.

Replacing Dunham, when he left the principalship of the Campus School, was Virginio (Dit) Piucci, former athlete, father of two pairs of twins, and veteran of classroom teaching on all levels from second grade through graduate school. "Dit" Piucci has a fortunate combination of youthful energy, initiative, imagination, and fortitude—and a reputation among his staff for "getting things done."

Most recent addition to the administrative family is George Kopp, director of graduate studies, summer school, and extension. Kopp is a member of Kappa Delta Pi, Phi Delta Kappa, and also a veteran of World War II. He served as a navigator in the USAF in World War II and is now a Major in the reserves. He came here from Syracuse University, where he directed the Intensive Teacher Training Program.

In industrial arts, there have been four divisional heads since 1953. Previously mentioned was Gordon Wilber, who retired in 1957 to become a consultant to a team in the Philippines. He was for many years national chairman of the Board of Directors of Epsilon Pi Tau. G. Harold Sylvius, professor and chairman of the Department of Industrial Education, Wayne State University, has said of Wilber: "He has done more than any other person to present the case for industrial arts as general education."

Wilber was followed by Robert Helsby, all-around good fellow, and disciple of industrial arts in its broad modern sense. When Helsby left two years later to become deputy commissioner of labor of the state of New York, the position of acting head was assumed by Art Hauler, whose life story is one of dedication to his field. In fact, Hauler settled on industrial arts as a career while still in high school. Then, because family fortunes were at a low ebb, he took assorted jobs, including machine shop, pattern-making and foundry—an excellent background for his future work. In the years that followed, his work at Oswego and across the state has been so noteworthy as to earn him the nickname "Mr. I.A." In 1956 the Central New York Industrial Arts Club, the Mohawk Valley Industrial Arts Club, and the Syracuse Industrial Teachers Club tendered Hauler a testimonial for unselfish service and ardent conscientious duty in the field of industrial arts education. And in 1959 the New York Steering Committee for the Industrial Arts Section of the New York State Vocational and Practical Arts Association presented him its Outstanding Service Award, given annually to the person making the greatest contribution in industrial arts to New York State.

The present head, since 1960, is Paul DeVore, a man of wide achievements. As a youngster, he took a very active part in Boy Scout work, especially in the area of aquatics. From this experience stem most of his present-day hobbies—camping, ornithology, hiking and canoeing.

DeVore's varied professional experiences reveal unusual initiative and creativity. In Grove City, Pennsylvania, he developed a Scout camp named the DeVore Camp in his honor. At Oswego he developed a drawing and planning program based on the solution of problems through drafting—and demonstrating the relationships between drafting and the other laboratories of Oswego's industrial arts sequence.

Serving students of both divisions is Norman Whitten, formerly a very able social studies professor who once aspired to be a haberdasher, now dean of students and "chief steward of manners and morals" on campus. Whitten is a sartorially elegant New Englander and former college athlete, having been high point man in a winter sports meet at Lake Placid and winner of the New England cross-country championships. In World War II he served as a lieutenant of ski troops. He is adept at assisting students driven to desperation by dishonored index, deflated pocketbook or assorted undergraduate dilemmas. He is also unusual in his ability to stimulate student initiative and to guide their activities without dominating them.

Whitten is assisted by a dean of men, a dean of women and several assistant deans and student counselors. Dean of men is Michael Patton, a member of Kappa Delta Pi, who received his B.S. at the University of Idaho and his Master's at Ohio State. The dean of women is Mrs. Thelma Herlin (A.B. Hood; M.A. Teachers College, Columbia). Assistant deans are Onnis Waid, Jill Periton, Stephanie McCandless, Zoé Watson and Peter McCandless.

Affiliated with this department are the Student Union (Ernest Bebb, director; Beverly Dowd, assistant director); food service (Robert Palmer, director; George Busher, assistant director); and the Health Center, under the direction of Dr. Kathaleen Perkins and nurse Louise Hess. Dr. Olin Mowry also acts as part-time physician. It should be noted, parenthetically, that students think enough of their health service to vote twelve thousand dollars annually for its operation.

In the special service area, none is more essential than the Lida Penfield Library, fulcrum of the academic life, recently stocked with almost 80,000 volumes transported from the old building in a gigantic student book brigade. This magnificent building, as well as several others on campus, were designed by Lorimer Rich, who gained distinction for his design of the Tomb of the Unknown Soldier. It has a seating space for eight hundred students, shelving for one hundred and fifty thousand volumes, and is equipped with listening room, reading room, microfilm viewing booths, seminar rooms, and a historical room. The present book collection has quadrupled since the present head librarian, Helen Hagger, arrived in 1945, and is growing at the rate of 5 per cent a year. The four assistant librarians are Zofia A. Drzewieniecki, Constance Hall, and Grace T. Manwaring, and Lois Prudom Stolp.

Three other services are especially concerned with recruiting the best possible candidates for the teaching profession and assisting them to find suitable positions upon graduation. White Warner, coordinator of Field Services, ranges over the state acquainting prospective students with the aims and purposes of teacher education generally and with this school's program in particular. Dorothy Mott, director of admissions, coordinates the interviewing and testing of incoming students. Richard Wheeler directs the Placement Service, which in 1959 found positions for 159 students at salaries ranging from $4,000 to $4,800 a year.

Other important administrative officers are Mary Hennessey, registrar; Carey Salander, financial secretary; and Gerald Bennett, engineer in charge of buildings and grounds. The two men in Bennett's department who have served Oswego longest are Richard Smith, employed in 1936, and Thomas Peckham, who came in 1942—both of them "alumni" of the Oswego Normal Campus School.

Until recent years the Normal School shortsightedly provided little in the way of secretarial services, which are of great importance to the efficiency of an institution. Representative of the outstanding secretaries are Ann Kray, Mary Brown, Helen Gilbert, Mildred Watts, and Margaret Christian—financial secretary during the days of Ralph Swetman.

Where the faculty as a whole is concerned—and there are 188 members at present—there is superb training and experience, effective antidotes to institutional stagnation. "Colleges count their blessings in terms of Ph.D.'s and scholarly publications," wrote William James of liberal arts colleges in 1903, "thus confirming the German notion that knowledge of subject is all that is needed to be a college teacher."

Teacher colleges were slow to follow suit, but, by the 1950's, they had caught the Ph.D. fever themselves. At Oswego, as elsewhere, staff members stoically resign themselves to achieving a doctorate or foregoing forever the award of full professorship.

Certainly the present faculty is far better prepared than that of any former administration. Every staff member has a degree of one kind or another.[1] Thirty-one per cent hold earned Doctor's degrees and 62 per cent Master's degrees. Of the twelve who hold only Bachelor's degrees, almost all are on temporary appointment or in specialized positions. Furthermore, over half those without doctorates are matriculated in programs directed toward advanced degrees.

Many institutions are found among faculty alma maters, making Oswego a melting pot of educational ideas. Bachelor's degrees held represent seventy-five institutions, Master's sixty, and Doctor's twenty-five, with Syracuse, Columbia and Cornell represented in that order for doctorates alone.

Many faculty members have studied in Europe. The number who have traveled abroad is too long to list. Suffice it to say that the present-day staff is a peripatetic one, and "nest habits" are frowned upon as provincial.

Turning now from faculty qualifications to staff problems and interrelationships, at least two conclusions appear justified. First, the present pattern of faculty relationships has long persisted and is typical of teacher-training institutions. Within the administration, a rough system of checks and balances exists, with boards and administrators checking each other, both subject to pressures from faculties, alumni, and public pressure groups and the whole system further checked by social forces from without. But institutional heads have remained dominant, and Oswego's history bears out the truth of a remark made by Brubacher: "In college government the president's role has been decisive. An Eliot or a Gilman could make his university world-famous, a poor president could set his school back fifty years." [2]

The second conclusion is that faculty gripes and problems at Oswego are typical of teacher-training institutions everywhere. Some reactions are clear-cut, some too diffuse to reveal any consensus. Some persons say the new merit system of promotion encourages better performance; others believe it defeats good morale. Some persons believe tenure a good thing; others, like Charles Yager, say: "We get all tangled up in security. We don't dare threaten our position by rocking the boat."

At any rate, many faculty members remain here year after year—for love of teaching, loyalty to the institution, or benefits accruing to State University staff members. These last include retirement, provisions for maternity leave, sick leave, sabbatical leave, leaves without pay upon special request, paid up insurance policies for one's beneficiaries, and tenure for those above the associate level who have served a specified period. Tenure was first urged by Thomas Jefferson, but the situation was not ripe for it until the twentieth century.

Salaries have also steadily improved, comparing favorably with other states but hardly as well with other professions. The regular-term salary range for the four academic ranks is presently as follows:

Instructor	$5140–$6250
Assistant Professor	$5570–$7250
Associate Professor	$6250–$8640
Professor	$7520–$12,220

Certainly such figures would seem astronomical to the Oswego faculty of a century ago when annual salaries of four hundred dollars were not uncommon!

CHAPTER 14

Oswego Student Life: 1960 Style

THE rapidly growing student body, now numbering 2,282 for the
regular session, is more cosmopolitan than ever. The vast majority are
out-of-towners, commuters constituting a mere fraction of the total. Three
in five are from metropolitan areas around Syracuse or New York City,
and all but a handful from New York State. Ten come from foreign countries, a few on special scholarships given to displaced persons after World
War II.

The entire college community welcomes these students. "A little of us
brushes off on them, and a little of them brushes off on us," says one
student. As for the foreign student's reaction, this statement by Austrian
Helga Lindbichler, '60, is typical:

> Some things I like—the sunsets, the lake, the informal friendliness.
> I am impressed by the way students run things at Oswego, and the fact
> that adults accept their decisions.
> Naturally, we foreign students have our problems, too. Our money
> doesn't go far; curricular adaptations should be made for us. For example,
> we need a survey of American history instead of minor details.

Francisca Hefti's reaction is also favorable:

> I am highly impressed and surprised, too, with the experience that
> people can be friendly just to make others feel happy, that authority,
> respect and humanity can be linked as they are here, making life easy
> and studying a pleasure. The interest that the administration and the
> teachers take in each student shapes the friendly atmosphere.

Francisca is from Switzerland and is getting her Master's degree from
Oswego in 1961, with a major in psychology.

Testimony to what they gained from Oswego also comes from the work
the foreign students perform upon returning to their native countries.
Maung Maung Gyi, '55, for example, holds the only industrial arts degree

236

in all Burma, and supervises industrial arts throughout his country.

Students come from the same social classes as ever—mostly lower-middle and middle-middle, with a few from upper-lower and upper-middle—the classes usually found at state schools and teacher-training institutions.

Aware of some tendency for teacher-training institutions to become the refuge for the academically less competent and of the pressing need for better teachers, Oswego has adopted steadily higher standards for screening applicants.

The present-day criteria are derived from high school credits, selective admissions examinations, personal interviews and health certificates, and in the fall of 1960 alone, 1,002 applicants were denied admission. Another 1,162 were accepted, of whom 750 actually came. In consequence, the median high school index of elementary students rose from 81.8 in 1956, to 85.7 in 1959, to over 86 in 1960, and almost all come from the upper half of their graduating class.

Students are far more clothes-conscious today. Even the boys are fashion-conscious, with ivy-league styles—heavy sweaters, short pants, and ankle-length shoes—having displaced dungarees and sloppy slacks. Depending on the occasion, the girl student wears heels, flats, sneakers, and shower clogs or spool-heel shoes; short plaid skirts, slacks, Bermuda shorts, or scoop-necked leotards or tights. Her coat is of camel's hair or of tweed with racoon collar. She wears the popular bouffant hair style with tresses arranged in puffs, making her face appear small and round.

Rules curb the coed's more extreme styles. In 1955, the Association of Women Students recommended skirts for classes—even on Saturdays—lest extension teachers should see them in dungarees and slacks. After four, "slacks and Bermudas are to be worn if desired, but dungarees are not recommended since they look messy and students are apt to wear sloppy shirts with them."

Students conform, too, in matters of daily routine, governed as they are by bells and schedules. Getting out of bed is a project in itself, encouraged by alarm clocks and books thrown by helpful roommates. The student attends several classes, browses in the library, then rushes for his mail, sharing with roommates the latest romantic epistle from the gal or guy back home. Meals are wolfed down, amid much calorie-counting, compensated for by several sundaes later on. From 7 to 10 P.M. are "quiet hours," so called because they are intended for study, but sometimes dedicated to bridge and gossip. Afterward there may be waterfights or raids of other floors, with toothpaste used to decorate walls and mirrors. Another prank is hiding alarm clocks in the counselor's room, each set to go off at a different hour. Finally, for the boy comes a late smoke, and for the girl, setting of pin curls and tumbling into bed, often well after midnight.

Hours unaccounted for in the foregoing are devoted to widely assorted activities, well adapted to a few who minor in classwork and major in campus. One may browse through the displays in the student union; he may relax before hi-fi or campus movie, ancient but free and generally fair. More popular, of course, is dating, easier to achieve for fellows than girls. With a boy-to-girl ratio of 1 to 1.5, the girls are the more predatory of the campus species. Especially keen is competition for Important Dates —such as for fraternity dances, or for Big Men on Campus. The losers, like good sports, pitch in and help the lucky ones get ready. They lend apparel, inspect the finished product, and lend motherly advice as their envied sisters float down to their dates in the lobby below.

Most popular non-varsity sport on campus is snack-barring—producing in the campus pub a scene of confusion. Around small tables hungry students dump into pitless stomachs an indiscriminate diet of Cokes, ice cream and potato chips. At other tables bridge fiends ply their tricks, while kibitzers knit sweaters for their boy friends. Occasionally a player struggles to his feet to feed the red-white-and-blue juke box grinding out its rhythms. Blending with the blare of bop is the buzz of campus gab and gossip, replete with the latest clichés. For here is the center of campus consumer research, where students share views on all the timely topics: the terrible test, the status of one's dieting, and techniques of winning dates and influencing profs.

Off campus, the 1961 student seeks out Vona's and Canale's for food, the Country Inn for atmosphere, and Buckland's for satisfying the herd-instinct, especially for the TGIF (Thank-God-It's-Friday) Club. The girl-seeking-a-date tries to get there early, to command an SP, or strategic position, where she will be noticed.

Organized recreations are equally prolific. In fact, joiners on campus may belong to fifteen clubs or more, according to a 1952 social psychology class, to gain prestige, security, and special benefits of the organization involved.

Of greatest importance, as always, is one's Greek affiliation, the more so since only one eligible student in three makes the grade. To accommodate even this fraction, there are currently six fraternities (Beta Tau Epsilon, Delta Kappa Kappa, Phi Sigma Phi, Psi Phi, Sigma Gamma, Sigma Tau Chi) and seven sororities (Alpha Delta Eta, Alpha Sigma Chi, Arethusa Eta, Phi Lambda Phi, Pi Delta Chi, Theta Chi Rho, and Alpha Epsilon).

Standards for matters like pledging and hazing are set by the Interfraternity or Intersorority Councils. Both groups require that pledges have an index of 2.0, and place a taboo on hard drinks in sorority houses.

As for manner of inducting fledglings, the Intersorority Council announced piously in 1952, "We're big girls now and ridiculous customs a thing of the past." Boys' reforms came later, when the 1959 hazing proved so hazardous as to evoke a special edict stopping it altogether—first such administrative interference in the history of the school. However, the circumstances were such that the students fully sanctioned the move.

Outside intervention was also necessary to dissociate local chapters from Greek organizations which practiced discrimination on the national level. At least one fraternity was open only to Christians as late as World War II. Finally State University ordered all student organizations, other than scholastic and religious ones, to sever their national fraternal affiliations and to eliminate discriminations in color, creed or national origin.[1]

Never since their founding has there been at Oswego any attempt to abolish the fraternal organizations altogether. "They give color to campus life," their advocates argue, "and they spark activities of many kinds." They have run the Greek games, operated the used book store, helped with the Red Cross Bloodmobile, addressed envelopes for the Crippled Children's Association, and assisted at the children's ward at the hospital. They have also sponsored less serious affairs, like Winter Weekend, Christmas carol serenades, float parades, and pie-eating contests.

The Greek organization also does much for its members.[2] It gives them a feeling of belonging, status, and security. It produces social know-how and poise. "I have seen some pretty rough diamonds acquire at least surface polish," says a fraternity sponsor. It sets standards of dress, behavior, and scholarship. In fact, in 1955 fraternities asked that the faculty report pledges whose work had fallen below par.

Nevertheless, an unvocal minority would abolish the Greek organizations, or at least open them to every would-be member. "There is an unhealthy striving to belong to this elite group," observed one faculty member. "And once membership is achieved, former friends are cut off." "The Greeks run the campus," said a second critic. "It's like the tail wagging the dog," added a third. "The independents have no organization, hence, little chance of winning campus elections." "Furthermore," said still another, "the Greeks encourage social arrogance. Though avowedly founded on brotherhood, gentle snobbery is their stock-in-trade." [3]

Worse is their effect on would-be members who fail to make the grade. "A youngster away from home for the first time has an imperative need to prove himself," says a member of the psychology staff. "Yet despite his best efforts he may find himself relegated to a lower-caste status. To make matters worse, the rejected one has no place to hide. In the sub-culture of the college campus one's status is terribly exposed."

Nevertheless, the great barriers to social equality on this, as on other campuses, cars and fraternities, remain. Advocates of equalitarianism and pedestrianism as yet find few adherents, at least few vocal ones.

Non-Greek social clubs have fared but poorly. The only current survivors are the Sons of the Wilted Wallet and the newly formed organization for the wives of married students. Other clubs are divided according to special classifications or groups. Each class has its organization, sponsoring such functions as Junior prom, Senior week, Senior ball, and class days.

The newest music organization is the Male Glee Club, indulging in such four-part harmonies as "Sippin' Cider Through a Straw" and "I've Got You Under My Skin." Religious and service organizations are the Canterbury Club (Episcopal), Hillel (Jewish), Newman Club (Catholic), Wesley Fellowship (Methodist), Oswego Christian Fellowship, the Lutheran Student Organization, and the Protestant Student Association, formerly the Oswego Protestant Youth Organization.

As for professional clubs, there are still Epsilon Pi Tau and Kappa Delta Pi, but the New York chapters of the Future Teachers Association have become the Students of the Education Association of New York State. Professional clubs by departments are the Industrial Arts Club, the Mathematics Club, Science Club, Social Studies Honors Society, Mathematics Honor Society, and English Honor Society. Dramatics organizations are the Blackfriars, open to any student; Alpha Psi Omega, with membership by invitation only; and the Children's Theatre, which develops and produces plays and operettas with children from the school of practice.

Clubs reflecting recent interest in politics and world events are the International Relations Club, Political Club, Debating Club, the Young Democrats and the Young Republicans. Debates may be on topics of general or of special local interest such as: "*Resolved,* that Oswego should adopt a policy of de-emphasizing extracurricular activities." Also with the aim of expanding horizons are the student-exchange program, inaugurated on December 15, 1953, whereby students visit each others' campuses; and the Lake Shore Amateur Radio Club, which has contacted hams all over the world, including the Soviet Union.[4]

Since its origin, the *Oswegonian* has retained much the same flavor and function. It is still the chief organ of student opinion. "When we do not speak for all, the letters pour in," says faculty sponsor Mildred Larson. Her own function she describes as follows:

> I must make students aware of the best journalistic and typographic trends in our country; to acquaint them with the journalist's responsibility to his readers in presenting facts fairly and in giving all the facts possible. I have tried to set a "tone" which prevents students from think-

ing of the paper as a vehicle for their own personal ideas. . . . As an English teacher I read copy to check spelling and grammar but any material which requires rewriting is turned back to the individual reporter or to the editor.

Enthusiasm for athletics has accelerated of recent years because of a combination of coaching staff and winning teams. In fact, athletic victories are becoming another Oswego tradition. The wrestling team, for example, had an undefeated season in 1957. The soccer team won eight games and lost but three in 1959. In 1958 and again in 1960 Oswego won the Annual State University Invitational Basketball Tournament.

Meanwhile, individual athletes are setting new local records. In the 1959–60 basketball season, Ron Davis established an average of 23.5 points per game beating the previous record set by Ted Murray in 1956. Ron Benwell set a scoring record in soccer in 1959, and Ralph Maru, a baseball batting record in 1960.

Another milestone was affiliation, in 1958, with the Eastern Collegiate Athletic Conference and the National Collegiate Athletic Association, which necessitated addition of freshman teams and, as a consequence, expansion of the coaching staff.

Intramural sports are still sponsored by the Women's Athletic Association and the Men's Recreation Association. Both are nationally affiliated and set up intramural competitions in such sports as bowling, volleyball and basketball. They also check out equipment for use by individuals or by groups. Sports clubs are the Catalina Club, a synchronized swim and water-ballet group for women organized by Alice Reardon; the Bit and Spur, a coeducational riding club, begun by Marguerite Roberts Kranz in 1956; the recently reactivated Ski Club; and a Scuba Diving Club initiated by students Pio Venditti and Al Prysmont in 1960.

The 1959 summer activities included swimming, canoeing, golf, tennis, horseback riding, softball, camping, fishing, weekend tours, and a supervised playground for students' children. In addition, the men have intramural competition in football, basketball, volleyball, squash, handball, bowling and softball. And women's sports include volleyball, basketball, softball, golf, tennis, horseback riding, archery, bowling, badminton, skiing, and trampoline. Highlighting their program are intramural tournaments and sports days, when teams from colleges in the area compete.

All sports, intramural and varsity, are guided by an Athletic Coordinating Council composed of three faculty members and six students. Their task is to act in a general advisory capacity and as arbiters in case of dispute. For example, teams used to be christened by custom instead of decree, playing under a host of handles. Finally, in 1955, all teams became the Lakers, with the official sanction of College Council, alumni, and students.[5]

Another of their problems is to define the degree of varsity emphasis, always a controversial problem. Prominent persons like President William Harper of the University of Chicago and President Charles Adams of the University of Wisconsin have favored athletic teams as a factor in augmenting the drawing power of institutions. Still others claim that intercollegiate sports produce sportsmanship, loyalty to a cause, team play, opportunities for democratic organization and individualism. "It's the public's language," says Dr. Hermann Cooper, executive dean of the State University of New York. "If you have it, do it right. Unfortunately, however, we haven't the financial support we need; teachers colleges lack monied alumni."

Others deplore the trend athletics in this country have taken. They contrast the American emphasis on mass enthusiasm and winning teams with the more wholesome British emphasis on the amateur spirit. Another criticism is the staggering cost. "Block-O has achieved another rape of the student body treasury," wrote an *Oswegonian* editor in 1955, citing $275 paid for the annual Block-O Banquet. Time taken from studies is another drawback.

In any case, varsity is no real issue at Oswego. "I'm the world's most non-athletic human being," confesses Professor Francis Hulme, "so what I say must be taken with a grain of salt. On some campuses athletics is the be-all and end-all of existence, but we haven't an unhealthy worship here." And he seems to be right. The majority bask in the glory of winning teams, but their world does not fall apart when their team takes a trouncing.

Major varsity sports continue to be soccer and basketball, with baseball a poor third because of the late spring. The interest in restoring football continues to fester without as yet having come to a head.

Besides regularly scheduled activities, there are many special occasions, including formals. There are also more serious concerns. There's Moving Up Day, instituted in 1955, when *rites de passage* are performed, student awards made, and class queens crowned. There is Religious Emphasis Weekend, instituted in 1954 and planned around some theme, for instance, "Time Out for God" in 1959. The Founders Day and Honors Convocation, October 12, 1960, featured an address by Harold Taylor, prominent author and educator. Latest entry to the parade of perennial events was the Festival of Arts, instituted in 1960 to create awareness of new arts developed in the twentieth century, and the first Homecoming Celebration, also established in 1960.

There are other special occasions created by time or circumstance. In this category was the student parade April 28, 1960, on behalf of desegregation. While many student parades were held over the country about this time, the local demonstration was respected for its dignified restraint. There were no brass bands, no wild orgies of emotion. While some deplored the relatively small number of students who took part, it should be recognized that no attempt was made to incorporate those who simply sought fanfare. Also timely was the survey in which students picked Richard Nixon and John Kennedy as Republican and Democratic Presidential candidates for 1960, a clairvoyant selection subsequently endorsed by both parties.

A further antidote to excess fun and frolic is service activity. A Community Chest quota of $1,500 was raised in 1960 by such activities as car wash, talent show, games carnival, and renouncement of one meal in the cafeteria, which earned $300.

Where the community is concerned, students have a good record. They may complain about the lack of local entertainment, and townspeople may grumble about the fraternity house next door, but town-gown hassles are unknown to this campus.

As for faculty-student relations, the chasm has become a furrow, but the gap remains. Students still comment that faculty members here are friendlier than their high school teachers. And there is no infallible side of the teacher's desk, though the grade-conscious student lets the prof have last word.

The student body may be roughly divided in many ways. The upstaters look on downstaters as brash and noisy, the downstaters on upstaters as hicks. Incoming math-science students preen themselves as prize plebes, while their peers look on them as intellectual snobs.

There's also the age-old status differentiation of lower and upper classmen, though less so than formerly. Time was when Freshmen bowed to Seniors and catered to Sophs. Samuel Eliot Morison noted: "The custom of 'fagging' whereby lower class members ran errands and served as unpaid servants for upper classmen were imported from England. An upper classman might say, 'Go to my room, take from it a pitcher, fill it from a pump, etc.'" [6] G. Stanley Hall called the practice a form of predatory aggression, and compared it to the primitive rites of savage peoples.[7]

Nowadays the not-so-lowly frosh serves a more painless apprenticeship. No longer is he ignored as the anonymous man on campus. A whole week is set aside in his honor, when he is treated to square dance, jam session, movies, coffee hour, picnic and freshman frolic. Nevertheless, he must still wear the green-and-gold beanie, bow to smokestacks, get upper-class autographs, and perform other painless but profitless rituals.

Not all the student's problems are social; he is also concerned over material matters—even food:

> The rolls at Oswego
> They say are mighty fine;
> One fell off a table
> And killed a friend of mine.

(Actually students like the food but griping about it is almost every school's tradition.)

More serious concerns include cars—how to pay for them, and where to park them. In 1958 only one in thirteen girls owned cars, but half the boys had them and believed them essential. Both sexes, in 1960, owned 564 cars among them.

An even greater concern is finance, especially for boys, who spend five dollars a week and up, pooled from family, vacation employment, or odd jobs through the year. Girls—who rely on Mom and Pop—generally spend from three to five dollars for miscellaneous items a week.

Needy students have recourse to far more loans and scholarships than ever before. Beginning in 1954, faculty and students have annually underwritten ten scholarships, equivalent to room rental and confined to the Freshman year. Three additional memorial loans and scholarships were recently established, one in memory of Professor James Moreland, another of Professor Jay Rudolph and his first wife Jessie, and a third of Carol King, popular young associate dean who died of a rare form of cancer.

There are also loans from outside. On the state level, in 1960, the New York Higher Assistance Corporation announced the guarantee of $6,500,000 in loans to needy college students. Federal loans had already become available, although only to students who signed a non-Communist affidavit—a stipulation many schools resent since such oaths are not required of other professional groups.

To insure that the student solve his problems, social or material, in socially acceptable ways, student governing services have expanded, now standing midway between the paternalistic treatment accorded women students of Sheldon's time and the autonomy of European schools. Student participation in government rather than self-government is still the policy, but the lead-them-by-the-hand philosophy is losing its grip. The Student Council coordinates all student organizations including the fifteen relating to sports which are under the Athletic Coordinating Council. For supporting these organizations, students assess themselves an activity fee, currently about twenty-five dollars a semester.

Oswego's student government, though fairly typical, and certainly less rigid than most, arouses conflicting faculty comment. Many approve it as sufficiently conservative to insure proper supervision, sufficiently liberal to foster independence. Others, here as elsewhere, remain suspicious of the student personnel movement and espouse relative autonomy instead.[8] "We wet-nurse students," says one faculty member, "and control their activities too rigidly. There is not the freedom to grow up and make decisions that there is on a liberal arts campus." "I think that the boys' rules are all right but girls are treated like children," asserts another. "What's sauce for the goose should be sauce for the gander!"

One move toward student autonomy was abolition of compulsory chapel in 1953, partly because students had come to exceed in number places to seat them. It could hardly be called a moral victory, for protests against chapel had stemmed more from boredom than from any more fundamental conviction.[9] At any rate, the present-day chapel committee faces a challenge to make programs sufficiently stimulating to lure students to attend them.

A conflict of far shorter duration arose over school colors which, since the early days, had been green and gold. In 1959, however, the band created a furor by purchasing uniforms in red and navy. About the same time, a group of students, finding no official record of school colors, favored a change from green and gold to green and white. The battle still rages, with nothing as yet officially decided.

Nor yet fully settled is the question of a school song. Many alumni still prefer Caroline Scales's song, "O, Blue Ontario's Waters," while present students acknowledge "Voices Fill the Air," but neither is "official." Maurice Boyd, chairman of the Music Department, reports that some people dislike the present song, and suggests laughingly that before long we may have a third. Anyhow, some other historian will have to record the outcome.

Emerging from all the conflicts and experiences we have described is the student's reaction to his school, a somewhat mixed one today. All are proud of its great history and all still convinced its professional training is sound. But they feel some inferiority, too, having been brain-washed with the propaganda that teacher-training institutions are inferior to liberal arts schools, and state schools to private ones. "They have been exposed to prestige thinking," explains one staff member. "Our girls took to body mechanics more readily when shown pictures of Smith girls taking such work."

Certainly, the 1961 student lacks the campus chauvinism of Sheldon's day or the passionate partisanship of Yale men, but the picture steadily brightens. The difference shows in the comments below, the first by an alumnus of 1951, the second by one of 1960:

My high school guidance counselor said to me, "You are crazy to go to Oswego Normal." Let's face it, there was not much campus then. Some of the high school campuses beat this one.

When I go out debating, I don't have to say I'm from a teachers college any more. I can say, "I'm from the State University of New York, College of Education at Oswego." It sounds impressive. It raises others' respect for us and makes us feel good.

Perhaps a lack of conspicuous chauvinism may derive partially from the present-day student's tendency to view himself critically—encouraged by world crisis and attacks on education. When Professor William McGarvey suggested to a class of Seniors that college letters be given to those who successfully completed practice teaching, the reaction was "What do such symbols matter? We are after substance, not symbols."

Concrete evidence of the student's hunger for solid substance exists in data concerning use of the library. According to Head Librarian Helen Hagger:

> Present facilities have been used to the utmost. The number of students using the Main Library for research and study purposes during the 1960 college year totaled 85,650. Students using the temporary corridor facilities numbered 22,831. Averaging these figures, we find that each student had need of the library resources sixty-three times during the college year. . . . A significant commentary on the type of usage is the fact that only 4 per cent of the total overnight circulation involves books on reserve; the remaining 96 per cent are books the student wants to read on his own.

Perhaps the soundest evidence of strong morale lies in the heightened alumni activity, channeled through fifty-seven active chapters as far west as California. Over 350 of them, including the oldest living graduate, Emma Dashley, '84, attended the Alumni Banquet of 1960, a vast increase over other years. A special feature was the presentation at the graduation exercises of the first Distinguished Alumnus Award, to be awarded annually, to Benjamin Van Oot, '05, longtime head of industrial and vocational education in the state of Virginia.

Contributing heavily to mounting morale is the campus, often acclaimed the finest in the state. Still cherished is the venerable main building; still revered the weather-beaten statue which guards it; and still admired its unexcelled natural endowment. To the east are the red and green rooftops of the city, the smokestacks like giant needles piercing the sky, and the lighthouse keeping watch over the harbor. In summer the student delights in the lake's gold-flecked surface. And in winter he clutches his cap, and leans into the wind, awed by nature's most terrifying but magnificent tantrums. And sometimes he stands by the shore admiring the giant ice caves, produced by swells beneath the flexible ice fields, turning the piles of ice into cones.

But it is the new construction that instills in him a confidence in the future, and his step involuntarily quickens to the rhythm of hammers and buzz of saws. He gazes upward at the skeletal girders silhouetted against the sky like great spiders, and at the men astride them like so many agile insects. He strides along new sidewalks, picks his way over boards and muddy trails, then relaxes over stretches of newly laid sidewalks. Sometimes he leaps over little pools of stagnant water or turns up his nose at the hot-tar odor. Presently he raises his voice to greet a friend above the din of drills and grind of steam shovels.

For Oswego at the century mark is a school on the move, growing in strength. And while the young student occasionally grumbles about the mud and the noises, he secretly relishes being identified with his school in its era of growth.

CHAPTER 15

Recent Developments

THE past decade at Oswego has seen many important events, arranged by man or by nature. In fall, 1953, a committee of the American Association of Colleges for Teachers Association evaluated and reported favorably on the college. In 1958 the St. Lawrence Seaway opened, offering bright prospects for the town and, indirectly, the college. An unplanned event was the Big Snow in December, 1958, deepest in the history of Oswego. The town was cut off from the outside world, the college shut down, and the Campus School children bedded down for one night in the gymnasium. . . . Throughout the period came a succession of important professional meetings—convocations, symposia, workshops, and conferences—for the benefit of the area served by the college.

Recent years have also seen alumni activity revitalized, with Robert Helsby as first regularly employed alumni executive secretary and Mrs. Hilda Bohall as president. In 1957 these two established a Fifty-Year Club, composed of alumni who had graduated a half-century ago or more. This organization superseded the Half-Century Club begun in 1937 by Isabel Hart. In 1960 the June alumni program was expanded from a one-day banquet and torchlight ceremony to a big three-day alumni weekend.

The biggest event of them all—at least for recent years—is the Centennial Celebration, for which this history is specially prepared. Commemorative events begin with the Elementary Education Conference on April 19, with a major address by Dr. Hermann Cooper, executive dean of teacher education for State University, because of his important role in New York teacher education. They culminate in the Convocation on Founder's Day, including an address by President of State University Thomas Hale Hamilton and the dedication and naming of several new buildings. Features will include a twenty-minute motion picture in color and a television program—both showing highlights in the history

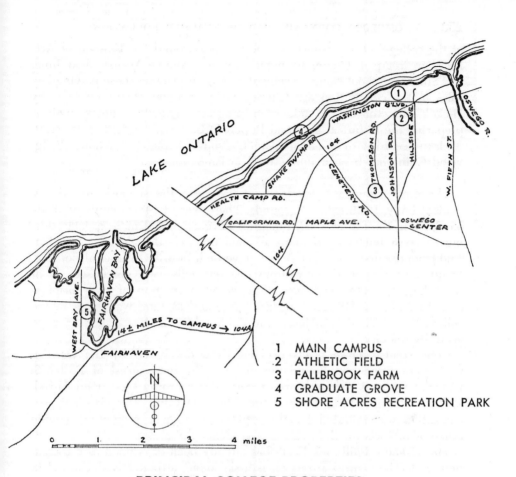

LAKE ONTARIO

OSWEGO R.

WASHINGTON B'LVD.

SNAKE SWAMP RD.

CEMETERY RD.

THOMPSON RD.

JOHNSON RD.

HILLSIDE AVE.

W. FIFTH ST.

HEALTH CAMP RD.

CALIFORNIA RD.

MAPLE AVE.

OSWEGO CENTER

104

104

WEST BAY AVE.

FAIRHAVEN BAY

14± MILES TO CAMPUS → 104A

FAIRHAVEN

N

0   1   2   3   4 miles

1   MAIN CAMPUS
2   ATHLETIC FIELD
3   FALLBROOK FARM
4   GRADUATE GROVE
5   SHORE ACRES RECREATION PARK

PRINCIPAL COLLEGE PROPERTIES
AS OF 1961

of the college. Other events will be focused around the Festival of Arts Program in April, Commencement Day and Alumni Weekend in June; and Summer School Commencement in August. Among those playing key roles in the celebration are Charles Wells, general chairman; Dorothy Hickok, director of the television program; Theodore Beers, who is preparing the historical film; and Rupert Stroud, who is writing its script. And, in accord with common custom, a souvenir plate of famous Wedgwood China has been manufactured in England.

The most significant development has been the school's growth—in student body, facilities and grounds. There were 1,148 students in 1952–53; 2,282 in the fall of 1960. Facilities have expanded more quickly during the past ten years than in all nine previous decades put together. And from the first President Brown gave high priority to student housing. In quick succession six off-campus resident halls were purchased, all of them large private residences obtained at a fraction of their original cost. In addition, Hillcrest, a former orphans' asylum, was given to the college by the Children's Home, and Fallbrook Farm, former home for the aged, by the city.

Concurrently, large tracts of land were purchased by the Oswego College of Education Foundation, whose directors consist of Foster S. Brown, Charles S. Turner, Carey P. Salander, Dorothy Mott, Paul Alfred, William Purvis, Hilda Bohall, and Mary McCann Murphy. This organization was initiated for the express purpose of promoting a wide range of projects for the welfare of students and alumni.

The 150-acre Fallbrook Farm has already been developed as a recreation area. The central attraction is a ski lodge, attractively decorated in knotty pine, with ski equipment area, snack bar and fireplace. A huge picture window overlooks the ski tow, toboggan slope, and outdoor riding ring. Adjacent are the modern stables, indoor riding arena and tack room. The sylvan setting roundabout provides picknicking spots and riding trails.

Another tract of eighty acres, located on Snake Swamp Road and formerly known as Dowie's Grove, and two adjacent properties will eventually be equipped with cabins, bathing beach, camping area, and picnic ground. It will also provide tenting and cottage facilities for graduate summer school students.

Several factors led to the enormous growth of the main campus, after nine decades of snail-like expansion: national prosperity, the college boom, parental support, and two administrators with unusual vision—Hermann Cooper and Foster Brown. "Parents are more interested in housing, about which they know much, than in curriculum, about which they know little," says Hermann Cooper. The public corroborated Dr.

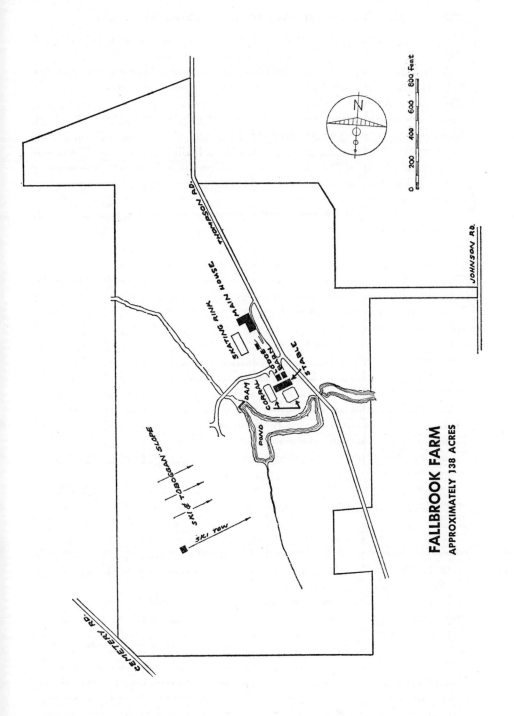

FALLBROOK FARM
APPROXIMATELY 138 ACRES

CEMETERY RD.

SKI TOW

SKI & TOBOGGAN SLOPE

POND

DAM

CORRAL

LODGE

BARN

STABLE

SKATING RINK

MAIN HOUSE

THOMPSON RD.

JOHNSON RD.

N

0   200   400   600   800 Feet

Cooper's assertion by endorsing a bond issue which authorized $250 million for capital development of State University.

In consequence, one giant building after another has risen under the present administration. All are of the latest design; no Gothic towers are these, binding us to a distant past. First came the Mary V. Lee Health and Physical Education Building in 1958. Then, directly on the lake shore appeared Lakeside Dining Hall (1958), and three new dormitories—Johnson Hall in 1958, Riggs and Waterbury Halls in 1960. Another one is now under construction. Each of these buildings presents far-ranging vistas of Lake Ontario, which lies directly below. Also affording a magnificent panorama of the lake and town is the Lida E. Penfield Library, informally nicknamed Hagger's Hut after the present boss of books and stacks. Next to rise will be a mathematics and science building, including roof observatory, radiological and botanical laboratories, and an education building jointly housing the Campus School, Education and Psychology Departments, Audio-Visual Center and Educational Clinic. Anticipated, though not yet programmed, are a fine arts building, field house, and additional dormitories. All told, Oswego has come a long way from the single cloakroom where Miss Jones held her classes.

None of these buildings had been given names until special ceremonies were held for that purpose on November 9, 1959. At that time Lee Hall was named for Mary V. Lee, pioneer woman physician and member of the Sheldon faculty (1874–92); Waterbury Hall for Edwin M. Waterbury (1884–1953), editor and publisher of the *Oswego Palladium-Times* and chairman of the former Board of Visitors; and Johnson Hall for Harold B. Johnson (1880–1949), editor and president of the *Watertown Daily Times*, chairman of the Board of Visitors, who contributed to developing this institution into a degree-granting college.

Also in 1959 Lonis Hall was named for Ernest J. Lonis (1878–1954), alumnus, state legislator and member of the Board of Visitors who, like Harold Johnson, assisted the Normal School to attain college status. The Lida S. Penfield Library was named for Lida S. Penfield (1873–1956), formerly chairman of the English Department; and Hewitt Union for Jesse Merle Hewitt (1898–1918), the first student of the Oswego State Normal School to be killed in World War I.

Two years later, in 1961, other buildings, subsequently erected or soon to be erected, as well as several residence halls and streets, were named as follows: The Main Administration Building was named Sheldon Hall in honor of the founder; the Education Wing of the Education Building, Poucher Hall in memory of the second principal and his wife Matilda Cooper Poucher; the Campus School Wing, Swetman Hall for the fourth principal; the Mathematics-Science Building for the long-time campus favorite, Richard Piez; a residence hall for Caroline Scales, outstanding

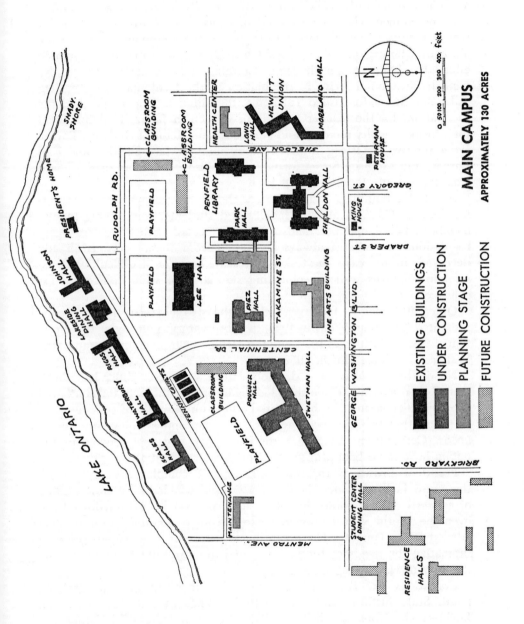

MAIN CAMPUS

APPROXIMATELY 130 ACRES

EXISTING BUILDINGS

UNDER CONSTRUCTION

PLANNING STAGE

FUTURE CONSTRUCTION

N

0 50 100 200 300 400 Feet

LAKE ONTARIO

SHADY SHORE

PRESIDENT'S HOME

JOHNSON HALL

LAKESIDE DINING HALL

RIGGS HALL

WATERBURY HALL

SCALES HALL

MAINTENANCE

TENNIS COURTS

CLASSROOM BUILDING

PLAYFIELD

POUCHER HALL

SWETMAN HALL

CENTENNIAL DR.

RUDOLPH RD.

PLAYFIELD

PLAYFIELD

CLASSROOM BUILDING

CLASSROOM BUILDING

PENFIELD LIBRARY

PARK HALL

LEE HALL

PIEZ HALL

TAKAMINE ST.

FINE ARTS BUILDING

HEALTH CENTER

LOWIS HALL

HEWITT UNION

MORELAND HALL

SHELDON AVE.

SHELDON HALL

GREGORY ST.

KING HOUSE

PETERMAN HOUSE

DRAPER ST.

GEORGE WASHINGTON BLVD.

MENTAO AVE.

BRICKYARD RD.

STUDENT CENTER & DINING HALL

RESIDENCE HALLS

253

teacher of English. The living centers formerly known as Draper, Piez, and Ontario are to be called the Carol King House for a popular young dean of women who recently died of cancer; the Farnham House for former faculty member Amos Farnham; and the Peterman House for the alumnus who organized the Boys' Club (N.Y.C. alumni) and promoted efforts to obtain campus housing. Certain roads on campus were also named: Centennial Drive in recognition of the Centennial Celebration; Takamine Street for Hideo Takamine, the alumnus who established the foundations for the teacher training of women in Japan; Rudolph Road for a former faculty member and generous benefactor of students; Barnes Drive for two of Oswego's most famous alumni, Mary Sheldon and Earl Barnes; and Mollison Street for Gilbert Mollison, chairman of the board from the school's founding until 1911.

Names for buildings and streets are chosen by a committee representing College Council, alumni, faculty and students from among faculty members, board members and alumni. In accord with State University regulation, names must always be chosen from among persons already deceased. In any case, the task is not easy, because of difficulties in assembling data as well as conflicting standards of what constitutes excellence.

Other additions to facilities include the six-inch refracting telescope presented by Lillian Wells in 1955, the observatory built under the direction of George Pitluga in 1956, and the carillon bells given by Mr. and Mrs. Walter P. Phillips, also in 1956.

Nor is the end of campus development in sight. No sooner had President Brown assumed office than he began paving the way for continued expansion. Then, in 1955, he initiated a long-range study of college needs to insure that facilities be practical, aesthetic, and adequate for future needs. Certainly no unit of State University and few schools in the nation have more beautiful grounds or greater potential for growth.

President Brown warns, however, against complacency, even with these new facilities, since the bumper crop of war babies is now coming of age. All the temporary buildings have not yet been torn down—not even the World War I appendage to the main building, appropriately labeled "The Tunnel." These ramshackle structures, however, serve to dramatize the needs of the College, and are carefully included on the itinerary of visiting legislators.

Conditions like these are the inevitable manifestations of growing pains. State institutions must justify buildings in order to get them; facilities therefore lag behind. "We are in a state of bursting our swaddling clothes," says Frank Hulme, "and instruction suffers." Furthermore, communications have become difficult. The left hand doesn't know what the right hand is doing. Students even fail to recognize the

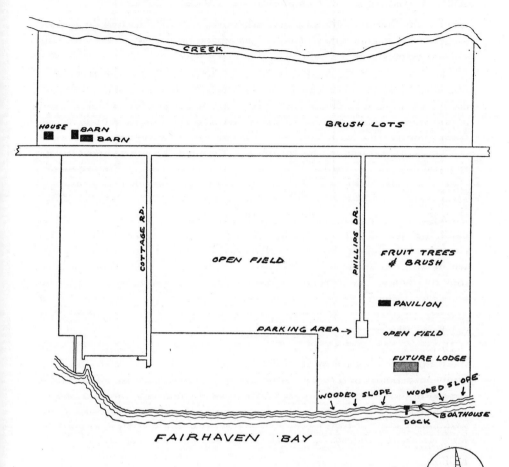

CREEK

HOUSE BARN BARN

BRUSH LOTS

COTTAGE RD.

PHILLIPS DR.

OPEN FIELD

FRUIT TREES & BRUSH

■ PAVILION

← PARKING AREA →

OPEN FIELD

FUTURE LODGE

WOODED SLOPE   WOODED SLOPE

DOCK   BOATHOUSE

FAIRHAVEN BAY

0 50 100   200   200   400 feet

N

SHORE ACRES RECREATION PARK
APPROXIMATELY 80 ACRES

faculty member who gives them a ride down the hill. Meanwhile, departments have become increasingly specialized and less concerned with college interests as a whole.

The adverse effects of growth, however, have been outnumbered by its benefits. More students call for better and more varied facilities—blue chips in raising the college stock. They are necessary for evolution from a post-high-school program to university status; campus morale profits from identification with something big and growing bigger.

The parallel between the fortunes of Oswego the town, and Oswego the college has persisted. Many college towns have one industry and that, education, but not Oswego. Actually, the city has one cardinal asset: it is the first port-of-call on many ocean-going vessels coming through the newly opened St. Lawrence Seaway. The city's effort to capitalize on its assets, coordinated by the State Port Authority, the Chamber of Commerce, and civic enterprise, called Operation Oswego, was revitalized during the 1950's, the same period that the college undertook its phenomenal burst of expansion. One significant outcome was the choice of Oswego by Aluminium, Ltd., for a thirty-million-dollar plant, and students joined with townspeople in a parade on February 21 to celebrate the event.

However impressive Oswego's recent growth may be, expansion even more epochal seems now in the offing. On January 18, 1961, the State University Board of Trustees submitted to Governor Nelson Rockefeller a $600 million, ten-year program which held important implications for every unit within the University including Oswego. The program, if implemented, will by 1970 involve expanding the full-time student capacity from 42,000 to 145,000 and tripling the annual operating costs to $155 million.

The Colleges of Education at Buffalo and Albany would immediately become multipurpose institutions while the other nine would incorporate liberal arts and sciences at the upper division levels. Students, therefore, could transfer from the University's network of two-year colleges to the Colleges of Education to complete their liberal arts degrees. This provision would assume special significance at Oswego, because the Master Plan calls for the establishment of community colleges in the three populous counties which ring Oswego County—Onondaga, Jefferson, and Monroe. In consequence, Oswego has been assigned the fifth highest student quota for the four-year colleges within State University, with certain of the enrollments projected for 1970 as follows: the Long Island Center, 13,000; Buffalo, 8,000; Albany, 6,200; Harpur (at Endicott), 6,000; Oswego, 5,000; Brockport, 3,330; Cortland, 3,400; Oneonta, 3,560; Plattsburg, 2,875; and Potsdam, 2,450.

The plan would also call for a full-time Master's degree program in the Colleges of Education. The program is currently carried on through extension and summer school courses.

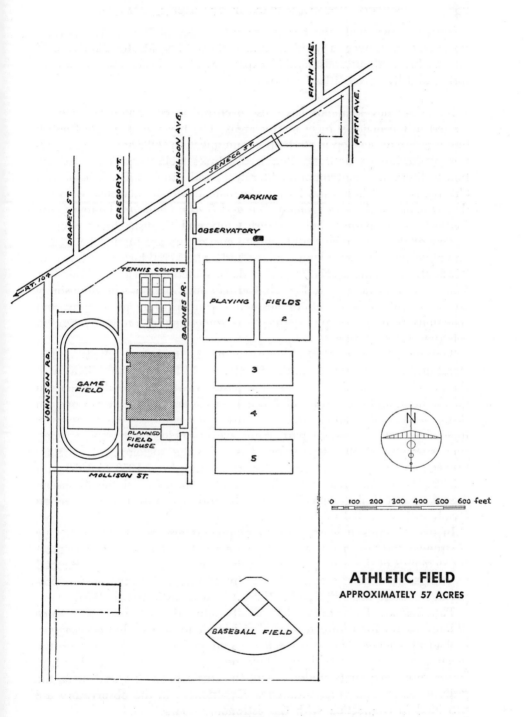

ATHLETIC FIELD
APPROXIMATELY 57 ACRES

Foster Brown hails the board's report as one of the most important documents in Oswego's hundred-year history. "The Master Plan will, of course, bring about considerable expansion of staff, classrooms, laboratories, and living facilities," he said.

Important developments have also occurred in curriculum, as demonstrated in the major subject matter areas. The basic aims of the English offerings are to develop in students communication skills and an appreciation of the literary heritage. Required courses include speech, introduction to literature, contemporary literature, and composition. The newest elective is world literature. Extracurricular activities connected with the department are the *Oswegonian, Pen and Brush, Ontarian,* Drama Club, Radio Club, Debating Club, English Club, and English Honor Society.

Two of the more recent additions to curriculum are foreign languages and philosophy. Foreign language has had a checkered history at Oswego; it was strongly emphasized in earlier days, sometimes deleted altogether. Languages now taught are French, German and Spanish. The philosophy course—including logic, ethics, aesthetics, contemporary philosophy, and selections from major philosophers—is something of an innovation in this type of institution.

The aim of the social studies instructors is "to help students understand and assume responsibilities for the world in which they live, with the present explained in terms of the past." All students study American government, and the history of Europe, Africa and Asia. Latin American history is treated as an elective. Recently, great emphasis has been given to Africa, and the eastern part of the world, including Russia. A long-time specialty of the department has been the sociology of religion; Oswego was one of fifteen centers participating from 1953 to 1958 in a pilot study in this area under the general sponsorship of the American Association of Colleges for Teacher Education and the specific direction locally of Seward Salisbury.

In mathematics at least three developments are worthy of note. One is stronger interest in this area, largely a result of the challenge to meet the demands of the new space age. Another is a concern for fundamental meanings, not merely applications. In addition, a program for preparing teachers of secondary mathematics was instituted in 1957.

The Science Department has as its aim "the increase of science literacy useful for future teachers." All students study physical science, biological science, and earth science and geography. Features of the geography course are field trips, both on and off campus. A harbor trip, for example, acquaints students with the steam plant, the coal dock, the grain elevator, and other industries. Experiences in the observatory are provided in connection with the astronomy course.

An important innovation in this area, as of fall, 1958, was the initiation of opportunities to specialize in biology, chemistry, physical science or earth science. Groups of hand-picked students keep instructors on their toes and communicate their interests to other students.

Another science, psychology, is included in the departments of education in all the State University Colleges of Education except Oswego and Albany, where it is a separate department. The Oswego system has its advantages. Every student learns the fundamentals of personality theory, human development, and educational psychology from a specialist. In fact, the department chairman, Donald Snygg, author of the classic work *Individual Behavior,* is one of the foremost authorities in America in the field of phenomenological psychology. Here are two of the numerous testimonials to the importance of this book—actually only one of Dr. Snygg's publications in this area:

> The initial publication of *Individual Behavior* excited the psychological world with its thesis that behavior can be understood only in terms of the individual's personal frame of reference. Subsequent research by many investigators has lent support to this perceptual view of behavior.[1]

> Probably Donald Snygg deserves more credit than any other person for really pushing the perceptual approach in the U.S., despite the steady scorn of the behaviorists. Responding to his call—issued twenty years ago—for a phenomenological system of psychology, a number of us have been making studies which demonstrate the fruitfulness of this orientation in various fields—such as intergroup relations, education, psychotherapy, and rehabilitation.[2]

A wide offering of electives in the Psychology Department permits interested students to establish sufficient background for graduate work in guidance or educational psychology—specialties for which teacher training is excellent preparation. Finally, the presence of a Psychology Department makes possible such services as testing.

The Music Department proclaims a dual purpose: "to give students a chance to grow in music and to prepare elementary students to utilize music in classroom teaching situations." Requirements differ to some extent according to levels students are preparing to teach. For example, all students take music appreciation, but only those majoring in early childhood education are required to take piano and to teach rote songs. New electives include music appreciation in opera, in symphony, and in contemporary music. And recent trends indicate a greater emphasis on music appreciation, on student music organizations and on liberalization of course content.

The aim of the Art Department is simply "to give students fuller realization of man's need for art and its role in living." Reflecting these aims in the required course for elementary education Juniors is the blending of art education, art psychology, and crafts.

Liberal arts colleges normally accord greater attention to art than does a school of this type. "However," says Aulus Saunders, chairman of the Art Department, "Oswego has two striking advantages in this area. For one thing, we have wonderful outdoor work space. The lake and surrounding scenery are ideal. We can get into the country in a hurry. Second, our industrial arts specialty would seem to help make this campus a natural for a major in art."

Also a part of the academic offering, despite its professional-sounding name, is physical education, required of all students for the first two years. Emphasis is on recreational habits and skills which carry over into later life. Both women's and men's departments offer team sports, bowling, swimming, social dancing, trampoline, horseback riding, and archery.

Among the purely professional offerings, are the elementary education curricula which follow: Graduates from the four-year early childhood program receive certificates licensing them to teach nursery school through grade three. Students who complete the elementary education program are permitted to teach in the elementary grades. And those who take the junior high program can, after four years and one summer, obtain a provisional certificate to teach English or citizenship education in the junior high schools of the state. Permanent certification hinges on satisfying requirements for teaching at least one major subject in the academic field. Still others obtain the elementary education degree with an industrial arts minor, as discussed elsewhere.

The current elementary education program, as initiated in 1959, may be outlined as follows. A course in observation and child development is followed by a sequence of three four-semester-hour laboratory courses. The first, designed to give the student a better introduction to teaching as a profession, consists of some eighty clock hours of participation in the Campus School program. He becomes acquainted with the philosophy and function of the elementary school, and with applications of child development concepts to classroom situations. The second laboratory course deals with language arts and social studies, the third with mathematics and science. Concurrent laboratory experiences include work in the children's library, and in the curriculum, reading, and audio-visual laboratories, besides observation of demonstration lessons and further participation in classroom work.

Next comes student teaching with specific problems treated in seminar discussions. Currently over three hundred students are assigned by Coordinators Theodore Moss, Kenneth Jones, and James Hastings to public school systems over the state, including the New York City and Utica-Rome areas, where resident supervisors are assigned.

Important additions to the professional curriculum are the junior and senior high school programs. The junior high school program, added in 1956, permitted students to earn an extension of their elementary certification to cover teaching in the junior high schools in the areas of English, mathematics, science, and social studies—limited after 1959 to English and social studies. In many schools the junior high program is simply added onto the elementary curriculum, but here it is organized around three blocks—general education, arts and mathematics-science. The five-year senior high program for training secondary mathematics and science teachers was instituted in the fall of 1959.

The fulcrum of the education program remains the Campus School. I. B. Poucher's statement of fifty years ago would be equally fitting today: "From the time when the memory of man runneth not to the contrary, the practice school experience has been regarded as the most important one in the normal course."

The present school encompasses nursery school through grade nine, with two groups on each grade level. In addition, the school has its own library, health service, and cafeteria, where lunches are provided for twenty-five cents with milk for three cents extra. Three-fourths of the children, all unselected, are drawn from adjacent districts and one-fourth from the city. In 1956, the program was expanded to include the ninth grade, thus making possible a junior high program.

In Campus School, as on college level, criticism has led to re-examination of methods and goals. More emphasis is placed on depth and thoroughness. Skills, even drill, while perceived as merely a means to an end, have regained respectability. Foreign language instruction begins in the fourth grade. Higher education's concern for mathematics and science has filtered to this level. The elementary science movement has gained new strength, being far richer in ideas and better adapted to children than was the first such movement of the 1870's. Also evident is an increased flexibility. For instance, mathematics-science students are sectioned but, except in the area of the specialty, are placed with other students. A distinctive feature is the opportunity for both sexes to take shop and home economics.

The co-curricular program is rich and varied. The Children's Theatre class, initiated in 1959, directs Campus School plays. Last year's offering included *Why Indians Wore Moccasins,* and *Strictly Puritan.* In 1960, the Campus School joined the St. Lawrence Valley Educational Television Council. Kinescopes developed under the Regents Educational Television Project are made available to classrooms. Recent programs include a science series for kindergarten through grade two, and special music films featuring orchestral instruments. Still other co-curricular activities stress science—notably the Annual Science Fair and camp trips to Racquette Lake.

Service projects are frequent. Constance Bond's fifth grade sponsored a Campus School drive to collect school supplies for Philippine schools. The drive was closed with a Philippine dinner, featuring coconut and pineapple chips, banana bread and Philippine punch.

Coordinating the professional program is the Professional Council, initiated by Charles Turner and composed of persons representing major areas and activities within the division and chaired by the director of the Division of Elementary Education.

Two interdepartmental courses, instituted in 1955, run the gamut of the main disciplines. Both courses give students a broad understanding of man and his relation to the universe as seen from the point of view of different academic areas. In "The Nature of Man" course, man is seen from the points of view of biology, physical and social science, humanities and religion. The "Frontiers of Knowledge" course treats outstanding issues and developments in biology, physical and social science and the way they relate to society.

The "Frontiers of Knowledge" course became the first to be offered by the college on television in 1957. Second was a course in American literature by Dr. Francis Hulme. "I got some very flattering letters," he confesses. "Most of those who got something from it were seeking informal, delightful entertainment in an area with which they were already acquainted."

Industrial arts education can claim an assortment of goals. It is said to increase social effectiveness and help build habits of analysis, planning concentration, and appreciation of materials. Industrial arts education at Oswego currently constitutes a phase of general education, meeting youth's common needs in an industrial society. The aim for junior high school is exploratory, while the senior high is more directly concerned with occupational choice.

Industrial arts offerings at present are of four types. (1) Elementary education students take a two-semester-hour program, learning to use tools, and, in a group project, to help children working together. (2) The majority of the I.A. students continue to take the regular industrial arts major certifying them to teach from kindergarten through grade twelve, though almost all of them teach on the secondary level. (3) The elementary industrial arts program includes electives in elementary education, and a laboratory course. It is for the industrial arts student who proposes to take charge of an elementary school program. (4) Conversely, the elementary education industrial arts program is for the elementary student who takes a special program of industrial arts electives in order to guide crafts and construction activities in the elementary school. Since this program is something of an innovation its coordinator, Robert Babcock, has outlined its main points:

> The elementary student has a two-semester-hour required laboratory course. He first makes something useful, something for which he feels an immediate need. It may be a book rack or something else for his dormitory room. He then constructs a number of individual items using a variety of materials. Then the class makes several group projects so they will have some understanding of the problems of different kinds of children working together. At this time we have no electives in industrial arts for elementary education students but one is certainly coming.
>
> The E.E.I.A. program actually begins in the Sophomore year with a series of laboratory courses—four-semester-hour courses meeting eight hours a week. In the first course, they have drawing and planning, interpreting ideas on paper. They must be able to explain plans to classroom teachers and children. The second course deals with group projects, such as may be suitable for third grade arithmetic, sixth grade health and safety, etc. They run the gamut of learning and grade levels. They also learn to get materials ready for teachers and children.
>
> As Sophomores they have participation just as other students do, but they are supposed to help out wherever possible with activities involving their specialty. Then in the Junior year they learn the nature of a demonstration, and construction experiences with a wide variety of materials are included. They perform and evaluate each other. Their practice teaching consists in nine weeks in the common branches; in nine operating out of a shop.
>
> In their Senior year they have a seminar to correct weaknesses, to experiment, and to learn to administer an industrial arts program—designing a laboratory, ordering materials, etc.
>
> When they graduate they receive a common branch certificate as well as a certificate indicating their preparation for this area—given first in 1959.
>
> As adviser to the E.E.I.A. students, I've noticed that they get to be a little clique, or like a family. It helps build morale. They help each other. One boy with a high index helped others who were in some scholastic difficulty.

The foregoing curricula—as revised—went into effect September, 1959, representing the first important modifications since 1936. Additional work became required in psychology, music, art, science, and mathematics. To permit a realistic setting for methods, the methods and materials course was combined with the general shop to become an applied methods laboratory. Greater concentration was permitted in some technical area, to meet the challenge of the senior high school. Many central schools now have more than one shop teacher, making it desirable that each have his own specialty. Furthermore, since the growth of junior high school shops, the senior high school shop often requires more advanced work than it did formerly. Finally, advanced progress in technology necessitates depth of preparation. In order to permit incorporation of all these essentials, electives were somewhat reduced.

Naturally, the shops themselves reflect the expansion in aims and curriculum. According to Frank Robinson, chairman of the Department of Laboratories:

> Most laboratories are organized on a basis of wood, metal, and electricity—even in teacher-training institutions. Some add a hobby-crafts course, including basketry, photography, and leather. In addition to all these, we have graphic arts, textiles, ceramics, and transportation. The transportation laboratory has great breadth. Most schools concentrate either on marine, aircraft or auto mechanics. We divide transportation into land, sea, and air. We are now concerned with learning experiences leading to the understanding of space travel and astronautics.

The driver education program is also strong, taking due cognizance of its status as the fastest growing high school subject of the past decade.

Addenda to the regular curriculum include graduate work, extension courses, and foreign study. The graduate program, initiated in 1947, was placed under a full-time director of graduate, extension, and summer session programs in 1959. Programs leading to a Master of Science degree are offered in elementary school education, industrial arts education, vocational industrial education, junior high school education, English, social studies, secondary school science, elementary school administration, and since 1959, a program for permanent certification of elementary school principals and supervisors. In addition, an intensive teacher training program is provided for liberal arts graduates who wish to make a career of elementary school teaching.

The program is rapidly expanding. Twelve hundred and fifty students attended the summer session of 1959 alone, with 623 presently seeking the Master of Science degree. Also flourishing is the extension program which, in spring, 1960, offered twenty-seven extension courses in centers up to one hundred miles away.

Incorporated into the summer school program are various professional and cultural features such as conferences, workshops, lectures, and reading hours—as well as a wealth of recreational opportunities. Especially noteworthy are inexpensive school-sponsored tours to the Niagara frontier, St. Lawrence Seaway, and Canada. Nor can we forget another local summer school feature—the weather. With cool breezes, lake front, and an average temperature of seventy degrees in July, Oswego has all the virtues of a summer resort.

A relative newcomer to the curriculum is the foreign study program sponsored by State University in cooperation with the Experiment in International Living. Since the idea is to dig deep into the culture of a country and to get to know the people, students actually live for several weeks in local homes. The place chosen for the trip depends on one's aim. "We went to Germany in 1957," explains Fred Winn, "to show economic revival of Europe after the war. Sweden was chosen in 1958 because it represents the middle way between the socialistic and capitalistic systems in terms of its cooperative movement. This year Erwin Palmer will take a group to Greece, Italy, and Majorca for studying backgrounds of world literature with emphasis on mythology." Other groups were taken by Charles Wells to Greece in 1958 and to Austria in 1960.

The program is continuing to expand. "We are talking now of a full year abroad," says Mr. Winn. "We may try a pilot experiment of thirty students from a college for a semester, then continue for a year in the Junior year."

Various services have been added under the present administration, some of them quasi-curricular, some non-curricular, but all contributing to the student's effectiveness or ultimate adjustment. A placement service, added in 1953, poses certain problems. "Many students have difficulty making up their minds," says Clarence Ridgeway, director of placement from 1953 until 1960. "Some of them have very special requirements in mind. Nevertheless, in the year 1958–59 alone, 159 students were placed through this office at salaries from $4,000 to $4,800."

A Reading Center was organized in 1956, which is being equipped by its present director, Robert Canfield, with all the latest devices and materials for diagnosis and instruction. Already instituted by former president Harvey Rice, but expanded in scope and program by Foster Brown, is the Student Personnel Office, "apostledom of the abundant life." And contributory to this aim is a course designed for the specific purpose of instructing student counselors, taught jointly by members of the personnel staff, with consultants from other departments.

An over-all appraisal of program and College might begin with industrial arts, a field so young that it naturally—and fortunately—remains in a state of flux. Flexibility will make it easier to adapt to the following needs which, according to several professors, remain to be met—both at Oswego and in the country at large:

(1) Industrial arts as a phase of general education should be ex-

tended to all children, of whatever educational level or intelligence grouping. To date, industrial arts has been largely confined to junior high. High school courses have been largely vocational, and lower-grade shops have hardly existed at all. The shop has also been a dumping ground for the dull with little challenge for the bright. Oddly enough, no concern was expressed for the girl, despite repeated assertions that industrial arts is general education.

In fact, Barbara A. Griffin, '61, only woman majoring in industrial arts at present, indicates that hers is a somewhat anomalous position.

> People always ask me the same questions: "Whatever made you decide to take I.A.?" "Don't you find it hard?" I believe the most difficult thing has been finding suitable answers for these questions.
>
> Having a woman in the shop was a completely new experience for most of the men in my classes. However, we all worked together, helping each other with our weak spots. They quickly got used to working next to a woman, for instance, on a lathe.
>
> I am under the impression, however, that the teachers regarded me as a crazy female who was biting off more than she could chew. One of them actually told me that I would never get an I.A. degree—just because I was a girl! Some of them tried to make things easier for me, others the opposite. Few judge both sexes equally.
>
> However, every minute I have spent in I.A. has been worth it—and I have every intention of finishing.

(2) More effective ways must be found of realizing industrial arts' basic aim—interpretation of an industrial society. Diehards reject this aim as watering down the program. Others espouse it in principle, but pronounce it unrealistically broad. Still others favor retaining this aim as their ideal, approximating it as well as they can.

(3) For implementing such broad aims, a first requirement is finding instructors whose specialty is their versatility. They must have had sufficient breadth of training to interpret major industries as they exist today, and enough depth of insight to show how technical areas relate to society. "All too often the I.A. man is merely a technician," says Robert Babcock; "he knows how to use a hammer and how to show others how to use it. The trouble is that we often make the student a better hammerer, without making him sufficiently rounded." Furthermore, the rare instructors who fulfill the desired requirements are often siphoned off into other areas, especially administration, guidance, and industry. Some way must be found of making shop instruction sufficiently attractive to retain talent in shops.

(4) As for non-technical aspects of the curriculum, at least two deficiencies are apparent—experience with children and general culture.

The industrial arts student has less educational psychology than the elementary student and far less opportunity to observe and work with children. He also needs a stronger background in the fine arts and in English composition. Yet, lest his index should suffer a blow, he rarely uses his electives to strengthen areas of weakness. Carlton Gerbracht, however, makes an interesting observation: "Industrial arts students simply are not willing to devote the length of time required for all the proficiencies—professional, technical, and general culture—that an industrial arts teacher needs. Nevertheless, isn't it better to have someone carry on with a college education than to have a carpenter provide such training?"

> Time was when students in school shops made things without knowing why [asserts Frank Robinson]. A student might make a garden stake, sharpened on one end with a hole in it for a piece of string. It had no meaning for the child but it was sometimes displayed at state fairs. It was an exercise. This approach was the result of the Russian influence. Lee Hornbake in the thirties brought about a change. He saw children in a rut carrying on busy-work. He used the areas-of-living approach based on needs of people—food, clothing, and shelter. He also exercised ingenuity in setting up equipment—for example, he adapted a big metal drum for foundry work.

> Nowadays the prime aim is helping students to understand and appreciate contemporary culture and industrial society. The child smells smoke, hears noise, and sees the products that come out of industry; he does not just hear about them. [Carlton Gerbracht]

Quite naturally the aim to interpret the whole society has tended to dissolve barriers between different areas of industrial arts and to encourage correlation with other subjects.

> We tell the science people we would like for them to demonstrate principles in terms of certain examples. When our students are working with metal, the science professor may explain various chemical reactions in terms of the metal being used. The same applies with relation to the Mathematics Department. [Frank Robinson]

Meanwhile the industrial arts–vocational education controversy has gradually subsided into a truce of sorts based more on expediency than on logic. As Carlton Gerbracht commented, "The relationship between these areas is becoming blurred and will disappear below the college level but not beyond. There is no evidence of industrial arts making inroads on the college level outside teacher education."

Many industrial arts men are coming to believe that solid improvement will require at least two essentials. One is more adequate research, the other a five-year program. After all, the industrial arts instructor requires proficiency in three areas—technical, professional, and general culture.

The situation with regard to the over-all college program, here as elsewhere, proves confusing. Our perception can easily become distorted by ill-founded attacks on education which, like baseball, has become an All-American pastime. In fact, Hermann Cooper asserts that the schools have become the scapegoat for society's failures. Fortunately, however, Oswego has refused to be stampeded. Where elementary education is concerned, several trends are apparent, here as throughout the country.

(1) First, the trend toward electives has reversed, since Russia's Sputnik sent American educators scurrying to restore basic fundamentals. Henceforth, the curricular diet would be "steak and potatoes" with cafeteria service suspended. Faculties would write the prescription for what constitutes the good life or the good education.

(2) But the full life can best be transmitted through teachers who are first of all well-educated human beings—hence, the increase in ratio of liberal-cultural to professional courses, which now represent 27.7 per cent of the total, against a national average of 31.5 per cent. However, some educators oppose any further reduction of the professional requirement, agreeing in spirit with Glennon, who noted that "less than one year's professional studies [is] required of teachers [as compared with] four years for veterinary medicine. We seem to value the care, feeding, and growth of livestock as being four times as important as the growth, development, and teaching of human beings." [3]

(3) Another trend is toward general education for the first two years, then three of professional training, with the fifth year devoted largely to it. According to former dean Thomas Miller: "The state teachers colleges may disappear as the high school populations double. Not all young people want to be teachers; hence, state schools must provide general education while selecting a few to go on with teaching."

(4) A concomitant development has been further differentiation of curricula and multiplication of courses. Differentiation is a reflection of an age of specialization, and the proliferation of courses at least partially an expression of vested interests. A department may acquire greater prestige and larger staff through maintaining a broad offering.

(5) Simultaneously there has been increased overlap among the various disciplines. As knowledge has expanded and interrelationships have grown more complex, subject matter boundaries have blurred. Each subject expands into related fields.

(6) A sixth trend is toward striving for respectability and a reaffirmation

of faith in knowledge. "What is so mere about a fact?" we have begun to ask ourselves. Conscious of taunts hurled at education we are striving to overcome the notion that teacher-training is shallow. Faculty members are constantly urged toward sound evaluation and challenging assignments.

Be that as it may, no clearly defined philosophy integrates the total college effort. We have smoked out weaknesses, without having welded together what remains. Clear imperatives are hard to discern. Programs grow more through accretion than through reason. For motivation we have continued to rely on the time-worn props of deans' lists, academic honors, and grades. Except in laboratory courses we still use largely lecture-discussion, meagerly flavored with audio-visual or other techniques.

Such educational philosophy as we have is syncretistic and neutralistic. Students are often served up casseroles of warmed-over Dewey, seasoned with ideological miscellany. There is, nevertheless, a dualism of sorts on campus, with some of the staff dedicated to humanism and others entrenched in pragmatism, each group privately viewing the other as unredeemed.

Obviously, the educational counterpart of Einstein is needed, but he has not yet arrived. Meanwhile, some of us bridle at criticisms of education despite private misgivings. Oswego simply shares with schools everywhere and with the country at large the inevitable lag in society's effort to discover philosophical answers to meet the demands of a fast-moving age. In fact, a period of exploration—although it might involve considerable stumbling—may be preferable to settling down comfortably, but prematurely, to any specific philosophy that would rapidly become outmoded.

There are several reasons for the relative dearth of research designed to discover answers to these questions—and help lead us out of the wilderness. Persons who are at once artist-teachers and research enthusiasts are not easy to find. Our primary requirement is classroom competence, and this is not necessarily correlated with a bent for research. Nor is the way easy for those with such dual inclinations. They lack secretarial help and struggle under a heavy teaching load, besides being expected to participate in campus and community life.

Fortunately, however, creative output at Oswego has recently taken a giant surge forward. Faculty publications during the past decade have probably outnumbered all those since Sheldon's time put together. More and more offices are acquiring computers; more and more staff members, a taste for research. And Dr. Brown, fully aware of the need, promises administrative backing to the extent that funds and facilities permit.[4]

When asked to assess the school's over-all status, staff members are generally vague. "It's like asking a fish what it's like to be wet," said one. Some point out constructive features, highly meritorious, but fairly typical of well-run teacher-training institutions.

> Ninety per cent of Oswego graduates immediately embark on teaching careers. More than 90 per cent of the others enter the services, and then teach.

> The most distinctive thing we do is our supreme effort to give first-hand classroom experiences throughout the program. As compared with other units, we use our campus school more for pre-student experiences in readiness rather than as a laboratory for student teaching.

> We have always had a good practice teaching program. In some colleges the boy goes out and gets into his red convertible in front of his fraternity house, drives down and teaches a class, and returns to his fraternity house. That is all there is to his teaching experience—no real contact with school and community.

> One of the school's major assets is its friendliness. Another is the wealth of organizations. Everyone has a chance to develop leadership.

Others questioned offered explanations for the failure of individual schools to achieve uniqueness on the current scene.

> As I teach in various institutions I am impressed by likenesses. Regionalism has become a myth; we all see the same movies, eat out of the same cans. We all benefit by America's faith in education.

> One reason we appear to do little new is that much has been done. We are in the position of the liberal in politics [who] has a hard time finding anything to fight for now. We have gotten many things we were screaming for before.

> We are now using what we know. Instead of making a big deal of individual needs we are simply meeting them.

> The tendency now is to try to preserve the best of new and old, and to consolidate our gains. There is more satisfaction, less confusion.

We are naturally cautious about claiming special merit for current achievements; however, recent testimonials from distinguished persons over the country indicate a continuing respect for what Oswego is doing. Several statements from authorities in the field of industrial arts provide an index to the school's reputation:

Those of us who have had the opportunity to be invited to your campus to meet with your faculty and students have gone away with a keen appreciation of the outstanding contribution that the program at Oswego has consistently made to industrial arts education through the years. [G. Harold Silvius, Chairman of the Department of Industrial Education, Wayne State University, Detroit, Michigan]

It has always been my real pleasure to think of Oswego as the first teacher education institution in the field of industrial arts. [Kermit A. Seefeld, Professor of Industrial Arts, University of California, Santa Barbara]

When I discuss Oswego [I always refer to it as] one of the four or five outstanding institutions for training I.A. teachers at the birth of the movement. [John F. Friese, professor emeritus of Industrial Arts Education, the Pennsylvania State University]

I have always heard of Oswego as one of the few top institutions for the preparation of industrial arts teachers. [William Micheels, professor and chairman, Industrial Education, University of Minnesota]

Oswego, I believe, more than any other teacher-education institution in America has influenced and contributed to the development of Industrial Arts as an important phase of public education in the United States. [S. Lewis Land, head of the Department of Industrial Education, Pennsylvania State University, University Park, Pennsylvania]

Reports concerning the Elementary Education Division are equally favorable. The College receives letters, too numerous to quote here, commending the performance of Oswego's graduates as classroom teachers. What impresses their employers most is the way they "take hold in a classroom," reflecting a preparation which integrates theory and practice.

In addition to these views, one senses a something new in the air, a belief that the school is in process of seeking a new stellar orbit. The spurt in growth of student body, the growing campus, a progressive and efficient administration—all foreshadow the shape of good things to come. However, we can become preoccupied with yet unrealized goals of the future. We can succumb to the temptation to gaze into our crystal ball and ebulliently predict a wonderful future. Prospects indeed look bright, but forecasting is a precarious business. The bell tolls and bids us come to grips with the present.

Hence, it is well that we have paused to refresh our historical perspective. It is healthy to have seen that we cannot take growth for granted. However, as in the case of Lot's wife, the backward look can spell one's doom. One can grow misty-eyed with nostalgia, basking in past glory. The historian's true function is to siphon off the wisdom of the past, to tap the reservoirs of experience.

We must, therefore, not linger in the shadow of past prestige, nor harbor Utopian illusions for the future. We must not live *down* to the tradition of inferiority among teacher-training institutions, but live *up* to the Sheldon tradition. We know full well that the promise of the future lies in learning from the past but making the most of the present. As true today as ever are these words read on the occasion of the school's Semi-Centennial Celebration in 1911:

> The clock strikes and it is not the evening hour but noon-time in the life of the school. The time for reminiscences is not yet; *that* belongs to the eventide of life. There is labor still to occupy our thought. Only as the past throws inspiration into the future may we safely dwell upon it.

> "Still as the spiral grew
>   He left the past year's dwelling for the new;
>   Stole with soft step its shining archway through,
>   built up its idle door,
>   Stretched in his last found home and knew the old no more." [5]

Notes

CHAPTER 1

1. Vincent J. Glennon, *The Road Ahead in Teacher Education* (Syracuse: Syracuse University Press, 1957), pp. 7–8.
2. Leonard W. Richardson, *The Normal School Idea* (Albany: J. B. Lyon, 1900), pp. 1–2.
3. A. D. Mayo, "American Common Schools in New York, New Jersey, and Pennsylvania During the First Half Century of the Republic," *U.S. Commissioner of Education Report*, 1895–96, p. 219.
4. *Report of Special Committee of the Assembly on the State Normal Schools* (Albany: Weed, Parsons, 1879).
5. *Annual Report of the New York Superintendent of Instruction*, 1904, pp. 27–31.
6. Donald Snygg, "Significance of the Oswego Movement in Education," in Oswego Historical Society, *Ninth Publication* (Oswego: Palladium-Times, 1945), pp. 59–65.
7. *Ibid.*, p. 60.
8. Mary Sheldon Barnes (ed.), *Autobiography of Edward Austin Sheldon* (New York: Ives-Butler, 1911), pp. 135–37.
9. *Oswego Commercial-Times*, February 10, 11, 14, 1862.
10. John Churchill, *Landmarks of Oswego County* (Syracuse: D. Mason, 1895), p. 447.
11. Thomas E. Finegan, *Teacher Training Agencies* (Albany: University of the State of New York, 1917), p. 270.
12. J. P. Gordy, *Rise and Growth of the Normal School Idea in the United States*, United States Bureau of Education, Circular of Information, No. 8 (1891).
13. *Oswego Daily Times*, February 23, 1864.
14. Finegan, *op. cit.*, p. 269.
15. *Oswego Daily Palladium*, February 10, 1872.
16. *Ibid.*, February 7, 1872.
17. Finegan, *op. cit.*, p. 269.
18. Mary Sheldon Barnes, "Edward Austin Sheldon," in *First Half Century: State Normal and Training School* (Oswego: Radcliffe Press, 1913), pp. 40–51.
19. *Report of the State Superintendent of Public Instruction of New York*, 1878, pp. 35–37.
20. Charles Harper, *Development of the Teachers College in the United States* (Bloomington, Illinois: McKnight and McKnight, 1935), pp. 125–26.

21. L. C. Mossman, *Changing Conceptions Relative to the Planning of Lessons* (New York: Teachers College Bureau of Publications, Columbia University Press, 1924), p. 31.
22. Christian Gauss, "How Good Were the Good Old Times," in *The College Years*, ed. A. C. Spectorsky (New York: Hawthorn, 1958), pp. 81–88.
23. Jerome Allen, *Education of Teachers in the State of New York and a Brief History of Normal Schools* (Albany: State Department of Education, 1880).
24. *Oswego Daily Palladium*, June 15, 1865.
25. *Oswego Palladium-Times*, October 7, 1939.
26. William M. Aber, "The Oswego State Normal School," *Popular Science Monthly*, Vol. 43 (1893), pp. 51–76.
27. Gauss, *op. cit.*, p. 85.

CHAPTER 2

1. *Catalogue of the Oswego State Normal and Training School*, 1862.
2. Jerome Allen, *Education of Teachers in the State of New York and a Brief History of Normal Schools* (Albany: State Department of Education, 1880).
3. G. E. Walk, "Decade of Tendencies in Curricula of State Normal Schools," *Education*, Vol. 37 (1916), pp. 209–29.
4. Thomas Gray, "Methods of Instruction and Courses of Study in Normal Schools," *Papers on School Issues of the Day*, IV (Syracuse: Bardeen, 1889).
5. *Report of the New York State Superintendent of Public Instruction of New York*, 1877, p. 29.
6. *Report of the United States Commissioner of Education*, 1893–94, p. 473.
7. Donald Snygg, "Significance of the Oswego Movement in Education," in Oswego Historical Society, *Ninth Publication* (Oswego: Palladium-Times, 1945), pp. 59–65.
8. Ned Dearborn, *The Oswego Movement in American Education* (Teachers College Contributions to Education, No. 183; New York, Columbia University, 1925), p. 60.
9. *Ibid.*, p. 69.
10. *Ibid.*, pp. 40–41.
11. Mary Sheldon Barnes (ed.), *Autobiography of Edward Austin Sheldon* (New York: Ives-Butler, 1911), pp. 135–37.
12. *Historical Sketches Relating to the First Quarter Century of the State Normal and Training School at Oswego, New York* (Oswego: R. J. Oliphant, Printer, 1888), pp. 88–89.
13. *Minutes of the Board of the Oswego Normal and Training School*, January 27, 1876.
14. E. A. Rice, *A Brief History of Physical Education* (New York: A. S. Barnes, 1932), pp. 175–83.
15. Elizabeth Sheldon Alling (ed.), *Hermann Krüsi's Recollections of My Life* (New York: Grafton Press, 1907), pp. 227–29.
16. *Minutes of the Board of the Oswego Normal and Training School*, August 28, 1886.

17. Dorothy Dockstader, *History of the Oswego Kindergarten.* Unpublished.
18. William M. Aber, "The Oswego State Normal School," *Popular Science Monthly,* Vol. 43 (1893), pp. 51–76.
19. A. B. Mays, "Industrial Education," in Walter S. Monroe (ed.), *Encyclopedia of Educational Research* (Rev. ed.; New York: Macmillan, 1950).
20. Lee Hornbake, "Professional Progress in Industrial Arts Education," *Epsilon Pi Tau Founder's Day Address* (Columbia, Ohio: Epsilon Pi Tau, 1951).
21. *Historical Sketches Relating to the First Quarter Century of the State Normal and Training School at Oswego, New York* (Oswego: R. J. Oliphant, Printer, 1888), p. 91.
22. Eugene D. Fink, *History of the Development of Industrial Education and of Industrial Arts Education in the Oswego State Normal School.* Unpublished Master's thesis, New York University, 1933.
23. Richard K. Piez, *Manual Training in the Oswego State Normal School.* Unpublished.
24. Richard K. Piez, "Development of Manual Training at Oswego," in Eugene D. Fink, *op. cit.*
25. Robert Davis Helsby, *A Comparative Analysis of Three Structured Groups from All Industrial Arts Graduates of the State University Teachers College at Oswego, New York from 1925–55.* Unpublished Doctor's thesis, Cornell University, 1958.
26. J. H. Pestalozzi, *How Gertrude Teaches Her Children,* Vol. II, trans. by Holland and Tucker (Syracuse: Bardeen, 1892), p. 325.
27. Richard K. Piez, "The Oswego State Normal and Training School, An Interpretation," Oswego Historical Society, *Tenth Publication* (Oswego: Palladium-Times, 1943), pp. 1–10.
28. Lewis Anderson, *History of Manual Training and Industrial School Education* (New York, D. Appleton, 1926), pp. 108–10.
29. Gordon Wilber, *How Was Pestalozzian Object Teaching Related to Practical Arts and What Oswego Did (1860–1900) to Contribute to Its Development.* Unpublished.

CHAPTER 3

1. Edward Austin Sheldon, *Autobiography.* Unpublished portion of original manuscript.
2. Mary Sheldon Barnes (ed.), *Autobiography of Edward Austin Sheldon* (New York: Ives-Butler, 1911), pp. 68–71.
3. *Ibid.,* p. 57.
4. A. E. Winship, *Great American Educators* (Chicago: Werner School Book Company, 1900), pp. 145–61.
5. Edward Austin Sheldon, "Report to the Second Quarterly Meeting of the Orphan and Free School Association, July, 1849," in Oswego Historical Society, *Eighteenth Publication* (Oswego: Palladium-Times, 1955), pp. 55–57.
6. James Corso, *The History of Oswego State Teachers College* (1861–1944), (Syracuse: Onondaga Historical Association), p. 5. Unpublished.
7. Barnes, *op. cit.,* p. 96.

8. Andrew P. Hollis, *The Contribution of the Oswego Normal School* (Boston: D. C. Heath, 1898), p. 83.
9. Barnes, *op. cit.*, p. 114.
10. Mary Sheldon Barnes, "Edward Austin Sheldon," in *First Half Century: State Normal and Training School* (Oswego: Radcliffe Press, 1913), p. 41.
11. Anna Sheldon Howe to Ralph Waldo Swetman, March 29, 1941.
12. Hollis, *op. cit.*, pp. 91–92.
13. Jesse B. Sears and Olin D. Henderson, *Cubberly of Stanford* (Stanford, California: Stanford University Press, 1957), p. 123.
14. *Oswego Alumni Bulletin,* Vol. 12, March, 1955.
15. J. C. Park, "Some Facts About Personalities, Curriculum, Evolution, and Contributions to American Education from 1862 to 1939," *Vocationist,* Vol. 7 (December, 1938).
16. *Ibid.*
17. Sarah J. Walter to I. B. Poucher, June, 1898.
18. Mary Sheldon Barnes, "Sheldon's Home Life," in *First Half Century; State Normal and Training School* (Oswego: Radcliffe Press, 1913), pp. 43–44.
19. David S. Jordan, "Perplexities of a College President," *Atlantic Monthly,* Vol. 85 (1900), pp. 488–89.
20. William A. Neilson (ed.), *Charles William Eliot and His Beliefs* (New York: Harper, 1926), pp. 217–39.
21. Elizabeth Sheldon Alling (ed.), *Hermann Krüsi's Recollections of My Life* (New York: Grafton Press, 1907), p. 223.
22. *Minutes of the Board of the Oswego State Normal and Training School,* Vol. 8 (July 7, 1875), p. 203.
23. J. S. Brubacher and Willis Rudy, *Higher Education in Transition* (New York: Harper, 1959).
24. W. D. Agnew, *Administration of Professional Schools* (Baltimore: Warwick and York, 1924), p. 138.
25. H. G. Good, *A History of American Education* (New York: Macmillan, 1956), p. 215.
26. Cora A. Brown to Ralph W. Swetman, April 29, 1936.
27. Alling, *op. cit.*, p. 217.
28. William M. Aber, "The Oswego State Normal School," *Popular Science Monthly,* Vol. 43 (1893), p. 71.
29. Richard Piez, "Early Days at the Normal," *Oswego Palladium-Times,* January 13, 1943.
30. "Our Faculty," *Sequoia,* Vol. I (March 30, 1892), p. 234.
31. Edward Howard Griggs, *The Story of an Itinerant Teacher* (Indianapolis: Bobbs-Merrill, 1934), pp. 69–71.
32. *Ibid.*
33. *Oswego Palladium-Times,* June 26, 1924.
34. *Historical Sketches Relating to the First Quarter Century of the State Normal and Training School at Oswego, New York* (Oswego: R. J. Oliphant, Printer, 1888), p. 89.
35. Earl Barnes, *Autobiography.* Unpublished.

36. *Forum,* Vol. 17 (May, 1894), pp. 340–44.
37. J. M. Pangburn, *The Evolution of the American Teachers College,* Doctor's thesis; Teachers College, Columbia University, 1932, p. 117.
38. Lena Hill Severance, "Case of the Normal Schools," *Journal of the Association of Collegiate Alumnae,* Vol. 8 (1915).
39. *Report of the Superintendent of Public Instruction of New York, 1900,* p. 237.
40. *Minutes of the Board of the Oswego Normal and Training School,* January 18, 1868.
41. Mary V. Lee and Mary Sheldon Barnes, *Up the Saguenay* (Fredonia, New York: C. R. Burchard, 1875).

CHAPTER 4

1. W. H. Maxwell, *Proceedings of the Dedication of the New York Educational Building,* p. 55.
2. *Catalogue of the Oswego Normal and Training School, 1888,* p. 29.
3. *Ibid.,* pp. 6–18.
4. Lena Hill Severance to Ralph W. Swetman, July 2, 1924.
5. Mary Sheldon, undated, unsigned essay written sometime between 1874 and 1885.
6. Charles Wells, "A Century of Public Entertainment in Oswego," in Oswego Historical Society, *Ninth Publication* (Oswego: Palladium-Times, 1945), p. 36.
7. Claude Bragdon, *More Lives Than One* (New York: Knopf, 1938).
8. *Minutes of the Board of the Oswego State Normal and Training School,* July 11, 1868.
9. *Ibid.,* February 23, 1863.
10. Samuel Elliot Morison, *Three Centuries of Harvard* (Cambridge: Harvard University, 1936), p. 116.
11. Roy J. Honeywell, *Educational Work of Thomas Jefferson* (Cambridge: Harvard University Press, 1931), pp. 143–45.
12. Clarence P. Shedd, *Two Centuries of Student Christian Movements* (New York: Association Press, 1934), pp. 26–31.
13. *Harvard College Records, I,* Colonial Society of Massachusetts, Collections, Vol. 15, p. 24.
14. *Catalogue of the Oswego State Normal and Training School, 1888,* p. 25.
15. Mary Alling Aber to I. B. Poucher, June 20, 1898.
16. Andrew W. White, *Autobiography,* Vol. I (London: Macmillan, 1905), pp. 348–49.
17. *Oswego Commercial Times,* April 8, 1865.
18. *New England's First Fruits* (London: 1643), pp. 31–32.
19. *Catalogue of the Oswego State Normal and Training School,* January 23, 1862.
20. Ina L. Cooper Lane, '91, to author, 1960.

21. Lena Hill Severance to Ralph W. Swetman, December 11, 1940.
22. S. S. Randall, *History of the Common School System of the State of New York* (New York: Ivison, Blakeman, Taylor, 1871), pp. 340–41.
23. W. S. Smith, '77, in letter to the editor of the *New York Herald*, March 17, 1877.
24. *Catalogue of the Oswego State Normal and Training School, 1888*, p. 22.
25. Leonard W. Richardson, *The Normal School Idea* (Albany: J. B. Lyon, 1900), p. 127.
26. *Historical Sketches Relating to the First Quarter Century of the State Normal and Training School at Oswego, New York* (Oswego: R. J. Oliphant, Printer, 1888), p. 119.

CHAPTER 5

1. *Report of the New York State Superintendent of Public Instruction*, 1897, p. 1,065.
2. Lena Hill Severance to R. W. Swetman, June 6, 1939.
3. Henry Barnard's *American Journal of Education*, Vol. 12 (1899).
4. *Oswego Commercial Times*, June 30, 1864.
5. Frank Pierrepont Graves, "Doctor Sheldon's Posthumous Contribution to Education," *Vocationist*, Vol. 21 (October, 1932), p. 1.
6. P. R. Radosavljevich, "The Oswego Movement and the New Education," *Educational Forum*, Vol. 2 (1937), pp. 90–100.
7. E. A. Sheldon to Mary Sheldon Barnes. Unpublished, date unknown.
8. *Oswego Palladium-Times*, October 30, 1957.
9. George Ripley and A. P. Hollis, "Dr. E. A. Sheldon and the Oswego Movement," *Education*, Vol. 18 (1898), pp. 545–54.
10. *Cincinnati School Report for 1857*, pp. 75–76.
11. Address by John W. Cook in *Journal of Proceedings and Addresses of the N.E.A.*, p. 89.
12. E. P. Cubberly, *The History of Education* (Boston: Houghton Mifflin, 1920), p. 380.
13. *Ibid.*, p. 394.
14. S. C. Parker, *History of Modern Elementary Education* (Boston: Houghton, 1912), pp. 340–41.
15. Donald Snygg, "Significance of the Oswego Movement in Education," in Oswego Historical Society, *Ninth Publication* (Oswego: Palladium-Times, 1945), pp. 64–65.
16. *Ibid.*
17. Nicholas M. Butler, *History of Education in the United States* (New York: American Book Company, 1910).
18. J. P. Gordy, "Rise and Growth of Normal School Idea," *Bureau of Education Bulletin*, No. 8 (1891).
19. *History of Oswego County, New York, 1789–1877* (Philadelphia: L. H. Everts Company, 1877), pp. 123–24.

20. Elizabeth Sheldon Alling (ed.), *Hermann Krüsi's Recollections of My Life* (New York: Grafton Press, 1907), pp. 230–31.
21. *Circular of Information*, Bureau of Education, No. 8 (1891).
22. A. D. Mayo, "The Normal School in America," in *Historical Sketches Relating to the First Quarter Century of the State Normal and Training School at Oswego, New York* (Oswego: R. J. Oliphant, Printer, 1888).
23. A. P. Hollis, *The Contribution of the Oswego Normal School* (Boston: D. C. Heath, 1898), p. 111.
24. H. G. Good, *A History of American Education*, (New York: Macmillan, 1956).
25. Hollis, *op. cit.*, p. 49.
26. *Semi-Centennial Historical Sketch and Notes, Winona State Normal School, 1860–1910.*
27. Copy of mimeographed letter sent by E. A. Sheldon.
28. *Contributions of North American Normal School Women in Argentina.* Unpublished research by Vanetta Warren.
29. Alice Houston Luiggi, *Sesenta y Cinco Valientes* (Buenos Aires: Editorial Agora, 1959).
30. *Homenaje a la Fundadora y Primera Directora de la Escuela Normal de Maestras de Jujuy, Señorita Juana Stevens* (Buenos Aires: Imprenta Lopez, 1939).
31. Lena Hill Severance to R. W. Swetman, June 6, 1939.
32. James Riggs, *Round the World* (Oswego: Radcliffe Press, 1934).
33. Based on information supplied the writer by Toguko Takamine, by Takashi Kurusawa, and "The Educational System of Japan," *Report of U.S. Commissioner of Education for 1890–91*, Vol. I.

CHAPTER 6

1. Howard P. Moore to Ralph W. Swetman, April 7, 1941.
2. *Minutes of the Board of the Oswego Normal and Training School*, October 9, 1908.
3. *Ibid.*, March 31, 1908.
4. *Oswego Palladium-Times*, June 30, 1911.
5. *Minutes of the Board of the Oswego Normal and Training School*, July 1, 1911.
6. R. K. Piez writing in the *Oswego Palladium-Times*, July 24, 1936.
7. Joseph C. Park to Eugene Fink, November 28, 1932.
8. *Annual Report of Superintendent of Public Instruction of New York*, 1901, p. 14.
9. Thomas E. Finegan, *Teacher–Training Agencies* (Albany: The University of the State of New York, 1917).
10. *Catalogue of the Oswego Normal and Training School, 1903–04.*
11. W. R. Harper, *The Trend in Higher Education* (Chicago: University of Chicago Press, 1905).

12. *Report of the Commissioner of Education in New York*, Vol. 2 (1915), p. 154.

13. Erna Kaska, *Oneonta Experience in Building a Professional Education Sequence* (Menasha, Wisconsin: Collegiate Press, 1944).

14. *Annual Report of Department of Education of New York State*, Vol. 2 (1915), pp. 153–54.

15. *Minutes of the Board of the Oswego State Normal and Training School*, June 25, 1912.

16. Herman L. Offner, *Administrative Procedures for Changing Curriculum Patterns for Selected State Teachers Colleges* (New York: Teachers College, Columbia University, 1944).

17. *Minutes of the Board of the Oswego State Normal and Training School*, July, 1911.

18. *Syracuse Post-Standard*, December 28, 1907.

19. E. E. White, *The Art of Teaching* (New York: American Book Company, 1901), pp. 106–16.

20. *Report of the Superintendent of Public Instruction of New York*, 1901, p. 557.

21. *Minutes of the Board of Oswego Normal and Training School*, September 16, 1913.

22. J. L. Meriam, *Normal School Education and Efficiency in Teaching*, Contributions to Education, Series No. 1 (New York: Teachers College, Columbia University, 1905).

23. *The Vocationist*, Vol. 27, March, 1937.

24. H. G. Good, *A History of American Education* (New York: Macmillan, 1956).

25. *Report of the Commissioner of Education of New York*, 1913, p. 94.

26. *Minutes of the Board of Oswego Normal and Training School*, October 9, 1908.

CHAPTER 7

1. *Catalogue of the Oswego State Normal and Training School, 1903–04*.

2. Alma Bevis, *Diets and Riots* (Boston: Marshall Jones, 1936).

3. Ben Van Oot to Edith Tallerton, April 5, 1945.

4. *Oswego Palladium-Times*, November 12, 1909.

5. *Ibid.*, November 19, 1919.

6. *Ibid.*, January 19, 1910.

7. *Oswego Daily Times*, May 4, 1910.

8. *Oswego Palladium-Times*, November 18, 1909.

9. *Catalogue of the Oswego State Normal and Training School, 1899*.

10. *Oswego Palladium-Times*, November 11, 1933.

11. From unsigned student notebook called *History of the Normal School*, 1899.

12. *Oswego Daily Times*, June 26, 1900.

13. Class poem by Jeanne Grossen Ashley, '07.
14. *Oswego Daily Times,* January 20, 1910.

CHAPTER 8

1. Thomas E. Finegan, *Teacher Training Agencies* (Albany: University of the State of New York, 1917).
2. *Laws of 1931 of New York State,* p. 314.
3. *Oswego Palladium-Times,* September 9, 1931.
4. *Ibid.,* August 6, 1931.
5. *The Vocationist,* Vol. 7 (December, 1918).
6. *Oswego Semi-Weekly Times,* March, 1918.
7. Harriet Stevens, *The Normal School in the War.* Unpublished handwritten manuscript.
8. Eugene D. Fink, *History of the Development of Industrial Education and of Industrial Arts Education in the Oswego State Normal School,* Master's thesis; New York University, 1933.
9. *Oswego Palladium-Times,* October 22, 1917.
10. A. E. Fitzelle, *Origin and Development of the Normal School System of New York State,* Doctor's thesis; New York University, 1928, p. 72.
11. H. Suzzallo, "The Reorganization of the Teacher Profession," *N.E.A. Proceedings* (1913), pp. 362-79.
12. J. E. Russell, "Professional Factors in the Training of High School Teachers," *Educational Review,* Vol. 45 (1913), pp. 217-36.
13. L. C. Mossman, *Changing Conceptions Relative to the Planning of Lessons* (New York: Teachers College Press, 1924), pp. 34-36.
14. *Catalogue of the Oswego State Normal and Training School, 1915-17.*
15. Dorothy Dockstader, *The Oswego Kindergarten,* Unpublished.
16. *Ninth Annual Report,* State of New York, Educational Department (1913), pp. 37-39.
17. *Minutes of the Board of the Oswego Normal and Training School,* September 19, 1919.
18. *Oswego Palladium-Times.* Undated clipping.
19. "Changed Relations with Normal School," in *Mayor's Annual Report for 1916* (Oswego: John F. Murphy, 1917), pp. 79-80.
20. *Journal of the Regents Meetings,* March 25, 1920, p. 584.

CHAPTER 9

1. *Oswego Palladium-Times,* November 1, 1913.
2. A. E. Fitzelle, *Origin and Development of the Normal School System of New York State,* Doctor's thesis; New York University, 1928, pp. 126-27.
3. J. M. Pangburn, *The Evolution of the American Teachers College,* Doctor's thesis; Teachers College, Columbia University, 1932, p. 107.

4. Fitzelle, *op. cit.*, pp. 224–28.
5. *The Vocationist*, Vol. 12 (October, 1923), p. 10.
6. The *Oshwakee*, 1919.
7. *Scribner's Magazine*, Vol. 46 (November, 1919), pp. 572–75.
8. Henry Seidel Canby, *Alma Mater: The Gothic Age of the American College* (New York: Farrar and Rinehart, 1936), pp. 125–31.
9. Henry D. Sheldon, *History and Pedagogy of American Student Societies* (New York: D. Appleton, 1901), pp. 172–92, 221–29.
10. J. S. Brubacher and Willis Rudy, *Higher Education in Transition* (New York: Harper, 1959), pp. 122–23.
11. Howard Savage, *American College Athletics* (New York: Carnegie Foundation for the Advancement of Teaching, 1929), pp. 13–20.
12. *Catalogue of the Oswego State Normal and Training School, 1922–23*, pp. 32–33.

CHAPTER 10

1. W. C. Ruediger, "Regent Tendencies in the Normal Schools of the United States," *Educational Review*, Vol. 27 (March, 1907), p. 87.
2. *Oswego Palladium-Times*, May 25, 1942.
3. Ralph W. Swetman, *Report to Hermann Cooper on Staff Preparation, Staff Load, and Needed Addition to the Faculty and Faculty Organization.* Unpublished.
4. *Oswego Palladium-Times*, December 6, 1935.
5. E. U. Rugg, "The Trend Toward Standardization in Teachers College," *N.E.A. Proceedings*, 1927, p. 921.
6. James Mulhern, *History of Education* (New York: Ronald, 1946), p. 627.
7. *Oswego Palladium-Times*, May 9, 1934.
8. *Oswegonian*, December 18, 1936.
9. *Ibid.*, January 26, 1935.
10. *Ibid.*, September 13, 1935, p. 1.
11. Lee Hornbake, *Industrial Arts in the Elementary School*, Doctor's thesis: Ohio State University, 1942.
12. Charles H. Judd, *Preparation of School Personnel* (New York: McGraw-Hill, 1938), pp. 9–40.
13. A. B. Hart, "The Teacher as a Professional Expert," *School Review*, Vol. 1 (1893).
14. *Oswego Palladium-Times*, June 26, 1924.
15. *Ibid.*, September 4, 1933.
16. *Ibid.*, February 1, 1947.
17. Lena Hill Severance to R. K. Piez, April 24, 1939.
18. R. K. Piez to Lena Hill Severance, April 24, 1939.
19. *Oswego Palladium-Times*, October 10, 1947.
20. Aulus Saunders, handwritten diary.
21. *Oswego Palladium-Times*, January, 1820–1940.
22. W. Seward Salisbury, "Oswego State College in War Times," Oswego His-

torical Society, *Tenth Publication* (Oswego: Palladium-Times, 1946), pp. 66–79.

CHAPTER 11

1. Alice Swetman, "Ralph Waldo Swetman," *Oswegonian,* June 2, 1947.
2. *Oswego Palladium-Times,* April, 1947.
3. *Green Cap Annual,* 1937–38.
4. *Green Cap Annual,* 1941–42.
5. Harry S. Warner, *Alcohol Trends in College Life* (Methodist Board of Temperance, 1938), pp. 5–6.
6. Stephen Vincent Benet, *The Beginning of Wisdom* (New York: Henry Holt, 1921), pp. 54–55.
7. Henry T. Claus, "The Problem of College Chapel," *Educational Review,* Vol. 46 (1913), pp. 177–87.
8. *Oswegonian,* October 23, 1936; February 13, 1938.
9. *Oswego Palladium-Times,* November 2, 1936.
10. Maurice S. Sheehy, *Problems of Student Guidance* (Baltimore: Dolphin Press, 1929).
11. Ralph Waldo Swetman to Mrs. Mary Blaikie, June 17, 1945.

CHAPTER 12

1. *Who's Who in American Education,* Vol. 18 (Nashville: Who's Who in American Education, Inc., 1957–58), p. 784.
2. Merle S. Kuder, *Trends in Professional Opportunities in the Liberal Arts College* (New York: Teachers College, Columbia University, 1937), Chapter 11.
3. S. E. Morison, *Three Centuries of Harvard* (Cambridge: Harvard University Press, 1936), p. 197.
4. *Oswego Palladium-Times,* September 26, 1947.
5. *Oswego Palladium-Times,* June 20, 1952.
6. Agnew, Walter, *Administration of Professional Schools for Teachers* (Baltimore: Warwick and York, 1944).
7. *Oswegonian,* October 14, 1947.
8. *Oswegonian,* May 15, 1951.
9. Robert M. McIver, *Academic Freedom in Our Time* (New York: Columbia University Press, 1955).
10. *Oswegonian,* May 4, 1948.

CHAPTER 13

1. Figures compiled by Charles Turner.
2. J. S. Brubacher and Willis Rudy, *Higher Education in Transition* (New York, Harper, 1959).

CHAPTER 14

1. *The New York Times*, October 9, 1953, p. 29.
2. *Oswegonian*, January 30, 1960.
3. *Ibid.*, February 26, 1957.
4. *Ibid.*, February 17, 1960.
5. *Oswego Alumni Bulletin*, March, 1955.
6. Samuel Elliot Morison, *Harvard in the Seventeenth Century*, Vol. 1 (Cambridge: Harvard University Press), pp. 58–59; 65–66.
7. G. Stanley Hall, "Student Customs," *Proceedings of the American Antiquarian Society*, 1900–10, p. 97.
8. Abraham Flexner, *Universities, American, English, German* (New York: Oxford University Press, 1930), p. 68.
9. Arthur H. Cole (ed.), *Charleston Goes to Harvard* (Cambridge: Harvard University Press, 1940), p. 65.

CHAPTER 15

1. James C. Coleman, *Personality Dynamics and Effective Behavior* (Chicago: Scott, Foresman, 1960), p. 466.
2. Report of a symposium presented at the annual convention of the American Psychological Association, September 2, 1960.
3. Vincent J. Glennon, *The Road Ahead in Teacher Education* (Syracuse: Syracuse University Press, 1957), p. 16.
4. Foster Brown, in speech before assembly, August 3, 1960.
5. Anna B. Herrig, "Honor to Whom Honor Is Due," in *History of the First Half Century of the Oswego State Normal and Training School* (Oswego: Radcliffe Press, 1913), p. 180.

Appendix

Additional Information on
CERTAIN ADMINISTRATIVE PERSONNEL

(Mrs.) ZOFIA A. DRZEWIENIECKI: asst. librarian; appointed 1960. Master of Law, U. of Warsaw. *Offices:* secty. of Polish Consul-General, Berlin; bd. director, Polish YMCA in Palestine, Egypt, Italy, Great Britain; asst. ed., Polish weekly. In charge U. of Chicago P. O.

HELEN J. HAGGER: head librarian; appointed 1945. B.S. in Lib. Sci., Syracuse; M.S. in Lib. Sci., U. of Illinois. *Member:* Beta Phi Mu. *Honors:* past pres. State University Librarians.

(Mrs.) CONSTANCE HALL: asst. librarian; appointed 1959. A.B., St. Lawrence; B.L.S., U. of Buffalo; M.A. in Lib. Sci., U. of Mich. *Military Service:* Lt. USNR (WAVES). *Member:* Tau Kappa Alpha; Mortarboard. *Interests:* photography, horseback riding.

LOUISE HESS: nurse; asst. prof.; appointed 1953. R.N., St. Luke's Hospital, N.Y.C.; R.D.N., Columbia School of Dental Hygiene; B.S., Syracuse. *Reserve Status:* Major in ANCRes.

(Mrs.) GRACE T. MANWARING: asst. librarian; appointed 1958. B.S. in Lib. Sci., Syracuse. *Interests:* gardening, flower arranging, collecting old glass and china.

DOROTHY MOTT: assoc. prof.; director of admissions; appointed 1946. A.B., Antioch; M.A., Columbia; professional diploma in Student Personnel Admin., Columbia. *Military Service:* Major, USMC (WR), W.W. II. *Offices:* chrmn. Oswego Housing Authority; Bd. of Directors, Oswego Hospital; Bd. of Directors, Oswego County Historical Society.

KATHALEEN PERKINS: prof.; appointed 1957. B.S., Russell Sage; M.D., Albany Medical College.

(Mrs.) LOIS PRUDOM STOLP: asst. librarian; appointed 1950. B.S., State U. of N.Y. Coll. of Ed. at Geneseo; M.S., Oswego. *Interests:* music, church work.

WHITE WARNER: coordinator of field services; appointed 1951. B.S., State U. of N.Y. Coll. of Ed. at Geneseo.

RICHARD WHEELER: director of placement; appointed 1957. A.B., N.Y. State Coll. for Teachers at Albany; M.A., Syracuse.

The Instructional Staff:

THE ENGLISH DEPARTMENT

CHARLES WELLS: prof. and chrmn.; appointed 1940. B.S., N.D. State Coll.; M.A., Ed. D., Columbia. Directed State U. of N.Y. foreign study courses in Europe. *Member:* Kappa Delta Pi; Phi Delta Kappa; Board of Directors, N.Y. State Speech Assn.; First White House Conference on Child Health and Protection. *Interests:* gardening and oil painting.

HELEN BUCKLEY: assoc. prof.; appointed 1949. B.S., M.S., Syracuse. *Author: Grandfather and I; Grandmother and I.*

ANITA BULLARD: asst. prof.; appointed 1957. A.B., M.A., Syracuse. *Member:* Phi Beta Kappa; Phi Kappa Phi. *Interest:* play production.

ROBERT F. CREGO: prof.; appointed 1948. A.B., Hamilton Coll.; M.A., Syracuse; Ph.D., N.Y.U.

JOHN FISHER: asst. prof.; A.B., Champlain Coll.; M.A. (teaching fellow), U. of Mich. *Member:* Alpha Psi Omega. *Interest:* antiques.

KINGSLEY HENDRICK: instr.; appointed 1960. A.B. (cum laude), Syracuse. *Interests:* church organist and choir director.

(Mrs.) ELIZABETH HODGKINSON: instr.; appointed 1960. B.S., M.A., Bowling Green State U.

FRANCIS HULME: prof.; appointed 1949. A.B., North Carolina; M.A., Emory; Ph.D., U. of Minn. *Member:* Phi Beta Kappa; Phi Mu Alpha. *Honors:* "United Nations Speaker" for Syracuse-Utica District; Fulbright professor. Hong Kong. *Interests:* fills Protestant pulpits, music, travel, raises fancy bantams. Author (poetry): *Come Up the Valley; A Mountain Measure;* "Loving Was Tenderness," a ballad set to music.

JOHN KINGSTON: asst. prof.; appointed 1958. A.B., Hartwick; M.A., U. of Ill. *Member:* Alpha Psi Omega; Delta Psi Omega. *Interests:* antiques, N.Y. State history and folklore, theater, gardening, travel.

MILDRED LARSON: prof.; appointed 1949. A.B., M.A., N.Y. State Coll. for Teachers at Albany; Ph.D., N.Y.U. Course in photogrammetry. *Member:* Signum Laudis (Albany); Delta Kappa Gamma; vice president, publicity chairman, State A.A.U.W. *Interests:* mathematics, photography, coin collecting, folklore, writing for children.

ERWIN G. PALMER: prof.; appointed 1946. A.B., Syracuse; M.A., Breadloaf School of English; Ph.D., Syracuse. *Member:* Kappa Phi Kappa; Alpha Psi Omega. *Interests:* gardening, mythology.

VERNON RANK: assoc. prof.; appointed 1946. A.B., M.A., Penn. State U. *Interests:* politics, Kiwanis. *Honors:* alderman, city of Oswego, 1949–51.

(Mrs.) OLLA G. RICKETT: assoc. prof.; appointed 1959. A.B., N.Y. State Coll. for Teachers at Albany; M.A., Syracuse. Also studied at McGill U. in Canada. *Interests:* Children's theater, radio and TV production, French-speaking theater of Montreal.

SANFORD V. STERNLICHT: asst. prof.; appointed 1959. B.S., Oswego; M.A. (with distinction), Colgate. *Honors:* poetry awards from *Writer's Magazine* and from the Poetry Society of Norfolk, Va. *Member:* Kappa Delta Pi. *Interests:* writing, poetry.

RUPERT STROUD: prof.; appointed 1944. B.Ed., Eastern Ill. State Coll.; M.A., U. of Ill.; Ph.D., Syracuse. Ped.D. (honorary), Eastern Ill. State Coll. *Interests:* trailer travel, carpentry, sailing.

DOROTHY P. WELLS: assoc. prof.; appointed 1953. B.S., Columbia; M.S., Syracuse. Studied in England. *Interests:* creative writing, travel, religious instruction.

PHILOSOPHY

CHRISTOPHER RUSSELL: asst. prof. philosophy; appointed 1959. A.B., Colgate; M.A., U. of Ill. *Member:* Delta Phi Alpha.

FOREIGN LANGUAGES

JOSEPH DE CAMP: asst. prof. foreign languages. B.A., M.A., Penn. State; Diploma, U. of Madrid (exchange student from Penn. State). *Member:* Phi Sigma Iota. *Interests:* golf, singing.

SOCIAL STUDIES DEPARTMENT

SEWARD SALISBURY: prof. and chrmn.; appointed 1936. B.S., M.S., Ph.D., Cornell. *Fellow:* American Sociological Assn. *Author: Religion in America; Religion and the College Student. Honors:* Grants from State U. Research Foundation for research in area of attitudes and behavior of college students.

FAIZ ABU-JABER: asst. prof.; appointed 1960. A.B., M.A., Syracuse. *Honors:* fellowships from Asia Society. *Member:* Pi Sigma Alpha. *Interests:* Ping-Pong, tennis, soccer, writing Arabic poetry.

FRED BARTLE: asst. prof.; appointed 1956. A.B., M.A., N.Y. State Coll. for Teachers at Albany.

JOHNSON COOPER: assoc. prof.; appointed 1947. Attended Oswego Campus School. A.B., Wesleyan; M.A., Syracuse. *Office:* pres. Gerritt A. Smith Library Board. *Reserve Status:* exec. officer, Intelligence Research Unit, conducting area studies for Army Intelligence.

WALTER M. DRZEWIENIECKI: asst. prof.; appointed 1959. B.S., Military Academy, Ostrow, Poland. Diploma, British Coll. of General Staff, Haifa, Palestine. B.S., Wisc. State Coll.; M.A., U. of Chicago. Formerly a major in Polish Armed Forces. *Author: The German-Polish Frontier.*

ROBERT FRUMKIN: asst. prof.; appointed 1957. A.B., Upsala Coll.; M.A., Ohio State U. *Offices:* editor-in-chief and art editor, *Heritage;* editor, *Ethos;* research editor, *Journal of Human Relations. Honors:* listed in *Who's Who in the East; Who's Who in New York;* winner of medals and ribbons in art.

Member: Alpha Kappa Delta; Psi Chi; Kappa Delta Pi. *Interests:* oil paint-ing, drawing, creative writing, tennis, judo, piano playing, hiking.

PAUL GOODWIN: assoc. prof.; appointed 1947. B.Ed., State U. of N.Y. Coll. of Ed. at Brockport; M.A. (fellowship), Syracuse. *Interests:* music, garden-ing, traveling, trailering.

NORMAN F. KEISER: prof.; appointed 1956. B.S., Penn. State Teachers College, Bloomsburg; M.A., U. of Scranton; D.S.S., Syracuse. Director of research committee, Operation Oswego. *Author: Economics.*

KERMIT KUNTZ: assoc. prof.; appointed 1947. A.B., Franklin & Marshall; A.M., U. of Penn. *Interest:* American history.

JOHN MC CONKEY: asst. prof.; appointed 1956. B.S. (cum laude), Oswego; M.S. Syracuse. *Member:* Kappa Delta Pi; Phi Delta Kappa. *Honors:* listed in *Who's Who in Amer. Coll. & Univ. Interests:* choral groups, politics.

FRANK SCHOLFIELD: prof.; appointed 1955. B.S., Southwest Mo. State Coll.; M.A., Ph.D., U. of Colo. Fulbright professor, U. of Karachi, Pakistan.

CHARLES M. SNYDER: prof.; appointed 1946. A.B., A.M., Bucknell; Ph.D., U. of Penn. *Offices:* pres. Oswego County Historical Society. *Author: The Jacksonian Heritage. Reserve Status:* Lt. U.S. Naval Res. *Interest:* state and regional history.

FREDERICK WINN: assoc. prof.; appointed 1946. A.B., N.Y.U.; M.A., Columbia. Studied in Switzerland. Conducted State U. of N.Y. travel-study groups to Sweden and Germany.

THE MATHEMATICS DEPARTMENT

EMMET STOPHER: prof. and chrmn.; appointed 1957. A.B., Miami U.; B.S. Ed., Kent State U.; M.S., Ph.D., U. of Ia. *Member:* Phi Kappa Phi; Sigma Xi; Sigma Pi Sigma; Phi Eta Sigma; Pi Mu Epsilon; Kappa Mu Epsilon; Blue Key; Phi Beta Kappa; past chrmn. Kansas Section Math. Assoc. of America.

LOUIS R. DE RITTER: assoc. prof.; appointed 1960. B.S., St. Lawrence U.; M.Ed., U. of Rochester. *Member:* Pi Mu Epsilon; Pi Delta Epsilon; Kixioc. *Interests:* music, sports.

FREDERICK FISCHER: asst. prof.; appointed 1960. B.A., Wesleyan U.; M.A., Michigan State.

JOHN HOOKER: asst. prof.; appointed 1959. B.A., Yankton College; M.A., U. of Minn. *Interest:* music.

JOHN KOKEN: assoc. prof.; appointed 1960. A.B., M.A., U. of Mo. *Member:* Sigma Xi; Kappa Mu Epsilon; Pi Mu Epsilon. *Interests:* yatching, boat building.

JOHN SCHLUEP: assoc. prof.; appointed 1959. B.A., Hartwick Coll.; M.A., Columbia. *Reserve Status:* Lt. Comdr. USNR. *Interest:* remodeling houses.

ROBERT SLOAN: prof.; appointed 1959. B.S., U.S. Naval Academy; M.S., Ph.D. U. of Ill. *Member:* Sigma Xi, Pi Mu Epsilon, Kappa Mu Epsilon. *Author: In-troduction to Modern Mathematics. Interest:* vocal music.

JOHN WALCOTT: assoc. prof.; appointed 1956. B.S., M.A., U. of Mich.; Ph.D., U. of Ill. *Interest:* music (French horn).

THE SCIENCE DEPARTMENT

HAROLD O. POWERS: prof. and chrmn.; appointed 1948. B.S., Edinboro (Pa.) State Teachers Coll.; M.S., Ph.D. (fellowship), Syracuse. *Member:* Fellow, Amer. Assoc. Advancement of Science; Sigma Xi. *Interests:* photography, fishing.

FRANKLIN COWLEY: asst. prof.; appointed 1959. A.B., Antioch; M.Ed., Cornell. *Interests:* electronics, home repairs.

GIRGIS B. GHOBRIAL: asst. prof.; appointed 1960. A.B. (with honors), U. of Alexandria, Egypt; Diploma (with honors) in Psych. and Ed. from Cairo; M.A., Institute of Higher Studies, Cairo; M.A., Ph.D., U. of Minn. *Member:* Phi Delta Kappa. *Interests:* travel, photography.

NORRIS W. GOLDSMITH: prof.; appointed 1957. A.B., Ph.D., Cornell. *Honors:* Sigma Xi; Naval Ordnance Development Award. *Interests:* writing essays, composing music, singing, dancing.

ORLA LOPER: assoc. prof.; appointed 1947. A.B., M.A., Cornell. *Member:* Oswego Housing Authority. *Author: Basic Electricity—D.C. Fundamentals.*

J. ARMSTRONG MILLER: prof.; appointed 1959. B.S., Franklin & Marshall; Ph.D., U. of Penn. *Interests:* music, athletics.

P. A. MONROE: prof.; appointed 1958. B.S., M.S., U. of Idaho; Ph.D., Indiana U. *Reserve Status:* Second Lt., USAR. *Interests:* fishing, golf.

GEORGE PITLUGA: prof.; appointed 1941. A.B., Columbia; M.A., Ed. D. (Dean's Scholar), Columbia; studied art in Mexico. *Author: Science Excursions into the Community. Reserve Status:* Lt. USNR. *Interests:* painting.

HAROLD RICHARDSON: prof.; appointed 1954. A.B., Colgate; M.A., Columbia; Ed.D., N.Y.U. *Offices:* audio-visual officer, Afghanistan; science ed. consultant, Indonesia. *Author: Audio-Visual Aids. Producer* (movies): *Yellowstone National Park; Indonesia; Afghanistan; Geysers and Geyser Action. Member:* Phi Delta Kappa. *Interests:* photography, music.

ROBERT STIRLING: assoc. prof.; appointed 1948. B.S., Danbury State Teachers Coll.; M.A., T.C., Columbia. *Reserve Status:* Captain, USAF. *Member:* Kappa Delta Pi. *Interests:* mineralogy, music.

M. MELVINA SVEC: assoc. prof.; appointed 1947. A.B., M.A., U. of Wisc.; studied in England. *Offices:* secty., pres., Natl. Council for Geog. Education. *Award:* Huntington Memorial Prize for compositions on Eurasia. *Co-author: Workbook for the United States and Canada. Member:* Alpha Omega Gamma. *Interests:* travel, photography, piano, writing.

PAUL SHAVER: asst. prof.; appointed 1960. A.B., M.S., Syracuse. *Interests:* choir work, fishing, outdoor activities.

CHARLES VIGH: asst. prof.; appointed 1959. B.A., Peabody Coll.; M.A., Ohio State. *Interests:* photography, travel, camping.

JOHN WEEKS: asst. prof.; appointed 1957. B.S., Cornell; M.S., Syracuse. *Interests:* nature study, ornithology, music, art, lay preacher.

HAROLD WILLIAMSON: asst. prof.; appointed 1960. A.B., M.S., Syracuse. *Interests:* woodworking, gardening, photography.

ERNEST G. WISE: assoc. prof.; appointed 1948. B.Ed., State U. of N.Y. Coll. of Ed. at Fredonia; M.A., Columbia; Ph.D., Syracuse; studied in Italy. *Military Honors:* Bronze Star; combat infantryman's badge, W.W. II. *Interests:* golf, travel.

CHARLES B. YAGER: prof.; appointed 1936. A.B., Central Coll. (Mo.); M.S., Ph.D., U. of Iowa. *Member:* Phi Lambda Upsilon; Sigma Xi. *Interest:* fishing.

THE PSYCHOLOGY DEPARTMENT

DONALD SNYGG: prof. and chrmn.; appointed 1937. A.B., Neb. State (Wayne); M.A., U. of Ia.; Ph.D., Toronto U. Offices: council member, Amer. Psych. Assn.; chrmn. Comm. on Relations with Ed.; Natl. Soc. of Coll. Teachers of Ed., chrmn. Ed. Psych. Div.; N.Y. State Psych. Assn. director. *Co-Author: Individual Behavior.*

HERBERT EICHLER: asst. prof.; appointed 1959. A.B., M.S., in Ed., Coll. of City of N.Y.

PAUL HUTKO: asst. prof.; appointed 1959. B.S., Penn. State U.; M.A., U. of Conn. *Interests:* sports, sports cars.

WILLIAM MC GARVEY: prof.; appointed 1941. B.S., Ursinus; M.S., and Ed. D., Temple. *Member:* Phi Delta Kappa, Epsilon Pi Tau. *Offices:* past pres. N.Y. State Iris Society. *Interests:* amateur geneticist (pheasants and irises).

OWEN PITTENGER: prof.; appointed 1955. B.S., George Williams Coll.; M.S., Ed. D., U. Ill. *Member:* Phi Delta Kappa; Kappa Delta Pi. *Interests:* hypnotism, extrasensory perception.

FREDERICK RATZEBURG: prof.; appointed 1959 (also at Oswego 1953–54; 1955–57). A.B., Willamette U.; Ph.D., Syracuse. *Member:* Sigma Xi.

DOROTHY ROGERS: prof.; appointed 1946. A.B., M.A., U. of Ga.; Ph.D. (fellowship), Duke. Studied at Natl. Univ. of Chile. *Member:* Phi Kappa Phi; Kappa Delta Pi; Delta Kappa Gamma; Phi Beta Kappa. *Honors:* Educator's Award, Delta Kappa Gamma Society. *Author: Jeopardy and a Jeep; Mental Hygiene in Elementary Education. Interests:* travel, photography.

HERBERT VAN SCHAACK: assoc. prof.; appointed 1956. B.S., Oswego; M.S., Ph.D., Cornell. *Interests:* tennis, sailing, human relations in industry.

LUCY WING: assoc. prof.; appointed 1959. A.B., B.S.L.S., N.Y. State Coll. for Teachers at Albany; M.A., Columbia. *Honors:* International Delta Kappa Gamma Society Scholarship; Syracuse tuition scholarship. *Member:* Pi Lambda Theta; Delta Kappa Gamma. *Co-Author: Developmental Trends in Preferences for Goals That Are Difficult to Attain. Interests:* photography, growing gladioli, stamp and antique button collecting.

THE MUSIC DEPARTMENT

MAURICE BOYD: prof. and chrmn.; appointed 1947. B.M., M.A., Ph.D., U. of Wisc. *Offices:* chrmn. Wisc. State Music Assn.; chrmn. N.Y. State Coll.

Section Music Assn. *Military Honors:* European theater, W.W. II: awarded Purple Heart, Bronze Star, Silver Star. *Interests:* sports, photography.

KENNETH FALKNER: prof.; appointed 1955. B.M. Ed., Westminster Coll., Pa.; M.A., U. of Conn.; Ph.D., State U. of Ia. *Interests:* musician, USNR; woodworking.

DOROTHY HICKOK: assoc. prof.; appointed 1947. B.S.M., Drake; M.M., Eastman School of Music. *Member:* Mu Phi Epsilon, Pi Lambda Theta. *Interests:* sewing, golf, bowling, educational TV.

SYLVIA IRWIN: asst. prof.; appointed 1957. A.B. (valedictorian, magna cum laude), Westmar (Ia.) Coll.; M.M., Northwestern. *Member:* Pi Kappa Lambda. *Interest:* piano.

PAUL ROGERS: assoc. prof.; appointed 1948. B.S., State U. of N.Y. Coll. of Ed. at Potsdam; M.A., Columbia. *Interest:* home workshop.

JAMES SOLURI: asst. prof.; appointed 1960. B.S., M.Ed., State U. of N.Y. Coll. of Ed. at Fredonia; M.M. (fellowship), U. of Mich. *Interests:* sports (tennis), drama, acting.

THE ART DEPARTMENT

AULUS W. SAUNDERS: prof. and chrmn.; appointed 1937. A.B., Westminster Coll. (Mo.); M.A., Washington U.; Ph.D., U. of Iowa. *Honors:* Fellow, Intl. Institue of Arts & Letters; awards for paintings in various art exhibitions. *Member:* Kappa Delta Pi; Sigma Xi. *Interests:* painting, cycling, camping.

ALLEN BREMMER: asst. prof.; appointed 1960. B.S., M.A., U. of Missouri; M.F.A., Cranbrook Academy of Art. *Honors:* exhibited St. Louis, Kansas City, Detroit, and Munson Williams Institute; Vernon R. Evans Prize, 1961. *Interests:* music (classical and jazz), fishing, sports.

DAVID M. CAMPBELL: asst. prof.; appointed 1957. B.A., M.A., Ohio State. *Specialty:* printmaking. *Award:* 1956 Prix de Rome Architectural Prize.

JOSEPH F. SCHOENFELT: assoc. prof.; appointed 1946. B.S., Indiana State; M.A., Columbia; M.F.A., U. of Guanajuato. *Reserve Status:* Lt. Cmdr. USNR. *Honors:* court of honor, N.Y. State Craftsmen; listed in *Who's Who in American Art;* Macelhaney Art Award. *Member:* Phi Delta Kappa. Author: *Designing and Making Handwrought Jewelry. Interest:* flying.

ROBERT STEINEN: prof.; appointed 1946. B.F.A., Pratt Institute; M.A., Columbia; Ed.D., Peabody. *Honors:* Perry Scholarship (Pratt Institute); Carnegie Scholarship (Columbia); St. Gaudens Medal for draftsmanship. *Member:* Phi Delta Kappa. *Interests:* photography, expert on guns, Civil War history.

ROBERT M. SULLINS: asst. prof.; appointed 1960. A.B., M.A., U. of Wyoming. *Honors:* Phi Kappa Phi; Fulbright Scholarship, Paris; Robert Ahl Memorial Scholarship, U. of Wyoming. *Interests:* mountain climbing, photography, jazz.

DEPARTMENT OF MEN'S PHYSICAL EDUCATION

GARDNER WELLS: assoc. prof.; director of health and physical education program and chrmn. men's dept. (acting); appointed 1959. B.S., State U. of N.Y. Coll. of Ed. at Cortland; M.S., Syracuse. *Honors:* Fulbright lecturer, Iraq; coached Bagdad All-Stars, winners of Iraq national championship. *Reserve Status:* Capt. Medical Corps, USAR. *Interests:* fishing, hunting.

DAVID A. CAMPBELL: assoc. prof.; director intramurals; appointed 1950. Fredonia Normal, 1938; B. S., State U. of N.Y. Coll. of Ed. at Cortland (varsity player: soccer, basketball, track, cross-country); M.S., State U. of N.Y. Coll. of Ed. at Brockport. *Member:* Phi Delta Kappa; Phi Epsilon Kappa; AAHPER; pres. Health-Phys. Ed. Section of Assn. of N.Y. State Teachers Coll. Faculties. *Interests:* photography, camping.

BRUCE DICK: asst. prof.; appointed 1959. B.S., State U. of N.Y. Coll. of Ed. at Cortland (varsity player: soccer, swimming, lacrosse), listed in *Who's Who in American Colleges;* M.S., Indiana U. *Interests:* sports, calling square dances.

JOHN GLINSKI: assoc. prof.; director of athletics; appointed 1958. B.S., State U. of N.Y. Coll. of Ed. at Cortland (varsity player: baseball, basketball); M.A., U. of Mich. *Interest:* basketball.

ERNEST B. LUONGO: asst. prof.; appointed 1957. B.S., M.S., State U. of N.Y. Coll. of Ed. at Cortland (varsity player: baseball, soccer). *Interest:* fishing, hunting.

WALTER NITARDY: asst. prof.; appointed 1959. A.B., Columbia College; M.A., T.C., Columbia. *Interest:* photography.

DAVID SEE: asst. prof.; appointed 1955. B.S., M.Ed., Springfield Coll. (Mass.); (varsity player: soccer, wrestling, lacrosse, crew). *Reserve Status:* Lt. Cmdr. USNR; commanding officer, USNR Surface Divn., Oswego. *Interests:* wood carving; music.

DEPARTMENT OF WOMEN'S PHYSICAL EDUCATION

LOUISE OSTBERG: assoc. prof.; chrmn. women's phys. ed., appointed 1945. B.S., M.Ed., U. of Minn. *Interests:* gardening, photography, travel.

JOAN HUFF: asst. prof.; appointed 1958. B.S. (cum laude), Russell Sage; M.A., Michigan State. *Offices:* secty., eastern zone N.Y. State Health Phys. Ed. Recreation Assn. *Interests:* skiing, tennis, travel.

(Mrs.) MARGUERITE ROBERTS KRANZ: asst. prof.; appointed 1956. B.S., Skidmore, M.S., Syracuse. *Interests:* skiing, teaching riding.

MARY ANN RICCIO: instr.; appointed 1960. B.S., State U. of N.Y. Coll. of Ed. at Brockport. *Interests:* golf, travel.

AUDIO-VISUAL DEPARTMENT

THEODORE H. BEERS: assoc. prof.; director, Audio-Visual Center; appointed 1949. A.B., M.A., Tufts; M.Ed., U. of Vt. *Honors:* pres. N.Y. State Audio-Visual Council. *Author:* lab. manual for audio-visual equipment operation. *Interests:* music, photography, carpentry.

JOHN PETERSON: asst. prof.; asst., Audio-Visual Center; appointed 1960. A.B. (great distinction), San Jose State; M.S. (with distinction), Indiana U. *Interests:* experiments in perception, communication via visual design.

THE PROFESSIONAL CURRICULUM: ELEMENTARY AND SECONDARY DIVISION

SHERWOOD DUNHAM: prof., chrmn.; appointed 1955. B.Ed., State U. of N.Y. Coll. of Ed. at Fredonia; M.A., Columbia, Ed.D., U. of Buffalo. *Honors:* Three air medals, W.W. II; chrmn. Elem. Principals, western zone (N.Y.). *Member:* Kappa Delta Pi. *Interest:* gardening.

DOUGLAS ALDRICH: asst. prof.; appointed 1960. B.S.Ed., Mansfield State College (Pa.); M.Ed., St. Lawrence. *Interests:* classic cars, music, refinishing furniture.

ANTHONY BARRACO: assoc. prof.; appointed 1956. B.Ed., State U. of N.Y. Coll. of Ed. at Geneseo; M.Ed., Syracuse. *Interest:* sports.

VERNA E. BERGEMANN: assoc. prof.; appointed 1956. B.Ed., State Univ. Coll. of Ed. at Brockport; M.S., State Univ. Coll. of Ed. at Buffalo; *Offices:* secty. and state representative, Niagara Falls Teachers' Assn. *Interests:* gardening, bowling.

NEVART BOGHOSIAN: asst. prof.; appointed 1956. B.S. (cum laude), M.S., State U. of N.Y. Coll. of Ed. at Cortland. *Interests:* travel, reading, golf.

ROBERT CANFIELD: prof.; director of Reading Center; appointed 1951. B.Ed., M.S.Ed., State U. of N.Y. Coll. of Ed. at Fredonia; Ed.D., Syracuse. *Member:* Phi Delta Kappa. *Interest:* music (choral work).

ROBERT DELANCEY: asst. prof.; appointed 1959. B.Ed., State U. of N.Y. Coll. of Ed. at Brockport; M.A., U. of Mich. *Reserve Status:* Pharmacists mate, USNR. *Interests:* small boat maintenance and sailing.

FRANCES DISBROW: asst. prof.; appointed 1960. B.S., T.C. Columbia. *Interests:* travel, boating, camping, collector of dolls, also of relics from foreign lands.

GORDON EDDY: assoc. prof.; appointed 1960. B.S., State U. of N.Y. Coll. of Ed. at Buffalo; M.A., Niagara. *Interests:* target shooting, bowling, hunting.

MABEL HAWKINSON: assoc. prof.; appointed 1946. B.S., M.A., U. of Minn. *Member:* Kappa Delta Pi, Delta Kappa Gamma. *Interest:* gardening.

WALTER HOBBS: prof.; appointed 1959. B.S., M.A., Ohio State; Ed.D., T.C. Columbia. *Member:* Phi Delta Kappa, Kappa Delta Pi, Phi Mu Alpha. *Interests:* sailing, science gadgets, camping, outdoor life, photography, electronics, music, classic automobiles.

KENNETH JONES: prof.; appointed 1954. A.B., Bates; M.A., Ed.D., T.C. Columbia. *Reserve Status:* Lt., USNR. *Member:* Delta Sigma Rho, Phi Delta Kappa, Kappa Delta Pi. *Consultant:* State U. of N.Y.—Ford Foundation Education Project, Indonesia.

HAROLD J. KEELER: prof.; coordinator of field services; appointed 1948. B.S. Syracuse; M.S., D.Ed., Cornell. *Interest:* sports.

R. LEE MARTIN: prof.; appointed 1950. B.S.Ed., M.A., Ed.D., U. of Mo. *Offices:* past pres. Mo. State Adm. Assn.; state adviser to Students of Ed. Assn. of N.Y. State. *Interests:* book collecting, camping, fishing.

ROBERT P. MC MANUS: prof., and chrmn. of secondary education; appointed 1954. A.B., Ind. State Teachers; M.A., Ed.D., T.C. Columbia. Director of education advisory teams in Tokyo-Yokohama areas; director of Educational Assistance Program of the U.N. to Korea. *Honors:* Commendations from U.S. Govt. and Govt. of Korea for educational work in Japan and Korea. *Interests:* music, writing, sports cars, gourmet cooking.

MARY MILLER: assoc. prof.; appointed 1955. B.E., M.E., Oswego; M.L.S., Syracuse. *Member:* Delta Kappa Gamma; Beta Phi Mu. *Offices:* chairman, primary section, N.Y. State Teachers Assn. (central zone). *Interests:* furniture refinishing, swimming.

THEODORE C. MOSS: prof. and chrmn. of Dept. of Elem. Ed.; appointed 1958. B.E., State U. of N.Y. Coll. of Ed. at Fredonia; M.A., T.C. Columbia; Ed.D., U. of Buffalo. *Member:* Phi Delta Kappa.

CLARENCE TREXLER: assoc. prof.; appointed 1959. A.B.Ed., M.Ed., Wash. Coll. of Ed.; Ed.D., T.C., Columbia. *Co-author: Teacher's Guides for Grades 3–6*, of the New ABC's Science Series.

KATHRYN VACHA: assoc. prof.; appointed 1957. A.B., Iowa State Teachers Coll.; M.A., Ed.D., T.C. Columbia. *Member:* Kappa Delta Pi; Pi Lambda Theta. *Interests:* gourmet cooking, music.

ALVIN WESTCOTT: asst. prof.; appointed 1959. B.S., State U. of N.Y. Coll. of Ed. at Oneonta; M.A., Syracuse; graduate fellow, Syracuse U. *Interests:* photography, oil painting, stamp collecting, tropical fish, music.

THE CAMPUS SCHOOL

VIRGINIO L. PIUCCI: principal, prof.; appointed 1956. B.E., State U. of N.Y. Coll. of Ed. at New Paltz; M.A., T.C. Columbia; Ed. D., U. of Fla. *Member:* Phi Kappa Phi; Phi Delta Kappa; Kappa Delta Pi. *Interests:* politics, camping.

MABEL LESHER ARCHBOLD: nurse assistant, prof.; appointed 1951. (Early schooling in China.) A.B., Bucknell; B.N., R.N., Yale. *Honors:* Vice-pres. Nurse Educators group, State U. of N.Y. Colleges of Ed.; *Who's Who of American Women* (1959); fellow of American School Health. *Interests:* knitting, crocheting, service clubs, church work.

CONSTANCE BOND: grade 5; assoc. prof.; appointed 1955. B.S., M.S., Oswego. *Member:* Kappa Delta Pi. *Author: Kalootie's Christmas* (children's operetta). *Interests:* creative dramatics, music, sports.

RICHARD BENJAMIN: director of phys. ed.; asst. prof.; appointed 1959. B.S., State U. of N.Y. Coll. of Ed. at Brockport; M.E., Springfield Coll.

RAYMOND B. BRIDGERS, JR.: jr. high; assoc. prof.; appointed 1958. A.B., M.Ed., William and Mary; Ed.D. (graduate assistant), Duke. *Honors:* pres. Kappa Delta Pi chapters at William and Mary and at Duke. *Interests:* phonograph records, pear farm.

CRAYTON BUCK: grade 6, asst. prof.; appointed 1960. B.S., Lock Haven State Coll. (Pa.); M.Ed., Penn. State U. *Interests:* hunting, fishing.

DONALD BUCK: jr. high; assoc. prof.; appointed 1948. B.Ed., Oswego; M.S., and Ed.D., Syracuse. *Member:* Phi Delta Kappa.

(Mrs.) DOROTHY CLARK: grade 3; assoc. prof.; appointed 1948. B.E., and M.S., Oswego. *Honors:* Originated *Ten O'Clock Scholar* (TV program) at Oswego. *Member:* Kappa Delta Pi. *Interest:* dramatics (director of Oswego Players).

BETTY CONE: music; asst. prof.; appointed 1960. B.S., Ithaca College; M.M., Eastman School of Music. *Member:* Kappa Lambda. *Interests:* sports, knitting.

CONSTANCE FAUST: foreign lang.; instr.; appointed 1960. A.B., Swarthmore; M.A., Albany State Teachers Coll.

LORETTA FRISSORA: grade 6; asst. prof.; appointed 1960. B.S., Boston U.; M.Ed., State Teachers College at Boston. *Interests:* art, theater, music.

MARY ANN GLANCY: grade 2; instr.; appointed 1960. B.S., Oswego. *Author:* children's books.

HAZEL HEWITT: kindergarten; assoc. prof.; appointed 1947. B.S., M.S., Syracuse. *Interest:* golf.

DUDLEY LAMBERT: jr. high; asst. prof.; appointed 1958. B.E., Oswego. *Interests:* scenery design, skiing, photography, painting, music (electric organ), and house remodeling.

ESTHER NORTHRIDGE: kindergarten; assoc. prof.; appointed 1953. B.S., Potsdam. *Interests:* traveling, camping, music.

FRANCES OLER: art consultant; assoc. prof.; appointed 1950. B.A.A. in Ed., Phila. Museum College of Art; M.Ed., Penn. State U. *Interests:* work with cerebral palsied children, painting children.

JOSEPHINE E. PARKHURST: grade 4; asst. prof.; appointed 1948. B.S., M.S., Oswego. *Honors:* past natl. pres. Woman's Relief Corps, Aux. Grand Army of Rep.; apptd. by U.S. Grant III, to serve on Natl. Civil War Centennial Commission (Women's Divn.). *Interest:* politics.

RALPH PLANT: shop; asst. prof.; appointed 1960. B.S., Oswego; M.A., T.C., Columbia. *Member:* Epsilon Pi Tau. *Interests:* collector guns and antiques; foreign cars.

THOMAS PODDI: grade 4; instr.; appointed 1960. B.A., Syracuse; M.S., State U. of N.Y. Coll. of Ed. at Oneonta. *Interests:* literature, outdoor sports.

WALTER RICHMOND: jr. high; assoc. prof.; appointed 1958. A.B., Syracuse; M.A., Syracuse. *Honors:* Natl. Science Foundation Research Grant, Cornell; Natl. Science Foundation Fellowship Grant, Syracuse.

(Mrs.) BEULAH COUNTS RUDOLPH: asst. coll. librarian; appointed 1937. A.B., Park College (Mo.); B.S. in Lib. Sci., U. of Southern Calif.; M.S. in Lib. Sci.,

U. Ill. *Member:* Pi Kappa Delta; Beta Phi Mu; Phi Kappa Phi. Chairman Campus School Librarians of N.Y. State Faculties Assn. *Interests:* collector dolls and figurines of characters from children's literature, textiles with literary themes from children's books, book markers, travel.

MARION STRICKLAND: grade 3; asst. prof.; appointed 1947. B.S., U. of Buffalo; M.A., Columbia. *Honors:* Fulbright Exchange Teacher, United Kingdom. *Interest:* travel.

(Mrs.) AMELIA WHELAHAN: grade 9; asst. prof.; appointed 1952. B.E., M.S., Oswego. *Interests:* dramatics, little theater groups, collecting old glass and china, politics.

MAUREEN WILSON: instructor; appointed 1961. B.S., State Univ. Coll. of Ed. at Brockport; *Offices:* pres., Band; *Interests:* trumpet, boats.

MATILDA WORDELMAN: grade 1; assoc. prof.; appointed 1943. Ph.B., Chicago; M.A., Columbia. *Author: The ABC of Manuscript Writing. Interests:* travel, international relations, collecting textiles and ceramics.

THE ELEMENTARY EDUCATION INDUSTRIAL ARTS DEPARTMENT

ROBERT J. BABCOCK: assoc. prof., and coordinator of elementary education industrial arts; appointed 1957. B.S., Oswego; M.A., N.Y.U. *Member:* Epsilon Pi Tau. *Offices:* past pres., Great Neck Teachers Assn. *Co-author: Industrial Arts for Grades K–6. Interest:* hi-fidelity recordings.

RICHARD HALL: asst. prof.; appointed 1958. A.B., M.A., Western Washington Coll. *Member:* Epsilon Pi Tau; Kappa Delta Pi. *Interests:* hunting, fishing, rock collecting, mountain photography.

ELIZABETH HUNT: asst. prof.; appointed 1956. A.B., Berea Coll.; M.S., Oswego; I.A. certification, E. Carolina Coll. *Member:* Epsilon Pi Tau. *Author: Electrical Demonstrations for Elementary School. Interests:* music, camping, inventing games.

DEPARTMENT OF INDUSTRIAL ARTS LABORATORIES

FRANK E. ROBINSON: prof. (drawing) and chrmn.; appointed 1948. B.S., M.Ed., Ed.D., U. of Mo. *Interests:* religion, philosophy, craftwork, carving.

WILLARD ALLEN: assoc. prof. (transportation); appointed 1954. B.S., Oswego; M.Ed., Penn. State Coll. *Member:* Epsilon Pi Tau, Iota Lambda Sigma. *Author* (textbook), *Know Your Car. Interests:* house building, photography.

AUSTIN BLAKE: asst. prof. (ceramics); appointed 1960. B.S., M.S., Oswego. *Member:* Epsilon Pi Tau. *Interests:* camping, canoeing.

JOSEPH BRACO: asst. prof. (electricity); appointed 1957. B.S., M.S., Oswego. *Interests:* electronics, trailering.

RAYMOND L. CORNWELL: assoc. prof.; coordinator of graphic arts; appointed 1958. B.S. (with high distinction), M.S., Stout State Coll. (Wisc.). *Offices:* past pres. N.W. Wisc. Graphic Arts Educators Assn.; past pres. Wisc. Audio-

Visual Ed. Assn. *Member:* Epsilon Pi Tau; Phi Delta Kappa. *Honors:* 1956 Danforth Teachers Grant. *Interests:* photography, home shop, bookbinding, maps.

ARTHUR GREER: assoc. prof. (coordinator metal laboratories); appointed 1954. B.S., Gorham (Me.) State Teachers Coll.; M.Ed., Penn. State U. *Offices:* past state chrmn. (Maine) New Eng. I.A. Assn. *Interests:* music (sings, and plays drums), golf, bowling.

WILLIAM HANKS: assoc. prof.; appointed 1957. B.S., M.A., Ball State Teachers Coll. *Honors:* past pres., Illinois I.A. Assn. *Member:* Delta Phi Delta; Epsilon Pi Tau. *Interests:* electronics; cartooning.

TAYLOR HARTER: assoc. prof.; coordinator of general laboratory; appointed 1947. B.S., Oswego; M.Ed., Penn. State. *Member:* Iota Lambda Sigma; Phi Delta Kappa; Epsilon Pi Tau. *Interest:* duck hunting.

ROBERT HELLER: instr. (graphic arts); appointed 1959. A.B., Montclair (N.J.) State Coll. *Offices:* state chrmn. N.J. Conf. in Citizenship. *Member:* Kappa Delta Pi, Epsilon Pi Tau. *Interests:* antiques, hi-fi, philosophy, hunting.

WILLIAM E. HUSS: prof., coordinator of drawing; appointed 1939. B.S., M.A., Ohio State; Ed.D., Penn. State U. *Honor:* member of Stanford University Overseas Mission to the Philippines. *Member:* Iota Lambda Sigma; Phi Delta Kappa; Epsilon Pi Tau. *Interests:* photography, watercolor painting, radio-electronics, ceramics, scouting, travel.

ROBERT MC WILLIAMS: assoc. prof., coordinator of textiles; appointed 1950. B.S., M.S., Oswego. *Honors:* one-man art show; highest natl. honors for textile fabrics; devised new technique for developing original designs by spraying.

CHARLES E. SHOEMAKER: assoc. prof. (electricity); appointed 1958. B.S., Oswego; M.A., Ohio State. *Interests:* amateur radio; oil painting.

DONALD SHUTTS: assoc. prof., coordinator of electricity; appointed 1956. B.S. (equiv.); M.S., Cornell. Vocational-Technical Elec. License, Buffalo. *Member:* Institute of Radio Engineers (only one in Oswego). *Interest:* electronic control developments.

JOHN SOMERVILLE: asst. prof. (general lab. and mech. drawing); appointed 1957. B.S., M.S., Oswego.

EARL S. SPAAR: assoc. prof. (wood lab and ceramics); appointed 1957. B.S., M.S., Oswego. *Member:* Epsilon Pi Tau, Kappa Delta Pi. Past pres., Mohawk Valley Ind. Ed. Club. *Honors:* merit citation State U. of N.Y. Coll. of Ed. at Oswego, Outstanding Teacher's Award, 1956. *Interests:* photography, model railroading.

CHARLES STEBBINS: asst. prof. (metalworking); appointed 1956. B.S., M.S., Oswego. *Member:* Kappa Delta Pi; Epsilon Pi Tau. *Honors:* listed in *Who's Who in Amer. Colleges and Univ. Interests:* carpentry, photography.

WILLIAM D. TODD: assoc. prof. (woodworking and mech. drawing); coordinator wood lab. B.S. (magna cum laude), Eastern Ky. State; M.Ed., U. of Ill. *Interest:* gardening.

THE INDUSTRIAL ARTS EDUCATION DEPARTMENT

ART HAULER: prof. and chrmn.; appointed 1925. B.S., Univ. New Hampshire; M.S., Syracuse.

SHERMAN F. DREYER: prof.; appointed 1960. B.S., M.S., Stout State College; Ed.D., U. of Okla. *Honors:* Distinguished Flying Cross, World War II, Laurett Award, Epsilon Pi Tau. *Member:* Phi Delta Kappa.

JAMES R. HASTINGS: prof. and chrmn, I.A. student teaching, B.S., Oswego; M.A., Ed.D., N.Y.U. *Offices:* vice-chrmn., I.A. Section Vocational & Practical Arts Assn.; member exec. committee, NYS Vocational & Practical Arts Assoc. *Honors:* Gordon O. Wilber Award. *Editor: Viewpoints Magazine. Reserve Status:* Capt. *USAF* (aircraft engineering) reserve officer, Air Materiel Commander. *Member:* Epsilon Pi Tau; Phi Delta Kappa. *Interests:* photography, gardening, cabinetmaking, travel.

CARL GERBRACHT: prof.; appointed 1954. B.S., State U. of N.Y. Coll. of Ed. at Buffalo; M.A., Ph.D., Ohio State. *Member:* Alpha Society (Buffalo); Kappa Delta Pi; Epsilon Pi Tau (Laureate Citation for contribution to professional literature); Phi Delta Kappa. *Co-Author: Industrial Arts for Grades K–6.* Now I.A. adviser to ICA Mission to Brazil.

PAUL T. HISER: prof.; appointed 1948. B.S., M.A., Ohio State; Ed.D., U. of Md. *Offices and honors:* meritorious service citation in W.W. II; natl. vice-pres., Amer. Council I.A. Teacher Ed.; N.Y. State rep., Amer. I.A. Assn.; trustee of Phi Chapter of Epsilon Pi Tau. Laureate Citation of Epsilon Pi Tau. *Member:* Phi Delta Kappa.

JOHN KOWALSKI: assoc. prof.; appointed 1954. B.S., Oswego; M.A., N.Y.U. *Offices:* pres. Driver & Safety Educators Assn. of N.Y. State; Board of Directors, American Driver Education Assn. *Honor:* Gordon O. Wilber Award. *Interests:* aviation, scouting.

J. RICHARD PFUND: assoc. prof.; appointed 1957. B.S.Ed., M.A., Kent State U.; Advanced Cert. in Ed., U. of Ill. *Interests:* boat building, sailing.

CHARLES W. PHALLEN: prof.; appointed 1958. B.S., Otterbein Coll.; M.A., Ph.D., Ohio State. *Member:* Phi Delta Kappa, Epsilon Pi Tau. *Interests:* trailering, visiting other institutions.

GEORGE RADCLIFFE: assoc. prof.; appointed 1957. B.S., Neb. State (Kearney); A.B., M.A., Texas A.&M.

JOHN STORM: prof.; appointed 1949. B.S., M.S., Syracuse; Ed.D., Cornell. *Offices:* treas., membership chrmn., and pres., N.Y. State Voc. and Practical Arts Assn. *Reserve Status:* Lt. USNR. *Honors:* First recipient of Gordon O. Wilber Award.

WILLIAM S. REYNOLDS: assoc. prof.; appointed 1954. B.S. (magna cum laude), Oswego; M.Ed., Penn. State U. *Honors:* first recipient of Mary E. Laing Scholarship; Regents War Service Scholarship. *Interests:* gliding, aviation, camping.

Index